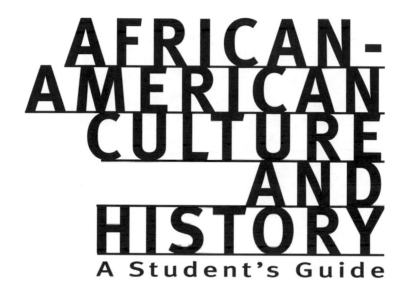

AFRICAN-AMERICAN CULTURE AND HISTORY

A Student's Guide

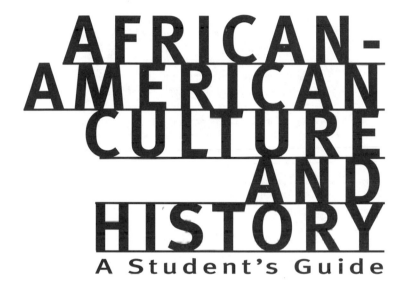

AFRICAN-AMERICAN CULTURE AND HISTORY
A Student's Guide

JACK SALZMAN
Editor-in-Chief

James S. Haskins
Consulting Editor

Evelyn Bender
Kathleen Lee
Advisors

volume **4**
Q-Z
INDEX

Macmillan Reference USA

an imprint of the Gale Group
New York • Detroit • San Francisco • London • Boston • Woodbridge, CT

Macmillan Reference USA
1633 Broadway
New York, NY 10019

Gale Group
27500 Drake Rd.
Farmington Hills, MI 48331

Editorial and Production Staff

David Galens, *Project Editor*
Kelle Sisung, *Developmental Editor*
Kathy Droste, *Illustration Editor*
Shalice Shah, *Permissions Associate*
Mark Milne, Pam Revitzer, and Larry Trudeau, *Contributing Editors*
Tim Akers, Rebecca Blanchard, Elizabeth Bodenmiller, Anne Marie Hacht, and
    Tara Atterberry, *Proofreaders*
Robert Griffin, *Copyeditor*
Tracey Rowens, *Senior Art Director*
Randy Bassett, *Imaging Supervisor*
Pam A. Reed, *Imaging Coordinator*
Dan Newell, *Imaging Specialist*
Kay Banning, *Indexer*
Geraldine Azzata, *Further Resources Compiler*

Elly Dickason, *Publisher, Macmillan Reference USA*
Jill Lectka, *Associate Publisher*

Printing number
1 2 3 4 5 6 7 8 9 10

LIBRARY OF CONGRESS CATALOGING-IN-PUBLICATION DATA

African-American culture and history: a student's guide / Jack Salzman, editor-in-chief.
    p. cm.
    Adapted from the five-volume Encyclopedia of African American culture and history published by Macmillan in 1996; revised for a sixth- to seventh-grade, middle school audience.
    Includes bibliographical references and index.
    ISBN 0-02-865531-1 (set : hardcover : alk. paper) – ISBN 0-02865532-X (vol. 1 : alk. paper) – ISBN 0-02-865533-8 (vol. 2 : alk. paper) – ISBN 0-02-865534-6 (vol. 3 : alk. paper) – ISBN 0-02-865535-4 (vol. 4 : alk. paper)
Afro-Americans—Encyclopedias, Juvenile. 2.
Afro-Americans—History—Encyclopedias, Juvenile literature. [1.
Afro-Ameridans—Encyclopedias.] I. Salzman, Jack. II. Encyclopedia of African-American culture and history.

E185 .A2527 2000
973'.0496073—dc21

Table of Contents

VOLUME 1

Table of Contents

VOLUME 2

Table of Contents   ▪▪▪

VOLUME 3

Table of Contents

VOLUME 4

Preface

The history and culture of African Americans is to a great extent the history and culture of the United States. But as much as we may now accept this as a truism, it was not always so. It was not until the second half of the twentieth century that students and historians of the American experience began to document and carefully study the lives of people of African descent. Until then our knowledge of a people who comprise almost 15 percent of this country's population was shamefully inadequate. In 1989 Macmillan Publishing Co. decided to redress this situation by publishing a major reference work devoted to the history and culture of African Americans. I was asked to serve as editor of the new work, and in 1996 the five volume *Encyclopedia of African-American Culture and History* was published.

The encyclopedia contains close to two million words and covers all aspects of the African-American experience. In the few years since its publication it has come to be recognized as a mainstay in most high school, public, and academic libraries. *Rettig on Reference* (April 1996) found the set to be "scholarly yet accessible and immeasurably informative." *CHOICE* (1996) praised its "clear and succinct writing style" and its "breadth of coverage of general biographical and historical data." It received a Dartmouth Award Honorable Mention and appeared on every list of 1996 best reference sources. After spending six years compiling the encyclopedia it was gratifying to read, in *American Libraries* (May 1997), that the work "is of enduring value and destined to become a standard reference source."

The enthusiastic response to *Encyclopedia of African-American Culture and History* convinced us that students would benefit from a work with similar scope but one rewritten for a wider audience. *African-American Culture and History: A Student's Guide* is that work. It incorporates the same editorial criteria we used for the original encyclopedia : articles include biographies of notable African Americans, events, historical eras, legal cases, areas of cultural achievement, professions, sports, and places. Readers will find entries on all 50 states, 12 major cities, and 15 historically black colleges.

This comprehensive four-volume Student's Guide has 852 articles— arranged alphabetically—of which 597 are biographies and 255 are events, eras, genres, or colleges, states, or cities. Although for the most part articles in this set are based on entries from the original encyclopedia, our Advisory

Board recommended that we also cover several contemporary popular topics and figures. Entries were chosen to reflect the school curriculum and have been updated through Summer 2000.

African-American Culture and History: A Student's Guide has been carefully designed for younger readers, and professional writers have crafted the articles to make them accessible for the intended audience. In addition, readers will find that articles are enhanced with numerous photographs and sidebar materials. Lists, quotations, extracts from primary sources, interesting facts, and chronologies are to be found in the margins. A system of cross-references makes it easy to explore the Student's Guide. Within the text, terms and names set in boldface type indicate that there is a separate entry for this subject. Additional cross-references appear at the end of many entries. A comprehensive index for the entire set appears at the end of volume 4. A list of "Further Resources" in Volume Four includes books, articles, and web sites and will provide a starting point for students who are beginning to explore the extraordinary history and accomplishments of African Americans.

Many people have provided invaluable help with *African-American Culture and History: A Student's Guide*. In particular, I would like to single out Jill Lectka and David Galens of the Gale Group and Kelle Sisung. I would also like to thank our editorial advisors, Evelyn Bender, Librarian, Edison High School in Philadelphia; and Kathleen Lee, Librarian, John P. Turner Middle School in Philadelphia. Thanks, too, to Jim Haskins, Professor of Education, University of Florida and author of numerous books for young adults. These three professionals provided valuable guidance as I developed the article list and helped design the margin features. It was at their urging that we included curriculum-related web sites in the resources list. Finally, to Becca, Phoebe, Jonah, and Libby, who soon will be able to make use of these volumes: thank you for being as wonderful as you are and for bringing so much to me and Cec.

Jack Salzman
New York City

Contributors

The text of *African-American Culture and History: A Student's Guide* is based on the Macmillan *Encyclopedia of African-American Culture and History,* which was published in 1996. We have updated material where necessary and added new entries. Articles have been condensed and made more accessible for a student audience. Please refer to the Alphabetical List of Articles on page xi of the first volume of *Encyclopedia of African-American Culture and History* (also edited by Jack Salzman) for the names of the authors of the articles in the original set. Their academic affiliations are noted in the Directory of Contributors. This title also includes entries from the Supplement to *Encyclopedia of African-American Culture and History* published by Macmillan late in 2000. The Supplement has its own Alphabetical List of Articles and Directory of Contributors. Here we wish to acknowledge the writers who revised entries from those two publications and wrote new articles for this set:

Sheree Beaudry
Craig Collins
Stephanie Dionne
Rebecca Ferguson
David Galens
Robert Griffin
Cathy Dybiec Holm
Paul Kobel
Paula Pyzik-Scott
Ann Shurgin
Kelle Sisung
Larry Trudeau

Quarles, Benjamin

HISTORIAN
January 28, 1904–November 16, 1996

Born in Boston, Massachusetts, the son of a subway porter, historian Benjamin Quarles entered college at the age of twenty-three. He received a bachelor's degree from Shaw University (Raleigh, North Carolina) in 1931 and a Ph.D. degree from the University of Wisconsin in 1940. He taught at Shaw, served as dean at Dillard University (New Orleans, Louisiana), and chaired the history department at Morgan State University (Baltimore, Maryland).

Building on the research of earlier black historians, Quarles confirmed the existence of a rich documentary record of African-American life and culture. He also proved wrong white historians who doubted that blacks could write objective history. Quarles's writings were based on careful research and showed his ability to present both sides of historical issues. His essays in the *Mississippi Valley Historical Review* in 1945 and 1959 were the first by a black historian to appear in a major historical journal.

Quarles's interest in race relations led to his study of the way in which blacks and whites have shaped each other's identity on individual and group levels. His topics included President Abraham Lincoln (1809–1865), abolitionist John Brown (1800–1859), the **abolition** movement, the **American Revolution** (1775–83), and the American **Civil War** (1861–65).

Quarles authored two textbooks, *The Negro in the Making of America* and *The Negro American: A Documentary History*. He was also a contributing editor to *Phylon* and associate editor of the *Journal of Negro History*.

Quilt Making

Although quilts were not needed in the warm climate of Africa, slaves in the American South learned the art of quilt making to provide warmth during cold winters in drafty cabins. Slave women used brightly colored scraps of cloth from plantation sewing rooms to make quilts with beautiful geo-

THE HARRIET QUILTS

Two quilts called the Harriet Quilts, made by a Georgia woman named Harriet Powers (1837–1911), are among the most unusual examples of nineteenth-century African-American quilt art. Powers was born into slavery near Athens, Georgia, but became free in 1863. She was the wife of a farmer and made quilts as a hobby.

Different from "crazy quilts" or quilts with geometric designs, the Harriet Quilts show scenes made by appliquéing or stitching patterns against a solid background. This technique is similar to the centuries-old tradition of royal tapestry making in the Republic of Benin (formerly Dahomey) in West Africa. Powers might have learned this technique from Dahomean slaves who were still being brought to central Georgia well into the 1800s.

One of the Harriet Quilts is in the Smithsonian Institution's (Washington, D.C.) National Museum of American History, and the other is at the Museum of Fine Arts in Boston, Massachusetts. The quilt at the Smithsonian, completed around 1885, shows eleven scenes from the biblical Old and New Testaments. The other was made in 1898 and shows fifteen scenes that combine religious and astronomical symbolism.

metric designs. At the end of the twentieth century, southern African-American women still host "quilting bees," in which a group gathers to piece together a quilt in three layers—the design top, the cotton interlining, and the cloth backing.

Certain types of quilt making probably began with the woven and appliquéd (using a cutout design fastened to a larger piece of cloth) cloth made in West and Central Africa. African-American geometric quilt patterns were handed down from generation to generation. Some of the most popular are Sawtooth, Single Irish Chain, Double Irish Chain, Pineapple, Wedding Ring, Rising Sun, Triangles, and Lone Star. One of the most common patterns is the Crazy Quilt, in which scraps of materials are sewn together without specific designs. This type of quilt probably originated in the Deep South. Other African-American quilters sewed long strips of cloth, often made by stitching small pieces together, into a quilt top. This method of making cloth from long strips is also a West African tradition.

In 1996 African-American photographer and folklorist Roland L. Freeman (1936–) published *A Communion of the Spirits: African American Quilters and Their Quilts*, a book of photographs and stories. Historian and quilter Carolyn Mazloomi created *Spirits of the Cloth* (1998), a collection of 150 quilts by modern African-American quilters.

African-American artist Faith Ringgold (1930–) is known for her "story quilts," which tell of her life experiences and address issues affecting all black women. The "quilts" are made from painted panels with patchwork around the edges and text at the bottom.

Radio

African-American radio first developed in the early twentieth century with "blackface" radio (1920–41). This was characterized by the use of African-American music and humor by white entertainers, who imitated blacks with charcoal-blackened faces for a mostly white listening audience. Popular black music styles like **blues** and **jazz** were also first performed on the radio by whites, as were black-humor shows such as *Amos 'n' Andy*, radio's first mass success.

A few black entertainers and actors were hired by the radio industry in the pre–**World War II**, but for the most part they were restricted to playing stereotyped roles. During the **Great Depression** (1930s), a number of black actors and actresses who auditioned for radio parts were told that they needed to be coached in the art of black dialect by white coaches if they wanted the jobs.

Jazz was a popular expression of black culture broadcast over the airways in the 1920s and 1930s. The first black musicians to be broadcast regularly were New York bandleaders **Duke Ellington** (1899–1974) and Noble Sissle (1889–1975).

Black characters began to be added to soap opera scripts, and a radio series produced by the federal government dramatized the participation of blacks in past wars. By the end of World War II radio was forced to turn to local markets in order to survive as businesses and thus discovered a growing African-American audience. This led to the emergence of radio stations that appealed to blacks and the rise of the African-American disc jockey (DJ).

By the end of the 1940s there was a growing number of DJs in urban black communities ready to take advantage of the new "Negro-appeal" formats springing up on stations throughout the United States. By 1956 more than 400 radio stations were broadcasting black-appeal programming. Each of these showcased its own African-American DJs, who were the centerpiece of the on-air sound.

During the 1950s, African-American radio DJs also had a profound effect on commercial radio in general. Some stations—such as WLAC in Nashville, a high-powered AM outlet heard at night throughout the South—devoted a hefty amount of their evening schedules to rhythm and blues records. In addition, the white disc jockeys at WLAC (John R., Gene Noble, Hoss Allen, and Wolfman Jack) adopted the on-air styles, and even dialect, of the black DJs. Many of their listeners, both black and white, thought that WLAC's disc jockeys were African Americans. This was also the case on WJMR in New Orleans, where the white DJs who hosted the popular Poppa Stoppa Show were actually trained to speak in black dialect by the creator of the show, an African-American college professor named Vernon Winslow. Other white DJs who became popular by emulating the broadcast styles of their black counterparts included Dewey Phillips in Memphis; Zenas "Daddy" Sears in Atlanta; Phil Mckernan in Oakland, California; George "Hound Dog" Lorenz in Buffalo, NY; and Allen Freed in Cleveland. Freed moved on to become New York City's most famous rock and roll disc jockey, before his fall from grace as the result of payola scandals in the early 1960s.

The chain operations not only established standardized top forty soul formats at their respective outlets, thus limiting the independence of the black DJs they employed, but they also eliminated most of the local African-American news and public-affairs offerings on the stations.

Payola, the exchange of money for record airplay, was a common practice throughout the radio industry. It was an easy way for disc jockeys to supplement the low wages they were paid by their employers. Hence, many well-known black DJs were adversely affected by the payola exposés. Some lost their jobs when their names were linked to the ongoing investigations, and an unfortunate few were even the targets of income-tax-evasion indictments. The industry's solution to the payola problem was the creation of the "top forty" radio format, which in effect gave management complete control over the playlists of records to be aired on their stations. Formerly, the playlists had been determined by the individual DJs. This change led to the demise of both the white rock-and-roll disc jockeys and the black "personality" DJs associated with rhythm and blues, and then "soul" music. Black-appeal stations were centralized even further by the emergence of five soul radio chains in the 1960s, all of which were white-owned and -managed. By the end of the decade, these corporations controlled a total of twenty stations in key urban markets with large African-American populations like New York, Chicago, Memphis, and Washington, D.C. The chain operations not only established standardized top forty soul formats at their respective outlets, thus limiting the independence of the black DJs they employed, but they also eliminated most of the local African-American news and public-affairs offerings on the stations.

The 1970s brought the era of black-owned and black-controlled radio operations. In 1970, of the more than 300 black stations, only 16 were owned by African Americans. During the next ten years the number of black-owned stations rose to 88, while the number of black-oriented stations rose to 450.

By 1990 there were 32 public FM stations owned and operated by black colleges and universities in the United States. These stations are not subject to the ratings pressures of commercial radio, allowing more freedom in programming news, public affairs, talk, and cultural features. The growth of black public radio has expanded the variety and diversity of African-American programming found on the airways, while also increasing the number of blacks working in radio.

Ragtime

Ragtime was the first African-American music that played a significant role in American popular culture. It reached its peak from the late 1890s through about 1915. Ragtime took some elements from **the blues,** and **jazz** is said to have been an offshoot of ragtime. Ragtime is characterized by a particular rhythm called syncopation, which alters the regular musical accent by stressing the weak beat. This gives it the uneven, "ragged" effect from which it gets its name.

Ragtime first gained public attention at the 1893 World's Fair in Chicago, Illinois. The term "ragtime" first appeared in print in about 1896 on published music such as Ernest Hogan's (c. 1860–1909) "All Coons Look Alike to Me," which had a syncopated chorus with its "Negro 'Rag' Accompaniment."

Vocal Ragtime

The earliest ragtime songs were called "coon" (a disrespectful term for blacks) songs and had lyrics that suggested blacks were lazy, greedy, or violent. Sheet music drawings showed African Americans with exaggerated features. However, this drew little protest from the black community of the time, and many respected blacks, such as composer **Will Marion Cook** (1869–1944) and poet-lyricist **Paul Laurence Dunbar** (1872–1906), contributed lyrics to ragtime.

Early ragtime songs by black artists include Howard and Emerson's "Hello! Ma Baby" (1899) and Bob Cole (1868–1911) and J. Rosamond Johnson's (1873–1954) "Under the Bamboo Tree" (1902). By around 1905 ragtime had lost its openly racial quality and had come to include any strongly rhythmic popular song. White composer Irving Berlin's (1888–1989) hit song "Alexander's Ragtime Band" (1911), is often thought of as the high point of ragtime.

Instrumental Ragtime

Ragtime was played on piano and by marching and concert bands, dance orchestras, and in combination groups like xylophone and marimba bands or mandolin-banjo groups. Piano ragtime was the most popular. Like the later musical style jazz, piano ragtime was often improvised, or made up as the performer played. Solo piano ragtimers played on the vaudeville stage, in saloons and dance halls, and in home parlors. Ragtime songs were also favorites on the mechanical player piano.

Blues influenced ragtime composers, and what later came to be known as the classic blues form made its earliest appearances in piano rags. The first blues song to become popular was **W. C. Handy**'s (1873–1958) "Memphis Blues" (1912), which combines blues and ragtime sections. The term "blues" was often used to refer to many rags.

Shocking New Music

When ragtime came on the scene during the 1890s, nothing like it had ever been heard. It was new music that captured the restless energy of the United States. Young Americans, regardless of race, embraced ragtime as their own music. Many older whites opposed ragtime and tried to discredit it as unoriginal. They feared that young whites were being "infected" by ragtime.

Some African-American church groups thought ragtime was sinful because it was played in saloons and used for dancing. Middle-class blacks avoided ragtime because it was associated with the lower class. The *Negro Music Journal* (1902–03) encouraged blacks to listen to classical music and denied that ragtime was an African-American expression. Ragtime thrived in spite of this opposition.

Ragtime Composers and Performers

Tom Turpin was the first black composer to have a piano rag, "Harlem Rag," published (1897). Turpin was a St. Louis, Missouri, saloon keeper and an important figure in the development of St. Louis ragtime.

DANCING TO RAGTIME

Ragtime music was closely tied to dancing. At first the two-step was most popular, with variations such as the slow-drag. The cakewalk was popular throughout the ragtime years but was saved for exhibitions and contests.

From 1910 to 1915 many new dances were created to ragtime, including the one-step, the fox-trot, turkey trot, and grizzly bear, along with new types of waltzes like the Boston, the hesitation, and the half-and-half. The Latin American tango and maxixe were performed to syncopated music and became part of the ragtime scene around 1915.

Ragtime bandleader James Reese Europe, who formed the Clef Club for New York City's black musicians, was also music director for the popular white dance team of Irene and Vernon Castle, who were the first white entertainers to hire black musicians. Beginning in 1914, Europe helped to create a demand for black music and black dance-band musicians.

Between 1897 and 1899 more than 150 piano rags were published, the most important being **Scott Joplin**'s (c. 1867–1917) "Maple Leaf Rag" (1899). Music publisher John Stark called Joplin's music "classic ragtime." Others who wrote this type of ragtime were black Missourians James Scott (1885–1938) and Louis Chauvin. White composers like J. Russel Robinson and Paul Pratt also wrote classic ragtime.

New York City, with its lively entertainment and music-publishing industry, called Tin Pan Alley, attracted many ragtimers. Some of the better pianists developed a style known as "stride." Among the leaders of this style were **Eubie Blake** (1883–1983), James P. Johnson (1894–1955), and Luckey Roberts (1887–1968). Black musical theater in New York included a great deal of ragtime.

Composer and bandleader **James Reese Europe** (1881–1919) became one of the most influential musicians on the late ragtime scene in New York. He formed the Clef Club in 1910, an organization and booking agency for New York's black musicians. Pianist "Jelly Roll" Morton (1885–1941), one of the greatest early jazz musicians, was active from the early ragtime years but did most of his publishing and recording during the 1920s and 1930s. Although many black performers were admired during the ragtime years—including a number of women performers—those who left no recorded or published music have been largely forgotten.

Ragtime gave rise to jazz between 1915 and 1920. At first there was little difference between the two, but by the end of World War I (1914–18), jazz had replaced ragtime as the most important native music of the United States. However, ragtime continued to be played, and many jazz musicians, such as instrumentalist Peter Bocage (1887–1967), considered themselves ragtimers.

Ragtime Revival

A revival of ragtime music took place during the 1970s, and since that time a number of new ragtime performers, white and African American, have recorded the old ragtime tunes. The revival is considered to have been led by white musician Max Morath (1926–), called "The Ragtime Man." Among others to record at the turn of the century are pianists Glen Jenks and Dan Grinstead (*Ragtime, Bigtime*, 1995) and Frank French and Scott Kirby (*Bucktown in the '90s*, 1995); stride pianist Tom Roberts, who brought back Luckey Roberts' few recordings with *Roberts Plays Roberts* (1999); white musician Jo Ann Castle (*Ragtime Favorites* 1995); and the St. Louis Ragtimers, a band that has been performing and recording since the late 1960s.

Rainey, Gertrude Pridgett "Ma"

SINGER
April 26, 1886–December 22, 1939

Ma Rainey, known as "the mother of **the blues**," supposedly coined the term "blues" after she began singing the mournful songs she heard another young woman sing in tent shows. Rainey became one of the most loved blues and vaudeville (a variety show) singers of the early twentieth century. She sang about the worries of country folk, white and black, in the traditional style of the rural South.

Born Gertrude Pridgett, the second of five children of Thomas and Ella Pridgett of Columbus, Georgia, Rainey performed in a local show, "A Bunch of Blackberries," at age fourteen. At eighteen she married tent showman Will Rainey, and they began traveling from town to town as a comedy song-and-dance act, the Assassinators of the Blues, accompanied by the Rabbit Foot Minstrels.

She left her husband after twelve years but continued to play on the tent circuit as a solo act. She sang with jug bands and with small jazz bands that sometimes included well-known musicians like **Coleman Hawkins** (1904–1969).

Rainey's first recording was "Moonshine Blues," produced in 1923. She recorded ninety-three songs, many of which she wrote. Although less popular than her fellow blues singer **Bessie Smith** (1894–1937), Rainey had a loyal following until her last days on the tent-show circuit, in the 1930s. She retired to Columbus, Georgia, where she opened her own theater.

Randolph, Asa Philip

LABOR AND CIVIL RIGHTS LEADER
April 15, 1889–May 11, 1979

Asa Philip Randolph organized the Brotherhood of Sleeping Car Porters labor union and was a civil rights leader. Randolph migrated from

Florida to New York City in 1911 and settled in the African-American neighborhood of Harlem. He attended the City College of New York, where he took courses in history, philosophy, economics, and political science and became active in the Socialist Party (a political party that calls for collective ownership of property and for political power to be exercised by the whole community).

In 1917 he and his friend Chandler Owen founded and began editing *The Messenger,* a monthly journal subtitled *The Only Radical Magazine Published by Negroes.* The journal campaigned against **lynching**s in the South, opposed America's participation in World War I (1914–18), counseled African-American men to resist being forced to register for military service, and urged blacks to participate in trade union movements.

In 1925 a delegation of Pullman porters (baggage handlers who worked on railroad sleeping cars; the "Pullman car," designed for sleeping or entertaining, was named after its inventor, George Pullman) approached Randolph with a request that he organize their workforce into a labor union. Randolph undertook the task—a decision that launched his career as a national leader in the fields of labor and civil rights. But establishing the **Brotherhood of Sleeping Car Porters** was a far more difficult task than he had anticipated. Not until 1937, after Congress had passed supportive labor legislation laws, did the Brotherhood of Sleeping Car Porters become recognized as the official representative of the porters.

The brotherhood's victory in 1937 also began Randolph's career as a national civil rights leader; he emerged from the struggle with Pullman as one of the more respected figures in black America.

In 1941 Randolph organized the March on Washington. Faced with Randolph's threat to lead a people's march on the nation's capital, President Franklin D. Roosevelt (1882–1945; president 1933–45) issued an order banning the exclusion of blacks from employment in defense plants. That

breakthrough brought Randolph to the forefront of black leadership. The March on Washington movement disintegrated by the end of the 1940s. By then, however, Randolph had secured another historic executive order—this one from President Harry S. Truman (1884–1972; president 1945–53), in 1948, outlawing segregation in the armed services. Scholars were to see Randolph's movement as one of the most remarkable in American history.

Randolph's methods influenced the civil rights leader Dr. **Martin Luther King Jr.**'s (1929–1968) 1963 March on Washington. Randolph participated in the march, which he called the "March for Jobs and Freedom."

In 1964 President Lyndon B. Johnson (1908–1973; president 1963–69) awarded Randolph the Presidential Medal of Freedom, the nation's highest civilian honor. Randolph spent the remaining years of his active life working on labor issues. He died in 1979, at the age of ninety.

Rangel, Charles Bernard

U.S. CONGRESSMAN
June 11, 1930–

Charles Rangel is a longtime member of the U.S. House of Representatives from New York. Rangel was born and raised in the Harlem neighborhood of New York City. He dropped out of high school in his junior year and worked at odd jobs until 1948, when he enlisted in the U.S. Army. He was sent to South Korea, where he was stationed for four years and served in the **Korean War** (1950–53), earning a Bronze Star Medal of Valor and a Purple Heart.

After the war Rangel returned to high school in New York and received his diploma in 1953. He then entered the New York University School of Commerce, earning a B.S. degree in 1957. Rangel went on to St. John's University Law School, where he obtained his degree in 1960. After law school, Rangel worked as an attorney and provided legal assistance to civil rights activists. In 1961 he was appointed an assistant U.S. attorney in the Southern District of New York.

Rangel began his career in politics in 1966, when he was elected to represent central Harlem in the New York State Assembly. He served two two-year terms in the legislature.

Rangel moved into national politics in 1970, when he narrowly defeated **Adam Clayton Powell Jr.,** who had represented **Harlem, New York** since 1945. Once in office, Rangel immediately established as his top priority the elimination of the drug trade.

In the 1970s Rangel took a leading position as an antiwar congressman. He consistently voted to reduce the **military** budget, opposed the development of the B-1 bomber and nuclear aircraft carriers, and vigorously criticized the **Vietnam War** (1959–75) in Southeast Asia. Rangel's liberalism extended to domestic issues as well. He voted for busing to desegregate schools, the creation of a consumer-protection agency, and the implementation of automobile pollution controls.

Rangel gained national exposure in 1974 as a member of the House Judiciary Committee during the impeachment hearings for President Richard Nixon. That year he was also elected chairman of the **Congressional Black Caucus.** In 1975 Rangel became the first African American appointed to the House Ways and Means Committee. Rangel obtained the chairmanship of the influential health subcommittee of the Ways and Means Committee in 1979. In 1980 Rangel became a member of the Democratic Steering and Policy Committee, and in 1983 he was made a deputy whip by Speaker of the House Tip O'Neill. He was also appointed chairman of the Select Committee on Narcotics.

In 1989, as chairman of the House Narcotics Task Force, Rangel led a congressional delegation to the Caribbean and Mexico to help coordinate the international crackdown on drugs. In 1994 Rangel was challenged in the Democratic Primary by Adam Clayton Powell IV, son of the man he had unseated, but he emerged victorious.

Elected for his fourteenth term in 1996, Rangel continued to be one of the most influential members of the U.S. House of Representatives.

Rap

"Rap" is an African-American term that describes a stylized way of speaking that uses metaphor (use of one word or phrase in place of another to suggest a likeness between them; for example, "drowning in money" to suggest "rich"), repetition, rhyme, and "signifyin'" (indirect references). The term is credited to the 1960s civil rights activist **"H. Rap" Brown** (1943–), whose adopted name, "Rap," showed his mastery of a "hip" way of speaking called "rappin'". The roots of rap can be traced from southern oral (spoken) traditions—such as toasts, folktales, **blues,** and game songs like "hambone,"—to northern urban street jive.

Jive is a way of talking that emerged in inner-city communities as the model for rap around 1921 and grew on all levels in the urban environment—from the church to the street corner. It was also used in the literary works of noted black writers and in the speech of **jazz** musicians. By the 1960s jive was redefined and given a newer meaning by H. Rap Brown, who laced his political speeches with signifyin', rhyme, and metaphor.

With the overselling of popular dance forms of the 1970s and the ongoing club gang violence, African-American youths, particularly in New York City, left the indoor scene and returned to neighborhood city parks, where they created outdoor dance clubs featuring a disc jockey, or deejay (one who plays records), and an emcee (master of ceremonies, or announcer). These circumstances increased the development of rap music, which is marked by four distinct phases: the mobile deejay (c. 1972–78), the rappin' emcee and the emergence of the rap music form (1976–78), the early commercial years of rap music (1979–85), and the explosive sound of rap in the musical mainstream (1986–1990s).

By the late 1980s rap music had moved from the inner city into mainstream popular culture. The African-American "hip-hop" style not only

included street art forms but also created an attitude seen in dress, gestures, and language associated with street culture. The introduction of "techno-pop"—music created on synthesizers and drum machines—in rap music gave rise to "sampling," the digital reproduction of prerecorded sounds. Other factors that broadened the appeal of rap in popular culture were the rise of female rap artists and the different sounds of rap: party rap, political rap, "gangsta" rap, and eclectic rap (a cross between party and hardcore rap).

Rap music not only became musically diverse but culturally diverse as well. A few white rap artists existed in the shadows of their African-American counterparts, but others, like the Beastie Boys, House of Pain, and Eminem, crossed over into wider acceptance in the 1990s. Also, by the late 1980s the rap scene expanded to include Spanish-speaking performers (whose raps are called "Spanglish").

By the beginning of the 1990s, rap had achieved first-time success in the American mainstream as seen by its use in advertising, fashion, and other musical genres (categories). But despite its popularity, rap created much controversy among critics, who considered its lyrics to be too hardcore and sexually descriptive. Although much of rap's controversy remains unresolved, it continues to appeal to listeners because of its artful use of street jive and funky beats. (*See also* **Social Dance.**)

Rastafarians

The Rastafarians are followers of a religious movement that began in Jamaica during the early twentieth century. In the United States, the Rastafarian movement has been more cultural and is most often associated with a general Afrocentrism (centered on African life and culture) and the popular music known as **reggae.**

The Rastafarian movement began in Kingston, Jamaica, with Christian preachers who were influenced by the teachings of Jamaican labor organizer and black nationalist **Marcus Garvey** (1887–1940), founder of the **Universal Negro Improvement Association (UNIA)** (1914). Garvey traveled to the United States in 1916 to develop a plan to settle African Americans in a new black-governed country in Africa.

Garvey predicted the rise of a powerful black king in **Africa**, based on a biblical Old Testament passage. When Prince Ras Tafari was crowned Haile Selassie I (1892–1975), king of Ethiopia, on November 2, 1930, Garvey's Christian followers believed this fulfilled his prophecy. The new king claimed to be a descendant of the biblical King Solomon and the Queen of Sheba, and the Jamaicans began calling him Jah Rastari, believing he was divine. The new movement became especially popular among Jamaica's poor, who welcomed a chance to better their lives.

These Jamaicans took the king's name, Ras Tafari ("Lion's Head"), and his royal title, Haile Selassie ("Might of the Trinity"), as religious symbols. Calling themselves Rastafarians, they let their hair grow into "dreadlocks," long, matted braids that resemble those worn by Ethiopian tribal warriors

**Jimmy Rasta, the "Rastafarian Man"
(Courtesy of the Jamaican Tourist Board)**

and priests. In doing so they were also following a biblical Old Testament passage that forbids the cutting of hair.

Rastafarians wear the colors of the Ethiopian flag—red, gold, and green—in knitted caps, belts, and badges. They also smoke "ganja" (marijuana) as a religious ritual they say brings them closer to God. Rastafarians are vegetarian and do not eat food that is processed or cooked with salt. They eat lots of fruit and drink homemade juices.

During the late 1960s and early 1970s, Rastafarian culture became popular among the "rude boys," rebellious young men in Kingston's ghettos, who adopted dreadlocks more as a style than a religion and danced to the Rasta-influenced Jamaican popular music, reggae.

Some of these young men, called "dreads," immigrated to the United States in the 1970s to take part in gang warfare over the drug trade and Jamaican politics in New York City. These dreads gave Rastafarians an often undeserved reputation for violence among the police.

As reggae music became more popular in the United States during the 1970s, African Americans and others began to join the Rastafarian movement. Jamaican singer Desmond Dekker's hit song "Israelites" (1968) and the 1969 film *The Harder They Come*, showing the ghettos of Kingston and urban Rastafarian culture, drew more Americans to the Rastafarian movement. Popular Jamaican reggae musicians and Rastafarians Bob Marley (1945–1981) and the Wailers and Peter Tosh (1944–1987) toured the United States throughout the 1970s, turning dreadlocks into both a political and a cultural statement.

In 1990 the U.S. Supreme Court ruled that Rastafarians could not be required to cut their hair in prison because they had a right to religious expression. Miami, Florida, hosted a Rastafarian gathering in 1994 that brought more than 200 delegates from several countries.

Although Rastafarians can be found in almost every African-American community in the United States, it is uncertain how many members the religion has because it has no churches and no organizational structure. Instead, Rastafarians prefer open discussion about politics, African history, and biblical interpretation. As a result, what it means to be a Rastafarian is always being redefined. (*See also* **Afrocentricity.**)

Rawls, Lou Allen

SINGER
December 1, 1936–

Singer Lou Rawls grew up in Chicago, Illinois, and became a member of the Baptist church choir at age seven. While still in high school, Rawls was performing in a local **gospel music** group. In the early 1950s Rawls moved to Los Angeles, California, where he was recruited by the Chosen Gospel Singers, with whom he made his first recording. In 1955 he joined the Pilgrim Travelers, with **Sam Cooke** (1935–1964) before entering the army. Three years later he left the service and rejoined the Travelers.

After the Travelers broke up in 1959, Rawls found work as a **blues** singer in various clubs in Los Angeles. He was performing at the Pandora's Box Coffee Shop for $10 a night when a producer at Capitol Records invited him to make an audition tape, which led to a record contract. In 1962 his first album was released. Rawls followed the album with **jazz** and blues pop songs such as "Love is a Hurting Thing" (1966), which reached number one on the **rhythm-and-blues** chart. Rawls made another album in the 1960s and began to make occasional television appearances.

In 1975 Rawls began a collaboration with Philadelphia International Records, combining his vocal style with a disco beat. In 1977 he won a Grammy Award for his album *Unmistakably Lou*. Since 1981 Rawls has sponsored the United Negro College Fund telethon, raising over $100 million through the early 1990s for the organization. In 1998 his new complex, the Lou Rawls Theater, opened in Chicago. Rawls started his own record lable—Rawls and Brokaw Records—in the 1990s and produced an album in 1998.

Lou Rawls: Selected Albums

Stormy Monday
(1962)

Lou Rawls Live
(1966)

All Things in Time
(1976)

Portrait of the Blues
(1993)

Seasons 4 U
(1998)

Ray, Charles Bennett

MINISTER, JOURNALIST
December 25, 1807–August 15, 1886

Charles Ray was born in Massachusetts. He studied theology at Wesleyan Seminary in Massachusetts in the 1830s and continued his studies at Wesleyan University in Middletown, Connecticut. He was ordained a Methodist minister in 1837 and later joined the Crosby Congregational Church. From 1845 until the 1860s, Ray served as pastor of Bethesda Congregational Church.

Ray was an active abolitionist (a person who worked to eliminate slavery) who worked as a "conductor" on the **Underground Railroad**. (The Underground Railroad was organized largely by African Americans to assist **fugitive slaves** and to obtain their freedom). From 1843 until 1858, Ray was a member and then secretary of the New York Vigilance Committee, which helped runaway slaves. He also served as a member of the American Missionary Association of New York and the Society for the Promotion of Education Among Colored Children. In addition, he was active in the African Society for Mutual Relief, the Congregational Clerical Union, and the Manhattan Congregational Association.

Beginning in 1846, Ray worked as a missionary in New York. In 1837 he was appointed general agent of *The Colored American*, an early African-American weekly publication, of which he became co-owner in 1839 and editor until its closing in 1842. Ray died in New York City in 1886. (*See also* **Abolition**.)

Reconstruction

Reconstruction is a period that began during the American **Civil War** (1861–65) and ended in 1877. It marked the first time the U.S. government took on the responsibility for defining and protecting Americans' civil rights. In the South, African-American men were for the first time given the right to vote and hold office, and they joined with white allies to bring the Republican Party to power. This made Reconstruction the first U.S. experiment in interracial democracy.

Reconstruction during the Civil War

President Abraham Lincoln's (1809–1865) Reconstruction program of December 1863 arranged for Southern states to be readmitted to the Union. The program gave blacks no part in rebuilding the South, however, and voting and holding office were still limited to whites.

Many Northern members of the Republican political party were unhappy with this plan, especially the group known as the Radicals, who had long favored granting equal rights to free blacks in the North. Early in 1865 Lincoln and the Radicals worked together to get congressional approval of the Thirteenth Amendment to the U.S. Constitution, which abolished **slavery** throughout the United States.

Soon after, a bill was passed creating the Freedmen's Bureau, an agency empowered to protect the legal rights of former slaves, provide education and medical care, lease land to blacks, and oversee labor contracts between freed slaves and their employers. In his last speech, shortly before his assassination on April 14, 1865, Lincoln talked of giving black veterans and educated blacks the right to vote.

The Presidents and Reconstruction

After Lincoln's death President Andrew Johnson (1808–1875) gave the states the power to manage their own affairs. White voters returned the upper class to power. They passed laws known as "black codes," designed to regulate the rights of free African Americans. Some states in the Midwest adopted black codes to restrict black rights and prevent more black immigration. The South adopted far more severe codes in an effort to reimpose the controls that existed under slavery.

Unhappy with Johnson's actions, Congress in 1866 overwhelmingly passed the new Civil Rights Bill, which defined all persons born in the United States, regardless of race, as citizens who were entitled to the equal benefits of all laws made to protect individuals and property. Congress also passed a bill extending the life of the Freedmen's Bureau, which had been established for only one year.

To Congress's surprise, Johnson vetoed both bills, saying they gave too much power to the federal government and took away the states' right to control their own affairs. Congress passed the bills anyway, then began to adopt its own plan for Reconstruction. In June 1866 it approved the Fourteenth Amendment, which established equality before the law as a basic right of American citizens, regardless of race, and made the federal government the protector of citizens' rights.

In March 1867, again over Johnson's veto, Congress adopted the Reconstruction Act. This act divided the South into five military districts and called for new state governments, with suffrage (the right to vote) no longer restricted because of race.

In 1868 the House of Representatives impeached (accused of misconduct in office) Johnson, and the Senate came within one vote of removing him from office. Soon after, the Republicans nominated former Civil War Union general Ulysses S. Grant (1822–1885) for president. Grant won the election, and in 1869 Congress approved the **Fifteenth Amendment,** prohibiting the federal and state governments from taking away any citizen's right to vote because of race.

Radical Reconstruction in the South

By 1870 all of the former Confederate states had been readmitted to the Union, and nearly all were under Republican Party influence. With African Americans making up about one-fourth of state legislators, the states drafted new constitutions that made government more democratic, modernized the tax system, established state-supported schools and hospitals, and guaranteed the rights of black citizens. Many institutions remained segregated by race, but by the 1870s more than half of black children were attending public schools.

CHRONOLOGY

Reconstruction

January 1, 1863
President Abraham Lincoln signs the Emancipation Proclamation, freeing all slaves in the South.

December 1863
Lincoln outlines his plan for Reconstruction.

Early 1865
Congress approves the Thirteenth Amendment, abolishing slavery throughout the United States.

April 14-15, 1865
Lincoln is shot and dies the following day; Vice president Andrew Johnson becomes president.

1865
The American Civil War ends.

April 1866
Congress passes the Civil Rights Bill. It is the first attempt to define and protect American citizenship rights.

June 1866
Congress approves the Fourteenth Amendment. It makes equality before the law a basic right of American citizens, regardless of race, and makes the federal government the protector of citizens' rights.

March 1867
Over Johnson's veto, Congress adopts the Reconstruction Act. Black men gain the right to vote. Most eligible African Americans register to vote.

THE MEANING OF FREEDOM

African-American slaves in the South were freed under the Emancipation Proclamation in 1863, and Reconstruction began about one year later. To the former slaves, this new freedom meant independence from white control—as individuals and as a community—and a great deal more.

Exercising their newfound freedom, former slaves traveled in search of better jobs or family members from whom they had been separated during slavery. A reporter met a freedman in 1865 who had walked more than six hundred miles searching for his wife and children. Many blacks moved to cities or towns where freedmen were more accepted.

Before the Civil War, nearly every Southern state had prohibited education for slaves. During Reconstruction adults as well as children filled schools established during and after the war. Northern societies, the Freedmen's Bureau, and state governments provided most of the funding for these schools, but often blacks themselves pooled their meager earnings to buy land, build schools, and hire teachers.

Churches had always played a central role in black communities, and black ministers became active in politics—more than two hundred held a public office during Reconstruction. Eager to play a part in their government, blacks organized meetings, parades, petitions, and conventions, demanding equality before the law and the right to vote.

Throughout Reconstruction black voters provided most of the Republican Party's support, although whites held most top offices. Still, more than 1,500 African Americans held positions of political power in the Reconstruction South, 14 in the U.S. House of Representatives and 2 in the Senate, as well as nearly 700 in state legislatures. The presence of these black officials and whites who supported them made a real difference in fairness to blacks in the South.

The Overthrow of Reconstruction

As African Americans gained new rights during Reconstruction, the South's traditional leaders—the planters, merchants, and Democratic politicians—became increasingly angry, claiming the new state governments were dishonest, inefficient, and controlled by blacks. They were determined to overthrow Reconstruction, restore white leadership, and regain their black labor force.

Reconstruction in Tennessee and Virginia ended as early as 1869 and 1870, when Democrats regained control of the governments. Elsewhere in the South a white terrorist organization called the **Ku Klux Klan** and others used violence to prevent blacks from voting and murdered many black, and some white, Republican leaders.

In 1870–71 Congress passed three Enforcement Acts outlawing terrorist societies. The acts made any crime aimed at taking away civil rights a fed-

FORTY ACRES AND A MULE

During Reconstruction many freed blacks yearned to farm their own land but were forced to work for white employers, who still held most of the property. In December 1864 Union General William T. Sherman (1820–1891), after capturing Savannah, Georgia, near the end of the Civil War, met with a group of the city's black leaders. They told Sherman that the best guarantee of freedom was to have land and "turn it and till it by our own labor." Four days later Sherman issued Field Order Number 15, setting aside the Sea Islands and part of the South Carolina and Georgia coasts for black settlement. Each family would receive forty acres of land, and the army would loan them mules to help work the land. This agreement resulted in the phrase "forty acres and a mule," which was heard throughout the South.

By June, forty thousand former slaves were settled on 400,000 acres of "Sherman land." In the summer of 1865, however, President Andrew Johnson ordered land in federal hands returned to its former owners, and blacks were forced to leave their forty acres. The result was a deep sense of betrayal that survived among the freed blacks and their descendants long after the end of Reconstruction.

eral offense. In 1871 Grant sent troops to arrest hundreds of accused Klansmen. The Klan ended after many were tried and jailed.

In 1873 the United States entered an economic depression that took Republican and presidential focus away from the South. President Rutherford B. Hayes (1822–1893), a Republican elected in 1876, ended federal intervention in the South in 1877, and Reconstruction came to an end.

Southern states disregarded the Fourteenth and Fifteenth Amendments and, beginning in the 1890s, stripped African Americans of the right to vote. Blacks found themselves caught in a web of segregation, poverty, and loss of political power. The South as a whole fell behind the rest of the nation in meeting its responsibilities to citizens. It also remained economically depressed well into the twentieth century. Not until the **Civil Rights movement** of the 1960s would the nation again address the issues of the Reconstruction period.

Redding, Otis

SOUL SINGER, COMPOSER
September 9, 1941–December 10, 1967

Otis Redding was one of the most powerful and original singer-songwriters of the 1960s and a star of Stax Records, the label that became internationally successful releasing gritty southern soul music. Redding grew up in Macon, Georgia. He began playing drums in school and was paid six dollars an hour on Sundays to accompany **gospel music** groups appearing on local radio station WIBB. Redding stayed in school until the tenth grade but quit to help support his family. He worked at a gas station, as a well digger, and occasionally as a musician.

As a singer, Redding began to win local talent contests with his spontaneous and tough vocal style. He traveled to Los Angeles, California, in mid-1960, where he recorded four songs, and then returned to Macon in 1961, where he recorded "Shout Bamalama." His break came in 1963, when he sang his song "These Arms of Mine" at a Stax recording session. When the record made it into the **Rhythm-and-Blues** Top Twenty in 1964, Redding's career was launched. Over the next five years, his popularity grew steadily through fiery live performances, hit singles, and critically praised albums.

Redding was able to capitalize on the liberal climate of the 1960s, crossing over to white listeners in the United States and in Europe. His performances in England were so popular that he was named Best Male Vocalist in a poll sponsored by the music publication *Melody Maker*. (This award had been won by white singer Elvis Presley for the previous eight years.)

Redding's death in a plane crash near Madison, Wisconsin, in 1967 came at the peak of his career. It left his fans wondering what might have been developing in Redding's music. "(Sittin' on) The Dock of the Bay," recorded three days before his death, revealed a different, introspective musical direction. It became his biggest hit record.

Otis Redding: Selected Recordings

"I've Been Loving You Too Long"
(single)

"Try a Little Tenderness"
(single)

"I Can't Turn You Loose"
(single)

Otis Blue
(album)

The Soul Album
(album)

The Great Otis Redding Sings Soul Ballads
(album)

Red Summer

During the summer and fall of 1919, twenty-five race riots erupted across the United States, the largest in Charleston, South Carolina; Washington, D.C.; Chicago, Illinois; Knoxville, Tennessee; Omaha, Nebraska; and Elaine, Arkansas. Whites usually started the riots, saying blacks had challenged their authority. Blacks defended themselves, shooting and beating their attackers. **James Weldon Johnson** (1871–1938), investigator for the **National Association for the Advancement of Colored People (NAACP),** called this period "Red Summer."

After **World War I** (1914–18) the rising cost of goods coupled with unemployment caused tension between blacks and whites. Northern whites were angered and frightened by the number of blacks who had migrated north during the war, and southern whites objected to blacks' new self-confidence and willingness to challenge racism.

Black soldiers came home from Europe, where they had been treated as equals by the French. Some had won medals for bravery, and all expected gratitude and employment opportunities. They received neither. There were seventy-six **lynching**s in a month and a half; a dozen of the victims were black veterans still in uniform.

Adding to the racial strife was the "Red scare." Americans feared that a revolution led by radicals, similar to the 1917 Communist revolution in Russia, might take place in the United States.

Red Summer convinced many African Americans that fighting in the war did not guarantee they would no longer be dominated by whites. Many blacks turned to militant action; others increased their commitment to civil rights protest or supported black nationalist leaders like **Marcus Garvey** (1887–1940), who wanted to create a self-governed nation for blacks in Africa.

Reed, Ishmael

AUTHOR
February 22, 1938–

Ishmael Reed was born in Chattanooga, Tennnesse, but was raised and educated in Buffalo, New York. In 1962 he moved to New York City to become a writer, where he met a group of young black writers from *Umbra* magazine and workshop, an important group in the **Black Arts movement** of the late 1960s and early 1970s. His first novel, *Free-Lance Pallbearers* (1967), a parody of **Ralph Ellison**'s *Invisible Man*, is a savage satire of the United States during the Vietnam War years (1959–75), personified by the president, Harry Sam, who literally eats American children.

In 1967 Reed moved to Berkeley, California, where he cofounded and published *The Yardbird Reader* (1972–76), a literary magazine that reflected his multiethnic spirit. His second novel, *Yellow Back Radio Broke-Down* (1969), a bizarre western, compares western culture unfavorably with black culture. His next novel, *Mumbo Jumbo* (1972), launches what is known as Reed's "countermythology," in which he challenges the Western tendency to ignore the influence of African civilizations. His later novels, including *Reckless Eyeballing* (1986) and *Japanese by Spring* (1993), all promote, in some way, this countermythology, which Reed calls Neo-HooDooism.

Even though Reed is known primarily as a novelist, he has produced a number of books of poetry, plays and essays. Among his poetry collections are *Conjure* (1972) and *New and Collected Poems* (1988). Mostly written in free verse, his poems are experimental, humorous, and satiric, and draw from many non-European cultures for their symbolism. Reed's essay collections include *Shrovetide in Old New Orleans* (1978), *Writin' Is Fightin': Thirty-Seven Years of Boxing on Paper* (1988), *Airing Dirty Laundry* (1993), and *Multi-America: Essays on Cultural Wars and Cultural Peace* (1997). In 1998 Reed was awarded the prestigious MacArthur Fellowship, or "genius grant."

Reggae

Reggae is a type of popular music that began in Jamaica and became successful worldwide during the late twentieth century. It has a medium-to-slow steady bass rhythm, with roots in calypso music of the West Indies and American rhythm and blues. In the 1990s reggae had a core black audience, but it appeals to all races, as a type of international music, known as World Beat.

Selected Reggae Recordings

Jimmy Cliff (and other artists)—*The Harder They Come*
(soundtrack; 1972)

Bob Marley and the Wailers—*Natty Dread*
(1974)

Burning Spear—*Marcus Garvey*
(1975)

Peter Tosh—*Legalize It*
(1976)

Lee "Scratch" Perry—*The Return of Pipecock Jackxon*
(1980)

Johnny Osborne—*Truth and Rights*
(1980)

Black Uhuru—*Anthem*
(1983)

Mighty Diamonds—*Reggae Street*
(1987)

Andrew Tosh—*Original Man*
(1988)

Ziggy Marley and the Melody Makers—*Conscious Party*
(1989)

Desmond Dekker and The Specials—*King of Ska*
(1998)

Shabba Ranks—*Get Up Stand Up*
(1998)

Third World—*Generation Coming*
(1999)

Toots and the Maytals—*20 Massive Hits*
(2000)

Roland Alphonso—*Something Special: Ska Hot Shots*
(2000)

Sugar Minott—*Ghetto-Ology Plus Dub*
(2000)

Linval Thompson—*Ride on Dreadlocks 1975–1977*
(2000)

Origins of Reggae

During the 1950s Jamaicans enjoyed U.S. radio broadcasts of rhythm-and-blues (R&B) songs recorded in New Orleans, Louisiana. These were often played on mobile "sound systems" at dances. In the 1960s Jamaicans began making their own records, on which island singers and musicians combined regional West Indian musical styles like calypso and mento with American R&B. This music was called "ska," after its scratchy guitar sounds. As the rhythm slowed to a medium tempo in later years, it was called "rock steady," and then finally—at its slowest—"reggae," after the 1968 song "Do the Reggay" by Toots and the Maytals.

Reggae Styles

The most well known reggae styles are "dub" reggae and "toasting" (or "deejaying"), which became popular during the late 1960s and early 1970s. Dub reggae uses studio sound effects, like echo, with booming bass and percussion. This style was introduced by producers such as Lee Perry and Augustus Pablo, who created unusual sound mixes in early recording studios.

Toasting began when Jamaican disc jockeys (DJs) began to chant rhythmically over the records they played to encourage dancers. They were imitating American radio DJs. Toasting is similar to the African-American musical style known as "rap." Made popular by reggae stars such as U-Roy and Big Youth, toasting records were played in the 1970s in U.S. cities with large West Indian populations, such as New York. Some people think toasting directly influenced the birth of American rap.

Reggae and the Rasatafarians

By the late 1960s reggae performers began to sing about Jamaican life and culture, especially the "rude boys," (local street gangs) and the religious group known as the Rastafarians. **Rastafarianism**, with roots in the Bible and in mysticism, began in Jamaica in the 1930s, offering the poor hope for a better future in an African homeland. Many Jamaican musicians were Rastafarian, so its terms and beliefs found their way into reggae songs.

From Jamaica to the United States

Most Americans were introduced to reggae during the 1970s through the Jamaican film *The Harder They Come* (1972), which starred reggae singer Jimmy Cliff (1948–) as Ivan Martin, a country boy who becomes a pop star and outlaw. The film has a reggae sound track and ran for several years in U.S. college towns and at art cinemas.

Around the same time, Americans discovered the Jamaican group Bob Marley (1945–1981) and the Wailers. Marley was the key performer who made reggae popular, through his many concert tours and albums of protest and love songs, including *Catch a Fire* (1973), *Natty Dread* (1974), and *Exodus* (1977). Marley became the face, voice, and symbol of reggae for most of the world. Singer Peter Tosh (1944–1987) split from Marley's band and became a top solo reggae performer until his death in 1987.

Jimmy Cliff, one of the best-known reggae artists, performs in concert (Corbis Corporation. Reproduced by permission)

Changing American Audience

Reggae's American audience was at first made up of white rock-music fans, who loved its exotic Caribbean flavor, its driving beat, and its message of separation from mainstream society. These fans had heard reggae on rock radio stations that played the ska hit song "My Boy Lollipop" (Millie Small, 1964) and the rock-steady classic "Israelites" (Desmond Dekker, 1968). Reggae later influenced the music of top white rock artists such as Paul Simon and Eric Clapton.

In the late 1970s a new rock music style—new wave—adopted many of reggae's rhythms and recording techniques, especially dub. Another emerging style, punk rock, contained lyrics that agreed with Rastafarian ideas about the fall of upper-class society and commercialism.

During the 1980s and 1990s reggae's black audience in the United States grew, partly because of the rising West Indian immigrant population and a growing interest in **Afrocentricity** (African culture), which reggae expresses through its Rastafarian influence. But the primary reason reggae caught on with African Americans is its "dance-hall style" songs—fast-talking toasting songs that are so similar to rap music. With a growing reggae audience, some performers have replaced traditional instruments with electronic keyboards and percussion, but others are returning to the old-style Jamaican reggae.

Religion

Religion has always been an important part of the lives of African Americans, through good times and bad. African-American religious beliefs have gone through several developmental stages over time. The one constant is that it has always provided a source of community and personal strength.

African American Religion up to the Civil War

In the American colonies and the early United States, most African Americans practiced the type of religion they were exposed to, which in most cases was Protestant evangelicalism. Protestantism is a form of Christianity that teaches personal moral strength and rejects the teachings of the Pope, head of the Roman Catholic Church. Evangelicalism, which literally means "pertaining to the Gospel," offers the teachings of the Holy Bible as a guide for life. African religions were brought with slaves, and elements of these religions survived in Christianity. But African religions were difficult to maintain in the context of **slavery** and the need to adapt to American culture. In the eighteenth century an African-American religious identity began to take shape.

By the time of the American **Civil War** (1861–65), approximately one out of every seven slaves belonged to an organized religion. Religion served two functions at this time: it served as a means to keep blacks obedient during slavery, and it provided a source of inner strength among slaves, who believed that everything would be made right in heaven.

In the North, free blacks were able to form their own churches. At many of these churches blacks prayed for enslaved African Americans in the South. Preachers taught blacks to be law-abiding citizens, knowing they had to prove to whites that free blacks posed no threat to society.

One of the more-popular black churches that formed at the time was the **African Methodist Episcopal (AME) Church.** Founded by **Richard Allen** in 1816, the AME Church attempted to establish a free form of government for the African-American community in addition to providing a source of

RELIGION AND THE FEAR OF SLAVE REVOLTS

When slaves were first brought to America they were not instructed on matters of faith because many whites believed that blacks did not have a soul. In addition, whites feared that if they introduced religion to blacks it might inspire them to rebel against slavery. However, once laws were created stating that practicing religion did not make blacks free from bondage, blacks were given greater liberty to practice a faith. In addition, many slave owners believed that introducing Christianity to slaves would make them more peaceful and less inclined to rebel.

spiritual growth. By the beginning of the Civil War, the AME Church had twenty thousand members.

Another religious group that generated a large following was the **Baptists.** The Baptist Church gets its name from the baptism ritual, in which the body is briefly placed under water in a symbolic purification from sin. The Baptist faith eventually became the most popular religion among African Americans, with some eight million members by the late twentieth century.

African-American Religion from the Civil War to World War II

After the Civil War, religion became a central part of African-American life in both northern and southern states. The role of women in African-American religion began to change after the war. Although women outnumbered men at church services, men dominated the religious leadership roles. However, in the 1900s many black religious denominations, such as the Holiness movement, began allowing women to be ordained in leadership positions. Some women who were frustrated by the largely male leadership established their own ministries in these groups.

The development of larger cities as a result of economic growth presented a problem for black churches. In 1910 nearly 90 percent of the black population lived in the South. Religion was stronger there among blacks because of racial discrimination and segregation laws that lessened economic and political opportunities for African Americans.

One problem black churches faced was the increasing movement of blacks northward in search of greater economic opportunity. Southern churches lost members, and northern churches became overcrowded. As a result, northern black churches began taking on more functions than they could handle, such as providing a place of worship, **education,** and a place to socialize.

By **World War I** (1914–18), tensions began to emerge between the existing northern black church culture and the flood of southern blacks. One of the biggest sources of conflict was the love of **gospel music** in the South, which was not a part of church services in the North.

The tension resulted in some blacks seeking out different forms of religion. However, the majority of blacks in the years after **World War II**

BLACKS SEEK OUT ALTERNATIVE RELIGIONS

In the years before World War II (1939–45) blacks began to experiment with different religions as a result of the crisis brought on by the Great Migration (massive movement of blacks to northern cities). In the late 1920s **Marcus Garvey** established the **Universal Negro Improvement Association,** which preached separation from white society in a "Back-to-Africa" movement. Although the organization attracted a large following, it began to fade when Garvey was forced to leave the United States in 1927.

Several small religious sects also developed but never generated national appeal among blacks. Blacks also began converting to Judaism and **Islam** at this time. Islam was made popular by **Elijah Muhammad,** one of the most influential leaders of the **Nation of Islam.** This religion became popular with black leaders such as **Malcolm X,** who saw Christianity as a means to keep blacks in oppression.

(1939–45) remained faithful to Christian denominations until black leaders found a way to accommodate the migration of blacks from the South. The solution came in the form of community service. Northern black churches began adopting programs to help African Americans solve everyday problems by offering economic and recreational activities. Baptist churches took on a community-development role, which created new responsibilities for black ministers. In addition to being religious leaders, ministers took on the task of helping blacks improve the secular (nonreligious) aspects of their lives.

Religion from the Civil Rights Movement to 2000

The most influential African-American figure during the 1960s was the Reverend **Martin Luther King Jr.** King's training in the Baptist tradition and his popularity as a preacher helped him become one of the most powerful political figures in U.S. history. King's nonviolent activism with the **Southern Christian Leadership Conference (SCLC)** laid a foundation of followers who took his lead in the fight against racism. Peaceful demonstrations of the **Civil Rights movement** were viewed by blacks as both religious and political events.

However, not all blacks believed in King's method of peaceful demonstration. Young blacks who wanted an immediate solution to racial injustice began the Black Power movement. Members of this movement believed in using any means necessary, including violence, to end racism. The Black Power movement caused several blacks to question the religion they were practicing. The movement claimed that even religion was an instrument used by whites to keep blacks down. Some blacks therefore began to seek out alternatives to Christianity, such as the **Nation of Islam,** an African-American organization founded on the practice of Islam, a religious faith with Middle Eastern and African origins. The majority of blacks remained within the Christian faith, but they began pressuring churches for more black leadership positions.

Black religious leaders of the twenty-first century face the challenge of unifying black religion across the globe. In the absence of a unified black church, several layers of black religious worship exist throughout the United States. Efforts have been made to construct a centralized black religious structure without much success. The Interdenominational Theological Center has made one of the most successful attempts at African-American "ecumenism" (worldwide unity within a religious group).

While religious leaders debate over how to unify the structure of black religion, religious practice within the African-American community will continue to enrich the culture and lives of African Americans, providing a constant source of personal and community strength. (*See also* **Christian Methodist Episcopal Church; Episcopalians; Jehovah's Witnesses; Mormons; Nat Turner's Rebellion; National Baptists Convention; Pentecostalism; Rastafarians; Roman Catholicism; Voodoo.**)

Black religious leaders of the twenty-first century face the challenge of unifying black religion across the globe.

Rhode Island

First African-American Settlers: The exact date when blacks first arrived in Rhode Island is unknown, although by 1637 American Indian warriors captured in the Pequot War were being exchanged for black slaves from the Caribbean.

Slave Population: Slavery became a mainstay of the colony's economy, making Newport one of the leading slave-trading centers in North America. Slaves were generally employed as house servants, although some became skilled or unskilled laborers. The presence of so large a black population created a strong community network, leading to the creation of what the slaves called " 'Lection Day," in which a body of black officials would be elected to govern the community.

Free Black Population: A gradual emancipation law was passed in 1784 declaring that all children born into slavery after March 1 of that year were to be free. Black Rhode Islanders left in droves, although others were attracted to a growing, developing, industrialized Providence. By the mid-1800s laws were in effect disfranchising black males (taking away their right to vote), forbidding interracial marriage, and segregating public schools.

Reconstruction: Responding to persistent racism, Rhode Island blacks organized themselves to serve their community through the formation of humanitarian societies, churches, fraternal orders, and newspapers.

The Great Depression: In the early decades of the twentieth century, black Rhode Islanders continued to suffer from discrimination in jobs, housing, and education. In spite of this, a number of black attorneys were admitted to the bar, and others owned and operated their own businesses.

Civil Rights Movement: Owing to efforts by leaders in Rhode Island's black community, by the 1970s African Americans began to be employed as college professors, bank tellers, schoolteachers, and policemen, although their numbers remained small.

Current African-American Population: According to U.S. Census Bureau estimates, the total black population in Rhode Island was 49,476 (5 percent of the state population) as of July 1, 1998.

Key Figures: Charles Walton (1948–), Rhode Island's first black state senator.

Rhythm and Blues

The term "rhythm and blues" was created by white-owned record companies in the 1950s to describe music created by black musicians for black listeners. Also known as "R&B," the music was a combination of the **jazz, the blues,** and **gospel music** popular in black communities after **World War II** (1939–45). During the 1950s R&B gave birth to rock-and-roll music and became the most popular music in the United States and the world.

Early Influences on Rhythm and Blues

Jazz music of the 1920s and 1930s had the most influence on the R&B sound. Jazz was so popular during this period that the 1920s came to be known as "the Jazz Age." The music was created by black musicians, and its main purpose was to get people dancing. In the 1940s many bands featured saxophonists who played in a style that drove dancers to faster and wilder steps. One of the greatest bandleaders and saxophonists of this time was Louis Jordan. His biggest hits, including "Is You Is or Is You Ain't My Baby?" (1944) and "Let the Good Times Roll" (1945), are now considered classics.

Vocal groups of the 1940s—known as "doo-wop" groups—also helped develop the distinctive rhythms and vocals that characterize R&B music. After World War II dozens of important vocal groups dominated black popular music. Groups such as **The Platters** ("Only You," 1955) and The Clovers ("Love Potion Number Nine," 1959) used simple arrangements with few instruments to highlight their vocal style.

The blues music of the late 1940s and early 1950s, which featured loud guitars, also influenced R&B music. The best examples of this influence are **Muddy Waters** and **B. B. King**. Female blues singers also made the rhythm-and-blues charts in the 1950s and 1960s. **Etta James** recorded "Something's Got a Hold on Me" in 1962, a song that made her reputation as a rhythm-and-blues singer. **Dinah Washington** also had great success as an R&B singer, with records such as "Baby Get Lost" (1949) and "What a Difference a Day Makes" (1959).

The Coming of Rock and Roll

In the early 1950s the terms "rock and roll" and "rhythm and blues" described the same kind of music. As more white teenagers began listening to rhythm and blues, the term "rock and roll" was applied to white musicians such as Elvis Presley, Buddy Holly, and Roy Orbison. Their music copied elements of rhythm-and-blues style but was aimed at white audiences. However, black musicians remained crucial to the development of rock and

roll, even after the term was being applied mostly to white musicians. **Chuck Berry** was very successful with white audiences. His hits "Maybellene" (1955), "Johnny B. Goode" (1958), and "Sweet Little Sixteen" (1958) became immediate rock classics.

Doo-Wop Singers

In the 1950s and 1960s unrehearsed street-corner singing was an important part of African-American urban life. Solo rhythm-and-blues singers who drew on gospel and doo-wop traditions were among the most popular recording artists of the era. **Jackie Wilson** had a huge following for his "Lonely Teardrops" (1958) and "Higher and Higher" (1959). Ben E. King also worked with The Drifters before recording "Spanish Harlem" (1960) and "Stand by Me" (1960). Frankie Lymon and The Teenagers achieved great popularity with songs such as "Why Do Fools Fall in Love?" (1956) and "I'm Not a Juvenile Delinquent" (1956).

African-American Soul Music

By 1964 black popular music had acquired a new name: "soul." This music, which features both shouting and slower musical rhythms, bloomed alongside the black pride movement of the 1960s. The music was made for black listeners and was part of a new culture that celebrated black values and black styles in hair and clothing. Soul music also confronted political issues that were important to African Americans during the 1960s. **James Brown**, who had been a successful recording artist throughout the 1950s, forever linked soul music and the Black Power movement, with his song "Say It Loud, I'm Black and I'm Proud" (1968). **Aretha Franklin** is perhaps the most famous soul singer of all time. Her powerful, emotional voice made songs such as "Respect" (1967) and "Chain of Fools" (1967) into soul masterpieces.

The record company **Motown** Records became prominent during the 1960s, launching the careers of soul artists such as **Marvin Gaye**, **Stevie Wonder**, and **Gladys Knight**. Vocal groups such as **Smokey Robinson** and The Miracles, **Michael Jackson and the Jackson Family**, **The Four Tops**, **The Temptations**, and **The Supremes** also got their start as soul singers for Motown.

In the 1970s soul-style vocal groups remained popular. Groups like Earth, Wind and Fire and The Spinners, along with singers such as **Roberta Flack** and **Al Green**, created slow, emotional ballads and love songs. During the 1980s and 1990s Whitney Houston and Luther Vandross continued the tradition of the gospel-influenced singing style that characterizes soul.

The Late Twentieth Century and Alternative R&B

Although the category of rhythm and blues has changed since the 1950s, the term continues to describe the characteristics of African-American popular music. In the 1980s and 1990s, musicians such as **Prince**, Lenny Kravitz, and Living Color have taken inspiration from **Little Richard**, James Brown, and **Jimi Hendrix**. Younger musicians such as the group Boyz II Men have updated the close-harmony sound of the 1940s and 1950s. By the late 1990s there was a new movement called "alternative R&B," sung by

younger artists such as Des'ree, D'Angelo, and Groove Theory. Alternative R&B adds elements of hip-hop and swing music to the traditional blend of blues, jazz, and soul.

Riggs, Marlon Troy

FILMMAKER
February 3, 1957–April 5, 1994

Marlon Riggs was born in Texas and received his bachelor's degree from Harvard University (Cambridge, Massachusetts) in 1978. After a short stint as an assistant with a television station in Texas, he attended the University of California at Berkeley and in 1981 received a master's degree in journalism, concentrating on documentary (based on facts) filmmaking.

The next year, he began work as a filmmaker. In 1986 Riggs wrote, produced, and directed *Ethnic Notions*, a study of different stereotypes (preconceived ideas about a group of people, treating them all as having the same characteristics) of African Americans. The film won an Emmy Award for outstanding achievement in television in 1988. In 1987 Riggs became a professor at the University of California at Berkeley and taught there until his death.

In 1988 Riggs began work on a documentary about black gay men and received a grant for the film. Shortly after beginning the project, Riggs learned he was infected with the virus that causes AIDS. He claimed the diagnosis helped personalize the film. The finished work, a mixture of documentary film, poetry, and Riggs's personal memories, was released in 1989. In 1991 the film became the center of a national controversy after it was scheduled to be shown on a public television series. Its frank discussions of black homosexuality horrified conservative critics like Senator Jesse Helms of North Carolina. In 1992 conservative Republican presidential candidate Pat Buchanan used a section of the work in a campaign commercial. Riggs, in turn, complained that Buchanan and others misrepresented his work.

Riggs continued to produce works about the black gay male experience. He also produced films about other subjects. His last project was *Black Is . . . Black Isn't*, an unfinished documentary about African-American intellectuals. Although Riggs championed black culture and the fight against racism, he remained critical of blacks' homophobia (discrimination against gays) and silence on AIDS. Riggs died of AIDS at his home in Oakland, California, in 1994. (*See also:* **Film**)

Marlon Riggs: Selected Films

Tongues Untied
(1988)

Color Adjustment
(1989)

Anthem
(1990)

Non, Je Ne Regrette Rien/No Regret
(1991)

Roach, Max Lemuel

JAZZ DRUMMER, BANDLEADER
January 10, 1924–

Max Roach was raised in Brooklyn, New York, and studied music as a child with his mother, a **gospel music** singer. He also received music lessons in public school, and by age ten was playing drums in church bands. He performed in Coney Island sideshows such as the Darktown Follies while in

high school. During this time he also began frequenting Minton's Playhouse in **Harlem, New York**, where he met some of the leading **jazz** musicians of the day. In 1941 Roach graduated with honors. Soon after, he started performing regularly with saxophonist **Charlie Parker** (1920–1955), and by the next year he had a strong enough reputation to fill in for several nights with bandleader **Duke Ellington**'s (1899–1974) orchestra. In 1943 and 1944 he recorded and performed with **Coleman Hawkins** (1904–1969). In 1944 he also joined **Dizzy Gillespie**'s (1917–1993) quintet at the Onyx Club.

Roach redefined jazz drumming, and created a new solo role for modern jazz drum performance. By the end of the 1940s, Roach was recognized as one of the leading drummers in jazz. In the early 1950s he continued his prolific career while studying composition and tympani (a type of drum) at the Manhattan School of Music. From 1954 to 1956 he and musician Clifford Brown led the Clifford Brown-Max Roach Quintet, which pioneered the hard-driving jazz style known as "hard hop."

In the 1960s Roach began to combine his music with his politics, with a particular emphasis on racial oppression in both the United States and South Africa. His 1960 recording of *We Insist: Freedom Now Suite* explored the theme of racial oppression in the United States. In the 1960s Roach began to move away from appearing solely in strict jazz contexts. He began performing solo drum compositions as independent pieces. He also recorded original works for vocal choruses and pianoless quartets. In the 1960s Roach taught at the Lenox School of Jazz, and in 1972 he assumed a faculty position at the University of Massachusetts, in Amherst. In the 1980s Roach's amazingly productive career included performances and recordings with a jazz quartet, a percussion ensemble, and **rap** and hip-hop musicians and dancers.

During the 1990s Roach released a two-CD set titled *To the Max!* He also performed with his group, the So What Brass Quintet. Roach, who has lived in New York all of his life, has been recognized not only as one of the most important drummers in the history of jazz, but as one of the leading African-American cultural figures of the twentieth century, with a commitment to fighting racial injustice.

Robertson, Oscar

BASKETBALL PLAYER
November 24, 1938–

Oscar Robertson was one of the best guards in the history of professional **basketball**. He is known for his electrifying point-scoring ability and leadership skills.

Born in Charlotte, Tennessee, Robertson grew up in Indianapolis, Indiana, where he led his high school basketball team to two championships. After high school Robertson chose to attend the University of Cincinnati, where he became the first black to play for the team. During college Robertson was an All-American three times, and he led the 1960 U.S. Olympic team to a gold medal. He graduated from college in 1960 with a

ROBERTSON FILES SUIT AGAINST THE NBA

While president of the NBA Players Association, Robertson filed suit against the NBA because of its unfair trading policy. The "reserve clause" tied a player to a given team until that team wanted to trade him. This caused players to have lower salaries because they could not work out deals with other teams. Two years after Robertson retired as president, the lawsuit was decided in favor of the players.

degree in business and was drafted by the Cincinnati Royals of the National Basketball Association (NBA).

It did not take long for Robertson to make an impression in the NBA. In his first year he won the Rookie of the Year award, and in 1964 he was voted the NBA's Most Valuable Player (MVP). In 1969 Robertson was traded to the Milwaukee Bucks, who he helped win a championship in 1971. Robertson retired in 1974 with an amazing 26,710 points and 9,887 assists. Robertson was elected to the Naismith Basketball Hall of Fame in 1979. Robertson served as president of the NBA Players Association from 1965 to 1972, in which capacity he filed an important suit against the NBA that eventually allowed players to earn higher salaries. In 1981 Robertson began a chemical company in Cincinnati for which he now serves as president and chief executive officer.

Robeson, Paul

ACTOR, SINGER, POLITICAL ACTIVIST
April 9, 1898–January 23, 1976

Paul Robeson was a talented actor, powerful singer, and inspiring civil rights activist. An uncommonly brilliant student and athlete, Paul Robeson entered Rutgers College in New Brunswick, New Jersey, in 1916. Although he was the only black student there, he became immensely popular. After graduating in 1919, he moved to Harlem (a black neighborhood in New York City) and in 1920 entered the law school of Columbia University in New York. To support himself he played professional football on weekends and later turned to acting.

Graduating from law school in 1923, Robeson served briefly in a law firm. Then, chafing at restrictions on him as a black, and urged on by his wife, Eslanda, he left the practice of law for the stage. He enjoyed immediate success, earning a place among the Provincetown (Massachusetts) Players, a production company cofounded by the famed playwright Eugene O'Neill (*The Emperor Jones; Long Day's Journey into Night*). In 1925 he launched his career as a singer of African-American spirituals and folk songs from around the world. He then traveled to Europe and Great Britain, where critics hailed his acting.

In the 1928 London production of the musical *Show Boat*, his stirring rendition of "Ol' Man River" took his popularity to new heights. Although he triumphed again when *Show Boat* opened in New York in 1930, Great Britain was the scene of many of his greatest achievements. In the following years he starred there in a number of plays, including *Othello* (1930), and *Stevedore* (1933). Robeson also had prominent roles in almost a dozen films, including *Sanders of the River* (1935), *Show Boat* (1936), and *Proud Valley* (1941). In most of these efforts, his depictions of a black man contrasted starkly with the images of subservience, ignorance, criminality, or low comedy usually seen on the Hollywood screen.

By the mid 1930s, Robeson became a supporter of progressive causes, including the rights of oppressed Jews and of freedom fighters in Spain. In London he befriended several students and intellectuals, such as Kwame Nkrumah, George Padmore, and Jomo Kenyatta, who would later be prominent in the freedom movements in Africa.

Robeson's political beliefs, including his support of communist politics, eventually ended his career. When Robeson refused to sign an oath opposing communism in 1950, his singing and acting careers in effect came to an end. He was was widely ostracized by whites and blacks.

In 1958 Robeson published *Here I Stand*, which combined **autobiography** with statements of his political concerns and other beliefs. He sang at New York's Carnegie Hall in what was billed as a farewell concert and also performed in California. As time passed, many people became more sympathetic toward Robeson's beliefs and more admiring of his talents.

At a seventy-fifth birthday celebration at Carnegie Hall in 1973, Robeson (whose illness kept him away) was saluted, in a more liberal age, by prominent blacks, liberals, and socialists as one of the towering figures of the twentieth century. In a message to the gathering, Robeson described himself as "dedicated as ever to the worldwide cause of humanity for freedom, peace, and brotherhood." He died in Philadelphia, Pennsylvania, in 1976.

Robinson, Bill "Bojangles"

TAP DANCER
May 25, 1878–November 29, 1949

Bill "Bojangles" Robinson was the most famous of all African-American tap dancers. Robinson demonstrated light footwork that was said to have brought tap "up on its toes" from the flat-footed shuffling style of the previous era. Born Luther Robinson in Richmond, Virginia, he was orphaned when both of his parents died, and he and his brothers were raised by his grandmother.

Robinson gained his nickname, "Bojangles," from the slang term "jangle," meaning "to quarrel or fight," after several teenage fights. He ran away to Washington, D.C., earning nickels and dimes by dancing and singing. He got his first professional job in 1892, performing in the chorus of a vaudeville show (a traveling stage show featuring music, dance, acrobatics, and comedy).

From 1902 to 1914 Robinson teamed up with fellow tap dancer George W. Cooper. They refused to wear the blackface makeup performers customarily used. Robinson was a gambler with a quick temper, and his arrest for assault in 1914 put an end to the partnership with Cooper.

After the split, Robinson convinced his manager to promote him as a soloist. After being booked at the Marigold Gardens Theater in Chicago, he became one of the first black performers to headline at New York's prestigious Palace Theatre.

Hailed as "the Dark Cloud of Joy," Robinson performed in vaudeville from 1914 to 1927. Onstage, Robinson's open face, flashing eyes, infectious smile, easygoing style, and air of surprise at what his feet were doing made him irresistible to audiences. Robinson always danced in split-clog shoes, in which the wooden sole was attached from the toe to the ball of the foot and the rest was left loose, allowing for greater flexibility.

Broadway fame came with an all-black revue, *Blackbirds*, of 1928, in which he sang "Doin' the New Low Down" while dancing up and down a flight of five steps. Robinson's performance was acclaimed by the major New York newspapers, and he was heralded by several as the greatest of all tap dancers. The dance Robinson performed in *Blackbirds* developed into his signature "stair dance." Largely in recognition of his Broadway success, Robinson was named honorary "Mayor of Harlem" by New York's Mayor Fiorello La Guardia (1882–1947). In 1939 he celebrated his sixty-first birthday by tapping down Broadway, one block for each year.

Robinson turned to Hollywood, which was largely closed to blacks, in the 1930s. His films included *Harlem Is Heaven* (1933), with an all-black cast. But of his many stage and film performances, those that brought him the most fame were his appearances with child star Shirley Temple.

A founding member of the Negro Actors Guild of America, Robinson performed in thousands of benefits in the course of his career and made generous contributions to charities and individuals. Nearly a hundred thousand people turned out to watch his funeral procession; the numbers testify to the esteem in which he was still held by his community and by the audiences who loved him. (*See also*: **Tap Dancing**)

Robinson, Frank

BASEBALL PLAYER, BASEBALL MANAGER
August 31, 1935–

Frank Robinson was the first African American to coach in major league **baseball.** Before coaching, however, he proved his baseball skills on the field with tremendous fielding and hitting precision.

Born in Beaumont, Texas, Robinson moved with his family to California at the age of four. In 1952 Robinson signed with the Cincinnati Reds. After playing in the minor leagues, Robinson got his chance to play for the Reds in 1956. By 1961 he was named the National League's Most Valuable Player (MVP). Robinson had his best season with the Baltimore Orioles in 1966, when he carried a .316 batting average, hit forty-nine home runs, won the

Triple Crown, and was named the American League and World Series MVP. Robinson retired with 586 career home runs (fourth highest on the charts at the time) and was the only player to be named MVP for both the American and the National leagues. He was elected to the Baseball Hall of Fame in 1982.

While Robinson was playing for the Cleveland Indians he was named head coach for the 1975 season, making him the first African American to coach a major league baseball team. Robinson went on to coach for the San Francisco Giants (1981–84) and the Baltimore Orioles (1988–91). He was named manager of the year in 1989. In February 2000 Robinson was named vice president of on-field operations for major league baseball. He is responsible for handling disputes such as rules violations and confrontations between players and umpires.

JACKIE ROBINSON'S ARMY CAREER

In the spring of 1942 Jackie Robinson was drafted to serve in the U.S. Army. When Robinson was denied to access to officer training school, he protested the decision with the help of heavyweight **boxing** champion Joe Louis. Robinson eventually earned the rank of officer and fought to improve conditions for blacks. Robinson was court-martialed (tried by a military court) for refusing to sit at the back of a bus; he was aquitted. At the time segregation laws forced blacks to sit in separate areas on public transportation systems.

Robinson, Jack Roosevelt "Jackie"

BASEBALL PLAYER, CIVIL RIGHTS LEADER, BUSINESSMAN
January 31, 1919–October 24, 1972

Jack Roosevelt "Jackie" Robinson was one of the best **baseball** players in the history of the game. He is celebrated as the first African American to break the color barrier in major league baseball.

Born in Georgia, Robinson was raised in Pasadena, California. During his childhood Robinson faced the ugliness of racial prejudice in the United States. Private and public facilities were segregated at the time, and whites attempted to force the Robinsons from their home. In high school Robinson was an athletic wonder. Apart from playing baseball, he was an All-American **football** player, an outstanding **basketball** player, and set records in the broad jump in **track-and-field.**

After serving in the **military,** Robinson played in the American Negro League. After playing seven months in the league, Robinson was asked to play for the Brooklyn Dodgers, making him the first black to play in the major leagues since the 1890s. Robinson started out playing for the Dodgers's farm club, the Montreal Royals, in the International League. He led the league in batting and helped the Royals win a championship. When

ROBINSON BOYCOTTS BASEBALL

Robinson held firmly to his commitment to end racism in the United States to the day he died. In the late 1960s Robinson became "bitterly disillusioned" with baseball and with American society in general. He refused to attend baseball events in protest of the absence of blacks in managerial positions. In his autobiography *I Never Had It Made* (1972), Robinson criticized American society for not doing more to bring an end to racial injustice. He ended his boycott on baseball in 1972 to attend a game in which he was honored for breaking the color barrier. In his speech he said, "I'd like to live to see a black manager." Robinson died of a heart attack nine days later.

Robinson joined the Dodgers in 1947, it sparked a wave of protest from whites. Robinson received death threats, and some players threatened to go on strike. However, Robinson kept his poise throughout the season and won the Rookie of the Year award (since renamed the Jackie Robinson Award).

During his ten years with the Dodgers, Robinson played outstanding baseball, batting .342 in 1949 and winning the National League's Most Valuable Player award. He led the Dodgers to six pennants (National League Championships) and one World Series Championship. His lifetime batting average was an astounding .311. He was elected to the Baseball Hall of Fame in 1961.

Robinson's achievements went beyond baseball. A man who rarely shied away from controversy, he was a leading civil rights spokesman, championing the fight against segregation (the separation of blacks and whites). Once Robinson established himself as a great player, he forced major league baseball to address its policies of discrimination. After retiring from baseball in 1956, Robinson gave speeches, worked as a newspaper columnist, and did fund-raising work for the **National Association for the Advancement of**

Jackie Robinson sliding past Yogi Bera's tag at home plate (AP/Wide World Photos. Reproduced by permission)

Colored People (NAACP). Robinson was also a successful businessman in the restaurant and construction industries.

Robinson, Smokey. *See* Robinson, William

Robinson, Sugar Ray

BOXER
May 3, 1921–April 12, 1989

Sugar Ray Robinson was one of the toughest boxers in history. He is known for his powerful punching ability, quick footwork, and flashy lifestyle outside the ring.

Born Walker Smith Jr. in Detroit, Michigan, Robinson moved with his mother to Harlem, New York, in 1933. He soon began **boxing** in a high school athletic club, using the identification card of a Ray Robinson. By 1939 he won the New York Golden Gloves award. He turned professional in 1940. A sportswriter described his technique as "sweet as sugar," giving him his name, "Sugar Ray." Robinson won his first forty fights before losing a decision to Jake LaMotta in 1943.

Robinson followed the lead of his friend and mentor, African-American boxer **Joe Louis.** He served in the **military** with Louis, with whom he put on boxing exhibitions to entertain the troops. At one point Robinson refused to go out on an exhibition until black soldiers were allowed to attend.

Robinson won the welterweight championship in 1946. In his first defense of the title he fought Jimmy Doyle, who died as a result of Robinson's blows. In 1951 he moved up to the middleweight division and fought a rematch against LaMotta. The fight was called the "St. Valentine's Day Massacre" because of the beating LaMotta sustained.

After losing and then regaining the title in the early 1950s, Robinson retired for a two-year period, during which he worked as a tap dancer. He reentered the ring in 1955 and regained the middleweight title. When Robinson retired in 1965, he had won the middleweight championship a record five times, with a record of 174 (with 109 knockouts). He was elected to the Boxing Hall of Fame in 1967. After retiring Robinson ran a nightclub and moved to Los Angeles, California, where he established a youth center in his name.

Robinson, William Jr. "Smokey"

SINGER
February 19, 1940–

Smokey Robinson: Selected Hits

"Shop Around"
(1960)

"The Tracks of My Tears"
(1965)

"Ooo Baby Baby"
(1965)

"The Tears of a Clown"
(1970)

Singer Smokey Robinson began performing early in life. In 1954, while still in high school in Detroit, Michigan, he formed The Miracles. The Miracles's distinctive sound was led by Robinson's quivering falsetto and tenor, along with other vocalists and instrumentalists. In 1958 Robinson signed with **Motown** Records and soon became important in the early successes of Motown. (Motown became the largest black-owned company in the United States and helped build the success of soul music.) Robinson was a popular performer, but he also became a significant songwriter and collaborator for Motown.

In 1972 Robinson left The Miracles in order to devote more time to his Motown executive position and songwriting, while beginning a successful solo career that produced seventeen albums. Robinson's vocal style is defined by his soft, sophisticated falsetto (high-pitched) singing. Although this style was popular with numerous **rhythm-and-blues** groups of the 1940s and 1950s, it was Robinson's highly influential solo style that was widely imitated by white "blue-eyed soul" vocalists of the 1970s to 1990s.

He was equally influential as a songwriter; his ballads defined the **Motown** sound. In 1986 he was inducted into the Songwriters' Hall of Fame, and he received a Grammy Award for "Just to See Her" in 1987. He released the album *Intimate* in 2000.

Rodney King Riot

On March 3, 1991, following a high-speed chase, black motorist Rodney King was subdued with extreme force and arrested by the Los Angeles Police Department for resisting and threatening police officers. The broadcast of a videotape by passing motorist George Holiday that depicted King being beaten and kicked by white police officers made King a symbolic victim of American racism and police brutality. King suffered multiple injuries and spent two days in the hospital before being booked. The Los Angeles County District Attorney dismissed all charges against King on March 7. A week later, the grand jury indicted the arresting officers—Sgt. Stacy Koon and officers Theodore J. Briseno, Laurence M. Powell, and Timothy Wind—on charges of assault with a deadly weapon and unnecessary assault. Mayor Tom Bradley responded to King's beating by establishing the Christopher Commission to investigate the LAPD. Releasing its findings in July, the commission documented the LAPD's systematic use of excessive force and racial harassment, finding that significant reforms in police procedure were required.

The King incident galvanized international attention on police brutality in Los Angeles. In the Semi Valley court trial, a jury of eleven whites and one Hispanic found the four officers not guilty. The verdict ignited one of the worst riots in the nation's history. On April 29, 1992, Los Angeles erupted into a racial volcano. Blacks brutally beat white motorists, burned and looted stores and other businesses for three days. In one horrific incident captured by television news cameras, white trucker Reginald Denny was pulled from his truck, beaten, shot, and robbed by four black men. President George Bush dispatched federal troops to the city. Riots broke out in other cities including San Francisco, Atlanta, New York, and Seattle. In May, the Los Angeles Board of Police Commissioners established a commission to study the performance of the LAPD during the riots. The Webster Commission found that failure of leadership in the LAPD and city government exacerbated the riots and called for reforms.

In 1993, the four officers were tried in federal court for violating King's civil rights. The jury convicted Koon and Powell and acquitted Briseno and Wind. No violent response resulted from the verdicts.

The riots following the King decision re-opened many racial wounds, showing to all Americans that, despite the advances of the civil rights era, there was still a racial divide in America. King's beating was proof for many that police power was being abused and that racial intolerance was part of that abuse. While many did use the riots to make a bold statement about the condition of race relations, others used the chaos as an opportunity to loot stores and indulge in reckless and random violence. Despite the lessons that should have been learned from the events of the King arrest and riots, police brutality against minorities continued in the late 1990s, with the brutal beating of Abner Louima in 1997 and the shooting death of Amadou Diallo in 1999—both defenseless black men attacked by white police officers—being standout cases. Another lasting effect of the riots became evident in racially charged court decisions. The trial of the "L.A. Four," the young men caught on videotape beating trucker Denny, resulted in the accused being found not guilty of the most serious charges. Many speculated that

such a decision was the result of fears that a guilty verdict would have touched off further rioting.

Rollins, Theodore Walter "Sonny"

SAXOPHONIST, COMPOSER
September 9, 1930–

Sonny Rollins began playing piano at the age of nine and later took up the saxophone. In the late 1940s he began playing professionally in New York, often with the greatest bebop musicians of the era, including saxophonist **Charlie Parker** (1920–1955) and trumpeter **Miles Davis** (1926–1991). He made his first recordings in 1949. His most significant early recordings have since become standards.

In 1955 Rollins, who had recovered from addiction to the drug heroin, joined the **Max Roach**-Clifford Brown quintet, the leading practitioners of the intense, bluesy style known as hard bop. Rollins played with the group until the death of trumpeter Brown in 1956. He then played again with Davis and began to lead his own groups.

Rollins recorded three albums in 1956 that showed his skill as a tenor saxophonist and a remarkable composer. The next two years were equally productive for Rollins, who recorded three albums, *Way Out West*, *Tenor Titan* and *Freedom Suite*. The latter was an early example of the growing concern among **jazz** musicians with the connection between the "freedom" of modern jazz composition and the struggle for the civil rights of African Americans.

Although by the end of the 1950s Rollins had become one of the leading saxophonists in jazz, he was increasingly dissatisfied with his playing. He retreated from public performing from 1959 to 1961 and began practicing

on New York City's Williamsburg Bridge. Rollins returned to playing in 1961, recording *The Bridge.* Rollins continued to record and perform. During this time his playing was unashamedly romantic, yet also capable of sharp statements, especially on ballads and popular tunes. He also took to leaving the bandstand while playing, and strolling around the nightclub, often wearing bells.

Rollins retired again in 1968, immersing himself in the philosophy and religion of India before reemerging in 1972. Rollins continues to record and perform throughout the United States, Europe, and Japan. At the beginning of the twenty-first century, he performed forty concerts a year. He declined to perform more, preferring to "live at home frugally" with his wife of forty years.

Sonny Rollins: Selected Works

The Cutting Edge
(1974)

Don't Stop The Carnival
(1978)

G-Man
(1987)

Roman Catholicism

African Americans have figured in the history of the Roman Catholic Church in the United States since the sixteenth century. The town of St. Augustine, Florida, established in 1565, was composed of Spanish-speaking Catholics, both white and black.

Although slavery was accepted by most Catholics, Catholic slaveholders had to abide by a special set of codes. They had to have their slaves baptized and instructed in the Catholic religion, and they could not separate slave families. Although these requirements were not always met by Catholic slaveholders, they nevertheless granted rights that did not exist for other slaves in the United States.

In the years before the American Civil War (1861–65), when many Protestant churches were divided by the issue of **slavery,** Catholic bishops did not get involved in the issue. Most Catholic leaders in Europe, on the other hand, were opposed to slavery; in 1839 Pope Gregory XVI condemned the **slave trade** and slavery itself.

After the **Civil War** the Catholic Church in the United States immediately began efforts to convert freed slaves to Catholicism. Bishops were made responsible for all blacks within their diocese (religious district). Catholic religious communities began preaching to and helping African Americans.

Black Catholics celebrated mass and preached to other blacks even before the Civil War, however. In 1824 three free black women began to live the religious life as nuns near Bardstown, Kentucky, under the guidance of a priest from Belgium. Mary Elizabeth Lange, a Haitian, created the first African-American community of nuns in 1829; it was known as the Oblate Sisters of Providence. In 1842 another community of black sisters was established, in New Orleans, Louisiana.

The first black priests in United States were three brothers who were the sons of an Irish slaveholder and his African-American slave. The oldest son, James Augustine Healy, in 1875 became bishop of Portland, Maine. He was the first black Catholic bishop in the United States. The third son, Patrick Francis Healy, became a Jesuit priest and a university president.

Because of their mixed race and light skin color, however, the Healys' African-American parentage was not publicly known. The first black priest who was clearly recognized as black was Augustus Tolton. Born a slave in Missouri and educated for the priesthood in Rome, Italy, he moved in 1886 to Chicago, Illinois, where he became the pastor of the first black parish in the United States.

The **Civil Rights movement** of the 1960s created a new sense of political activism among black Catholics. In 1968 the National Black Catholic Clergy Caucus and the National Black Sisters' Conference were formed. Harold Perry, the second black bishop in U.S. history, was ordained in 1966 as auxiliary bishop of New Orleans. By 1991 there were thirteen black bishops. In 1987 a group called the Black Secretariat was established as part of the National Conference of Catholic Bishops. This group functions as a bridge between the diocese and the concerns of black Catholics in churches that serve a large black population.

Ross, Diana

SINGER, ACTRESS
March 26, 1944–

Born in a low-income housing project in Detroit, Michigan, pop singer and actress Diana Ross has had nineteen number-one recordings on the pop charts, the most achieved by any solo performer to date. She first began singing in her church choir. In high school she studied dress design, illustration, and cosmetology, spending her free time singing on Detroit street corners with her friends Mary Wilson (1944–) and Florence Ballard (1943–1976). Betty McGlowan soon joined the group, and the quartet became known as the Primettes.

The group was later renamed the **Supremes,** and from the mid-1960s until 1970 they were one of the most popular groups in music, producing a string of hits. In 1970, however, Ross left the Supremes to pursue a solo career. She remained popular as a singer, releasing "Ain't No Mountain High Enough" in 1970, and also began a career as a film actress. Ross was nominated for an Academy Award for her performance as legendary singer **Billie Holiday** in *Lady Sings the Blues* (1972).

By the mid-1970s Ross was also considered a top disco singer, recording "Love Hangover" (1976) and "Upside Down" (1980). During this time Ross starred in the films *Mahogany* (1975) and *The Wiz* (1978). She reached the top of the pop charts again in 1981 with "Endless Love," a duet with Lionel Ritchie. In 1989 she released the album *Workin' Overtime*.

Ross continued strong into the 1990s, collaborating in 1991 with musician **Stevie Wonder** and other artists on *The Force Behind the Power,* a collection of contemporary ballads. She released several albums, including *Take Me Higher* (1995) and *Every Day is a New Day* (1999), and received critical acclaim for her role in the 1994 television movie, *Out of Darkness.*

In 2000 Ross was honored by the television music channel VH1 with "Divas 2000: A Tribute to Diana Ross," a television special which featured

popular singers Faith Hill, Mariah Carey, and Donna Summer covering Diana Ross and the Supremes tunes. In the summer of 2000 Ross toured the country with former members of the Supremes, Lynda Laurence and Scherrie Payne.

Rudolph, Wilma Glodean

ATHLETE
June 23, 1940–November 12, 1994

Olympian Wilma Rudolph holding her gold medals

Wilma Glodean Rudolph was an Olympic **track-and-field** runner who stole the show at the 1960 Olympic games in Rome, Italy. She is known for her athleticism and her commitment to helping others, particularly children.

Born in Bethlehem, Tennessee, Rudolph was the twentieth of twenty-two children. As a child she suffered from polio, a terrible sickness that caused her to lose use of her left leg. She was forced to wear a leg brace until the age of nine. By age twelve she was the fastest runner in her school.

Rudolph attended Tennessee State University, where she met track coach Edward Temple, who invited her to a summer training camp to help develop her track racing abilities. By 1956 she qualified to compete in the Olympic games in Melbourne, Australia, where her team won a bronze medal.

Rudolph was determined to return to the Olympics and win a gold medal. She joined the track team at college and trained vigorously. In the 1960 Olympics she became the first woman to win three gold medals. She became a superstar overnight.

However, in 1962 Rudolph retired from amateur competition at the peak of her career in order to pursue other interests. She graduated from college in 1963 and became a teacher and track coach at an elementary school. While teaching, Rudolph participated in several community service programs, including the Wilma Rudolph Foundation, which she formed in 1981. The organization is designed to help young athletes fulfill their dreams.

Rudolph won several prestigious awards. In 1960 she was chosen as the United Press Athlete of the Year; in 1973 she was inducted into the Black Sports Hall of Fame; in 1980 she was inducted into the Women's Sports Hall of Fame; and in 1983 she was inducted into the U.S. Olympic Hall of Fame. Rudolph has served as a role model and inspiration for thousands of African-American and female athletes, as well as for people with disabilities.

Russell, Nipsey

COMEDIAN
October 13, 1923–

Nipsey Russell entered show business before the age of six as a member of a dance team, the Ragamuffins of Rhythm. As an adult, he served four years as a captain in the U.S. Army and attended the University of

Cincinnati in Ohio, where he earned a bachelor's degree. In 1948 he moved to New York City to become a comedian. Russell was one of the first black **comedians** to perform without making references to his or her race. This brought him the national attention that allowed him to move into mainstream clubs.

One of the first African Americans to be invited to appear on television talk shows, Russell was a frequent guest on *The Tonight Show*. On the *Les Crane Show* (1964-65), he was the first African American regularly employed as a master of ceremonies on a national television program. He was also the first black to appear on television game shows, such as *Matchgame*, where he became known for his ability to improvise poetry.

In 1978 Russell was singled out for praise by film critics for his song-and-dance performance as the Tin Man in the movie *The Wiz*. Throughout the 1980s Russell appeared on such television programs as *The Love Boat* and *As the World Turns*, in addition to performing his stand-up act in clubs in Atlantic City, New Jersey, and Las Vegas, Nevada. In 1986 he appeared in the film *Wildcats*, and in 1992 he had a part in the Eddie Murphy movie *Boomerang*. In 1993 he had a small part in *Posse*, a black western film, and in 1994 he repeated his original television role in the film version of *Car 54, Where Are You?* Russell also appeared in the Home Box Office (HBO) historical documentary *Mo' Funny: Black Comedy in America* (1993).

Rustin, Bayard

ACTIVIST
March 17, 1910–August 24, 1987

Bayard Rustin was a civil rights leader and political organizer. He was born in West Chester, Pennsylvania, in 1910, the last of nine children. Reared by his mother and grandparents, local caterers, he grew up in the relatively privileged setting of a large mansion in town.

He attended college at West Chester State, then moved to **Harlem, New York,** during the 1930s, where he had an artistic lifestyle, attending classes at City College, singing with **jazz** groups and at nightclubs, and gaining a reputation as a chef.

His public personality and organizing skills brought him to the attention of A. Philip Randolph, who recruited him to help develop his plans for a massive March on Washington to secure equal access to defense jobs for African Americans. Randolph arranged for Rustin to meet with A. J. Muste, the head of the antiwar group, the Fellowship of Reconciliation (FOR). Muste made Rustin a staff member for FOR, and Rustin also continued as a youth organizer for the March on Washington movement.

With his reputation as an activist in politics, Rustin was able to offer advice to the members of FOR, who began a new nonviolent action organization, the **Congress of Racial Equality (CORE).** Until 1955 Rustin held a variety of offices within both groups, conducting weekend and summer institutes on nonviolent direct action in race relations. In 1947 he worked closely with Randolph again in a movement opposing **military** training and a segregated military.

Rustin's commitment to nonviolence and racial equality cost him dearly. In the summer of 1942, refusing to sit in the black section of a bus going from Louisville, Kentucky, to Nashville, Tennessee, he was beaten and arrested. The following year, unwilling to accept either the validity of the military draft or the conscientious-objector status (refusing to serve in the armed forces for religious or moral reasons) he was jailed as a draft resister and spent twenty-eight months in prison. Following his release, in 1947 he proposed that a racially integrated group of activists undertake a bus trip through the South to test a recent U.S. Supreme Court decision on interstate travel. The trip was essentially peaceful, although participants encountered violence outside Chapel Hill, North Carolina, where Rustin and three others were charged with violating the segregation laws. Rustin and the others were convicted and sentenced to thirty days hard labor on a chain gang. His continuing visible role in racial policies brought him additional arrests and beatings.

Rustin left CORE and FOR in 1955 to serve as a publicist for the **Southern Christian Leadership Conference (SCLC).** In 1963, as Randolph renewed his plans for a massive March on Washington, he proposed Rustin as the coordinator for the national event. Rustin successfully managed the complex planning for the event and avoided violence. He was named executive director of the A. Philip Randolph Institute in 1964, while continuing to lead protests against militarism and segregation.

Rustin spent the rest of his life writing and speaking in support of civil rights issues. (*See also* **Civil Rights Movement.**)

Bayard Rustin (AP/Wide World Photos. Reproduced by permission)

Saar, Betye Irene

ARTIST
July 30, 1926–

Betye Brown was born in Los Angeles and attended public school in Pasadena, California. She earned a degree in design from the University of California at Los Angeles in 1949 and married artist Richard Saar shortly thereafter. She worked as a costume designer before resuming formal art training in the late 1950s. In graduate school she mastered the techniques of graphics, printmaking, and design.

After 1967 Saar turned to what would become her characteristic style: three-dimensional "assemblage" boxes. An early example is *Black Girl's Window* (1969), in which a black girl presses her face and hands against a glass pane, surrounded by images of the supernatural.

Saar's boxes often criticized negative stereotypes (preconceived notions about an entire group of people) of African Americans. In *The Liberation of Aunt Jemima* (1972), she transformed the passive black female figure featured on boxes of pancake mix into a militant revolutionary (someone who fights for major changes). Saar later made more personal, autobiographical assemblage boxes, exploring her mixed heritage of Native American, Irish, and African descent as well as her spiritual beliefs.

During the 1970s Saar traveled to the countries of Haiti, Mexico, and Nigeria. These trips, as well as visits to the Field Museum of Natural

History in Chicago, Illinois, resulted in a series of altarpieces (works of art to decorate church altars) reflecting African, Caribbean, and Asian cultures. For example, *Dambella* (1975) contains references to Haitian **voodoo** with its ritualistic animal parts and snakeskin.

In the 1980s and 1990s Saar began experimenting with room-size works. Using recycled materials, she created "found treasures" to stir emotion and memories in the viewer. *Mojotech* (1988) explored the relationship between technology and magic, containing computer-system circuit boards as well as traditional religious objects.

Since 1983 Saar has been awarded several commissions to create installations for public places. She was one of two artists chosen to represent the United States in the 1994 São Paulo Biennial (occurring every two years) art exhibition in Brazil.

Sam and Dave

POPULAR MUSIC GROUP

Samuel Moore (1935–) and Dave Prater (1937–1988) teamed up as the Sam and Dave duo in 1958. The soul singers had their first hit, "You Don't Know Like I Know," in 1965.

Sam and Dave exemplified "the Memphis sound." Both had begun their careers as gospel singers, and their music combined elements of gospel and the sad and jazzy sound of **rhythm-and-blues.** Their hit songs included "Hold On, I'm Coming" (1966), "Soul Man" (1967), and "I Thank You" (1968). The duo became popular with both white and black audiences.

Sam and Dave split up in 1970. They both pursued unsuccessful solo careers but reunited several times during the 1970s. They briefly regained the spotlight in 1979, when their song "Soul Man" was used in the film *The Blues Brothers.* Dave Prater died in a car crash in 1988.

Sanchez, Sonia

WRITER, POET
September 19, 1934–

Sonia Sanchez was born Wilsonia Benita Driver in Birmingham, Alabama. During her childhood in the South as well as in Harlem, she was outraged by the way American society mistreated black people, and this anger transformed her from a shy, stuttering girl into one of the most vocal writer-activists in contemporary literature. She studied at Hunter College in New York and at New York University, and in the early 1960s she began publishing poems under her married name, Sonia Sanchez, which she continued to use professionally after a divorce. *Homecoming* (1969), her first collection of poetry, attacked racial injustice in angry voices from the street.

While the struggle of African Americans in a white society is her major subject, Sanchez has also critiqued struggles within the black community. *Sister Sonji*, a play produced in 1972, is about a young woman fighting the sexism of the black revolutionary movement. Sanchez herself left the

Nation of Islam in 1975 because the organization would not change its policy on assigning an inferior role to women.

Books by Sanchez include several poetry collections, including *homegirls & handgrenades* (1984) and *Like the Singing Coming off the Drums* (2000), juvenile fiction, plays, and numerous contributions to collections and recordings as an essayist and editor. She has recieved several major awards, and her 1997 poetry collection, *Does Your House Have Lions?* was nominated for a National Book Critics Circle Award. In 1998 Sanchez published *Shake Loose My Skin*, a look back at her thirty years of work.

Santeria

Santeria, or "saint worship," is a religion that combines the spiritual beliefs of the Yoruba people of West Africa with Roman Catholicism. The Yoruba people believed in the supreme God, Olodumare, and in lesser gods known as "orishas." The Yoruba people taken as slaves to sugar plantations in Cuba were baptized in the **Roman Catholic** Church (according to the laws of the church, Catholic slaveholders had to baptize their slaves).

Slaves soon recognized similiarities between Catholic saints and orishas. Eventually, each orisha was matched to a Catholic saint and came to be known by both the African and Christian name. For example, Orula (an orisha) and St. Francis of Assisi (a Catholic saint) describe the same spiritual being. The followers of this new religion, called "santeros," continued to honor their spiritual ancestors. They communicated to the orishas by making animal sacrifices and other offerings, such as food or clothing. In modern Santeria, community service is also a method of worship.

After a Cuban revolution in 1959, a large number of Cubans fled their country for the United States, bringing the religion of Santeria with them. In southern Florida, which has a large Caribbean-American population, roughly seventy thousand people practice Santeria.

The Society for the Prevention of Cruelty to Animals has protested the ritual slaughter of animals on several occasions. One town in Florida even passed an ordinance banning animal sacrifice. But followers of Santeria argued in court that such laws were hypocritical in a society where animals are killed daily for food, especially since in Santeria the animal sacrificed is often eaten afterward. In June 1993 the Supreme Court removed the ban on religious animal sacrifices, saying that it discriminated against religious practice.

Savoy Ballroom

Known as "the Home of Happy Feet," the Savoy Ballroom, in the **Harlem** district of New York City, was the top showcase for the greatest big bands and dancers of the swing era (from about the mid-1920s to the late 1950s). Swing music was played mainly by large **jazz** dance bands, with a steady, lively rhythm.

The Savoy opened in 1926 at 596 Lenox Avenue, between 140th and 141st Streets. It had two mirrored flights of marble stairs that led up to a chandeliered lobby, and to the Orange-and-Blue Room, which measured 200 by 500 feet and could hold up to seven thousand people. There were two bandstands, a disappearing stage under multicolored spotlights, and a vast dance floor that was worn down and replaced every three years.

In spite of its elegance, the Savoy Ballroom attracted a working-class audience that paid low admission prices for an evening of swing dancing. Unlike the Cotton Club and others, which had strict racial boundaries, the Savoy welcomed both black and white patrons and performers.

Every notable black big band—and many white ones—performed at the Savoy. Often, more than one band played in an evening, alternating tunes and sets in a "battle of the bands." Among the most memorable was the 1938 victory of a band led by Chick Webb (1909–1939) over an orchestra led by **Count Basie** (1904–1984).

Al Cooper's Savoy Sultans served as the house band. Among the many other famous bandleaders and musicians appearing at the Savoy were **Duke Ellington** (1899–1974), **Louis Armstrong** (1901–1971), **Ella Fitzgerald** (1918–1996), **Coleman Hawkins** (1904–1969), Benny Carter (1907–), **Charlie Parker** (1920–1955), and Jimmie Lunceford (1902–1947). Edgar Sampson, an arranger and saxophonist with Webb's band, composed the ballroom's anthem, "Stompin' at the Savoy" (1934).

The dancing at the Savoy was as outstanding as the music. This was where the energetic and acrobatic style of swing dancing known as Lindy hopping (named for American aviator Charles A. "Lindy" Lindbergh) developed in the 1930s. Dancers such as Leon James, Shirley "Snowball" Jordan, George "Shorty" Snowden, and "Big Bea" created and perfected dances like the Itch and the Big Apple. The extraordinary dances invented at the Savoy Ballroom came from the interaction between dancers and bands as well as the unwritten rule against dancers copying one another's steps. In the mid-1930s a new generation of Lindy hoppers, including Frankie Manning (1914–), Norma Miller (1919–), and "Pepsi" Bethel (1923–), developed leaping "air steps" like the "hip to hip," the "side flip," and the "scratch."

The Savoy Ballroom was a remarkable example of an interracial cultural meeting place during the 1930s and 1940s. It flourished as long as white audiences saw Harlem as an attractive and safe place for nightlife. However, with the economic decline of Harlem after **World War II** (1939–45)—and with the rise of bebop and rock 'n' roll music—the owners of the Savoy found it harder to bring in large audiences and book new big bands each week. The Savoy Ballroom closed its doors in the late 1950s. The building was torn down in 1958 to make way for a housing project. (*See also* **Social Dance.**)

Sayers, Gale Eugene

PROFESSIONAL FOOTBALL PLAYER
May 30, 1943–

Football great Gale Sayers was raised in the poor northside district of Omaha, Nebraska. A high school **track-and-field** and football star, he enrolled at the University of Kansas at Lawrence in 1962. At Kansas, Sayers was a two-

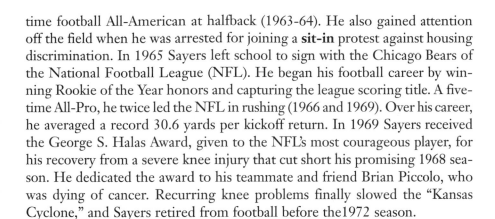
time football All-American at halfback (1963-64). He also gained attention off the field when he was arrested for joining a **sit-in** protest against housing discrimination. In 1965 Sayers left school to sign with the Chicago Bears of the National Football League (NFL). He began his football career by winning Rookie of the Year honors and capturing the league scoring title. A five-time All-Pro, he twice led the NFL in rushing (1966 and 1969). Over his career, he averaged a record 30.6 yards per kickoff return. In 1969 Sayers received the George S. Halas Award, given to the NFL's most courageous player, for his recovery from a severe knee injury that cut short his promising 1968 season. He dedicated the award to his teammate and friend Brian Piccolo, who was dying of cancer. Recurring knee problems finally slowed the "Kansas Cyclone," and Sayers retired from football before the 1972 season.

After retirement, Sayers returned to the University of Kansas, completing his undergraduate degree in 1974 and receiving a master's degree in education in 1977. He served as assistant athletic director at the University of Kansas and as athletic director at Southern Illinois University in Carbondale (1976-81).

Three years later, in 1984, Sayers founded Crest Computer Supplies in Skokie, Illinois. By 1994 the company ranked thirty-second on Black Enterprise's Top 100 Industrial/Service Companies and registered $43 million in annual sales.

Sayers was inducted into the Pro Football Hall of Fame in 1977. His autobiography, *I Am Third*, was published in 1970.

Scalawags

During the period after the American **Civil War** (1861–1865) known as **Reconstruction,** Northern and Southern states struggled to "reconstruct" or reunite the Union (the United States), which had been torn apart by war. There was also a struggle in the Southern states between whites who were members of the Republican Party and whites who were members of the Democratic Party. Whites who were members of the Republican Party and who had been born in the South were known as "scalawags." They were also called "white Negroes," because many of them supported black rights.

The Republican Party was particularly popular in North Carolina, Tennessee, Alabama, and Arkansas. In general, scalawags favored debtor relief, low taxes, and restricting the voting rights of former Confederates (people in the South who supported a separate Southern government). And while they were willing to recognize the political and civil rights that had been newly promised to blacks, they strongly opposed legislation that would integrate schools and public facilities.

"Scalawags" came from all walks of life and were drawn to the Republican Party for a number of reasons: some were eager for the economic opportunities the party promised; others saw political opportunity that had been denied before the war. A number of them, however, were whites with small farms and had never owned slaves. They were drawn to the Republican Party because they hoped Republican economic policies would help them recover from the losses they suffered during the war.

Some famous scalawags included James L. Alcorn, one of the largest planters in the Yazoo-Mississippi Delta, who became Mississippi's first Republican governor; businessman Rufus Bullock, Georgia's first Reconstruction governor; and South Carolina congressman Simeon Corley.

As Reconstruction continued, the economic progress promised by the Republican Party did not materialize. In addition, blacks began to demand more rights; in response, Democrats directed violence against white Republicans. As a result, the number of scalawags decreased. In some areas, however, including eastern Tennessee and western North Carolina, the Republican Party remained a political force long after the end of Reconstruction. (*See also* **Carpetbaggers.**)

Schmoke, Kurt

MAYOR
December 1, 1949–

Kurt Schmoke was born in Baltimore, Maryland. After attending Baltimore public schools, he graduated from Yale University (New Haven, Connecticut) in 1971. He then studied for two years at Oxford University, Great Britain, as a Rhodes Scholar. He earned a J.D. degree from Harvard Law School (Cambridge, Massachusetts) in 1976. Following a brief period at a prestigious Baltimore law firm, he joined the President Jimmy Carter's administration (1977–81) in Washington, D.C., serving on the White House Domestic Policy Staff and in the Department of Transportation.

In 1978 Schmoke returned to Baltimore as assistant U.S. attorney. On September 16, 1982, he won the Democratic primary and then the election for the office of Baltimore state's attorney, the chief prosecuting officer for the city. This office gave him the visibility to run for mayor. Schmoke's opponent was Clarence "Du" Burns, the first black mayor of Baltimore. Schmoke's margin of victory in the 1987 September primary was narrower than expected. He won two more races for the mayoralty, in 1991 and in 1995, before announcing his decision not to seek another term in 1999.

Schomburg, Arthur Alfonso

BOOK COLLECTOR
January 24, 1874–June 10, 1938

With his broad knowledge and passion for African-American history, book collector Arthur Schomburg was an inspiration to a generation of historians. Born in San Juan, Puerto Rico, he was largely self-taught and immigrated to the United States in 1891. Schomburg worked in a New York City law office and at Bankers Trust Company, while building a collection of African-American books and materials to demonstrate the documented existence and significance of black history.

In 1911 Schomburg cofounded the Negro Society for Historical Research with John Edward Bruce, and in 1922 he became president of the

short-lived American Negro Academy. Among his many pamphlets and bibliographical studies is "The Negro Digs Up His Past," published in **Alain Leroy Locke**'s *The New Negro* (1925).

In 1925 the New York Public Library established a special Negro Division. The next year, the Carnegie Corporation purchased Schomburg's vast collection of books, manuscripts, and artworks for $10,000 and donated it to the library. Another Carnegie grant enabled Schomburg to become manager of his own collection in 1932. His collection now forms the core of the present Schomburg Center for Research in Black Culture, the largest collection of materials by and about people of African descent.

Arthur Schomburg (standing second from the right) with the staff of the Negro Society for Historical Research (AP/Wide World Photos. Reproduced by permission)

Schuyler, George S.

JOURNALIST
1895–September 6, 1977

George S. Schuyler was considered to be one of the best journalists of his time. His move from radical socialist to arch conservative later in life was controversial.

Schuyler was raised in New York and dropped out of high school to enter the U.S. Army. After his military service, he was active in the labor movement. He was living in New York when the **Harlem Renaissance**, an exciting period of cultural growth, began around 1917. Schuyler's work spurred on some of the excitement of those times. In 1923 Schuyler joined the radical black newspaper *The Messenger* as a columnist and assistant editor. He later became its managing editor. The publication was considered so fiery that several southern members of Congress brought it under investigation.

Schuyler moved on to do publicity for the **National Association for the Advancement of Colored People (NAACP)**. His first book, *Racial Intermarriage in the United States*, was published in 1929. In 1931 Schuyler published two more novels. The first, *Black No More*, was a scathing satire featuring black people enabled to become white by taking a chemical. The second, *Slaves Today: A Story of Liberia*, told of a black elite that avenged wrongs done by whites in the United States, gathered an army and air force, and moved to Africa, where the genius of black scientists carved out a black empire.

From 1927 to 1933 Schuyler published nine essays. Shortly thereafter, he began working for the *Pittsburgh Courier*, where he would remain for forty years. Although he published furiously, he noted that his primary interest was in "having enough money to live on properly." He supplemented his $60 weekly salary by publishing in several white journals.

Schuyler and his wife, Josephine, had a daughter, Philippa Duke Schuyler (1931–1967). An extraordinarily talented child, she became a noted concert pianist. She was killed at age 35 in a helicopter crash. George Schuyler died in 1977.

Science

From colonial times, before the **American Revolution** (1775–83), scientific methods were used to study different races. The primary goal of the scientific study of race was to prove that blacks were inferior to whites, so that racial prejudice might seem acceptable. Although science has added to the problem of racial injustice in the United States, black scientists have disproved theories about black inferiority through their own scientific achievement.

Racial Concepts

The idea of racial classification was greatly influenced by the work of English naturalist Charles Darwin (1809–1882). Darwin is considered the father of the theory of evolution, which holds that man grew and developed from lower life forms. In the eighteenth century Darwin and other scientists believed that blacks had not developed as far as whites had. One scientist, Georges Cuvier, called blacks the lowest of the human races.

In the nineteenth century new theories were developed that built on Darwin's work. Scientists began studying the size of the skull and other parts of the human body to explain physical, mental, and moral differences between races. This work was carried out primarily by white scientists and sponsored by the U.S. government. These theories had an important effect on the way blacks were viewed. Black scientists did not have a chance to form different theories, because they were banned from scientific organiza-

tions. In 1895 black scientists formed their own scientific organization called the National Medical Association. However, the organization did little to combat racist theories and views, because black scientists feared that such protest would damage their reputation.

The Science of Eugenics

In the early twentieth century more theories were developed that promoted racial prejudice, including a scientific field of study called "eugenics." Eugenics is the study of how to improve the hereditary qualities of a race. Eugenics studies had an impact on government policies. It captured the public imagination, bringing issues of racial inferiority into focus not only in natural science but in the social arena as well. In one study, called the **Tuskegee Syphilis Experiment** (1932–72), black men infected with the deadly disease syphilis were left untreated to see whether the disease affected blacks differently from the way it did whites. (In 1999 President Bill Clinton issued a public apology on behalf of the government agency that conducted the experiment.)

African Americans in Science

The damage done to blacks by the scientific community did not prevent African Americans from contributing to science. Blacks have contributed to scientific discovery since the 1700s. African-American mathematician **Benjamin Banneker** (1731–1806) helped a team of engineers and surveyors lay the foundation for the city of Washington, D.C. After the American **Civil War** (1861–65), blacks began creating their own colleges and universities, which prompted more blacks to enter the field of science. However, the programs developed at black colleges did not promote pure scientific study. Blacks interested in pure science had to study at white universities to receive the training necessary to conduct research.

It was not until the 1900s that science began to open up to blacks. Famous black scientists, such as botanist **George Washington Carver** (c. 1864–1943) and physician **Charles Richard Drew** (1904–1950), were recognized for achievements in agriculture and medicine.

During **World War II** (1939–45), Americans saw beyond race and religion in an effort to defeat a common enemy. Blacks began to earn national acclaim for scientific discovery. Edwin Roberts Russell and Benjamin Franklin Scott helped with research on the atomic bomb. Blacks began creating their own scientific associations to encourage research, such as the National Institute of Science.

In the 1960s the field of science opened up more to blacks as a result of the **Civil Rights movement.** Since that time, the number of black scientists has increased significantly. However, only a small percentage of American scientists today are black. (*See also* **Shirley Jackson.**)

Science Fiction ▪▪▪

Scholars have a hard time providing an exact definition of science fiction. A mixture of fantasy and science, science fiction has been around, in one form or another, for centuries. However, not until the twentieth century did it emerge as its own genre (or field) of fiction.

The 1960s was perhaps the most important decade for the development of science fiction. During this time, the audience for science fiction began to grow. The focus of some science fiction also shifted from outer space to inner space, from a focus on technologies of the future to the possibilities of the human mind.

Samuel R. Delany is the first African-American writer committed to the field of science fiction. He has written more than two dozen books since he was first published in 1962. Although not an activist during the Civil Rights movement, he benefited from the rise of a new black culture that felt free to experiment and participate more fully in American society. His success as a science-fiction writer encouraged other black writers contemplating a career in science fiction.

Octavia Estelle Butler, the first black female science-fiction writer, is best known for her novel *Kindred* (1979), which deals with time travel. Steven Barnes, author of *Gorgon Child* (1989), and Charles R. Saunders, author of *Imaro* (1981), are also important African-American science-fiction writers who emerged during the 1970s and 1980s.

In 1998 the award-winning mystery writer Walter Mosley entered the science-fiction arena with the novel *Blue Light.* That same year, a newcomer, Jamaica-born Nalo Hopkinson, joined the ranks of black science-fiction writers with the award-winning *Brown Girl in the Ring*, a novel that combines elements of science fiction and fantasy with Caribbean folklore and culture.

Hopkinson's second novel, *Midnight Robber*, was published in 2000. Also published that year was a collection of African-American science fiction, *Dark Matter: A Century of Speculative Fiction from the African Diaspora*, edited by Sheree R. Thomas. It features contemporary writers such as Butler and Hopkinson but also includes pieces by a wide range of African-American writers—such as the late black nationalist **W. E. B. Du Bois**—not usually known for science fiction.

Scott, Hazel Dorothy

PIANIST, SINGER
June 11, 1920–October 2, 1981

Hazel Scott was a multitalented musician and actress. Scott was born in Port-of-Spain, Trinidad. In 1924 her father obtained a teaching position in the United States, and the family moved to New York City.

Scott began playing the piano at age two and made her performance debut at age three in Trinidad. She began formal musical training when the family moved to New York. She made her first U.S. appearance as a five-year-old at New York's Town Hall.

In 1934 Scott's father died, and her mother took a job as a saxophonist in an all-woman band. A few months later, Scott's mother decided to organize her own band—Alma Long Scott's All-Woman Orchestra—with Hazel playing both piano and trumpet. In 1936, at age sixteen, Scott played with

the **Count Basie** Orchestra at the Roseland Ballroom and on a **radio** program broadcast on the Mutual Broadcasting System. By age eighteen, already a veteran of the road, Scott appeared on Broadway in the musical *Sing Out the News*. She then became a **film** actress in the 1940s and played herself in such films as *Something to Shout About* (1943), *Broadway Rhythm* (1944), and *Rhapsody in Blue* (1945).

In 1950 Scott hosted a summer **television** program, *Hazel Scott*, becoming the first black woman to host her own television program.

In 1961 Scott moved to Europe after remarrying. Five years later, she returned to the United States. Upon her return, she made guest appearances on such television shows as *Julia* and *The Bold Ones*. Scott continued to perform in New York-area clubs until a few months before her death from cancer in 1981.

Scottsboro Boys

On April 9, 1931, an Alabama judge gave the death sentence to eight black teenagers: Haywood Patterson, Olen Montgomery, Clarence Norris, Willie Roberson, Andrew Wright, Ozie Powell, Eugene Williams, and Charley Weems. After trials in Scottsboro, all-white juries convicted the youths of attacking two white women.

The impact of the Scottsboro case was felt throughout the 1930s; by the end of the decade, it had become one of the great civil rights cases of the twentieth century. After the conviction, the International Labor Defense (ILD) took over the case and succeeded in obtaining a new trial for the defendants.

In Haywood Patterson's retrial, one of the victims took back her accusations and testified on behalf of the Scottsboro defendants. The jurors ignored her testimony and convicted Patterson and directed the judge to order the death penalty.

Judge Horton, convinced that Patterson and the other defendants were innocent, set aside the verdict, pointing out that the evidence was overwhelmingly in favor of the Scottsboro defendants. He ordered a new trial and announced that the defendants would never be convicted in his court. In the next election, however, voters defeated Horton and elected a new judge who presided over the new trial.

The trials that followed were terribly unjust. Horton's replacement, Judge William Callahan, barred defense evidence and belittled defense attorneys and witnesses. In the fall of 1933, all-white juries convicted both Patterson and Norris.

The ILD successfully appealed to the Supreme Court, on the grounds that African Americans had been excluded from Alabama juries. In *Norris v. Alabama* (1935), the Court accepted the defense argument, overturned the Norris and Patterson verdicts, and returned the case to Alabama for retrial.

In 1936, oversight of the case passed from the ILD to a coalition of civil rights organizations. This shift gave Alabama officials, by now embarrassed over the continuing judicial unfairness, an opportunity to compromise. The

The Scotsboro Boys pictured in Jail (Corbis Corporation. Reproduced by permission)

state dropped the charges against the four youngest defendants, and the other five received prison sentences from twenty years to life with the understanding that once publicity in the case had subsided, they would be quietly released. Despite the intense lobbying of national civil rights leaders (and the secret intervention of President Franklin Roosevelt), Alabama officials blocked their release. It was 1950 before the last of the Scottsboro defendants, Andrew Wright, received his parole.

Seale, Bobby George

ACTIVIST
October 22, 1936–

Robert "Bobby" Seale was a civil rights activist who helped found the **Black Panther Party.** The organization is known for promoting extreme action, even violent means, to bring an end to racial injustices in the United States.

Born in Dallas, Texas, Seale moved with his family to California before he reached the age of ten. Seale joined the U.S. Air Force when he was eighteen and was sent to Texas to train to be an aircraft mechanic. After training, Seale worked on an air force base in South Dakota for three years before being discharged. He then attended Merritt College in Oakland, California, where he took an interest in improving the African-American community.

Seale joined the Afro-American Association (a militant organization dedicated to fighting racial inequality) in 1961 and later formed his own group, the Soul Students Advisory Council. The council was formed to end the policy of drafting blacks to serve in the **Vietnam War** (1959–75). After hearing the inspiring speeches of black leader **Malcolm X,** Seale formed the Black Panther Party with his friend **Huey Newton.** The goals of the party were black freedom, full employment for blacks, and equal opportunity for blacks. The party also fought against police brutality against blacks.

Black Panthers co-founders Bobby Seale (left) and Huey Newton (AP/Wide World Photos. Reproduced by permission)

Three years after forming the Black Panther Party, Seale changed his political outlook. He began seeing the problem of inequality as a class struggle rather than a conflict between races. He decided to give up working with the Panthers, saying he did not want to "fight racism with more racism." Seale retired from the Black Panther Party in 1974, and in the 1980s he started a youth program called Youth Employment Strategies. The program encourages black students to pursue doctoral degrees.

Secession

The idea of secession, or withdrawing from one country to form a separate one, was behind one of the most important events in U.S. history, the **Civil War.** In the mid-1800s states in the American South considered breaking from the Union (the United States) and forming their own country, in large part to preserve their institution of **slavery.** Southerners supported slavery not only because they saw blacks as unequal citizens but also because their economy depended on slavery. Slaves helped them run their plantations. Eleven states eventually seceded from the Union and were prepared to go to war to preserve slavery and their livelihoods.

Southerners first began to see a threat to slavery when it was decided that California would be admitted to the Union as a "free state" (blacks would be considered free rather than the property of whites). The rise of the Republican Party further threatened Southerners because the Republicans opposed slavery. Southerners saw secession as a legal alternative (to revolution) because the Constitution does not specifically prohibit secession. In December 1860 South Carolina voted to secede from the Union, and two months later, Mississippi, Alabama, Florida, Georgia, Louisiana, and Texas followed. Although many Southerners did not want to leave the Union, they were forced to join in because they were a minority.

States in the upper South, such as Virginia, Tennessee, Arkansas, and North Carolina, were undecided about seceding. However, when the Confederate army attacked Fort Sumter in 1861 (officially beginning the Civil War (1861–65) these states were forced to make a decision. All of these states chose to fight for slavery (except the northwestern part of Virginia, which later became West Virginia). Four other "slave state" (Kentucky, Delaware, Missouri, and Maryland) decided to fight alongside the Union. The nation fell into four years of destructive war to resolve the issue of slavery. Although the North preserved the Union, the force that drove the country to war, racism, still exists today.

Seminole Wars

During the eighteenth century **American Indians** from various tribes arrived in Florida, fleeing the expansion of white settlers into tribal lands and wars with other Indian tribes. These Indians were called Seminoles, which means "runaways." After their arrival the different groups of Seminoles created alliances among themselves.

African Americans also became members of these alliances. Most were **fugitive slaves** known as "Maroons." Maroon villages selected their own leaders, who participated in Seminole affairs. African Americans fought with Indians in the First Seminole War (1817–18), the Second Seminole War (1835–42), and the Third Seminole War (1855–58) against the U.S. Army.

The U.S. government wanted Seminole land for white settlers, and it wanted to discourage other slaves from running away and joining the Seminoles. The First Seminole War began when General Andrew Jackson (1767–1845) destroyed several Seminole settlements and captured many Indians and blacks. As a result of the war, the Seminoles and blacks were driven deeper into Florida, some as far south as the Everglades.

African Americans worked as interpreters between the Seminoles and the government, and they also spoke out against the Indian Removal Act of 1830, a law requiring all American Indians in the southeastern United States to be moved west of the Mississippi River. The Indian Removal Act eventually led to the Second Seminole War. Throughout the war Seminole blacks served as strategists, interpreters, spies, and warriors. The war led to the deaths of some 1,500 American soldiers. The Seminoles also suffered heavy losses. By 1842 they had been almost completely removed from their land and relocated to Oklahoma.

Despite the government's promise that Seminole blacks would not be returned to **slavery,** slave hunters and traders kidnapped groups of African Americans from their Seminole communities. As a result, some African Americans followed Wild Cat, a Seminole Indian leader, to Mexico in 1850, in order to escape. Seminoles who remained in Florida continued to attack white communities and soldiers. But by the time the Third Seminole War ended (in 1858), almost all of the remaining Seminoles, both Indian and black, had been killed or relocated. When the last group of about 150 Seminoles left Florida in 1858, only two blacks accompanied them.

Sengstacke, Robert Abbott

PHOTOGRAPHER, NEWSPAPER EDITOR, PUBLISHER
May 29, 1943–

Robert Sengstacke is a well-known photographer, journalist, editor, and publisher who has worked for some of the top magazines and newspapers in the United States.

At age fourteen he received a box camera from his father, and his aunt gave him a film-developing set. In 1959 Sengstacke purchased another camera and an enlarger and organized a **photography** studio in his parents' basement.

In 1964 Sengstacke went to work as staff photographer for the *Chicago Defender,* a newspaper published by his father. Sengstacke also became the first non-Muslim appointed as a staff photographer for *Muhammad Speaks,* the newspaper of the **Nation of Islam.**

During the 1960s Sengstacke began to view photography as an art and as a powerful tool that African Americans could use to document their own history. The **Civil Rights movement** became the central subject of Sengstacke's photographs, and he became known for his images of such civil rights leaders as Rev. **Martin Luther King Jr., Jesse Jackson,** and **Ralph Abernathy.** Sengstacke also photographed demonstrators at various civil rights marches.

In 1971 Sengstacke became vice president of Sengstacke Newspaper Enterprise. During that year he also worked as a photographer on assignment in Mississippi for *Ebony* magazine. During the 1970s he photographed for the Black Press. He also became general manager of the *Tri-State Defender* in Memphis, Tennessee, in 1975, and four years later was appointed editor and publisher.

During the 1980s Sengstacke began working for Eastman Kodak and the *Phil Donahue Show.* He also took on assignments for *Essence,* *Jet Magazine, Negro Digest, Life Magazine,* the *Washington Post,* and the *New York Times.* Sengstacke became president of Sengstacke Newspaper Enterprise in 1988.

Since the mid-1960s, Sengstacke has exhibited photographs in colleges throughout the United States. He was appointed executive editor of the *Chicago Daily Defender* in 1993.

Shange, Ntozake

PLAYWRIGHT, PERFORMER
October 18, 1948–

Ntozake Shange was born Paulette Williams in Trenton, New Jersey. She took the Zulu name Ntozake ("she who comes with her own things") Shange ("she who walks like a lion") in 1971. Shange grew up in an upper-middle-class family very involved in political and cultural activities. She earned degrees in American studies from Barnard College (New York) in 1970 and the University of Southern California in 1973.

Shange's writing is marked by unique spelling and punctuation, partly to establish a recognizable style, but also as a reaction against Western culture. Much of her work blends music, drama, and dance, and it is brutally honest and reflective. Her best-known work is the play *for colored girls who have considered suicide/when the rainbow is enuf* (1976). Despite many upsetting scenes, the work is optimistic, showing the "infinite beauty" of black women. The play opened on Broadway in September 1976 and played there for almost two years before going on a national and international tour.

Shange is a highly productive author whose other published plays include *a photograph: lovers in motion, boogie woogie landscapes,* and *spell #7.* She has published several volumes of poetry, a book of children's literature, and two novels. Many of these works have also been adapted into theatrical form. Her writing is collected in *See No Evil: Prefaces, Essays, and Accounts, 1976–1983* (1984), and she is a major contributor to the collection *The Beacon Best of 1999: Creative Writing by Women and Men of All Colors.*

Sharecropping

During **Reconstruction** (1865-77), the twelve-year period of rebuilding that followed the **Civil War** (1861-65), a system of labor called sharecropping developed in the South. Landowners needed workers to plant their fields and harvest the crops. Former slaves needed to work for wages so they could support themselves and their families. But the South's economy was wrecked. Formerly well-to-do plantation owners now had no money to pay laborers. A new system of farm labor was developed. African Americans, along with poor whites, worked in the cotton, rice, and tobacco fields without pay on a regular basis. However, they did so with the promise of being payed at the end of the growing season.

How the System Worked

In sharecropping arrangements, the landowner either sold the harvest at market and gave each of his laborers a share of the earnings, or he gave the laborers their share of the crops to take to market and sell on their own. During the growing season, when the field hands were hard at work and had only the promise of being paid in the future, they were able to "buy" goods on credit. Local stores (owned by whites) operated this way, and sometimes the plantation owners set up stores where workers could purchase supplies on credit. But goods were priced in a way that made it hard for black work-

SHARE-TENANCY

A variation of sharecropping was share-tenancy. In this system, groups of families worked a small farm for themselves. In exchange for the labor they provided in the landowner's fields, the landowner "gave" the workers a plot of land that they could plant and harvest for themselves. Share tenants were a conservative workforce. Although they might have resented their condition and the landowner, rarely did these feelings result in activism.

ers to get ahead or even stay out of debt. Also, the landowner subtracted his planting expenses from the workers' shares, leaving the laborers with little or nothing to show for their toil at the end of the growing season.

Other Problems for Sharecroppers

The system of sharecropping had other problems as well. Many white overseers, the men who supervised work crews, had been "drivers" during the days of slavery. Some black laborers suffered abuses at the hands of these bosses. The federal Freedmen's Bureau sometimes was called on to intervene in such cases but abuses continued. There was also the problem of unfairness in earnings. Since African-American field hands worked in crews and on the promise of a future share of profits, at the end of the growing season the hard worker was given the same share as the slack worker. This problem was sometimes solved by landowners' allowing workers to choose their own crews. Work collectives (called "squads" or "associations") developed, with black workers joining a group of their choosing, which would contract with landowners for field jobs.

Crop failure was also a problem for sharecroppers. Poor weather or insects would destroy crops, leaving workers with little hope of future compensation. Yet another problem was that even after a good growing season, sellers could find that the market price of their crops was lower than they had expected. Such was the case with cotton during the late 1800s. The textile industry, which makes clothing and other goods out of fabric, was booming. There was great demand for cotton with which to spin thread and weave fabric. Seeing this opportunity, many southern growers converted their fields to cotton. Before long there was too much cotton harvested and sold. With so much to choose from, the buyers controlled the market price. Soon cotton was worth very little money.

Nevertheless, these "share" systems of labor persisted. There were exceptions, such as the black southerners who were able to secure land from the government and settle in the West, where many set up successful farms of their own. But like their sharecropping counterparts in the South, these farmers were at the mercy of weather conditions and market changes. It was not until World War I (1914-18) that African Americans in the South began migrating in great numbers to the North, where they found factory and service jobs in industrialized cities. This migration changed the economic outlook of many black Americans. (*See also Economics.*)

Jazz saxophonist Wayne Shorter (Archive Photos. Reproduced by permission)

Shorter, Wayne

JAZZ SAXOPHONIST, COMPOSER
August 25, 1933–

Wayne Shorter is a **jazz** saxophonist who contributed to the popularity of jazz in the 1950s and 1960s. He is known for experimenting with music and was a leader of the avant-garde (new, or experimental) jazz movement of the 1960s.

Born in Newark, New Jersey, Shorter originally wanted to be a painter and sculptor. However, he fell in love with music when he began playing the clarinet at age sixteen. He later switched to the tenor saxophone. Shorter graduated from New York University in 1956 with a degree in music.

After serving in the **military** for two years, he worked with famous saxophonist **John Coltrane** before being hired to work for **Art Blakey**'s Jazz Messengers (known as a training program for jazz musicians). Blakey was so impressed with Shorter's performing and composing that he made him

director. During this time, Shorter created his own sound, which was later displayed on his recordings *The Big Beat* (1960), *The Witch Doctor* (1961), and *The Freedom Rider* (1961).

In 1964 Shorter joined **Miles Davis**'s quintet (group of five musicians) in New York City. During his six years with the band, Shorter expanded his creativity by taking up the soprano saxophone and combining jazz with rock music. Some of his hits during this period were "Footprints," "Pinocchio," and "Dolores."

In 1970 Shorter broke with Davis and formed a new band called Weather Report. The band concentrated on blending jazz with rock music, creating the album *Heavy Weather* (1976).

Shorter played with different musicians throughout the 1970s and 1980s, including V.S.O.P (a group made up of Davis's rhythm section), **Herbie Hancock,** and Carlos Santana. Shorter continues to create music, reinventing his sound—which he says is something all artists should do from time to time.

Sickle-Cell Disease

Sickle-cell disease is a genetically acquired disorder of the red blood cells. A person who inherits the sickle-cell gene from both parents is born with the disease; a person inheriting the gene from only one parent is known as a sickle-cell carrier. Sickle-cell disorders in the United States are concentrated in areas where there are large groups of African Americans, such as the Northeast, the Midwest, and the rural South. About 8 percent of the African-American population is believed to carry the sickle-cell gene or trait. This gene was first introduced into the Americas through the **slave trade.**

Sickle-cell disease (preferred to the older term "sickle-cell anemia") can also be found among the populations of West Africa, the Caribbean, Guyana, Panama, Brazil, Italy, Greece, and India. Carriers of the disease have some immunity to the form of malaria—a disease transmitted by mosquitoes—that can cause death. This immunity made it possible for many African slaves to live and work on the humid, swampy rice plantations of South Carolina and the Chesapeake region.

The sickle cell, so called because of its curved, sickle-like shape, was not named until 1910, when Dr. J. B. Herrick described the blood cells of an anemic patient. In 1949 American chemist Linus Pauling (1901–1994) discovered the chemical abnormality that causes red blood cells to sickle.

Several organizations have been established for education and research about the disease, including the National Association for Sickle-Cell Disease. Numerous hospitals have centers for the study of sickle-cell disease, including the Columbia University Comprehensive Sickle-Cell Center at Harlem Hospital in New York City. These organizations raise funds for research and treatment of the illness. Government funding for research has risen since the early 1970s. Attempts to cut federal research support in the 1980s drew opposition from many African-American organizations.

Symptoms of sickle-cell disease usually appear in children after six months of age. Older patients may have pain in the larger bones, chest, back, joints, and abdomen and can develop bleeding in the eyes and the brain. Treatment for sickle-cell patients commonly calls for pain medication. Intravenous fluids are prescribed to prevent dehydration.

Although no cure exists, methods of treating sickle-cell patients have improved since about 1975. People with sickle-cell disease, once expected to live only to their forties, now enjoy longer and healthier lives.

Simone, Nina

SINGER
February 21, 1933–

Eunice Kathleen Waymon, known by her stage name Nina Simone, is a famous **jazz** singer. She is best known for her politically inspirational songs during the 1960s.

Born in Tryon, North Carolina, Simone was introduced to music at a very young age. Her mother encouraged her to play the piano at age three. By the time she was just six years old, she became the pianist at her family's church. Simone trained extensively to become a concert pianist at the prestigious Curtis Institute of Music in Philadelphia (1950–53) and the Juilliard School in New York City (1954–56).

It was not until 1954 that Simone stumbled upon her singing career. One night she was asked to sing, in addition to playing the piano, at a nightclub, and she was an instant hit.

Although Simone has been labeled as a jazz singer, her range of music cannot be accurately contained within one category. She has combined **the blues** and **folk music** and was inspired to compose songs with political meaning during the **Civil Rights movement**, including "Mississippi Goddam," "Four Women" (which she wrote with African-American poet **Langston Hughes**), "Old Jim Crow," and "Don't Let Me Be Misunderstood."

In the 1970s Simone performed internationally and later moved to Paris, France. Her **autobiography**, *I Put a Spell on You*, was published in 1991. Simone continued to live in France in 2000. However, to the delight of her fans, she returned that year to the United States to perform at the Oriental Theater in Chicago, Illinois.

Simpson, Orenthal James "O. J."

FOOTBALL PLAYER
July 9, 1947–

Orenthal James "O. J." Simpson was one of the greatest running backs in the history of the National Football League (NFL). Unfortunately, Simpson's accomplishments on the field have been overshadowed by the trial for his wife's murder, of which he was acquitted.

O. J. Simpson (second from right) conferring with his "dream team" of lawyers during his murder trial (AP/Wide World Photos. Reproduced by permission)

Born in San Francisco, California, Simpson starred in **football, baseball, and track-and-field** in high school. Simpson attended the City College of San Francisco, where he set several junior college football rushing records. In 1967 he was highly sought after by college scouts and decided to attend the University of Southern California (USC). At USC Simpson showed superior ability running with the football. In 1967 he led his team to a college championship and won the Heisman Memorial Trophy (an award given to the best college football player of the year) in 1968.

In 1969 Simpson was drafted by the Buffalo Bills. After faltering his first three seasons he broke out in 1972 with 1,251 rushing yards. The following year Simpson became the first running back to rush for over 2,000 yards in a single season. In 1976 he set the single-game rushing record, with 273 yards against the Detroit Lions.

Simpson retired from football in 1979 and was inducted into the NFL Hall of Fame in 1985. After retiring, he began a successful **television** career as an announcer. He also began a **film** and commercial acting career. He appeared in the television miniseries *Roots* (1977) and in three *Naked Gun* films (1988, 1991, 1993).

However, Simpson's career and standing in the public eye came to a dramatic end when he was accused of murdering his former wife, Nicole Brown, and her friend Ronald Goldman in 1994. Suspicion focused on Simpson, who led police on a high-speed chase shortly after the murders. He was arrested and charged with the murders and was the focus of attention in one of the most highly publicized trials in U.S. history. During the trial, details of Simpson's life came out that disrupted his national following. After an eight-month trial he was found not guilty; however, in 1997 he was found guilty of wrongful death in a civil suit (civil lawsuits are different from criminal suits in that the standards for proving guilt are less rigid).

In 2000 Simpson began participating in a Web site business designed to rebuild his severely damaged reputation. In June 2000 Simpson regained custody of his children.

Sims, Howard Bernard "Sandman"

c. 1925–

Howard Bernard "Sandman" Sims was raised in a family of tap dancers. He had neither the money nor the desire for dancing school, so he learned to dance on the streets of Los Angeles, California, with the guidance of his older brother. He went to New York City in 1946 to become a boxer; while warming his feet, he used to delight his spectators by dancing. After breaking his hand in a fight, Sims turned to **tap dance.**

Sims used the gritty sounds of sand grating against the wood to enhance the rhythm of his movements. He became a well-known "sand dancer," admired by audiences for his athletic, original style and for the clarity of his tapping. For seventeen years he performed at Harlem's **Apollo Theater** as a comedian. As a dancer, he toured with the big bands, including **Duke Ellington**'s (1899–1974). Sims is featured in the 1979 documentary film *No Maps on My Taps* and appeared in the 1989 film *Taps*. In 1990 he was featured at an evening of tap dancing at the **Apollo Theater.**

Sit-Ins

A sit-in is a nonviolent protest during which participants sit down and refuse to leave a location until their demands are met. Sit-ins are credited with initiating the modern **Civil Rights movement.** A lunch counter sit-in in Greensboro, North Carolina, on February 1, 1960, by four African-American college students is generally regarded as marking a new phase in the struggle to achieve racial justice. The students sat down at a Woolworth's lunch counter to protest the establishment's refusal to serve African Americans. Despite insults, physical attacks, and arrests, the students returned again and again until all Woolworth's counters were integrated.

The use of sit-ins as a political strategy actually began much earlier. During labor unrest in the 1930s, strikers (employees who refuse to work until the employer meets certain demands) used the "sit-down." Workers simply sat down in factories until employers met their demands for better wages and working conditions. Because some of the early civil rights activists had once been engaged in economic struggles on behalf of workers, they were familiar with the success of the sit-down.

The sit-in, in a variety of forms—a "swim-in" at public pools, or a "pray-in" in segregated churches—became a vital part of the struggle. Because they were challenging local laws and customs upholding segregation, the participants were often arrested and jailed for their actions. Their strategy was to sit quietly and ignore all forms of verbal and physical abuse directed toward them until they were removed, arrested, or served.

As the civil rights campaign moved into its more assertive phase of Black Power activism after 1963, the nonviolent sit-in was not used as frequently. But for the past twenty years it had been an effective strategy in achieving the integration of all types of establishments. (*See also* **Martin Luther King Jr.; Student Nonviolent Coordinating Committee (SNCC); National Association for the Advancement of Colored People (NAACP).**)

Picketers protest lunch counter segregation, where the "sit-in" protests began (AP/Wide World Photos. Reproduced by permission)

Slave narratives of this period tell about passing from slavery in the South— a kind of hell on earth— to freedom in the North. Most follow a common outline: the slave reaches a personal crisis, such as the sale of a loved one, that causes him or her to decide to escape.

Slave narratives—the personal stories of African Americans who lived as slaves and escaped to freedom—made up most of the literature written by blacks before the American Civil War (1861–65). After slavery was abolished in the United States (1865), former slaves continued to write about their experiences. From 1865 to 1930 at least fifty former slaves wrote, or told to another person who then wrote down, book-length accounts of their lives.

Most of the major authors of African-American literature before 1900, including **Frederick Douglass** (1818–1895), **William Wells Brown** (c. 1814–1884), **Harriet Ann Jacobs** (1813–1897), and **Booker T. Washington** (c. 1856–1915), launched their writing careers through the slave narrative. During the **Great Depression** of the 1930s, the Federal Writers' Project gathered spoken personal histories and testimony about slavery from twenty-five hundred former slaves in seventeen states, generating about ten thousand pages of interviews that were published in eighteen volumes.

With the rise of the antislavery movement in the early nineteenth century came a demand for stories that would emphasize the harsh realities of **slavery.** These began to appear in print in the late 1830s and early 1840s. White abolitionists (those who worked to end slavery) believed that testimony of former slaves would touch the hearts of people in the North who were unaware of—or did not care about—the situation of African Americans in the South. These abolitionists often added a preface or appendix to slave narratives that introduced the writer as a person of good character and told what the narrative would reveal about the horrors of slavery.

Slave narratives of this period tell about passing from slavery in the South—a kind of hell on earth—to freedom in the North. Most follow a common outline: the slave reaches a personal crisis, such as the sale of a loved one, that causes him or her to decide to escape. Trusting in God, the slave endures hardship on the way to freedom but finally reaches the North. Often the former slave then takes a new name and dedicates his life to helping other slaves become free.

These slave narrative were widely advertised and were sold at abolitionist meetings throughout the English-speaking world, eventually selling tens of thousands of copies. The most widely read and debated American novel of the nineteenth century—white author Harriet Beecher Stowe's (1811–1896) *Uncle Tom's Cabin* (1852)—was greatly influenced by the slave narratives Stowe read. From them she gained models for some of her most memorable characters and ideas for the events in the novel.

The slave narrative reached its peak in 1845 with the publication of the *Narrative of the Life of Frederick Douglass, an American Slave, Written by Himself.* Selling more than thirty thousand copies in its first five years of publication, Douglass's book became an international best-seller. Abolitionist leader William Lloyd Garrison (1805–1879) stressed that Douglass's narrative represented the usual experience of slavery, but he also noted that Douglass presented his story from the viewpoint of a former slave who seeks mental as well as physical freedom. That view made Douglass's narrative stand out from the rest.

During the 1850s and 1860s slave narratives showed a complicated American social class system, in both the North and the South. Douglass, in *My Bondage and My Freedom* (1855), revealed that he had not found true freedom among the abolitionists, because some of the same attitudes toward blacks were present among Northern, as well as Southern, whites.

Harriet Ann Jacobs, the first African-American woman to write her own slave narrative, showed how sexual control by white masters made slavery especially oppressive for black women. Her autobiography, *Incidents in the Life of a Slave Girl* (1861), shows how she fought back against this oppression and gained freedom for herself and her two children.

The best-selling slave narrative of the late nineteenth and early twentieth centuries was Booker T. Washington's *Up from Slavery* (1901), a classic American success story. Because Washington's autobiography discussed black progress and interracial cooperation since the freeing of Southern slaves in 1863, it was more accepted by whites than were the autobiographies of former slaves who told of injustices to blacks in the post–Civil War South.

Modern black autobiographies, such as **Richard Wright**'s (1908–1960) *Black Boy* (1945), and modern novels such as **Ernest J. Gaines**'s (1933–) *The Autobiography of Miss Jane Pittman* (1971) and **Toni Morrison**'s (1931–) *Beloved* (1989), owe some of their form and theme to the pre–Civil War slave narrative. They especially recall the slave narrative as they explore the origins of psychological and social oppression and question the meaning of freedom for twentieth-century blacks and whites. (*See also* **Autobiography.**)

Slave Trade

The slave trade conducted across the Atlantic Ocean extended over four centuries—from the mid-1400s through the mid-1800s. It caused the removal of millions of African peoples from their homelands to forced labor in other parts of the world. The most significant population transfer of all time, it created an African diaspora (the spreading out of a people from their homeland to other lands) in North and South America and the Caribbean. It also changed the development of African society in ways that are still being discovered.

In the New World, African slaves helped to shape the social, economic, and political structure of nations and furnished essential ingredients of modern world culture. Yet the slave trade left a legacy of racism by establishing a connection between forced, unpaid labor and peoples of African descent.

Control of the Slave Trade

From its beginning in about 1444 the Portuguese controlled the Atlantic slave trade. Between 1630 and 1650 the Dutch took control of the sea and the trade. After 1650 the English and the French dominated the slave trade, which reached its peak from about 1650 to 1850. During the 1850s and 1860s, as the slave trade was being abolished in other parts of the world, the Spanish and the Portuguese regained control and continued to supply Brazil and Cuba with slaves until 1865.

THE MIDDLE PASSAGE

The slave trade is a monument to the cruelty that humans can inflict on other humans. The term "Middle Passage" has long been a synonym for horror and human suffering. It refers to the transport of slaves aboard ships from the African coast to the Americas.

It is estimated that between twelve and fifteen million Africans were shipped across the Atlantic Ocean during the four-hundred-year history of the slave trade. Many did not survive the journey. Conditions aboard the ships were crowded and unsanitary, and often there was not enough food or drinking water for the slaves.

In the early days of the trade, carpenters were hired to build platforms in the lower part of ships to hold the human "cargo." The space between decks was normally four to five feet, and slaves could not stand, and sometimes not even sit, upright. Under the worst conditions, they could be packed like sardines in compartments with poor ventilation and no room for bodily functions, including vomiting from seasickness.

Beginning in the late 1600s, Portugal regulated the number of slaves carried according to the size of the ship. It further decreased the number during the 1800s. Great Britain had similar restrictions beginning in the late 1700s.

Conditions were at their worst during the 1800s as illegal traders placed themselves beyond regulation. Steamships, introduced by Americans as a method for carrying slaves, carried more Africans but did not give them any more room and often placed them too close to the boiler, adding burning or scalding to the dangers of the journey.

Slaves were needed for the large-scale production of tropical staple crops like sugar and cotton. Plantation owners needed a constant supply of strong laborers, and Africa provided this labor. Early European slave traders obtained slaves through middlemen, usually Europeans who married and lived among Africans. They also cooperated with African slave traders, who gathered slaves and took them to the West African coast, where they were held until they could be shipped across the Atlantic. Captives taken in war were a good source of slaves, and the Portuguese sometimes initiated wars among African chieftains to get these captives. Europeans also sent black servants or employees into the interior of Africa to trade—or often to raid—for slaves.

Europeans paid for slaves with items like iron bars, gold, cowrie shells, copper bracelets, and various European-made goods. Traders bargained over "bundles" of slaves according to the goods they had to offer.

European slave traders had to stay informed of social and political conditions in Africa to be successful in the trade. For this reason their records are a source of valuable information about Africa and Africans.

During the 1400s the Portuguese used slaves for their own sugar plantation colonies on islands off the West African coast. They also shipped them to Europe and the Mediterranean region. When the land that would

Diseases such as dysentery were the greatest killers, however. These were sometimes contracted by African captives during the rainy seasons and developed on the voyage with a terrible outcome. Illness also began while slaves were being held on the African coast as traders waited to get a full "cargo" of captives before setting sail. These holding pens could be damp dungeons, floating ship hulks, or open stockades where slaves were exposed to the weather. They were chained, branded, and inadequately cared for.

Individual ship captains, however, tried to preserve as many lives as they could, for economic reasons. After the ship had left the African coast, some captains tried to make conditions as good as possible. (The greatest danger of an uprising came as the ship set sail from Africa.) Men were chained together below deck and women above, but pregnant women and children were allowed to roam free. Captives were fed twice a day and allowed some exercise on deck in good weather. The ship's crew sometimes washed the holding decks with vinegar and water. African women helped prepare the food—often favorites brought from Africa, such as rice, corn, and yams.

In spite of the terrible conditions of the Middle Passage, friendships and cultural exchanges formed among Africans on slave ships often lasted a lifetime for those who survived the journey. These survivors gained a sense of optimism and self-worth that carried them through a difficult life of slavery.

become South America developed its plantation system in the 1500s, most slaves were sold in Brazil.

By the end of the 1700s, the British controlled more than half of the slave trade. Most slaves went to sugar-producing regions in South America and the Caribbean, with fewer going to North America. Before the 1600s, about two thousand slaves reached the New World per year. By the 1700s that figure had risen to more than sixty thousand. Most African captives were taken from the western coast and central Africa.

Abolition of the Slave Trade

Denmark was the first country to outlaw the slave trade, phasing it out over a ten-year period beginning in 1792. During the American Revolution (1775–83), Britain's trade between North America and West Africa came to a temporary halt. During the 1780s a massive antislavery movement began in England. By 1807 the slave trade was abolished in Great Britain, and the nation freed all British-owned slaves in 1833.

Slavery was abolished in the French colonies in the West Indies in 1794. It was reinstated under the ruler Napoleon Bonaparte (1769–1821) in 1802 but was finally abolished in all French territories by 1848. The

A depiction of slaves being sold at auction (Archive Photos. Reproduced by permission)

Dutch slave trade was banned in 1815, and slavery was abolished in the Netherlands in 1863.

Antislavery groups in North America, especially the Quakers, began working to ban the trade during the late 1600s. Repeated attempts by the colonies to get their British governors to ban the slave trade were denied or ignored, because England received a large portion of the profits from crops produced in the colonies through slave labor. After the American Revolution the new United States widely prohibited or taxed the slave trade, and the U.S. Congress closed the trade in 1808.

There was no enforcement of this law, however, and slave smuggling became widespread as Southern planters realized the profit value of slave labor. Because the United States would not allow its ships to be searched, illegal slave traders often flew the American flag as a cover. It was difficult to get a conviction of slave traders when they were caught. Finally, in 1862, during the American Civil War (1861–65), the Union (the Northern side) agreed to mutual searches of ships on the part of both British and Americans, and this policy shut off the illegal slave trade.

The Spanish and the Portuguese, however, continued the trade in slaves south of the equator until 1865. Slavery itself continued in some forms in Cuba and Brazil until the late 1800s. Brazil received almost 40 percent of all African slaves, because the slave trade began earlier there and lasted longer than anywhere else. The Caribbean islands of Jamaica and Barbados received 8 percent and 4 percent of the slaves, respectively.

By contrast, the land that became the United States received only about 5 percent of the total number of slaves imported from Africa. Still, because crop production there allowed slaves to settle and produce children, the United States had the largest slave population in the Americas during the nineteenth century.

Slavery

Evolving over two centuries, from the mid-1600s through the 1860s, slavery in the United States was always controversial. Many believed a nation based on liberty and equality should not prosper from the bondage of others. Slavery became a major issue leading to the American **Civil War** (1861–65). The slaves themselves used their African heritage and their creativity to develop a distinctive culture and help to win their own freedom.

Development of Slavery

When the North American colonies were under British control, from their founding until the **American Revolution** (1775–83), slavery developed slowly. Slaves first arrived around 1619 in Virginia to help with tobacco growing, but historians believe they, like many whites, worked as indentured servants (workers who sell their labor for a given period of time). Records show that many blacks were free in 1625.

This began to change in the late 1600s, as black slaves became more available when England entered the slave trade. Slavery was written into law in Virginia and Maryland, and the status of slaves became lifelong and hereditary (their children also became slaves). By the turn of the 1700s, black skin had come to be associated with being the property of another.

South Carolina was home to some English planters who had lived on the island of Barbados, where slavery was well established. In the 1690s these planters turned to rice cultivation. Their African slaves' adaptability to the humid climate and immunity to malaria made them ideal for working year-round along the South Carolina coast. By the 1730s much of the region was planted in rice, and blacks outnumbered whites almost two to one, with newly imported Africans making up a large portion of the slave population.

This large black population changed South Carolina slavery. Whites and blacks increasingly lived apart, and whites began to exert more control over blacks. In 1739 this resulted in the **Stono Rebellion,** the largest slave uprising during the colonial period. It was followed by the passing of the Negro Act of 1740, instituting the harshest slave laws in the British mainland colonies.

By the time of the American Revolution, every colony had slaves. Northern colonies used them in trades such as shipbuilding, in household service, and as common laborers. Slaves made up more than 30 percent of New York City's laborers by the mid-1700s.

The largest number of African-born slaves arrived in the mid-1700s, the time that the American-born slave population was forming families and rais-

SLAVE LIFE ON THE PLANTATIONS

Plantation field slaves worked in gangs from sunup to sundown, about fifteen hours a day, with only Sundays and Christmas holidays off. In these gangs they talked, sang, and courted among themselves when the master was not close by. At harvest time whole families might turn out to pick the crops. Large plantations required their own carpenters, blacksmiths, millers, gardeners, and house servants. Slaves performed all of this work, and some were chosen as managers. Slaves who had free time after finishing their tasks could tend their own gardens, hunt and fish, or work on other projects.

From sundown to sunup slaves were left to themselves. African-American culture grew in these free times. African patterns found their way into basketry, quilts, pottery, and the making of instruments like the African banjo. African rhythms were kept through hand clapping, body-slapping, and foot-tapping, known as "playin' Jubba." Slaves used their food rations to make African-American dishes like hoecakes or cornbread and spiced meat dishes with West African seasonings. They built slave cabins with some African features, like pounded-dirt floors.

Slaves also told African folktales about trickster animals like Brer Rabbit and Brer Fox. Slave sacred songs, or spirituals, recalled the African call-and-response style of singing, and a religious dance called the "ring shout" was based on an African spiritual dance. Slaves also sang lullabies to quiet their children and sad tunes about life's sorrows.

More than anything else, slaves feared that economic hard times might cause the slaveholder to sell members of their family or send them away to work elsewhere. Because of this danger, slaves created extensive family networks, as in

ing children. Slave families gave the increasing black population an African-American, rather than African, quality from the mid-1700s on.

The American Revolution

During the American Revolution blacks laid the foundation for freedom. Thousands fled to northern towns or took refuge among **American Indians** in South Carolina and Georgia. Others fought on the side of the British, who promised them freedom for their service.

Maryland rewarded slaves who fought for the colonists with manumission (granting them freedom). Between 1782 and 1790 more than ten thousand slaves in Virginia were freed by masters believing in equal rights and Christian principles. Many other slaves used new manumission laws to purchase their own freedom.

In the 1790s, however, Southern whites again defended slavery and threatened to leave the Constitutional Convention of 1787 unless the new constitution protected their interests. Slavery was recognized by law, and in 1793 the government passed a **fugitive slave** law that authorized anyone finding a runaway slave to return the slave to the master.

West African culture. Aunts, uncles, cousins, and grandparents shared in raising children or took over if the parents died or were sold. Children learned crafts, proper work habits, and survival skills for dealing with white owners, called "puttin' on massa." Children helped work in the family garden and shared chores in the slave cabin.

On larger farms both parents were usually present, but on smaller ones the mother raised the children and the father visited whenever he could if on a nearby plantation. Fathers hunted, fished, gardened, and even stole to provide more food for their families.

By the 1850s slaveholders provided better food, clothing, and housing for their slaves. Southern whites claimed their slaves had better lives than people trapped in the "wage slavery" of Northern cities, where rootless workers labored long hours in poor conditions for low pay. In spite of better provisions, however, slaveholders still used whipping more than rewards to get their slaves to work harder.

Slave resistance was always present. African-born slaves escaped in large groups, hoping to form a "maroon" colony in the wilderness. By contrast, American-born slaves who were familiar with white culture and had job skills escaped as individuals to a city, where they could find work and blend with the population, making their recapture difficult. Field hands and domestic slaves, who were confined to the plantation, resisted in smaller ways, such as pretending to be ignorant or ill, breaking tools, stealing plantation goods, and running away to the woods temporarily to escape punishment.

The 1800s and the American Civil War

The U.S. **slave trade** had stopped during the American Revolution, but South Carolina and Georgia bought many slaves after the war and before the closing of the trade in 1808. Because established slaves were raising children, in the early 1800s the United States had the only slave population that was reproducing itself. Between 1808 and 1861 about forty thousand more slaves were illegally brought to the United States.

In 1800 the **Gabriel Prosser conspiracy** in Virginia shocked the upper South, and many took back their antislavery feelings, believing slavery was necessary to control the large black population. Once a national institution, slavery became a regional one, separating North and South by the early 1800s.

As the United States grew, slaves were used to work in lumberyards, mining, and a variety of trades. But the chief demand for slave labor still came from agriculture. During the 1800s cotton became the principal crop, and the center of slavery shifted from Virginia, South Carolina, and Georgia to the cotton plantations of Alabama and Mississippi.

Southern planters earned as much on their farms by using slave labor as Northern investors earned in manufacturing or in building railroads. By

Slaves picking cotton (Courtesy of the Library of Congress)

1860 slaves were the best investment in the South, even greater than land. The desire to own slaves for profit and social status made the protection of slavery the main political concern in the South and a root cause of the American Civil War.

The war caused many slaveholders to abandon their plantations, leaving the slaves on their own. Some claimed the land for themselves and began to farm it. Others left for cities in the North to find work. Some slaves spied for the Union army, and others joined to fight, realizing that every Union victory quickened slavery's end.

In 1862 Congress passed a law freeing slaves who crossed Union lines. Slaves did not wait for President Abraham Lincoln (1809–1865) to issue his Emancipation Proclamation in 1863. Old and young walked, swam, rode, and were carried over Union lines, making a stronger statement for **abolition** than any white person ever had.

More than 180,000 blacks served in the Union army and navy during the Civil War. Some 37,000 died, making **emancipation** something they earned through their own sweat and blood. Former slaves emerged from the Civil War with a lively African-American culture, new citizenship rights, and a strong sense of themselves as a people.

Slyde, Jimmy

TAP DANCER
1927–

Born James Godbolt and raised in Boston, Massachusetts, Jimmy Slyde by the age of twelve was studying the violin and **tap dance,** learning to "slide." With Jimmy ("Sir Slyde") Mitchell he formed the duo the Slyde Brothers and appeared in nightclubs and theaters. He became known for his lyrical, sophisticated rhythms and for the slides and glides that are the trademarks of his jazz-tap dancing. During the 1940s Slyde appeared with the **Count Basie** (1904–1984) and **Duke Ellington** (1899–1974) big bands. After Slyde won a small role in the film *A Star Is Born* (1954) with Judy Garland, choreographer (dance composer) Nick Castle provided him with studio space for work and teaching.

In the 1950s and 1960s Slyde performed at major **jazz** festivals around the world. Unable to find work in the United States, he moved to Paris, France, in 1972, where he worked in small jazz clubs. The performance group "One Thousand Years of Jazz Dance with the Original Hoofers" drew him back to the United States.

Slyde has also appeared in several films. He received a Tony nomination for his dancing in the 1989 Broadway production of *Black and Blue*. In the early 1990s he frequently appeared as a surprise guest at jazz clubs in New York City, where he taught the younger generation the fine points of jazz-tap dance. Slyde continued to perform at the turn of the century, including an appearance at the "Footnotes" concert in Los Angeles, California in 2000.

Smith, Ada "Bricktop"

ENTERTAINER, NIGHTCLUB OWNER
August 14, 1894–January 31, 1984

Ada "Bricktop" Smith, the owner of racially integrated European nightclubs, was born in Alderson, West Virginia. She has also been known by the extended name Ada Beatrice Queen Victoria Louise Virginia Smith; her parents could not decide what to name her, so they allowed their neighbors to contribute, and the result was the extended name. In 1898 the family moved to Chicago. Around 1920 Bricktop began singing and dancing full-time in vaudeville shows (traveling variety shows featuring song, dance, acrobatics, comedy). In the early 1920s Bricktop, whose nickname came from her bright red hair, also worked extensively in Los Angeles and New York.

In 1924 Bricktop moved to Paris, France, to perform at the Cafe Le Grand Duc. She quickly became friends with members of the American and European elite, including the Prince of Wales, the writer F. Scott Fitzgerald, **Josephine Baker,** and composer Cole Porter. In 1926 Bricktop opened her own nightclub, the Music Box. After she encountered trouble in securing a permanent operating license, she reopened the Grand Duc under the name

Bricktop's. During the late-1920s and 1930s, the elegant club was a focal point for the glamorous nightlife for both blacks and whites in Paris. That era lasted only until the coming of **World War II** (1939–45). In the late 1930s, after most Americans had fled Paris, Bricktop made broadcasts for the French government, but she too eventually returned to the United States.

After several unsuccessful business ventures, Bricktop returned to Paris in 1949. She found the city drastically changed, and the new Bricktop's that she opened lasted less than a year. She moved the club to Rome in the late 1950s, and she lived there until her retirement from nightlife in 1964. By the 1970s she was living in New York, and in 1972 she recorded "So Long Baby" with Cy Coleman. In the mid-1970s she began to perform again at nightclubs in New York. Bricktop died in New York in 1984.

Smith, Bessie

BLUES SINGER
April 15, 1894–September 26, 1937

Bessie Smith, "Empress of **the Blues**," considered by many to be the greatest of all blues singers, was born in Chattanooga, Tennessee, the youngest of seven children. Her father, mother, and two brothers died during her childhood, and Bessie and her brother Andrew earned coins on street corners with Bessie singing and dancing to her brother's guitar music.

When another brother became involved with a traveling tent show, Bessie left home in 1912 to join him, and a year later moved to Atlanta and became a regular club performer. Her singing was rough and unrefined, but she possessed a dazzling vocal style and powerful stage presence. On her tours, Smith attracted a growing number of black followers in the rural South, as well as recent immigrants to northern urban ghettos who missed the down-home style and sound. She was too raw and vulgar, though, for

THE DEATH OF BESSIE SMITH

The circumstances of Bessie Smith's death in 1937 after an automobile accident near Clarksdale, Mississippi, brought more controversy and attention from the white press than Bessie had received during her lifetime. While driving with her companion, their car rear-ended a truck and rolled over, crushing Smith's arm and ribs. Smith had bled to death by the time she reached the hospital. Her producer at the time, John Hammond, published an article, based entirely on rumors, claiming that Bessie had died unattended after a white hospital refused to accept her into the emergency room. The claim proved to be untrue, but writers spread—and exaggerated—the story without bothering to investigate it. Edward Albee's 1960 play *The Death of Bessie Smith* prolonged the myth, and for a time the singer was better known for the way she died than for what she had accomplished in her life.

Blues pioneer Bessie Smith

the Tin Pan Alley songwriters—black songwriters attempting to move into the well-paying world of phonograph recordings—and white record company executives found her brand of blues too strange and unpolished. As a result, Smith was not recorded until 1923, when the black buying public had already demonstrated a market for blues songs.

Two of Smith's first recordings, "Down Hearted Blues" and "Gulf Coast Blues," were huge commercial successes, and Smith was able to expand her touring to all of the major northern cities. By 1924 she was the highest-paid African American in the country, earning as much as two thousand dollars a week—then an enormous amount of money. She sang with passion about everyday problems, natural disasters, abuse and violence, unfaithful lovers, and the longing for love. She performed these songs with a dramatic style that reflected the memory of her own suffering and captured the mood of black people who had experienced pain and sorrow.

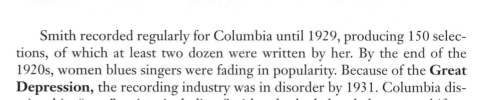

Smith recorded regularly for Columbia until 1929, producing 150 selections, of which at least two dozen were written by her. By the end of the 1920s, women blues singers were fading in popularity. Because of the **Great Depression,** the recording industry was in disorder by 1931. Columbia dismissed its "race" artists, including Smith, who had already begun to shift to popular ballads and swing tunes in an attempt to keep up with changing public taste. She changed her act and costumes in an attempt to appeal to club patrons, but she did not live to fulfill her hope of a new success with the emerging swing bands. On a tour of southern towns, Smith died in an automobile accident.

SNCC. *See* **Student Nonviolent Coordinating Committee**

Social Dance

Social dance refers to dances by individuals, couples, or groups done to the popular music of the time. Always changing, social dance remains as imaginative and flexible as the individual dancer. In the United States social dance began with a combining of African and European dance styles.

Slaves in colonial America carried on circle dances, animal dances, and others remembered from Africa. Plantation slaves sometimes had the opportunity to watch European dance styles at the master's balls. "Jig" dancing (named for fancy footwork, as in the jigs of the British Isles) was popular with slaves in the South and with free blacks in the North, where blacks and Irish immigrants lived and worked closely together.

Between the late 1600s and the early 1800s, African Americans began to dance in couples like Europeans, but they kept their shuffling steps and rhythmic movement of feet, limbs, and hips. After the 1820s white Americans began to copy African-American dance styles, a trend that continues today.

The Cakewalk

During the 1890s an African-American dance called the "cakewalk" became internationally famous. Its high-kneed strut probably imitated the upright posture of white ballroom dancers. Danced to early **ragtime** music of the 1890s, the cakewalk became popular in New York City's Broadway theater. New York held cakewalk competitions for white dancers, and dance teams traveled to Europe to perform. With its focus on the couple and individual dancers, the cakewalk was the key to modern dance of the twentieth century.

The cakewalk was slowly replaced by dances like the "turkey trot," "kangaroo hop," and "grizzly bear," which used gestures like pecking, flapping, and hopping, borrowed from African-American animal dances.

The Charleston and the Lindy Hop

With the 1923 Broadway show *Runnin' Wild*, a dance called the "Charleston" captured the heart of the American public. The Charleston

THE INCREDIBLE LINDY HOP

The lindy hop had wild movements similar to those of the Charleston, but with two outstanding characteristics. One was the "breakaway," when partners split apart or barely held on to each other with one hand. The other was the spectacular aerial lifts and throws, in which the men tossed their woman partners around their bodies or over their heads then pulled them through their legs and back to a standing position. The women seemed to fly, skid-land, then rebound again.

At the **Savoy Ballroom**, in New York City's Harlem neighborhood, the Lindy hop was renowned for its speed and aerials. The greatest big-band jazz musicians of the era played at the Savoy, and it became a showplace where the finest dancers tried to outdance one another. Whitey's Lindy Hoppers, a group of the Savoy's best dancers, toured the United States, appearing in movies, on Broadway, and at the 1939 World's Fair in New York City. The lindy hop spread throughout the world, first through newsreels and films, and then through American soldiers who introduced it in Europe and Asia during **World War II** (1939–45).

Known as the "jitterbug" in white communities, the Lindy hop could be danced to any kind of music. During the 1950s the Lindy changed tempos and became known as "rock and roll." The disco "hustle" of the 1970s looks like a highly ornamented lindy hop cut down to half time. Country-and-western "swing" dancing of the 1980s and 1990s resembles the Lindy hop framed by fancy arm work, and the South's "shag" is a regional variation of the Lindy hop.

was a wild, fast, angular dance, with the knees turning in and out and a forward-backward prancing step alternated with pigeon-toed shuffles and high kicks. It was so popular that the young women "flappers" who performed it became a symbol of the era. African-American dancer **Josephine Baker** (1906–1975) performed the Charleston in France, and it caught on throughout Europe.

In 1926 the **Savoy Ballroom** opened in **Harlem, New York**. It was the center of popular dance in New York City for the next thirty years. At the Savoy a new dance evolved alongside the Charleston, and in 1928 dancer Shorty Snowden named it the "Lindy hop," for American aviator Charles A. Lindbergh's 1927 solo flight across the Atlantic Ocean. The Lindy hop became an international craze and an American classic that reappeared in dances through the 1990s.

The Birth of Bebop

After the great dance halls closed during the late 1950s, smaller clubs opened, featuring five- or six-piece **jazz** bands, and with little room for dancing. These clubs fostered a new dance called "bebop." Dancers slipped and slid but basically stayed in place, appearing to gather energy into the center of the body. Bebop was danced mostly by men, although couples and small groups also performed. It used rapid splits that broke down to the floor

THE BUTT, WINDING, AND GRINDING

In 1988 singer Chuck Brown's hit song "The Butt" gave rise to a perfect example of an Africanized dance. "The Butt" has a bold call-and-response structure like many traditional African songs. Dancers who do the butt "get down" in a deep squat, place their hands on buttocks or thighs, arch their spines, nod their heads, and swivel the pelvis in figure eights.

The same dance was called "winding" in the 1990s and was performed by young black and white club goers to Jamaican reggae or go-go music (a Washington, D.C., musical style influenced by reggae).

As long ago as 1901, the same moves were called "the funky butt," and in the 1930s they were known as "grinding."

and rebounded up. It also had skating-hopping steps, with elbows pulled in and hands lightly paddling the air. Black singer **James Brown** (1933–) is probably the best-known entertainer to dance bebop.

Rock and Roll

Bebop and **rhythm and blues** influenced the development of rock and roll in the 1950s. The basic lindy hop was renamed "rock and roll" for the new musical style. Smooth footwork taken from bebop replaced the aerial throws. The "twist" became a dance craze in the early 1960s, introduced by black singer **Chubby Checker** (1941–). Close couple dancing came back in the 1950s, performed to a new singing style known as "doo-wop."

With the 1960s came a renewed interest in African animal dances, giving rise to the "Watusi," the "monkey," and the "jerk," followed by the "pony" and the "swim."

Breaking and Popping

With the explosion of **breakdancing** in New York City during the late 1970s, and a style called "popping" in California, dance styles underwent a radical change in the United States. "Breaking" was part of a larger cultural movement known as "hip-hop," established in New York City. It took in graffiti, spoken street poetry called "rap" music, religion, African-based philosophy, and dance.

Accompanying breakdancers were street disc jockeys (DJs) who developed two techniques. One is "scratchin'," or moving the record back and forth in the same groove to make a scratching sound. The other is mixing, or shifting between two turntables to mix parts of two records, creating new "breaks" in familiar songs. Along with these techniques, rappers used microphones to talk rhythmically over the music.

Breakdancing was performed mainly solo, by young black men of the ghettos. It has elements of a martial-arts dance that came to America with African slaves. Breakdancers dance upright then "break" down to twirl on

the floor. A dance style of the 1990s called "lofting" is a softer form of the original breakdance. Breakdancing's popularity faded in the United States in about 1984, but movies, satellite TV, and music videos introduced it to a new audience in Europe, Asia, and South America.

Popping and "locking" are other hip-hop dance styles, developed in California. In them the body seems to be broken into segments, and the joints of the arms and fingers seem to pop into sharp, brief freezes.

Freestyle Dancing

In the late 1980s and 1990s young adults created dances in which they gather in loose circles and dance apart from partners—or without a partner altogether. As in traditional African dancing, dancers crouch slightly, slide or stamp their feet, and jump into the air or dive down to the floor in shoulder rolls or belly slides. They shimmy their shoulders, swivel their hips, bob their heads, and hold positions briefly in freezes. Dances are named for the style of music played or are simply called "freestyle" because dancers combine steps however they choose.

South Carolina

First African-American Settlers: The first blacks to join the **American Indians** in South Carolina were African-Spanish slaves who rebelled against their captors and were left behind in 1526 when the Spanish abandoned their short-lived settlement.

Slave Population: African slaves were introduced in greater numbers in South Carolina after white settlers immigrated to the North American mainland from Barbados, where black slavery was prevalent. In 1790, two years after South Carolina became a state, there were 107,094 slaves; by 1860 that number had risen to 402,406.

Free Black Population: From the time of South Carolina's statehood, there was always a subset of free African-American residents. In 1790 there were 1,801 **free blacks** living in South Carolina, a number that rose to 10,002 in 1860.

Civil War: South Carolina was the first state to secede from the Union, helping to trigger the **Civil War** (1861–65). While some of South Carolina's blacks supported the Confederate cause and fought in its army, black support of the war was generally minimal.

Reconstruction: After the Civil War, male African Americans were able to vote freely and won majorities in both houses of the state legislature. Most whites preferred the exclusion of blacks from political power, however, and organizations such as the **Ku Klux Klan** violently opposed black enfranchisement (the right to vote). Between the mid-1800s and 1900, African Americans made up almost 60 percent of the state population; this changed, however, as a result of the Great Migration of the early 1900s, in which almost 275,000 blacks left South Carolina and headed north.

The Great Depression: Black migration out of South Carolina continued into the mid-1900s as rural poverty and segregation persisted; **World War II**

(1939–45) and the **Great Depression** intensified the desire to leave. Between 1940 and 1960 an estimated 339,000 African-American South Carolinians left the state.

Civil Rights Movement: The modern **Civil Rights movement** in South Carolina began in 1942 when a small group of black activists organized to challenge the all-white voting primary and to encourage black voter registration. Black leaders such as **Mary McLeod Bethune** and James McCain worked tirelessly to improve African-American educational opportunities and to end segregation. Schools in the state were integrated in the 1960s.

Current African-American Population: According to U.S. Census Bureau estimates, the total black population in South Carolina was 1,147,239 (30 percent of the state population) as of July 1, 1998.

Key Figures: Benjamin Elijah Mays (1894–1984), renowned black educator, preacher, and civil rights leader; **John Birks "Dizzy" Gillespie** (1917–1993), jazz trumpeter and composer; rock star **Chubby Checker** (1941–); **"Smokin' " Joe Frazier** (1944–), heavyweight boxing champion of the late 1960s.

(SEE ALSO **STONO REBELLION.**)

South Dakota

First African-American Settlers: The first black person recorded in South Dakota was York, a slave owned by William Clark of the Lewis and Clark expedition (1804–1806).

Civil War: In 1862, a year after Congress created the Dakota Territory, the new legislature considered a bill banning any black—enslaved or free—from entering the territory. The proposal was rejected, although the territorial government barred blacks from voting until the law was repealed in 1868.

Reconstruction: A few former slaves and freedmen entered South Dakota during the years after the Civil War (1861–65). The 1870 census counted only 94 blacks in the entire territory, or 0.7 percent of the total population. Most early South Dakotan blacks made their livings as dockworkers, woodcutters, cattle drovers, and farmers. Many blacks who moved to South Dakota after statehood in 1889 became homesteaders or settled in small towns.

The Great Depression: At the start of the 1920s there were 832 blacks in the state out of a total population of 636,547. The depressed economic conditions of the 1930s, however, challenged South Dakota's black residents, who joined the heavy migration out of the state. With black enlistments in the military, even more blacks left the state during **World War II** (1939–45).

Civil Rights Movement: Though remaining small in number, South Dakota's black community took encouragement from the national **Civil Rights movement,** and discrimination began to recede by the late 1950s. In the 1960s the state legislature banned racial discrimination in public places.

Current African-American Population: According to U.S. Census Bureau estimates, the total black population in South Dakota was 5,120 (0.7 percent of the state population) as of July 1, 1998.

Key Figures: Oscar Micheaux (1884–1951), pioneer novelist and filmmaker.

Southern Christian Leadership Conference

The Southern Christian Leadership Conference (SCLC) was founded in January 1957 by the Reverend **Dr. Martin Luther King Jr.** (1929–1968) and other young ministers who were active in local civil rights protest efforts across the South. It soon became the primary organization through which southern black churches made significant contributions to the struggle for civil rights for African Americans.

The SCLC drew together southern ministers who believed that black churches had a responsibility to be politically active. The organization also pulled together important protest campaigns that brought the southern struggle to the forefront of national attention and helped win passage of landmark federal civil rights legislation.

Three principal influences shaped the SCLC's founding. The first was the **Montgomery bus boycott** in Alabama in 1955–56, a successful local protest effort that brought King to national attention and made him the symbol of new black activism in the South. Second, young ministers in other cities seeking to follow the Montgomery example launched bus protests and sought a means of exchanging ideas and experiences. Third, northern civil rights activists began supporting the formation of a regional organization in the South that could spread the influence of Montgomery's mass movement and provide King a larger platform. The SCLC was composed not of individual members but of local organization "affiliates," such as civic leagues, ministerial alliances, and individual churches. King and the other ministers leading the conference focused on the right to vote and sought to develop a program, staff, and financial resources with which to pursue it.

In 1960 King and newly appointed director Rev. Wyatt Tee Walker (1929–) set out to design a direct assault on southern segregation. In a series of aggressive demonstrations, the SCLC put the violent acts of racist southern lawmen on the front pages of newspapers throughout the world. Civil rights rose as never before to the top of the U.S. national agenda. Within little more than a year, the Civil Rights Act of 1964 began changing southern race relations.

King was deeply convinced that the civil rights struggle should be expanded into the North to directly confront nationwide issues of housing discrimination and inadequate education and jobs. As a result, the SCLC in early 1966 shifted much of its staff and energies to an organizing campaign in Chicago, Illinois.

Following King's assassination on April 4, 1968, however, the SCLC's efforts to proceed with the campaign were spoiled by confusion within the organization. Tensions surrounding King's replacement, Rev. **Ralph D.**

Abernathy (1926–1990), as well as wider changes in the **Civil Rights movement,** led to the SCLC's decline. Only in the late 1970s, when another of the original founders, Joseph E. Lowery (1924–), assumed the SCLC's presidency, did the conference again become stable. In the last decades of the twentieth century, the SCLC continued to exist only as a shadow of the organization that had played such an important role in the civil rights struggle between 1963 and 1968.

Spanish-American War

During the short Spanish-American War (1898), African-American soldiers and officers served bravely at home and overseas, on the battlefield, and in the training camps, despite suffering overwhelming racism.

The war began in 1898 when the USS *Maine* exploded in Havana (Cuba) harbor. Twenty-two African-American sailors were among the two hundred sailors and officers killed. Suspecting Spanish involvement, the U.S. Army immediately began preparing itself for war and expanded all of its units to full strength. Some of the regiments reporting to battle had African-American officers, while others had large numbers of African-American soldiers and a few officers.

Black soldiers of the 10th cavalry at the Battle of San Juan Hill during the Spanish-American War

There were three major battles in the Cuban campaign, and the African-American units fought bravely in all three. In the battle at Las Guasimas, African-American cavalrymen joined other soldiers to rescue the famous "Rough Riders," who had come under attack. During the battle at El Caney, an African-American infantry unit attacked the enemy under heavy fire and suffered a large number of casualties. Private Conny Gray won a commendation for assisting his wounded captain to safety despite the heavy enemy fire. The assault on San Juan Hill involved three African-American regiments. While walking through the jungle, the regiments came under heavy attack and began to charge up the hill. The Spanish quickly retreated, and despite heavy losses, the regiments were widely praised for their bravery. Soon after this attack, the Spanish surrendered.

When they returned to the United States, the public honored all of the troops, including the African-American units. They participated in victory parades before returning to their regular duties. (*See also* **Military.**)

Spelman College

Founded: Spelman was founded in 1881 by Sophia B. Packard and Harriet E. Giles, two New England educators and members of the Women's American Baptist Home Mission Society (WABHMS), who were concerned over the lack of schools for black women in the American South.

History Highlights:

- 1882: American businessman John D. Rockefeller (1839–1937) pledges a $250 donation toward a building for the school, the first of several donations Rockefeller made to Spelman.
- 1884: The school is named Spelman Seminary in honor of Rockefeller's wife, Laura Spelman Rockefeller.
- 1924: Spelman begins offering a full range of college-level courses and changes its name to Spelman College.
- 1929: Because it is continually troubled by financial problems, the school enters into a contract with **Atlanta University** and **Morehouse College.** This partnership allows the schools to combine their resources and save costs.
- 1953: Spelman's first African-American president, Albert E. Manley, is appointed.
- 1957: The cooperation between Atlanta colleges that began in 1929 is expanded when Spelman, Atlanta University, and Morehouse are joined by several other Atlanta colleges to form the **Atlanta University Center.**
- 1960: **Martin Luther King Jr.** (1929–1968) delivers the Founder's Day address at Spelman.
- 1987: Dr. Johnnetta Betsch Cole becomes the first black woman president of Spelman College.
- 1988: African-American entertainer **Bill Cosby** and his wife, Camille, donate $20 million to Spelman College, part of which is used to build the Camille Olivia Hanks Cosby Academic Center.
- 1998: Dr. Audrey Forbes Manley becomes president of Spelman.

Location: Atlanta, Georgia

Known For: Spelman is the oldest black women's college in the United States.

Number of Students (1999–2000): 1,092

Grade Average of Incoming Freshman: B+

Admission Requirements: At least four years' college prep English; two years of science (at least one lab science); two years of math (algebra and geometry); two years of foreign language; SAT or ACT scores; recommendations from counselors and teachers; personal essay.

Mailing Address:
Office of Admission
Spelman College, Box 277
350 Spelman Lane
Atlanta, GA 30314

Telephone: (800) 982-2411

E-mail: admiss@spelman.edu

URL: http://www.spelman.edu

Campus: The 32-acre campus is located in the heart of Atlanta. The core of activity is the Manley College Center, which is home to administrative offices, the dining hall, and a food court. Other buildings include a science center, a fine arts building, a language laboratory, and a media center. Because Spelman is part of the Atlanta University Center, students are eligible to use many of the facilities located throughout Atlanta, including the Robert Woodruff Library, which contains over 500,000 volumes.

Special Programs: Women in Science and Engineering Scholars Program (WISE); students are required to participate in a special course called the African **Diaspora** in the World, which helps Spelman students develop an appreciation and understanding of the multicultural communities of the world.

Extracurricular Activities: Student Government Association; organizations, including the Spelman Glee Club, the Spelman-Morehouse Chorus, the Spelman-Morehouse Players; athletics (women's **basketball**, **track-and-field**, **tennis**, volleyball); school newspaper, the *Spotlight*; four sororities.

Spelman Alumni: Marian Wright Edelman (1939–), founder and president of the Children's Defense Fund; author **Alice Walker** (1944–); actress **Esther Rolle** (1920–1998); and Col. Marchelite Jordan, first woman commander of a U.S. Air Force base.

Sports

African slaves in the United States enjoyed sports, but they were only allowed to participate in certain activities, like **boxing, horse racing,** and ball games, on Sundays and holidays. Blacks did not gain wide acceptance in athletics in the United States until the mid-twentieth century. They now enjoy access to all professional sports, and many command multimillion-dollar salaries. However, racial issues are still evident in U.S. sports.

No Blacks Allowed

Blacks participated in all sports before the American **Civil War** (1861–65), but after the war and into the twentieth century they were barred from many sports. Blacks were successful in the boxing ring, and some were allowed to fight whites. In 1908 **Jack Johnson** (1878–1946) became the first black world heavyweight champion. Black jockeys dominated horse racing until about 1906, when increasing "whites only" policies began to force them out of the sport. Marshall "Major" Taylor, considered the best cyclist in the world between 1896 and 1910, was barred from the all-white American Racing Cyclists Union. The National Association of Baseball Players placed a formal ban on black players in 1867. Blacks were accepted in **football** throughout the 1800s and early 1900s, playing on northern college teams. A few blacks played professional football in the early 1900s, but in 1933 professional football leagues also barred blacks from playing.

Blacks Play Their Own Game

When all-black colleges were formed after the Civil War, they opened the door for blacks to play organized sports. Football and **tennis** were the first sports to develop on black college campuses, in the 1890s. **Baseball** followed in 1896. **Track-and-field** competitions were held at black colleges beginning in 1907. **Basketball** took longer to catch on—black colleges began forming teams just before World War I (1914–18).

Because of poor funding and a lack of training facilities, few blacks had a chance to compete in the Olympic Games before 1928.

Baseball was the first sport in which blacks developed their own professional leagues. Although some short-lived leagues were formed during the late1800s, it was not until after World War I that the first successful black league was formed, the National Negro Baseball League (NNL). In 1936 the Negro American League (NAL) was formed and competed against the NNL. Although the leagues gave blacks a chance to play professional baseball, they eventually suffered financial problems and disbanded during the 1950s.

In the 1920s blacks created their own basketball teams. Because professional basketball was poorly organized at the time, blacks were often given a chance to play against white teams. The two dominant black basketball teams were the Harlem Rens and the **Harlem Globetrotters.** The Rens were the first black-owned and black-staffed basketball team that earned its living full-time from playing basketball. The Globetrotters were still successful in 2000.

Shortly before World War I, blacks created the American Tennis Association (ATA). It was not until 1950 that **Althea Gibson** (1927–) became the first black woman to play in a U.S. Tennis Association tournament.

Blacks Are Allowed to Play

In 1945 the National Football League (NFL) withdrew its ban on blacks. The Cleveland (Ohio) Rams moved to Los Angeles, California, that year and signed two black players. In 1946 the Cleveland Browns—playing in the All-American Football Conference—introduced African-American football talent, and several other teams followed suit. By 2000 blacks had demonstrated remarkable skill at every position on the field.

Jackie Robinson (1919–1972) was the first black to break the color barrier in baseball when he joined the Brooklyn (New York) Dodgers in 1947. In 1950 the Boston Celtics's **Chuck Cooper** (1926–1984) became the first African American to play in the National Basketball Association (NBA). By the 1980s blacks dominated the ranks of professional basketball.

It was not until 1959 that blacks were allowed to play in Professional Golf Association events. Charlie Sifford became one of the first well–known black golfers. In 2000 African-American golfer **Tiger Woods** (1975–) became the top-ranking golfer in the world.

Integration on college campuses in the South came late. The University of Oklahoma was the first major southern university to recruit a black foot-

Baseball was the first sport in which blacks developed their own professional leagues.

BLACK ATHLETES AS ROLE MODELS

Despite the color barrier that prevented black athletes from participating in professional sports, African Americans were more than willing to serve as patriotic role models for the United States. Boxer **Joe Louis** (1914–1981) and Olympic track star **Jesse Owens** (1913–1980) were admired athletes who were used to raise money for armed services–related charities during World War II (1939–45). Posters of the heavyweight champion Louis had the caption "Private Joe says, 'We're going to do our part and we'll win because we're on God's side.'" Owens, who performed with excellence during the 1936 Olympics, inspired pride in the United States. African-American sports stars such as basketball players **Michael Jordan** and **Magic Johnson** became symbols of American success during the late twentieth century.

ball player, in 1958. Other southern schools quickly followed, and within ten years most were integrated. Basketball was slower to open up to blacks in southern colleges despite the clear presence of black talent at northern universities. Mississippi State University was the first southern college to break with tradition and play in the integrated National Collegiate Athletic Association (NCAA) tournament, in 1963. In 1966 a game between the University of Kentucky and Texas Western University marked a breakthrough in college basketball. Until that time, the University of Kentucky team had refused to play against blacks. But when the all-black squad at Texas Western defeated them, it became clear that blacks deserved to play at the college level.

Black Coaches and the Myth about Black Athleticism

In 1966 basketball player Bill Russell (1934–) became the first African-American head coach of a professional team. Russell led the Boston Celtics to two NBA titles, in 1968 and 1969. Baseball did not see its first black manager until 1975, when **Frank Robinson** (1935–) became manager of the Cleveland Indians. Professional football was the last to open its doors to African-American coaches, when **Art Shell** (1946–) became head coach of the Oakland (California) Raiders in 1989.

The difficulty that blacks have experienced reaching the coaching and managerial levels is directly related to a prejudiced view of blacks as being "athletic" but not as intelligent as whites. Because African Americans dominate many sports, some whites claim that blacks as a whole are physically gifted. Black athletes resent this claim, because it suggests that they do not have to work as hard to compete at a high level.

The most plausible explanation for the outstanding record of black athletic accomplishment during the late twentieth century is that young blacks choose sports as a chance for a successful career and a means of gaining respect among their peers. African-American sports superstars provide excellent role models for young blacks. Blacks have demonstrated tremendous ability in both amateur and professional sports, yet the fight against racial prejudice is unfinished.

St. Louis, Missouri

The city of St. Louis, Missouri, has held both hope and hardship for African Americans. Throughout its history, St. Louis's large black population struggled to gain education and basic civil rights. Problems with housing, education, health care, and unemployment continue to plague many black residents. In spite of its troubles, the city has been a center for developing black musical talents, and many of the greatest African-American musicians of all time have come from St. Louis.

St. Louis Beginnings

African Americans, both slave and free, lived in St. Louis from its founding in 1764. White authorities passed laws to prevent slaves from gathering in public, drinking, or associating with free blacks or with whites. In 1803, following the Louisiana Purchase, the district of St. Louis became part of the United States.

In 1825 free black leader John Berry Meachum founded the First African Baptist Church, probably the first independent black religious congregation west of the Mississippi River. He also opened a school for blacks, in spite of the state's ban on their education. Meachum bought black slaves, trained them in his carpentry shop, and then paid them wages so they could buy their freedom from him.

Before the American **Civil War** (1861–65), St. Louis was strongly proslavery. St. Louis slave Dred Scott (c. 1795–1858) made history when he tried to buy his freedom in 1846 and his owner refused. White lawyers helped Scott win his case in court, but the decision was overturned in 1857 by the U.S. Supreme Court in **Dred Scott v. Sanford**. Even as slavery declined in St. Louis, the city remained a major slave market and depot for slaves being shipped to the deep South.

Shortly before the Civil War a class of free blacks sprang up in St. Louis, and they soon outnumbered the slaves. Most were poor laborers with few civil rights, but a few were educated, owned property, and were even wealthy.

Nuns, priests, and a few free blacks started schools for black children during the mid-1800s. White authorities closed the schools if they knew African Americans were learning to read and write, so some were cleverly called "sewing schools."

The Civil War Years

When the Civil War broke out, St. Louis became a Union (the federal union of states, or the Northern side in the Civil War) outpost, and refugee slaves poured in, increasing the black population. In 1865, two years after President Abraham Lincoln (1809–1865) signed the Emancipation Proclamation, slavery was outlawed in St. Louis, and the ban on black education ended. St. Louis grew to become the third largest city in the United States. By the late 1800s, most blacks lived in two poor sections of town: Mill Creek Valley and Chestnut Valley, home of some famous African-American

ST. LOUIS: HOME OF GREAT AFRICAN-AMERICAN MUSIC

At the turn of the twentieth century, the Chestnut Valley district of St. Louis was home to such famous African-American ragtime musicians as **Scott Joplin** (1868–1917), called "the King of Ragtime." Joplin's house on Morgan Street (later Delmar Boulevard) is today a ragtime museum and center. Great blues artist **W. C. Handy** (1873–1958) made the city famous with his 1914 song "St. Louis Blues."

Along with Chicago, Illinois, and Memphis, Tennessee, the St. Louis area was known as a major center for blues and jazz before World War II. Some of its leading blues musicians were Lonnie Johnson, "St. Louis Jimmy" Oden, and Roosevelt Sykes. Big band jazz also became popular after the turn of the nineteenth century, especially bands playing on the Mississippi riverboats. Nightclubs were another place to find big bands, such as the Jeters-Pillars Orchestra and **Cab Calloway**'s (1907–1994) band. Two of the most important jazz trumpeters of all time, Clark Terry (1920—) and **Miles Davis** (1926–1991), came from the St. Louis area.

In the 1950s many significant blues and rock-and roll-musicians were based in St. Louis, including Ike and **Tina Turner** (1939—), **Chuck Berry** (1926—), and Albert King. The St. Louis-based Black Artists Group (1968–72) produced jazz talents like Hamiett Bluiett, Joseph and Lester Bowie, and Oliver Lake. St. Louis has also been the home of African-American entertainer Redd Foxx (1922–1991), comedian-activist **Dick Gregory**, and opera singers **Grace Bumbry** (1937—) and Felicia Weathers.

ragtime, blues, and **jazz** musicians. Ragtime, blues, and jazz are musical styles that are said to have risen out of African-American folk music of the South. All three have a characteristic rhythm called syncopation (pronounced sin-kuh-PAY-shun), and they are usually played on piano, guitar, horns, saxophones, and drums.

The Early Twentieth Century

In 1915 large numbers of southern blacks arrived in nearby East St. Louis, Illinois, in hopes of finding industrial jobs, but when race riots broke out in 1917 many fled across the Mississippi River to St. Louis, where they were protected. This new black population helped elect the city's (and state's) first black legislator, Walthall Moore.

Most blacks remained poor during the 1920s and 1930s because of employment discrimination against blacks, although a few, like beautician Annie Malone (1869–1957), became wealthy. After World War II (1939–45) blacks made the first successful challenges to discrimination in St. Louis. By 1949 city swimming pools and parks were opened to blacks, and Washington University was integrated. Public schools remained mostly segregated as late as 1965 because of segregated neighborhoods, even though some black students were bused to white schools.

The Civil Rights Era

During the Civil Rights Movement of the 1950s and 1960s, students and members of the **Congress of Racial Equality** (CORE) and the **National Association for the Advancement of Colored People** (NAACP) Youth Council held "**sit-ins.**" These were a means of peaceful protest in which a large group of blacks sat in public areas set aside for whites only. This action helped bring about desegregation and called attention to job discrimination against blacks.

By 1971 a poorly planned federal housing project for blacks had deteriorated so badly it had to be torn down. After the 1960s, however, education improved, black businesses became successful, and African Americans entered the government. In 1993 St. Louis elected its first black mayor, Freeman Bosley Jr.

St. Louis Today

Still, blacks in St. Louis face many difficulties. With industries closing, by 1990 the city had less than half its 1950 residents, but blacks made up almost half the population. A school desegregation plan adopted in 1976 was still not complete by 1991. In the early 1990s the black unemployment rate was as high as 34 percent, with 96 percent unemployment for black youth. From 1990 to 1996 St. Louis lost about 11.4 percent of its population. (*See also* **Missouri.**)

Stokes, Carl Burton

LAWYER, POLITICIAN
June 21, 1927–April 3, 1996

Carl Stokes was a noted lawyer and politician who served as a member of the Ohio Legislature, mayor, and judge, and as a U.S. ambassador.

Stokes was born and raised in Cleveland, Ohio. He attended the University of Minnesota at Minneapolis, receiving a B.S. degree in law in 1954 and completing his law degree in 1956. That same year, he and his brother Louis Stokes opened the law firm of Minor, McCurdy, Stokes and Stokes, in Cleveland.

In 1958 Stokes began his career in government when Cleveland's Mayor Anthony J. Celebrezze appointed him as an assistant city prosecutor. In the late 1950s Stokes became involved in the **Civil Rights movement,** and in 1958 he was elected to the executive committee of the Cleveland branch of the **National Association for the Advancement of Colored People (NAACP).** In 1962 Stokes entered **politics,** becoming the first black Democrat elected to the Ohio General Assembly. He was reelected twice and served through 1967.

In 1967 Stokes ran for the office of mayor of Cleveland. With the help of voter registration drives, Stokes easily defeated his opponent, becoming the first black elected mayor of a major American city. He was reelected in 1969 but decided not to run for a third term in 1971.

Stokes's administration succeeded in raising the city income tax to increase spending for schools, welfare, street improvement, the city zoo, and water purification.

In 1972 Stokes moved to New York City to work as a reporter and anchor for WNBC-TV. In 1980 he returned to Cleveland to serve as a senior partner in the labor law firm of Green, Schiavoni, Murphy, Haines and Sgambati. Three years later, Stokes successfully ran for a seat as Cleveland municipal court judge, a position he held through the early 1990s. In 1994

Stokes was appointed U.S. Ambassador to the Seychelles by President Bill Clinton. Suffering from poor health, he took an extended leave of absence from his post, and he died on April 3, 1996.

Stone, Sly ▪▪▪

MUSICIAN
March 15, 1944–

Sylvester Stewart, known to the world as Sly Stone, formed a band called Sly and The Family Stone, which was popular in the 1960s. He is credited for creating a unique blend of R&B, soul, funk, and rock.

Born in Dallas, Texas, Stone made his first musical recording playing drums and guitar at the age of four. In the 1950s he moved with his family to San Francisco, California. In 1964 Stone started working as a producer and songwriter for Autumn Records, which resulted in recordings by groups The Great Society and Bobby "The Swim" Freeman.

At the peak of one of the most racially tense moments in U.S. history—the 1960s—Stone formed an interracial band called The Family Stone. The band, which included both male and female musicians, performed a new breed of **rhythm-and-blues.** Its music, which blended **blues** with a funky soul and rock sound, was instantly popular. Among the albums Sly and The Family Stone produced were *A Whole New Thing* (1967) and *Dance to the Music* (1968). In 1969 the band performed at Woodstock and debuted its popular hit "Hot Fun in the Summertime."

Off the stage, Stone's life was filled with problems. He used drugs and alcohol heavily, and in the 1970s he was arrested on drug charges. He produced three records during the 1970s, all of which failed to catch on with the public. He produced albums in the late 1970s that were popular with critics but failed with the public. In 1981 Stone entered a drug-treatment center in an attempt to turn his life around. However, after staging a brief comeback, he once again got into trouble with the law. In 1985 he was arrested for failing to pay child support, and in 1989 he was arrested on drug charges. Although Stone's moment in the spotlight was brief, he made a lasting impression on performing artists. In 1993 he was inducted into the Rock 'n' Roll Hall of Fame.

Stono Rebellion ▪▪▪

In the early 1700s in South Carolina, black slaves outnumbered whites by a ratio of two to one. The slaves knew that if they tried to revolt, the numbers were in their favor. South Carolina slaves were also aware that revolts were being attempted elsewhere. A group of slaves planned a revolt, to take place on a Sunday, when whites would be least prepared to fight because of church and Sabbath (holy day) observances. Also, blacks were often not required to work on the Sabbath, so their absence from their daily chores would not be noticed.

On the Sunday morning of September 9, 1739, led by a slave named Jemmy, the slaves met near the Stono River to begin their revolt. They charged a store and killed two shopkeepers, taking guns and ammunition. They traveled to St. Augustine, Florida, ruled by the Spanish, fighting any whites who tried to stop them along the way. A military officer (William Bull) spotted the rebels and sent word for members of the militia to capture them.

In the ensuing fight several slaves were killed or captured, while a handful managed to escape. When the uprising was over, twenty whites and approximately forty slaves (out of the approximately eighty involved) had been killed. The Stono Rebellion of 1739 was the largest uprising of African-American slaves before the **Revolutionary War** (1776–79). (*See also*: **Slavery**)

Strayhorn, William Thomas "Billy"

COMPOSER, JAZZ PIANIST
November 25, 1915–May 30, 1967

The musician William "Billy" Strayhorn was born in Ohio but had most of his schooling, including private piano instruction, in Pittsburgh, Pennsylvania. He sought out **jazz** bandleader **Duke Ellington** (1899–1974) in December 1938, hoping to work with him as a lyricist. By 1939 Strayhorn had become a regular associate of the Ellington orchestra, contributing themes like "Day Dream" and "Passion Flower" and an arrangement that became the orchestra's theme, "Take the A Train." Strayhorn regularly contributed instrumental works like "Raincheck," "Chelsea Bridge," and "Johnny Come Lately" (all 1941). Ellington and Strayhorn frequently worked together, and they said in later years that they were unsure, once a work was completed, which one of them had actually composed the piece. Strayhorn came to the orchestra with a sophisticated knowledge of harmony, much of which he had worked out on his own. Ellington himself had knowledge only of basic harmony.

From the mid-1950s until his death, Strayhorn's collaborations with Ellington grew stronger. There were several extended works such as *Such Sweet Thunder*, *Suite Thursday*, and the *Far East Suite*. One of Strayhorn's final short works, the compelling "Blood Count," was written for the orchestra's alto saxophonist, **Johnny Hodges.**

Student Nonviolent Coordinating Committee

Black college students began a **sit-in** movement in 1960 that spread throughout the South. In response to this student civil rights activism, **Ella Baker** (1903–1986) of the **Southern Christian Leadership Conference (SCLC)** invited student protest leaders to a weekend conference in Raleigh, North Carolina. The student leaders, believing that existing civil rights organizations were too cautious in their methods, agreed to form a new group. They called this group the Student Nonviolent Coordinating Committee (SNCC, or "Snick") and elected student **Marion Barry** (1936–) as chairman.

SNCC gradually assumed a more assertive role in the **Civil Rights movement** and began to show its militancy and independence from the **National Association for the Advancement of Colored People (NAACP),** which worked for civil rights through the courts. From the fall of 1961 through the spring of 1966, SNCC shifted its focus from nonviolent protests of segregation to long-term voting rights campaigns in the Deep South. Full-time SNCC field secretaries worked closely with local leaders. SNCC workers mobilized black student protesters and organized marches that resulted in hundreds of arrests.

The group's bold actions did not overcome the segregationist opposition in many areas, and its voter registration campaign in rural areas achieved few gains, because of violent white resistance. SNCC's largest projects were in Mississippi, where its community-organizing efforts encountered fierce resistance from whites. Although SNCC's staff was composed mainly of native Mississippians, the campaign for voting rights in the state attracted increasing support from northern white college students.

Acknowledging the need for more outside support, the Council of Federated Organizations—a coalition of civil rights groups that was led by SNCC—launched a summer project in 1964 that was designed to bring hundreds of white students to Mississippi. The murder of three civil rights workers—two of them white—during the early days of the project brought national attention to the suppression of black voting rights in the Deep South.

After a brutal police attack in 1965 on a protest group marching from Selma, Alabama, to the state capitol in Montgomery, Alabama, SNCC militants cut many of their ties to the political mainstream. **Stokely Carmichael (1941–1998)** and other SNCC organizers helped establish an independent political group known as the **Black Panther Party.**

By the late 1960s, SNCC's ties to the **Black Panther Party** and its involvement in political issues in the Middle East had alienated many former supporters. In addition, its leaders' emphasis on social theories took time and attention from long-term community-organizing efforts. SNCC did not have much impact on African-American politics after 1967, although it remained in existence until the early 1970s.

Suffrage

African Americans were given the right to vote through the **Fifteenth Amendment** to the U.S. Constitution (1870). However, several barriers were set in place to prevent blacks from voting. It would be one hundred years after the amendment was passed—and only through political activism during the **Civil Rights movement** and decisions made by the U.S. Supreme Court—before blacks would finally begin to enjoy their constitutional right to vote.

Suffrage in the Nineteenth Century

African-American suffrage (the right to vote) was denied until three years after the American **Civil War** (1861–65). Initially, blacks were allowed

African-American Suffrage

1866
Civil Rights Act is passed.

1868
Fourteenth Amendment to the Constitution is ratified, granting citizenship to blacks.

1870
Fifteenth Amendment to the Constitution is ratified, giving blacks the right to vote.

1890–1910
Poll taxes, literacy tests, and grandfather clause are established in the South.

1915
Supreme Court case outlaws grandfather clause.

1920
Nineteenth Amendment to the Constitution is ratified, granting women the right to vote.

1964
Twenty-fourth Amendment to the Constitution is ratified, eliminating poll tax.

1965
Martin Luther King Jr. leads march in Selma, Alabama.

1965
Voting Rights Act is passed.

to vote in certain areas, such as Pennsylvania and New York, before the Civil War. However, the power to vote was officially taken away from blacks in every state by 1860. The Republican Party initiated radical changes to the structure of Southern politics after the Civil War. Initially, the right to vote was granted only to African-American men. Black women were excluded, because not even white women could vote until 1920. Perhaps the most important factor leading to black suffrage was the participation of blacks in the Civil War. Many blacks volunteered to fight in the Union (Northern) army, and the United States could not justify denying the right to vote to people who risked their lives to reunite the North and the South.

Citizenship was granted to blacks in 1868 with the adoption of the Fourteenth Amendment to the Constitution. However, the right to vote was not considered an important part of citizenship and was left out of the amendment. Although the right to vote is often considered to have been a natural extension of the Civil War, it was largely a result of keen political planning. Apart from a belief in equality, Northern Republicans granted blacks the right to vote in order to keep the old political system of the South from having too much power in the federal government.

Granting blacks the right to vote took more than ratifying (approving) a constitutional amendment. The federal government had to get involved on several occasions to keep the peace. White terrorist groups like the **Klu Klux Klan** and others were determined to keep blacks away from the polls. Despite the forces working against black voters, many risked their lives to cast their vote.

Another obstacle blacks had to face was the political group that developed in the South, which was determined to maintain old racist policies. Conservative Democrats set up barriers such as poll taxes and literacy tests to keep blacks from voting. A poll tax was a fee that people had to pay in order to vote. Because so few blacks could afford the extra expense, many did not vote. Literacy tests, to determine whether a voter could read and write, were required to prove that the voter was informed about political issues. Because many blacks did not have access to education, and because the tests were unreasonably difficult, many blacks were discouraged from going to the polls. The majority of whites could not pass the literacy tests either, but a rule called the "grandfather clause" excused many whites from having to take the test. The clause stated that if a man's grandfather had been a property owner, the man did not have to take a literacy test in order to vote. Because blacks were never given the chance to own property, they were never exempt from having to take literacy tests.

Suffrage in the Twentieth Century

During the early part of the twentieth century, blacks were prevented from voting in much of the South. This was a critical problem for democracy in the United States, because blacks made up a majority of the population in many regions of the South. The most important factor in a representative democracy (a government in which officeholders and lawmakers are elected by the people to represent them) is the right to vote. The all-white primary was another political device that kept blacks from voting. (Primaries are elections to determine which candidates will represent a given

REPUBLICANS VERSUS DEMOCRATS

Blacks originally favored the Republican Party, President Abraham Lincoln's (1809–1865) political party, because it abolished (eliminated) slavery. Another reason they favored the Republican Party was that the Democratic Party in the South set up barriers to black suffrage after blacks were given the legal right to vote.

However, by the 1930s many blacks began shifting their allegiance to the Democratic Party. This was a result of President Franklin D. Roosevelt's (1882–1945) New Deal programs, which enabled many blacks to recover from the **Great Depression** of the 1930s. Later Democratic presidents Harry S. Truman (1884–1972), John F. Kennedy (1917–1963), and Lyndon B. Johnson (1908–1973) advanced much of the civil rights legislation that granted civil liberties to blacks, including the right to vote without being harassed at the polls. (*See also* **Emancipation; Abolition.**)

party.) In the South, the Democratic Party dominated political affairs, and excluding blacks from primary elections meant there was no way for blacks to elect a candidate of their choice.

Beginning in 1915, several barriers to voting were shattered. The **National Association for the Advancement of Colored People (NAACP)** won an important Supreme Court case that outlawed the grandfather clause. In 1920 women were given the right to vote, and in 1944 the all-white primary system was ended by the Supreme Court. Before **World War II** (1939–45) only 5 percent of blacks in the United States voted. However, the war inspired greater pride in democracy. Blacks who risked their lives in the armed services came home determined to exercise their constitutional right to vote.

The Civil Rights movement led a fight to end discrimination at the voting booth. The struggle for voting rights reached a peak in 1965 when Rev. **Martin Luther King Jr.** (1929–1968) led a demonstration in Alabama. The march resulted in the ratification of the Twenty-fourth Amendment and passage of the Voting Rights Act of 1965, which finally brought an end to literacy tests. With barriers to voting broken down, blacks were able to win a greater number of elections to public office. By 1990 African Americans held more than seven thousand elected positions throughout the United States.

Sun Ra (Blount, Herman "Sonny") ▬▬▬

JAZZ BANDLEADER, PIANIST
May 1914–May 13, 1993

Born in Alabama, Herman "Sonny" Blount played piano as a child and led his own band while still in high school. In the 1930s he toured with a band and gradually gained a reputation as a sideman and arranger for shows.

Sun Ra: Selected Works

Sound of Joy
(1957)

The Heliocentric Worlds of Sun Ra
(1965)

Nothing Is
(1966)

The Solar Myth Approach
(1970–71)

Live at Montreux
(1976)

Sunrise in Different Dimensions
(1980)

Blue Delight
(1989)

From 1946 to 1947 Blount worked at Chicago's Club de Lisa, leading his own group and also serving as pianist and arranger for **Fletcher Henderson** (1897–1952).

In the late 1940s Blount completely reinvented himself, changing his name to Sun Ra and claiming the planet Saturn as his birthplace. His music had strong science-fiction overtones, and he made his motto Space Is the Place. At the same time, he also began to turn to ancient Egypt and Ethiopia for his spiritual outlook.

In 1953 he formed a big band called The Arkestra, and over the next forty years the group pioneered the use of modern improvisation and the spirit of free **jazz.** Sun Ra also established a core of remarkable soloists. Sun Ra was an accomplished pianist who never lost the energetic drive of his stride piano (a **ragtime** piano-playing style) roots. He was a pioneer in the use of electric instruments, playing the electric piano as early as 1956. He became well known as a composer of songs.

In Chicago during the 1950s, Sun Ra found his music rejected by established jazz musicians. However, he proved enormously influential to the new generation of musicians. In the late 1950s he started Saturn Records, which released dozens of his albums. In the early 1960s The Arkestra set up communal living quarters in New York and became a mainstay in contemporary JAZZ. In the 1960s and 1970s, The Arkestra continued to record and tour.

It was not until the late 1970s, when The Arkestra moved to Philadelphia, that Sun Ra began to incorporate traditional arrangements of tunes by **Jelly Roll Morton** (1890–1941), **Duke Ellington** (1899–1974), and **Thelonious Monk** (1917–1982) into its repertoire. Nonetheless, the Arkestra never lost its futuristic sound. During this time, Sun Ra directed circuslike concerts, complete with dancers and spectacular costumes, space-age prophecy, tales of intergalactic travel, and chants of "Next stop: Mars!" By the 1980s Sun Ra had become an internationally acclaimed figure, recording frequently and taking his extravagant show on tours in Europe and Asia. Sun Ra died in 1993 in Birmingham, Alabama.

Supremes, The

POPULAR MUSIC GROUP

The Supremes were one of the most successful music groups of all time. They smashed the color barrier in the pop market with their rise to national fame and, in the process, earned twelve number one hits and sold over twenty million records. Their songs are still played on the radio today and with each generation they win more and more fans.

Originally a quartet known as the Primettes, the group from Detroit, Michigan, had several personnel changes during its eighteen-year history. At the height of its popularity (1962-67), the Supremes included **Diana Ross** (1944–), Florence Ballard (1943–1976), and Mary Wilson (1944–). They were one of **Motown's** most successful all-girl groups and their wildly popular hits included "Where Did Our Love Go," "Baby Love," "Come See

About Me," (all from 1964), and three number one hits in 1965, "Stop! In the Name of Love," "Back in My Arms Again," and "I Hear a Symphony."

By 1965 the trio was appearing on countless television programs and touring around the world. In 1967 Cindy Birdsong (formerly with the popular group **Patti Labelle** and the Blue Belles) replaced Ballard, and the group was renamed Diana Ross and the Supremes. Ballard later sued Berry Gordy, the founder of Motown, and the other original Supremes, claiming she was forced to leave the group.

In 1970 Ross departed for a solo career, and Jean Terrell led the trio, but their popularity declined by 1973. When Terrell left the group in 1973, she wasn't replaced until 1975, when Scherrie Payne joined the new lineup. The Supremes officially disbanded in 1977, however, Mary Wilson continued to tour with other singers, still performing as the Supremes. In 1984 Wilson published *Dreamgirl: My Life as a Supreme.* In 1988 the Supremes (the original group featuring Ross, Wilson, and Ballard) were inducted into the Rock and Roll Hall of Fame.

Diana Ross continued to perform Supremes hits during her solo performances and in 2000 she launched an unsuccessful Supremes tour, performing with later Supreme members, Lynda Laurence and Scherrie Payne.

Tap Dance

Tap dance is a form of "percussive" (producing sound by scraping, striking, or shaking) dancing in which the feet are used to produce a rhythm to accompany the music.

Early Forms of Tap Dance

Tap dance evolved over hundreds of years and is a blend of African and European dance styles. The earliest African roots of tap dancing are associated with the **slave trade**. African slaves were forced to do a type of dance aboard slave ships in order to stay in good spirits and be physically fit for sale when the slave traders reached their destination.

Between 1600 and 1800, an African-American style of tap dance began to develop from African dance forms called "juba" and "ring-shouts." These were combined with European dances like the Irish jig, with its rapid toe-and-heel work. Juba featured shuffling footwork, hand clapping, and "hamboning," a way of using the body as a drum by slapping the thighs, chest, and cheeks with the hands to add rhythm. By 1800 a technique called "jigging" was added to tap dance. It featured a relaxed upper body with movement from the hips down and quickly shuffling feet. Jigging competitions were held as social events for slaves and freedmen.

Tap-Dancing Entertainers

Tap dance was an early form of black entertainment. One of the most influential dancers who helped bring African-American tap dancing into form was William Henry Lane (c.1825–1852). Lane was the first to break the color barrier in the dance entertainment world when he performed for white minstrel companies. Minstrels were dance and comedy shows put on by whites who painted their faces black and imitated black slaves. Blacks soon began to put on minstrel shows, and they became the earliest forms of black entertainment performed in public. The problem with minstrelsy was that it perpetuated negative stereotypes about blacks. Tap-dancing shows put on by companies such as Sam T. Jack's Creole Company and South Before the War helped introduced a form of black entertainment that did not carry on the degrading style of minstrel shows.

The popularity of vaudeville (variety shows) in the 1880s presented greater opportunities for blacks to perform on stage. Vaudeville further shaped tap-dancing styles. Dance teams such as Covan and Ruffin, Reed and Bryant, and Willams and Walker greatly improved on former styles. However, because of the social environment of the time, few blacks had a chance to perform for white audiences. Vaudeville put on two shows, one for blacks and one for whites.

Jazz Music and Modern Tap

Over the years, tap dance has been most influenced by **jazz** music. Jazz has long been associated with African-American culture, because blacks had the most impact on its development.

Modern tap dance developed when people started to click their shoes to the musical beat while dancing. Tap is different from other forms of dancing because its percussive sound is considered a musical instrument similar to the drums. In 1915—after experimenting with different types of shoes to produce the right sound—tap dancers began attaching small metal plates to their shoes to produce a louder click.

In the 1920s black tap dancers such as **Bill "Bojangles" Robinson** (1878–1949) and **John Bubbles** (1902–1986) began performing on Broadway, New York City's major theater district, as the popularity of tap dancing encouraged people to look beyond skin color. For the most part, however, entertainment was segregated in U.S. society, and black performers were forced to play in small nightclubs.

Hollywood Tap Dancers

In the 1930s and 1940s, Hollywood musicals were created that put tap dance in the national spotlight. Some well-known black dancers performed in Hollywood **films**, but most blacks were denied access. During this time, two of the more popular forms of black tap dancing were comedy routines and song-and-dance shows (called "the Class Act"). Some of the pioneers of the comedy style of tap were teams such as Slap and Happy, Stump and Stumpy, and Chuck and Chuckles. Among the famous song-and-dance teams were Johnson and Cole and Greenlee and Drayton.

Tap Dance Declines

In the mid-1940s tap dance went through a radical change as a result of the popularity of bebop, a jazz music style. Bebop had a much faster beat, which made it difficult for tap dancers to incorporate their routines. However, performers such as "Baby" Laurence found a way to keep tap dance alive by keeping pace with the quicker music. By the 1950s the popularity of jazz began to decline sharply for several reasons. Vaudeville and the variety act lost its appeal, and Hollywood stopped making tap-dancing films. A federal tax on dance floors caused many small dance businesses to collapse.

Tap-Dance Revival

In the 1970s tap dance began to regain popularity. Until then, tap dance was considered more of a hobby than an artistic dance form. However, tap dance achieved a higher artistic level when dancers began appearing in concert during the 1990s. As a result, it has received greater appreciation from the public and critics than ever before. (*See also* **Social Dance.**)

Tatum, Art Jr.

JAZZ PIANIST
October 13, 1909–November 5, 1956

Arthur "Art" Tatum, Jr. is considered by many to be the best jazz pianist in American history. He is known for the astonishing speed with which he played piano and his lasting impression on **jazz** music. His talent was even more remarkable considering he played without the use of his eyes.

Born in Toledo, Ohio, Tatum was partially blind. However, he was encouraged by his parents, both of whom were musicians, to take up piano playing. As a child he learned to play songs from the radio and then learned how to play the guitar, violin, and accordion. He received further musical training at Cousino School for the Blind and the Toledo School of Music. By 1926 Tatum was playing in local bands, and by 1929 he was hired by a Toledo radio station to do daily radio spots.

Two years later, he moved to New York City and built a reputation as being one of the best piano players around. He competed in traditional Harlem "cutting" contests (standoffs between musicians, with the crowd determining the winner), defeating many of his childhood idols. Shortly afterward, Tatum's career began to take flight. He recorded songs in 1933 and began touring nightclubs around the United States and England. Some of his popular recordings at the time were "Sweet Lorraine" (1940) and "Esquire Blues" (1943), which he made with saxophonist **Coleman Hawkins.**

Tatum played in different bands, but he received his greatest critical acclaim as a solo pianist. Tatum's music influenced some of the greatest performers in jazz, such as **Charlie Parker** and **Oscar Peterson.** Tatum was known as an interpreter of jazz music and for his ability to combine jazz with classical piano standards. Although Tatum suffered health problems stemming from overeating and alcohol abuse, he managed to record over one hundred solo performances from 1953 to 1955. In 1956 Tatum played to a crowd of nineteen thousand people at the Hollywood Bowl just before his death.

Television

Television was conceived as a form of commercialized mass entertainment. Its standard fare—comedy, melodrama, and variety shows—favors simple plot structures, family situations, light treatment of social issues, and reassuring happy endings, all of which limit character and thematic developments. Perhaps more than any other group in American society, African Americans have suffered from the tendencies of these shows to depict one-

-dimensional character stereotypes. In 2000, African Americans were prominent in all aspects of the television industry, and the effort for honest representation has continued.

Early Years

In the early years of television—the late 1940s to early 1950s—black performers appeared as guests on variety shows like Milton Berle's *Texaco Star Theater* and Ed Sullivan's *Toast of the Town*. They were also seen on quiz shows, amateur talent contests, and sporting events, especially boxing matches.

Rarely did African Americans host their own shows. Among the exceptions were the *Nat "King" Cole Show* (1956–57), and the *Mahalia Jackson Show* (1955).

African Americans were most visible in comedy, which linked television with the old minstrelsy tradition, in which blacks were portrayed as clownlike characters or as maids, chauffeurs, and shoeshine boys. In the 1920s radio programs carried on the minstrel tradition. Radio invented the situation comedy, which later became the most popular type of television program.

Drama

Blacks at first played only minor roles in television drama. Performers such as **Sidney Poitier** (1927–) had supporting roles in episodes of the *General Electric Theater* and others. The *Hallmark Hall of Fame* (1952–) produced "Green Pastures" in the late 1950s, a biblical drama featuring an all-black cast. The popular TV western almost never included African Americans, in spite of their importance to the real American West.

During the **Civil Rights movement** African Americans appeared on daily news programs and in network documentaries. The TV series *See It Now* reported on the movement as early as 1954, when the U.S. Supreme Court ruled to desegregate public schools. The NBC network's *White Paper* aired a five-part series on discrimination in housing, education, and employment, beginning in 1963.

African Americans also appeared in limited roles in dramas that explored social problems from the viewpoint of white professionals. One exception was *East Side/West Side* (1963–64), the first non-comedy in the history of television to cast an African American—played by **Cicely Tyson** (1939–)—as a regular character. The program showed the dreary realities of city life without artificial happy endings.

By 1965 top-rated programs featured African Americans in both leading and supporting roles. A turning point came with the series *I Spy* (1965–68), featuring black actor **Bill Cosby** (1937–) as an intelligent and cultured secret agent. *I Spy* was followed by *Mission Impossible* (1966–73), in which Greg Morris played an electronics expert on the espionage team. In *Mod Squad* (1968–73), Clarence Williams III played one of three undercover police officers.

By the end of the 1980s most top-rated shows featured at least one black character, and some racial restrictions were broken. MTM Enter-

AFRICAN AMERICANS WINNING EMMY AWARDS

An Emmy is an award given annually for excellence in different categories in television by the Academy of Television Arts and Sciences, founded in 1946. Awards are given for primetime (nighttime) programming and for daytime programming. African Americans began winning Emmys in 1959 and have received awards for achievement both on-screen and behind the scenes, as producers and directors.

prises produced successful programs featuring African Americans in the 1980s, such as *Fame*, about teens of different ethnic backgrounds coping with modern life.

The dramatic miniseries *Roots* (1977) and *Roots: The Next Generations* (1979) were unusually successful. For the first time in the history of television nearly 130 million Americans spent almost twenty-four hours watching a three-hundred-year saga about blacks journeying from Africa to slavery in America and finally to freedom.

In 2000 **Oprah Winfrey**'s (1954–) Harpo Films production of the series *Tuesdays With Morrie* was widely successful. Winfrey's daytime talk show has won several Grammy Awards.

Situation Comedy and Variety Shows

Situation comedy—with short episodes and a fixed set of characters—transferred easily from radio to television. One show to do this was ***Amos 'n' Andy,*** which began on radio in 1929, with white comedians Freeman Gosden and Charles Correll portraying the black main characters. Another radio show that moved to TV was *Fibber McGee and Molly*, with a main character, Beulah (for whom the television show was named) played on radio by white actor Marlin Hurt. When these shows moved to TV, African Americans got the starring roles.

Amos 'n' Andy, with its humorous, stereotyped main characters balanced by serious supporting characters, was the first all-black television comedy to introduce white audiences to the everyday lives of African-American families in New York City's Harlem neighborhood.

A number of African Americans enjoyed *Beulah* and *Amos 'n' Andy*, but many were offended by the stereotyped characters. The **National Association for the Advancement of Colored People (NAACP)** sued the television network for *Amos 'n' Andy's* demeaning portrayal of blacks. In 1953 the show was canceled, but individual stations showed reruns until 1966.

In the late 1960s two new comedy shows became the first in more than fifteen years to feature black stars. *Julia* (1968–71) and the *Bill Cosby Show* (1969–71) portrayed black families in everyday situations. In the 1970s came popular all-black family comedies like *Sanford and Son*, *The Jeffersons*, and *Good Times*.

PUBLIC TELEVISION AND CABLE NETWORKS

Local television stations, public television, and cable networks have provided important outlets for authentic African-American programming since the late 1960s. Examples are *Soul* (1970–75), a variety show produced by WNET in New York, and *Like It Is,* a public affairs show featuring outspoken host Gil Noble.

Public television has addressed African-American life and culture in series and special programs, like *The Righteous Apples* (1979–81) and *Eyes on the Prize* (1987 and 1990).

Syndication, the system of selling programming to individual stations, has been crucial for distributing popular shows like *Soul Train* (1971–), the *Oprah Winfrey Show* (1986–), and the *Montel Williams Show* (1992–). Winfrey has made a lasting mark on the media, as host of her own daytime TV talk show, producer and actress in both film and television, and in publishing.

Cable television has also made a wider range of programming possible. Robert Johnson started **Black Entertainment Television (BET)** in the early 1980s in the Washington, D.C., area. By the early 1990s it had expanded across the United States. Its programming includes black collegiate sports, music videos, public affairs programs, and reruns of shows featuring blacks, such as the *Cosby Show* and *Frank's Place.*

The cable network HBO presented the television movie *Introducing **Dorothy Dandridge*** starring black actress Halle Berry (1968–) in 1999. HBO also airs the successful black comedy the *Chris Rock Show,* featuring popular stand-up comedian Rock, as well as his comedy specials. The TNT network aired the television movie *Freedom Song* (2000), starring **Danny Glover** (1947–), about the effects of the Civil Rights movement on a small Mississippi town.

As late as 1969 children's programming did not include African Americans. The first to do so were *Fat Albert and the Cosby Kids* (1972–89) and public television's *Sesame Street* (1969–). These groundbreaking shows focused on the solution of everyday problems and the development of reading and basic math skills. Among other children's shows centered on or including African Americans are *ABC Afterschool Specials* (1972–), *Reading Rainbow* (1983–), *Saved by the Bell* (1989–), and *Carmen San Diego* (1991–).

The most significant comedies of the 1980s and 1990s were those in which black culture was explored on its own terms. The very successful *Cosby Show*—the first African-American series to top the annual Nielsen ratings—featured Bill Cosby as Dr. Cliff Huxtable and Phylicia Rashad as his lawyer wife, Clair, with their six children. Other successful black comedies of the 1990s were *Family Matters, Fresh Prince of Bel-Air, Sister, Sister,* and *Martin.*

The first successful variety show hosted by an African American was the *Flip Wilson Show* (1970–74). It featured white and black celebrity guests such as Lucille Ball, **Sammy Davis Jr.** (1925–1990), Bill Cosby, and **Richard**

The Temptations, one of Motown Record's cornerstone groups

Pryor (1940–). Wilson (1933–1998) became known for his outrageous comedy skits about black characters.

Although African Americans have had to struggle against both racial tension and the built-in limitations of television, they have become prominent in all aspects of the television industry and the effort for honest representation continues.

Temptations, The

POPULAR MUSIC GROUP

During their more than three decades of entertaining, the **rhythm-and-blues** quintet (a group with five members) the Temptations' has seen many personnel changes. First called the Elgins, original members were Eldridge Bryant, Eddie Kendricks, Paul Williams, Otis Williams, and Melvin Franklin.

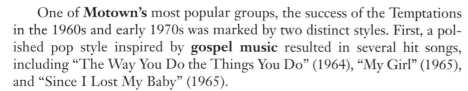

One of **Motown's** most popular groups, the success of the Temptations in the 1960s and early 1970s was marked by two distinct styles. First, a polished pop style inspired by **gospel music** resulted in several hit songs, including "The Way You Do the Things You Do" (1964), "My Girl" (1965), and "Since I Lost My Baby" (1965).

In the late 1960s the group came up with a new sound, "psychedelic soul," characterized by loud, brassy arrangements. This style produced another string of hits, including "Cloud Nine" (1969), "Psychedelic Shack" (1970), and "Ball of Confusion" (1970). After Damon Harris and Richard Street replaced Kendricks and Paul Williams, respectively, the group created one of its most important hits, "Papa Was a Rolling Stone" (1972), a powerful piece commenting on the despair of black family life. In 1989 the group was inducted into the Rock and Roll Hall of Fame.

Tennessee

First African-American Settlers: The first African Americans arrived in Tennessee with the settlers of the colonial period in the eighteenth century.

Slave Population: Most settlers of the territory were farmers living in east Tennessee, possessing one or two slaves. Tennessee joined the Union in 1796, and by 1800 over ten thousand slaves had entered the state.

Free Black Population: In 1826 the Manumission Society of Tennessee succeeded in banning the interstate slave trade. The invention of the cotton gin and opening of better farm lands made slavery too profitable, and in 1834 the state constitutional convention made slavery legal. The state's almost five thousand free blacks lost the right to vote and were barred from militia service.

Civil War: After Tennessee seceded from the Union in 1861, parts of the state were conquered and quickly occupied by the Union (northern) army. Tennessee blacks volunteered for the Union army in large numbers—nearly four thousand enlisted—and fought bravely in the **Civil War** (1861–65).

Reconstruction: In 1865, after accepting the Thirteenth Amendment, Tennessee was restored to the Union. While the efforts of freedmen's bureaus helped bring land, political office, and freedom to black Tennesseans, by the 1880s **Jim Crow** laws further restricted black activity. At the turn of the twentieth century, three-quarters of Tennessee's blacks worked on the land, although a few worked in trade and industry, in the iron foundries, or in sawmills, ports, and mines. Employment opportunities brought by **World War I** (1914–18) drew many blacks into the cities, sparking a wave of violence.

The Great Depression: After 1920 cotton prices remained chronically low, and the farm economy remained depressed until **World War II** (1939–45). The state's black urban population increased; Knoxville's and Chattanooga's populations more than doubled between 1910 and 1940. Interracial tensions escalated in the 1940s, leading to white rioting.

Civil Rights Movement: By 1960, 59 percent of the state's blacks had become registered voters. The **sit-in** movement of the 1960s led to the desegregation of public accommodations in a number of cities. The efforts of civil rights activists, however, were often met with violence; the Reverend Dr. **Martin Luther King Jr.** was assassinated in Memphis while speaking in support of a strike by garbage workers.

Current African-American Population: According to U.S. Census Bureau estimates, the total black population in Tennessee was 899,546 (16 percent of the state population) as of July 1, 1998.

Key Figures: Ida Bell Wells-Barnett (1862–1931), journalist and civil rights activist; author **Alex Haley** (1921–1992); civil rights leaders Rev. **Benjamin Hooks** (1925–); **Marion Barry,** former mayor of Washington, D.C. (1936–); Charley Pride (1938–), country singer and guitarist.

(SEE ALSO RED SUMMER; FISK UNIVERSITY.)

Tennis

Tennis has historically been known as a "white" sport, but African Americans have been playing tennis since it was introduced to the United States in 1874. Racial discrimination prevented blacks from competing in major events until the 1950s, but several blacks have had an impact on the sport.

At first, tennis was popular only among blacks in upper-class professions such as medicine, law, and teaching. In the early 1900s the popularity of tennis increased among blacks when it was introduced on black college campuses such as the **Tuskegee Institute (University)** and **Howard University.** By **World War I** (1914–18) tennis had spread to African-American communities in several areas of the United States.

Without a professional league in which to compete, blacks created their own tennis organization in 1916, the American Tennis Association (ATA). Through a combined effort of several black tennis players, the ATA held its first national tennis tournament one year later. Lucy D. Slowe, the women's champion, became the first African American to win a national title in any sport. The ATA led the way for African Americans to enter professional tennis in the United States by creating junior development programs in the 1930s to maintain interest among blacks.

In 1940 the color barrier was broken when the top-ranked men's tennis player, Don Budge, agreed to play a match against the top ATA player. Although Budge won the match, it opened the door for future interracial competitions. The professional women's league, the United States Tennis Association (USTA) refused to hold a similar event. However, black tennis player **Althea Gibson** (1927–) eventually broke into the white tennis world, winning the French Open tournament in 1956. As a result of Gibson's performance, the USTA agreed to allow black women to play in their events. In men's tennis, **Arthur Ashe Jr.** (1943–1993) broke the color barrier by winning the U.S. Open in 1968 and becoming the top-ranked player in the world the same year.

Although African Americans have always enjoyed the sport of tennis, their entrance into the professional ranks has been slow. In the late 1990s and 2000 the emergence of remarkable players such as the Williams sisters

(Serena and Venus Williams) has created greater interest in tennis among blacks in a sport largely dominated by whites.

Terrell, Mary Eliza Church

CIVIL RIGHTS ACTIVIST, WOMEN'S RIGHTS ACTIVIST
September 26, 1863–July 24, 1954

Mary Terrell was a college-educated civil and women's rights advocate at a time when few women could dream of achieving so much. She graduated from Oberlin College in Ohio in 1884 and traveled in Europe for two years.

After moving to Washington, D.C., with her husband, she was the first black woman appointed to the District of Columbia Board of Education. Terrell was an active member of the National American Woman Suffrage Association. She joined the Woman's Party picket line at the White House, and, after the achievement of the right to vote by women, was active in the Republican Party.

Women's international affairs involved her as well. She addressed the International Council of Women in 1904, in English, German, and French, the only American to do so.

Terrell participated in the founding of the **National Association for the Advancement of Colored People (NAACP)** and was vice president of the Washington, D.C., branch for many years. In 1892, she helped organize and headed the National League for the Protection of Colored Women in Washington, D.C., and she was the first president of the National Association of Colored Women in 1896.

Age did not diminish Terrell's activism. Denied admission to the Washington chapter of the American Association of University Women (AAUW) in 1946 on racial grounds, she entered a three-year legal battle that led the national group to reverse its position. In 1949, Terrell participated in **sit-ins,** which challenged segregation in public accommodations. Terrell also wrote articles on discrimination and racism as well as her **autobiography,** *A Colored Woman in a White World* (1940).

Terry, Sonny Saunders Terrell

BLUES MUSICIAN
October 24, 1911–March 12, 1986

Born Saunders Terrell in Greensboro, Georgia, Sonny Terry was raised on a farm and taught how to play the harmonica by his father. Two separate accidents in 1927 left Terry totally blind, and he later moved to North Carolina, where he met the country-**blues** guitarists Blind Boy Fuller and **Brownie McGhee.** The three of them wandered throughout the state during the 1930s and early 1940s, playing at local dances and recording songs. Terry was a creative and influential musician, best known for his "cross-note" technique (playing in a key other than the key of the harmonica) and his ability to produce special effects such as train whistles, animal cries, and moans.

In 1942 Terry and McGhee went to New York City and began a long recording and touring career together, sometimes recording and playing with white folksinger Woody Guthrie (1912–1967). Around 1970 Terry and McGhee split up due to personality conflicts, although they later occasionally reunited for concerts. After 1970 Terry usually performed solo or as the leader of a small band. He died in 1986, following a heart attack.

Texas

First African-American Settlers: Africans first arrived in Texas in the sixteenth century as part of Spanish exploring parties.

Slave Population: Free Africans and mulattoes (those of mixed descent) significantly outnumbered slaves in the Spanish period, but that would change abruptly with Mexican independence and American immigration in the 1820s. By 1836 the slave population numbered about 5,000, growing to 30,000 by the time of Texas's annexation in 1845, and reaching 182,000 in 1860. Most slaves worked as cowhands in ranching areas or on farms and plantations.

Free Black Population: A small free population of blacks lived in pre–Civil War Texas; in 1860 there were about one thousand. In the mid-1850s several thousand enslaved black Texans fled to Mexico to escape harsh treatment and living conditions.

Civil War: Because Union (Northern) troops never advanced beyond the fringes of the state during the **Civil War** (1861–65), Texas slaves had fewer chances to escape slavery than their counterparts in the eastern Southern states. As a result, only forty-seven black Texans served with federal armies. Some 250,000 African Americans would wait until June 19, 1865, for their freedom to be decreed by Union forces.

Reconstruction: In the years after the Civil War, confined largely to agricultural, unskilled, and service work, black Texans found their efforts rarely yielded more than a bare survival. Still, they quickly built institutions, particularly churches and schools, to serve their higher aspirations. Disfranchisement (loss of voting rights) and segregation prevailed in the first half of the twentieth century, and hundreds of African Americans were lynched between 1890 and the mid-1920s.

The Great Depression: With the discovery of vast oil reserves in the early 1900s, a new industrial economy emerged in Texas and saw the movement of blacks to urban areas to take advantage of job opportunities. By 1930 nearly two-thirds of the black labor force worked outside agriculture.

Civil Rights Movement: While Texas's booming economy and enormous growth helped lessen white resistance to black political and civil rights initiatives, African Americans still experienced significant obstacles such as continued lynchings and persistent school segregation.

Current African-American Population: According to U.S. Census Bureau estimates, the total black population in Texas was 2,430,061 (12 percent of the total population) as of July 1, 1998.

Key Figures: Norris Wright Cuney (1846–1898), prominent Republican party leader during the **Reconstruction** era.

(SEE ALSO **CARPETBAGGERS; LYNCHING**.)

Tharpe, Rosetta "Sister"

GOSPEL SINGER, GUITARIST
March 20, 1915–October 9, 1973

"Sister" Rosetta Tharpe was born Rosetta Nubin in Cotton Plant, Arkansas. She began playing guitar and singing in the Church of God in Christ, a Pentecostal church, and gained professional experience traveling with her mother, Katie Bell Nubin, a missionary.

Under the name Sister Rosetta Tharpe, she became popular in 1938 in New York. She performed in secular (not church-related) arenas such as **Harlem, New York**'s **Cotton Club**, a controversial practice for a gospel singer.

Tharpe landed a contract with Decca Records, becoming the first gospel singer to record for a major record label. In 1943 she performed at the **Apollo Theater**, the first time that a major gospel singer appeared there. Her 1944 rendition of "Strange Things Happen Every Day" was widely popular.

During the 1940s Tharpe performed in churches, concert halls, on radio, and eventually on television. She defended her unconventional career by explaining that all of her music was evangelical (religious). She was popular, however, because of her jazz and blues-influenced guitar playing. She eventually toured with **jazz** and **blues** artists, including Benny Goodman (1906–1986) and **Muddy Waters** (1915–1983), and with gospel groups such as the Caravans and the Dixie Hummingbirds.

Tharpe was also the first major gospel singer to tour Europe. Through her live performances and recordings, she popularized such songs as "That's All," "I Looked Down the Line," "Up Above My Head," and "This Train." (*See also*: **Gospel Music**)

Thomas, Clarence

JUSTICE OF U.S. SUPREME COURT
June 23, 1948–

Born in Georgia, Clarence Thomas attended Catholic schools, whose teachers he later credited with giving him hope and self-confidence. In 1967 Thomas entered the seminary. He decided to leave after hearing white classmates happily report the assassination of the Reverend Dr. **Martin Luther King Jr.** (1929–1968). Thomas transferred to Holy Cross College in Massachusetts and majored in English literature. He helped form the Black Students League and ran a free-breakfast program for black children.

Thomas entered Yale University Law School and was admitted to the bar in 1974. Shortly thereafter, he read the conservative African-American

Clarence Thomas, one of the most controversial Supreme Court Justices of the twentieth century (Courtesy of the Library of Congress)

economist Thomas Sowell's book *Race and Economics* (1975), which he later claimed as his intellectual "salvation." Thomas adopted Sowell's pro-market, anti-**affirmative action** theories.

In 1980 Thomas spoke at a meeting of black conservatives. He denounced the social welfare system for fostering dependency. The publicity Thomas's conservative views received won him the interest of the Reagan administration. In 1981 Thomas was named assistant secretary for civil rights in the Department of Education, where he drew criticism for refusing to push integration (legally enforced sharing of public facilities by blacks and whites) orders on southern colleges.

In 1982 Thomas was appointed chair of the Equal Employment Opportunity Commission, a federal agency. In 1989 President George Bush nominated Thomas for a seat on the U.S. Circuit Court of Appeals for the District of Columbia. The appointment was widely understood as preliminary to a possible Supreme Court appointment, as a replacement for aging African-American Justice Thurgood Marshall (1908–1993). In July 1991 Marshall retired, and Bush nominated Thomas as his successor. Bush claimed race had nothing to do with the nomination. Nevertheless, many blacks who opposed Thomas's conservative ideas felt torn by the nomination and supported him or remained neutral on racial grounds.

Thomas's confirmation hearings were highly charged and bitter. He refused to take a position on the *Roe v. Wade* (1973) abortion decision. On September 27, 1991, the Senate Judiciary Committee deadlocked on Thomas's nomination and sent it to the Senate floor without recommendation. Shortly after, testimony by Anita Hill, Thomas's former assistant who claimed he had sexually harassed her, was leaked to media sources. The committee reopened hearings to discuss the issue. The questioning of Hill and Thomas became a national television event and a source of universal debate over issues of sexual harassment. Despite the damaging publicity, Thomas was confirmed.

In his first years on the Supreme Court, Thomas voted consistently with the Court's conservative wing. Thomas remained bitter about the treatment he had received during his confirmation process. In 1993 he gave a controversial speech linking society's treatment of conservative African-American intellectuals to lynching. During the 1990s and at the beginning of the twenty-first century, Thomas regularly voted with his conservative colleagues on the Court in cases involving affirmative action, abortion, educational opportunity, the death penalty, and civil rights for gays and lesbians.

Thomas, Debra J. "Debi"

ICE SKATER
March 25, 1967–

A native of Poughkeepsie, New York, Debi Thomas moved to northern California with her family when she was a small child. Fascinated by an ice

Debi Thomas performs during the World Figure Skating Championships (Corbls Corporation. Reproduced by permission)

show she watched at the age of three, Thomas became a competitive skater by the time she was in junior high school.

Thomas also excelled academically as well as on the ice and became the first prominent female skater to attend college since the 1950s, graduating from Stanford in 1991.

Thomas thrilled audiences and pleased judges with her graceful choreography blended with a powerful athleticism. In 1985 she was named Figure Skater of the Year, and in 1986 she became the first black woman to win the United States and Women's World Figure Championships. That same year, she was named Amateur Female Athlete of the Year and Wide World of Sports Athlete of the Year. She faced injuries in 1987 but managed to place second in the U.S. and world championships. In 1988 she placed third in both the world championships and at the Winter Olympics.

Thomas turned professional in 1988, winning world championships in 1988, 1989, and 1991. In 1991 she won the World Challenge of Champions and also entered Northwestern University Medical School to study orthopedic and sports medicine, receiving her M.D. degree in 1994.

Thornton, Willie Mae "Big Mama"

BLUES SINGER
December 11, 1926–July 25, 1984

Born in Montgomery, **Alabama**, Willie Mae Thornton left home after her mother died, and she joined a **Harlem** stage act at age fourteen. In 1948 she moved to Houston, **Texas**, and sang with the Johnny Otis Rhythm and Blues Caravan. Her 250-pound size earned her the nickname "Big Mama," and she became popular for her rowdy, shouting style, as well as her outlandish behavior—she drank heavily and dressed in men's clothing, sometimes wearing a dress over trousers. "Hound Dog" (1953), a song later made famous by white singer Elvis Presley (1935–1977), was her only hit, but it enabled her to tour with **Johnny Ace** until Ace's suicide in 1954—an event from which Thornton's career never recovered.

Thornton struggled in the San Francisco Bay area until **the blues** revival of the mid-1960s created a demand for older blues singers. From then on, she performed at **jazz, folk music**, and blues festivals around the world.

White rock and blues singer Janis Joplin (1943–1970) remade Thornton's "Ball and Chain" into her signature song in 1968, but Thornton had signed away the copyright to the tune years before, and she earned no money for Joplin's version. She was frail from liver disease and weighed only ninety-five pounds when she died of a heart attack at age fifty-seven in a Los Angeles, California, boarding house.

Thurman, Wallace

WRITER
August 16, 1902–December 22, 1934

Born in Salt Lake City, **Utah**, Wallace Thurman began his literary career shortly after he left the University of Utah to begin studies at the University of Southern California. He had intended to study medicine but soon rediscovered an earlier love for writing. Having heard about the **Harlem Renaissance**, an artistic movement among New York's African Americans, Thurman decided to try forming a West Coast counterpart and began editing his own literary magazine. The magazine folded after six months, however, and Thurman left for New York soon after. The city became his lifelong residence.

Thurman's first important position in New York was as an editorial assistant at the revolutionary *Messenger*. The magazine eventually served as a forum for Thurman's work as well as that of other Harlem Renaissance talent, including **Langston Hughes, Arna Bontemps,** and **Zora Neale Hurston.** In 1926 Thurman joined with Hurston and others to produce an experimental magazine, *Fire,* but strangely enough, the magazine failed soon after the release of its first issue, when a fire swept through a basement where several hundred copies were stored.

Thurman also wrote critical articles on African-American life and culture for such magazines as the *New Republic* and the *Independent.* Black writers of the Harlem Renaissance, he claimed, tended too often to view their own people as "sociological problems rather than as human beings," and he urged them to write about the real and unique parts of black life and culture.

Thurman published his first novel, *The Blacker the Berry,* in 1929 to critical praise. Later that year, Thurman worked with a white writer, William Jourdan Rapp, on the play *Harlem,* which opened at the **Apollo Theater.** Based on the plot of one of Thurman's short stories, the play follows the introduction of a Southern black family to city life in Harlem. Thurman's second novel, *Infants of the Spring,* was an autobiographical—and sometimes sarcastic—look back at the Harlem Renaissance, which Thurman believed had failed to express the black identity in any real or meaningful way. His final novel, *The Interne* (1932), written in collaboration with Abraham L. Furman, was a "muckraking" novel exposing the corrupt conditions of City Hospital in New York. He became editor in chief of the book's publisher, Macaulay, in 1932, and two years later he went to Hollywood, California, to write scenarios for two films.

Hollywood life was a strain on Thurman, who became ill and quickly returned to New York. He had been physically frail all his life and was also a chronic alcoholic. Shortly after his return to New York, he was checked into City Hospital—the institution he had criticized so harshly in *The Interne*. After remaining six months in the "incurable" ward, Thurman died of consumption.

Till, Emmett Louis

July 25, 1941–August 28, 1955

Emmett Till was a **lynching** (murder) victim in 1955. Born and raised in **Chicago**, **Illinois**, he was fourteen when his parents sent him to LeFlore County, **Mississippi**, to visit his uncle. Till bragged about northern social freedoms and claimed to have a white girlfriend. His friends dared him to ask a white store clerk, Carolyn Bryant, for a date. Till squeezed Bryant's hand, grabbed her around the waist, and propositioned her. When she fled and returned with a gun, he wolf whistled at her.

Till's actions crossed southern social barriers between black men and white women. In Mississippi, the **Ku Klux Klan** enforced these barriers by the threat of violence. On August 28, 1955, Bryant's husband, Roy, and his half brother, J. W. Milam, abducted Till, brutally beat him, shot him in the head, and then dumped his naked body in the Tallahatchie River.

Till's mangled and decomposed body was found three days later. His uncle named Bryant and Milam as his assailants. The men were tried for murder but were acquitted by an all-white jury because the body was too mangled for positive identification.

Emmett Till's murder unleased a storm of protest and helped propel the growing **Civil Rights movement**. Pictures of Till's body in *Jet* magazine focused national attention on the trial. Till's death proved the violent depths of southern racism to many African Americans. Demonstrations and demands for laws against **lynching** came from African-American leaders and organizations. Black protests of the lack of federal intervention led to new legal measures, such as the Civil Rights Act of 1957.

In 1959 Milam all but confessed to Till's murder to journalist William Bradford Huie. The interview was published in 1959 in the book *Wolf Whistle*.

Tolson, Melvin Beaunorus

POET, EDUCATOR
February 6, 1898–August 29, 1966

Melvin Tolson was born in Howard County, **Missouri**, and later earned a degree from **Lincoln University** in Pennsylvania. With his wife, Ruth, whom he married in 1922, he would raise several highly successful children. In 1923 Tolson began teaching at Wiley College in Marshall, **Texas**, where he also coached one of the country's most successful debating teams.

As early as 1917, Tolson was writing poems and short tales, but his poetry did not really blossom until 1931 and 1932, when he was attending Colum-

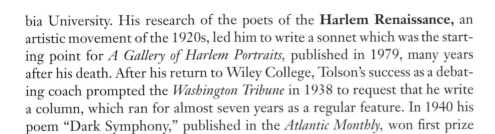

bia University. His research of the poets of the **Harlem Renaissance,** an artistic movement of the 1920s, led him to write a sonnet which was the starting point for *A Gallery of Harlem Portraits*, published in 1979, many years after his death. After his return to Wiley College, Tolson's success as a debating coach prompted the *Washington Tribune* in 1938 to request that he write a column, which ran for almost seven years as a regular feature. In 1940 his poem "Dark Symphony," published in the *Atlantic Monthly*, won first prize at the American Negro Exposition in **Chicago, Illinois.**

Tolson's later poetry became more scholarly and difficult for most readers; it tended to appear in small-circulation literary journals. It was during this period, however, that he published his most famous work, *Harlem Gallery* (1965), a long sequence of poetic portraits.

Tolson lived a colorful and eventful life, serving four terms as mayor of the town of Langston, Oklahoma, and, after a 1947 appointment, as poet laureate (a largely honorary position for distinguished poets) of the African nation of Liberia.

Toomer, Jean

WRITER
December 26, 1894–March 30, 1967

Born Nathan Pinchback Toomer in **Washington, D.C.,** Toomer changed his name in 1920. After his father abandoned the family and his mother died, he spent much of his childhood in his grandparents' home in Washington. After graduating from high school, Toomer spent a few months studying agriculture at the University of Wisconsin and then attended various colleges from 1916 to 1917.

By 1918 Toomer had written "Bona and Paul," a story that became part of *Cane* (1923), his masterpiece. This early story established a theme that Toomer would return to in most of his writing: the search for personal identity and harmony with other people. Throughout his life, Toomer, who had light skin, felt uncomfortable with the strict racial and ethnic classifications in the United States. Having lived in both white and black neighborhoods in Washington, and being of mixed racial heritage, he thought it ridiculous to define himself so simply.

After taking a position as substitute principal at a Georgia school, Toomer became inspired by the rural black people and their land—he felt that for the first time, he truly identified with his black heritage—and he poured out his admiration for them onto the pages that would become *Cane*. *Cane* was experimental in its form, a collection of stories, sketches, and poems. It did not sell many copies but was generally well reviewed and was especially praised by the writers who were then establishing what was to become the **Harlem Renaissance.**

Despite the critical praise for *Cane*, by 1924 Toomer was feeling restless and unhappy. His struggle with personal identity continued, and he soon fell under the influence of a French spiritual leader, Georges I. Gurdjieff. He wrote many works after 1924—plays, poems, short stories, novels, essays,

and more—but never achieved the success of *Cane*. Within a decade, he had dropped into obscurity.

It was not until the 1960s, with the renewed interest in earlier African-American writing and the republication of *Cane*, that Toomer gained a large readership and an influence on the young black writers of the day. From 1936 until his death, Toomer lived in Bucks County, Pennsylvania.

Tosi, Dewayne. *See* Chase-Riboud, Barbara

Toussaint, Pierre

BUSINESSMAN, PHILANTHROPIST, CANDIDATE FOR CANONIZATION
c. 1766–1853

Philanthropist (financial contributor to social causes, such as aid to the poor and to the arts) Pierre Toussaint was probably born in Haiti in 1766. As the house slave of planter Jean Berard, he was treated as a member of Berard's family. Later in life, he would give financial support to the Berard family. After his death, he would become a candidate for sainthood.

In 1787, during the early stages of a slave revolt, the Berards fled to New York City, taking Toussaint and his sister. Toussaint became a hairdresser and, while still a slave, opened a business of his own. He was popular with some of the wealthiest women in the city and became quite rich.

After his master died, Toussaint used his earnings to support his mistress (his master's wife, now head of the household). In 1809, upon her deathbed, Madame Berard granted Toussaint his freedom. He would continue to support her daughter for several years.

In 1811 Toussaint purchased the freedom of his sister and that of his future wife, Juliette Noel. Three years later, he did the same for a niece, whom he would support and educate.

Toussaint was a devout Roman Catholic and attended mass every day for sixty-six years. He and his wife took black orphans into their home and raised money in support of the Catholic Orphan Asylum for white children. He was the first person to support the building of a Roman Catholic church for French-speakers (now Saint Vincent de Paul's), giving one hundred dollars.

In the early 1990s the Roman Catholic Church began the process of his canonization (officially recognizing him as a saint). New York's Cardinal John O'Connor regarded Toussaint as a model of faith and charity. Opponents of his canonization saw him as passive and accepting of **slavery,** and therefore unworthy of sainthood.

Track-and-Field

African Americans are responsible for some of the greatest achievements in U.S. sports in the area of track-and-field. Blacks have won championships, won Olympic medals, and set world records in various track-and-field events. They have done particularly well in the 100- and 200-meter runs and in the long jump.

Track-and-field first became a popular sporting event in the United States in the late 1800s. A handful of blacks made an early impression on the sport. George C. Poage was the first black to win an Olympic medal (1904), and John B. Taylor was the first international star winning an Olympic gold medal (1908). However, it was not until after **World War I** (1914–18) that blacks began making their mark on track-and-field events.

After the war, universities with mostly white students began recruiting and training black athletes. In the 1920s William DeHart, a graduate of the University of Michigan, had an amazing career in the long-jump competition. The 1930s was the golden age of African-American sprinters. Eddie Tolan, Ralph Metcalfe, and **Jesse Owens** (1913–1980) opened the door for blacks in amateur track-and-field events by winning several college and Olympic competitions.

Owens had a huge impact on the sport and on the way black athletes were perceived in the social environment of the time. In 1935 he set three world records in track-and-field events, and in 1936 he won four Olympic gold medals.

Achievements by athletes such as Owens opened the door for African-American men to compete in track-and-field events, but it took much longer for black women to gain access to the sport. Leading the way for women was the Tuskegee Institute (now **Tuskegee University**), which dominated women's track-and-field competitions for a decade in the 1930s and 1940s. During this time, Lulu Hymes, a Tuskegee graduate, became the first black woman to win an Olympic gold medal (1948).

The 1940s and 1950s were dominated by the performances of William Harrison Dillard and Mal Whitfield in racing events. Blacks also began demonstrating skill in the decathlon (a rigorous competition with ten events) led by Milton Campbell, who set Olympic and world records. Women such as **Wilma Rudolph** (1940–1994) set new standards for female track-and-field competitors, winning three Olympic gold medals in 1960. The 1960s was a time of civil unrest in the United States, and many black athletes boycotted competitions. However, in the 1968 Olympics Bob Beamon delivered one of the most spectacular performances in the history of track-and-field, with his world-record long jump.

(SEE ALSO **JACKIE JOYNER-KERSEE**; **FLORENCE GRIFFITH-JOYNER**; **CARL LEWIS**; **EDWIN MOSES**; **SPORTS**)

Trotter, William Monroe

NEWSPAPER EDITOR, CIVIL RIGHTS ACTIVIST
April 7, 1872–April 7, 1934

William Trotter was the editor of *The Guardian* newspaper and an outspoken civil rights activist. Raised in a rich white Boston neighborhood, young Trotter absorbed the integration of beliefs of his father.

Elected president of his senior class by his white high school classmates, Trotter entered Harvard College in the fall of 1891. He graduated in 1895, and in 1899, he opened his own real estate firm.

Trotter was deeply concerned about worsening race relations in the South and signs of growing racial problems in the North. In March 1901, Trotter helped form the Boston Literary and Historical Association, which fostered intellectual debate among African Americans; he also joined the more politically active Massachusetts Racial Protective Association (MRPA).

With fellow MRPA member George W. Forbes, Trotter began his life work: the advocacy of civil and political equality for African Americans, by establishing the newspaper, *The Boston Guardian.*

The Guardian newspaper, which began publication in 1901, offered news and analysis of the African-American condition. Trotter also founded the Boston Suffrage League and the New England Suffrage League, through which he called for federal anti-lynching legislation, enforcement of the **Fifteenth Amendment**, and the end of racial segregation.

Trotter's political independence and confrontational style led him to disagree strongly with the ideas of **Booker T. Washington**. He resolved to wage the fight for racial justice through his own virtually all-black organization, the National Equal Rights League, or NERL (originally founded as the Negro-American Political League in April 1908). While Trotter attended the founding convention of the **National Association for the Advancement of Colored People (NAACP)** in 1909, he kept his distance from the white-dominated association; relations between NERL and the NAACP remained cool over the years, with occasional instances of cooperation to achieve common goals.

In an audience with President Woodrow Wilson in 1914, Trotter challenged the president's segregationist policies. Wilson, viewing his adversary as insolent and offensive, ordered the meeting to a close. The following year, Trotter led public protests against the showing of the racist film *The Birth of a Nation*. As a result of his efforts, the movie was banned in Boston.

In 1919, Trotter made his way to France for the Paris Peace Conference where the treaty ending **World War I** was drafted. He hoped to ensure that the treaty would contain guarantees of racial equality. Unable to influence the proceedings, he later testified against the treaty before the U.S. Congress. In 1926 Trotter again visited the White House to make the case against segregation in the federal government, this time before President Calvin Coolidge.

On April 7, 1934, Trotter either fell or jumped to his death from the roof of his apartment building. He was remembered as one who had made enormous personal sacrifices for the cause of racial equality.

Truth, Sojourner

ABOLITIONIST, SUFFRAGIST, SPIRITUALIST
c. 1797–November 26, 1883

Sojourner Truth was an amazing woman who became a preacher and a tireless antislavery activist. Sojourner Truth was born a slave with the name Isabella Bomefree in Ulster County, New York.

Isabella Bomefree, whose first language was Dutch, was taken from her parents and sold to an English-speaking owner in 1808. The owner mistreated her because of her inability to understand English. In 1810 John I. Dumont of New Paltz, New York, purchased Isabella Bomefree for three hundred dollars.

Isabella remained Dumont's slave for eighteen years. Dumont boasted that Belle, as he called her, was "better to me than a man." She planted, plowed, cultivated, and harvested crops. She milked the farm animals, sewed, weaved, cooked, and cleaned house. Isabella eventually had five children.

Although New York slavery ended for adults in 1827, Dumont promised Isabella her freedom a year earlier. When he refused to keep his promise, she fled with an infant child, guided by "the word of God" as she later related. She took refuge with Isaac Van Wagenen, who purchased her for the remainder of her time as a slave. She later adopted his family name.

In 1829 Isabella, now a Methodist, moved to New York City. She joined the African Methodist Episcopal Zion Church, where she discovered a brother and two sisters. She also began to attract attention for her extraordinary preaching, praying, and singing.

In 1843 Isabella became a traveling preacher and adopted the name Sojourner Truth because voices directed her to sojourn (stay temporarily in) the countryside and speak God's truth. In the fall of 1843 she became ill and was taken to Florence, Massachusetts, where black abolitionist David Ruggles took care of her. Sojourner Truth impressed the community's residents, who included a number of abolitionists, with her **slavery** accounts, scriptural interpretations, wit, and speaking abilities.

AIN'T I A WOMAN?

Well, children, where there is so much racket there must be something out of kilter. I think that 'twixt the negroes of the South and the women at the North, all talking about rights, the white men will be in a fix pretty soon. But what's all this here talking about?

That man over there says that women need to be helped into carriages, and lifted over ditches, and to have the best place everywhere. Nobody ever helps me into carriages, or over mud-puddles, or gives me any best place! And ain't I a woman? Look at me! Look at my arm! I have ploughed and planted, and gathered into barns, and no man could head me! And ain't I a woman? I could work as much and eat as much as a man—when I could get it—and bear the lash as well! And ain't I a woman? I have borne thirteen children, and seen most all sold off to slavery, and when I cried out with my mother's grief, none but Jesus heard me! And ain't I a woman?

Then they talk about this thing in the head; what's this they call it? [member of audience whispers, "intellect"] That's it, honey. What's that got to do with women's rights or negroes' rights? If my cup won't hold but a pint, and yours holds a quart, wouldn't you be mean not to let me have my little half measure full?

Then that little man in black there, he says women can't have as much rights as men, 'cause Christ wasn't a woman! Where did your Christ come from? Where did your Christ come from? From God and a woman! Man had nothing to do with Him.

If the first woman God ever made was strong enough to turn the world upside down all alone, these women together ought to be able to turn it back, and get it right side up again! And now they is asking to do it, the men better let them.

Obliged to you for hearing me, and now old Sojourner ain't got nothing more to say.

(Source: Soujourner Truth. Speech given at the Women's Convention, Akron, Ohio, 1851.)

By 1846 Sojourner Truth had joined the antislavery circuit, traveling with Abby Kelly Foster, **Frederick Douglass,** and William Lloyd Garrison. An electrifying public speaker, she soon became one of the most popular speakers for the abolitionist cause. Her fame was heightened by the publication of her *Narrative* in 1850, related and transcribed by Olive Gilbert. In 1851, speaking before a National Women's Convention in Akron, Ohio, Sojourner Truth defended the physical and spiritual strength of women, in her famous "Ain't I a Woman?" speech. In 1853 Sojourner's antislavery work took her to the Midwest, where she settled in Harmonia, Michigan.

During the **Civil War** Sojourner Truth recruited and supported Michigan's black regiment, counseled freedwomen, set up employment

operations for freedpeople willing to relocate, and initiated desegregation of streetcars in Washington, D.C. In 1864 she had an audience with Abraham Lincoln. Following the war, Sojourner Truth supported the **Fifteenth Amendment** and women's suffrage.

Sojourner Truth devoted her last years to the support of a black western homeland. In her later years, despite decades of interracial cooperation, she became distrustful of whites and became an advocate of racial separation. She died in 1883 in Battle Creek, Michigan.

Tubman, Harriet Ross

ABOLITIONIST, NURSE, FEMINIST
c. 1820–March 10, 1913

Underground Railroad leader Harriet Ross was born a slave in Dorchester County, Maryland. At age thirteen she was struck in the head

Harriet Tubman (left) pictured with six slaves she helped guide to freedom through the Underground Railroad (Courtesy of the Library of Congress)

with a two-pound lead weight when she placed herself between her master and a fleeing slave. For the rest of her life, she experienced sudden blackouts.

In 1844 Ross married a free black man, John Tubman, while remaining a slave herself. After her master died, it was rumored that she was among slaves that might be sold out of the state. Tubman responded by running away in 1849. When she returned for her husband two years later, he was remarried.

Tubman had become an agent on the **Underground Railroad,** a secret network that helped runaway slaves reach sanctuary in the free states or Canada. Assuming different disguises to assist runaways in obtaining food, shelter, clothing, cash, and transportation, Tubman rescued several family members, including her sister, brother, and parents. She traveled to the South nineteen times to assist approximately three hundred African-American men, women, and children.

Tubman had contact with many social leaders in the North. She helped **John Brown** (1800–1859) plan his raid on Harpers Ferry, Virginia, in 1859, and became friends with black Underground Railroad leader **William Grant Still** and white abolitionist Thomas Garrett.

In the **Civil War** (1861–66) Tubman served in the Union army as a scout, spy, and nurse. In 1862 she nursed both white soldiers and black slave refugees in South Carolina. Tubman also traveled behind enemy lines to gather information and recruit slaves. During 1865 she worked at a freedman's hospital.

After the war Tubman returned to Auburn, New York, where she helped support her family by farming. In 1869 Tubman married Nelson Davis, a Civil War veteran. That same year, she published *Scenes in the Life of Harriet Tubman*, written for her by Sarah H. Bradford.

Tubman believed that racial liberation and women's rights were inseparable issues. After the war she supported woman suffrage (women's right to vote) and formed a close relationship with women's rights fighter Susan B.

Anthony. She was a delegate to the first convention of the National Federation of Afro-American Women in 1896 (later the National Association of Colored Women).

When Tubman died at the age of ninety-three, she had become known as "the Moses of her people." Local Civil War veterans led her funeral march. (*See also* **John Brown's Raid at Harpers Ferry**)

Turner, Joseph Vernon "Big Joe"

BLUES SINGER
1911–November 24, 1985

"Big Joe" Turner was one of the pioneering **blues** and **rhythm-and-blues** "shouters." Born in Kansas City, Missouri, Turner worked as a bartender and singer in local nightclubs during the Great Depression (a period of economic hardship throughout the United States during the 1930s). He was soon in demand as a vocalist for local jump-blues and **jazz** bands, one of which was led by the great **Count Basie** (1904–1984).

Turner's recording career began in the late 1930s. He gained major exposure in a series of Carnegie Hall concerts in 1938 but continued to sing in primarily African-American clubs until he crossed over to a white audience with his recording of "Shake, Rattle, and Roll" in 1954. His recordings for Atlantic Records (1951–59) brought Turner to a larger audience, and he remained a popular performer, shouting standards such as "Roll 'em Pete" and "Piney Brown Blues" until his death.

Turner, Tina

POP SINGER
November 26, 1939–

Tina Turner is one of the first and best female rock-and-roll performers in the United States. Turner was born Anna Mae Bullock in Brownsville, Tennessee. She lived with her grandmother until the age of sixteen and then moved to St. Louis, Missouri, to live again with her mother. With her older sister Alline, she frequented nightclubs across the river in East St. Louis to see the popular Kings of Rhythm band, led by the rhythm and blues singer, guitarist, producer, and disc jockey Ike Turner. One night Anna Mae took the stage and sang with Turner and, soon after, she joined the group and went on tour with Ike and the Kings of Rhythm.

In 1960 Ike Turner declared that Anna Mae Bullock would be publicly known as "Tina," and announced that her first lead-vocal debut, "A Fool in Love" (1960), would be credited to Ike and Tina Turner. In 1962 Ike and Tina were married. The couple toured and recorded until 1974 as the "Ike and Tina Turner Revue," which featured Tina with her flamboyant backup singers and dancers, the Ikettes, accompanied by the Kings of Rhythm. They became one of the foremost groups of the 1960s. In 1971 they won a Grammy Award for "Proud Mary." Their other hits from this period include

"Nutbush City Limits" (1973) and "Sweet Rhode Island Red" (1974). In 1974 Tina Turner embarked upon an acting career, starring in the movie version of The Who's rock opera *Tommy*.

Ike and Tina Turner separated in 1975, Tina claiming she was the victim of frequent domestic abuse. Their divorce came in 1978, and Tina built her solo career. Her 1984 album *Private Dancer* marked her arrival as a solo performer. Turner won three Grammys for *Private Dancer* (1984), which included the song "What's Love Got to Do with It?"

By the mid-1980s Turner had become a major pop singer in her own right. In 1985 she resumed her acting career with the film *Mad Max 3: Beyond Thunderdome*, whose soundtrack included her performances of "We Don't Need Another Hero" and the Grammy-winning "One of the Living." After publishing her autobiography, *I, Tina*, in 1986, Turner released *Break Every Rule*, a best-selling album that also won another Grammy. In 1988, Turner announced that she was retiring from touring to focus on her acting career, but the following year she toured to promote her *Foreign Affair* album (1989). She served as consultant for the film *What's Love Got to Do with It?* (1993), which was based on her autobiography. Throughout the 1990s Turner remained an extremely active and popular performer. Her 1997 world tour rocketed her onto the list of top ten moneymakers in rock music circles.

In 1999 Turner began another worldwide performance tour at age 60. She also announced her intention to retire at the end of the tour.

Tuskegee Syphilis Experiment

In the early twentieth century, African Americans in the South faced many public health problems—caused mostly by poverty and inadequate medical care—and their death rates were much higher than those of whites. In response to these problems, the U.S. government created the Public Health Service (PHS) in 1912. One of the main concerns of the PHS was syphilis, a sexually transmitted disease.

In the 1920s the PHS developed a plan to control syphilis among African Americans in the South. Most doctors assumed that the higher rate of syphilis among blacks was caused by their having too many sexual partners. Doctors also believed that once infected, African Americans were too poor and ignorant to get medical care. To test these theories, the PHS selected black communities in six southern states and offered free treatment to those with syphilis. One of the communities was Tuskegee, in Macon County, Alabama.

Tuskegee was the home of the renowned Tuskegee Institute. Despite the presence of such a famous African-American college and hospital, blacks in the community suffered from the highest rates of syphilis in the South.

The PHS lost its private funding at the beginning of the **Great Depression,** in 1929, soon after the project began. It could not afford to treat the patients who had syphilis. Instead, the PHS decided to simply record the damage untreated syphilis had on black males. Many white southerners (including doctors) believed syphilis did not harm African Americans

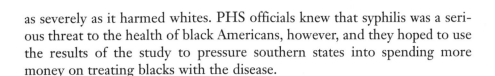

as severely as it harmed whites. PHS officials knew that syphilis was a serious threat to the health of black Americans, however, and they hoped to use the results of the study to pressure southern states into spending more money on treating blacks with the disease.

Although the original plan called for a one-year experiment, the Tuskegee study began in 1932 and continued until 1972, partly because many of the health officers were interested in the results of a long-term study. In order to secure their cooperation the PHS told Tuskegee residents they were going to treat people who were ill. They did not tell the men they had syphilis but instead simply told them they had "bad blood," a phrase local blacks used to describe a number of ailments. State health officials cooperated with the PHS in the experiment but required them to give the men at least enough medicine to keep them from spreading the disease. Therefore, all of the men received a little treatment but not enough to cure them. This small amount of treatment, however, flawed the study from the beginning.

As a result of the Tuskegee Study, approximately one hundred black men died of untreated syphilis. Many more went blind or insane, and still others endured lives of sickness from syphilis-related diseases. Throughout this suffering the PHS made no effort to treat the men, and on many occasions it took steps to prevent them from getting treatment elsewhere. As a result, the men did not receive penicillin (the cure for syphilis) when it became widely available after **World War II** (1939–45).

During the four decades of the Tuskegee study, the **Civil Rights movement** raised concern for the rights of black people, and the standards regarding the medical treatment of nonwhite patients changed dramatically. But these changes had no impact on the Tuskegee study.

The study ended in 1972 only because Peter Buxtun, an employee of the PHS, told the story to the press. At first, health officials tried to defend their actions, but public outrage quickly silenced them, and they agreed to end the experiment. As part of an out-of-court settlement, the survivors were finally treated for syphilis. In addition, the men—and the families of the dead—received small cash payments. Soon afterward, Congress passed new laws protecting the subjects of human experiments. In 1997 President Bill Clinton apologized to Tuskegee volunteers and their families on behalf of the American people. (*See also* **Diseases and Epidemics**.)

"We can look you in the eye and finally say on behalf of the American people, what the United States government did was shameful, and I am sorry."

—President Clinton speaking to volunteers from the Tuskegee Syphilis Experiment, May 16, 1997

Tuskegee University

Founded: Tuskegee University was founded in 1881 as the Normal School for Colored Teachers at Tuskegee in Alabama's Macon County.

History Highlights:

- 1881: Tuskegee Normal School is founded as the result of a political deal made between white Alabama legislators Arthur Brooks and Col. Wilbur Foster and a leading black citizen named Lewis Adams. If Adams guaranteed black votes in the area, Brooks and Foster would push for state funding ($2,000 per year) for a black teachers' school.

Booker T. Washington is chosen to organize the school, which begins with thirty students, ranging in age from sixteen to forty.

- 1882: As the school expands, Washington borrows money to purchase the Bowen estate, a nearby property that has been almost destroyed during the **Civil War**. Tuskegee students clean and rebuild the estate while attending classes, and Washington travels throughout the North to raise funds.

- 1896: Scientist **George Washington Carver** becomes head of the agriculture department and establishes the Agriculture Experiment Station.

- 1915: After Booker T. Washington's death, the school gradually changes its focus from an industrial college to a more academic-based program with an emphasis on science and technology. An industrial program focuses on learning farming and trade skills, with little emphasis on academics.

- 1937: The school's name is changed to the Tuskegee Institute.

- 1939–43: During **World War II** (1939–45), the U.S. Air Force trains more than nine hundred black pilots at Tuskegee, establishing the Tuskegee Airfield in 1941.

- 1968: During the **Civil Rights movement,** Tuskegee students briefly hold members of the board of trustees hostage in the hopes of changing campus policies.

- 1985: Tuskegee Institute becomes Tuskegee University.

Location: Tuskegee, Alabama

Known For: Tuskegee University has long been known for its emphasis on research and technology, a legacy started by George Washington Carver.

Number of Students (1999–2000): 3,080

Grade Average of Incoming Freshman: 3.0

Admission Requirements: SAT or ACT scores; four years of English, three years of math, two years of science, three years of social studies.

Mailing Address:
Tuskegee University
Office of Admission
Tuskegee, AL 36088

Telephone: (800) 622-6531

E-mail: admi@acd.tusk.edu

URL: http://www.tusk.edu

Campus: Tuskegee's 4,700-acre campus has been designated a National Historic Site by the U.S. Congress. It is located 30 miles east of Montgomery and 165 miles south of Atlanta. The campus includes the George Washington Carver agricultural and natural history museum, the Kellogg Conference Center, and a blending of newer structures and historic buildings, some of which were built by Tuskegee students from bricks made by the students.

Special Programs: International Center of Excellence for Biotechnology Research, National Center for Bioethics in Research and Health Care.

Extracurricular Activities: Student government, student newspaper, *Campus Digest*; four fraternities and four sororities; organizations, including honor societies, men's and women's glee clubs, theater groups; athletics (men's baseball, basketball, cross-country, football, tennis, track-and-field; women's basketball, cross-country, tennis, softball, track-and-field, volleyball).

Tuskegee Alumni: Daniel "Chappie" James Jr. (1920–1978), the nation's first African-American four star general; novelist **Ralph Ellison** (1914–1994); actor, director, writer Keenan Ivory Wayans; **Arthur Adams Mitchell Jr.** (1883–1968), the first black Democratic congressman.

Tyson, Cicely

ACTRESS
December 19, 1939–

Cicely Tyson is a gifted actress. Born to immigrant parents, she grew up in East Harlem in New York City. It was at Saint John's Episcopal Church in Harlem, where she sang and played the organ, that Tyson's theatrical talents surfaced.

In 1957 Tyson had a small part in the film *Twelve Angry Men*. Two years later she made her stage debut, starring in *Dark of the Moon*. Tyson was recruited in 1963 for a lead role in the CBS television series *East Side/West Side*, becoming the first African-American actress to be a regular on a dramatic television series. In 1968 she appeared in the film *The Heart Is a Lonely Hunter*, for which she received critical and public acclaim for her performance.

Tyson waited four years before doing film work again because of her decision not to accept roles that added to the negative stereotypes of African Americans. Then, in 1972, she accepted the role of Rebecca in the film *Sounder*. Her performance earned her an Academy Award nomination for best actress.

In 1974 Tyson received two Emmy Awards for *The Autobiography of Miss Jane Pittman*. She went on to play other socially conscious roles for television, including the part of Harriet Tubman in *A Woman Called Moses* (1976), Kunte Kinte's mother in *Roots* (1977), and Coretta Scott King in *King* (1978).

Tyson continues to be active in film and television, and in 1999 she began to sell a line of jewelry she designs under the name Jewels of Unity. (*See also* **Film**)

Tyson, Michael Gerald "Iron Mike"

BOXER
June 30, 1966–

Michael Gerald "Mike" Tyson is one of the most powerful and entertaining boxers of modern times. He is known for his street-fighting style as well as for his highly publicized run-ins with the law.

Born in Brooklyn, New York, Tyson was raised in a crime-ridden neighborhood. As a youth he committed street crimes such as muggings. When he was thirteen, he was sent to a detention center, where he met a boxing trainer named Cus D'Amato, who immediately noticed Tyson's potential. D'Amato became Tyson's trainer, friend, and legal guardian.

In 1984 Tyson won the Golden Gloves amateur heavyweight championship. Shortly afterward, he turned professional and instantly showed tremendous force in the ring. In his first fifteen fights, none of his opponents lasted more than four rounds against him. In 1986, at the age of twenty, Tyson became the youngest heavyweight **boxing** champion in history, defeating the reigning champ in two rounds. Tyson went on to win the World Boxing Association heavyweight championship (1987) and the International Boxing Federation (IBF) title (1987). One of his most impressive performances came the following year when he knocked out former IBF champion Michael Spinks in ninety-one seconds. Tyson developed a national following because of his powerful punching style and apparent invincibility.

Tyson's personal life has been a popular subject in the national media. After his father figure, D'Amato, died in 1985, his life seemed to take a turn for the worse. He split with his management team and contracted with controversial fight promoter Don King in 1988 and entered into a stormy marriage with actress Robin Givens (there were allegations that he beat Givens). In 1990 Tyson lost the heavyweight title, and in 1991 he was arrested and convicted of raping an eighteen-year-old girl in Indianapolis, Indiana. After Tyson's release from prison, he seemed to have put his personal affairs in order by converting to the religion of **Islam.** However, Tyson lost a fight against Evander Holyfield in 1996 during which he bit off a portion of Holyfield's ear. He was suspended from boxing because of the act, and in 1999 he was sent back to prison for beating up two motorists. In 2000 Tyson moved to Great Britain in an effort to revive his boxing career as well as remove himself from negative media in the United States. In June 2000 he defeated Lou Saveres in a thirty-six second match.

Uncle Tom's Cabin

Uncle Tom's Cabin; or, Life Among the Lowly (1852) is a novel written by white abolitionist (a person who worked to end slavery) Harriet Beecher Stowe (1811–1896). It was considered radical during its time. Stowe borrowed from the harsh realities of slavery to create a work of fiction that inspired fiery opposition to **slavery** throughout the American North.

Even though many in the South accused Stowe of intending to cause a revolution with the story, *Uncle Tom's Cabin* is just as hard on Northerners who defended slavery as it is on Southerners who owned slaves. It is also a basically Christian novel that revolves around changing individual feelings about slavery rather than collective struggle over the issue.

Stowe came from a prominent Connecticut family of public figures that included her father, clergyman Lyman Beecher; her sister, author Catherine Beecher; and her brother, clergyman Henry Ward Beecher. She was the wife of clergyman Calvin Stowe.

UNCLE TOM ON THE STAGE AND IN FILM

As popular as the book *Uncle Tom's Cabin* was, its long presence on the stage and in film were responsible for its enormous influence in the United States for more than half a century. In January 1852 an "anti-Tom" play appeared in Baltimore, Maryland. It was called *Uncle Tom's Cabin as It Is; The Southern Uncle Tom*. The dramatic conflict it began was a kind of on-stage introduction to the American Civil War (1861–65).

The *Uncle Tom* plays of George Aiken and H. J. Conway were the two main competitors during the 1850s. The rivalry between Aiken's and Conway's plays caused everything from journalistic debate to street fights, a warning of the sectional conflicts that would soon lead to civil war. Aiken's version told both Little Eva's and Uncle Tom's stories, combining them into the first full-length, night-long theatrical production in history. It opened in New York City in July 1853. Conway's play, which opened in Boston, used minstrel traditions and outright racism in a production that was only occasionally true to Stowe's novel. These two plays spawned dozens of offshoots, including comedies that made fun of the novel and focused on, for example, issues of Irish oppression.

Even after the Civil War, plays and films of *Uncle Tom's Cabin* continued to be produced well into the twentieth century (the first film version was released in 1903). They fueled the ongoing American political debate over race and the legacy of slavery.

Stowe was outraged by the Compromise of 1850, a group of legislative measures on the issue of slavery, which was increasingly dividing the Northern and the Southern states. The compromise (a "give-and-take" arrangement) included the Fugitive Slave Law of 1851, which provided for the return of runaway slaves to their owner. Stowe and other abolitionists believed this law gave federal approval to slavery in both the North and the South.

In response to this legislation, she wrote a story called "The Freeman's Dream" (1850). Soon afterward, she said she experienced a vision of an old black male slave being whipped to death. This image inspired her to write *Uncle Tom's Cabin; or, Life Among the Lowly*. It was first published as a series in the antislavery newspaper *National Era* in 1851–52 and was published in book form on March 20, 1852.

Uncle Tom's Cabin achieved immediate and long-lasting success. It sold 300,000 copies in its first year alone and inspired other books, plays and minstrel-show parodies, commercial takeoffs, and popular art and symbolism. The novel brought the national struggle over slavery into full public view and made it a fact of everyday life.

Uncle Tom's Cabin: The Story

The main characters in *Uncle Tom's Cabin* are the slave Eliza Harris, her husband, George, and their young son, Harry; Eliza's owner, Arthur Shelby;

Uncle Tom, a slave on the Shelby plantation in Kentucky; Evangeline (Little Eva) St. Clare and her father, a New Orleans slaveowner; abolitionist Aunt Ophelia, who comes to the St. Clare home to nurse Mrs. St. Clare; the abusive slaveholder Simon Legree; Legree's slaves Cassy and Emmeline; and Arthur Shelby's son George.

Eliza, George, and Harry—after learning of Shelby's plan to sell some of his slaves because he needs money—escape to freedom in Ohio, where they are sheltered by members of the religious group the Quakers. They fight off slave traders who have followed them, and George speaks passionately about their right to freedom. Soon George, Eliza, and Harry escape to Canada.

Meanwhile, Uncle Tom, who allowed himself to be sold in hopes of saving other slaves on the Shelby plantation from sale, meets Little Eva and her father. Eva insists that her father buy Tom. St. Clare is a gentle master, but he argues with Aunt Ophelia about the social system of slavery. He comes under the influence of Tom's religious beliefs. Little Eva dies, and her father decides to set Tom free, but before he is able to, he is killed trying to break up a fight in a bar.

Tom is sold again, this time to an abusive master, Simon Legree. Throughout the novel, Tom longs to return to his family, from whom he was sold away. Cassy, another of Legree's slaves, takes advantage of Legree's guilt over abandoning his mother. Cassy and Emmeline pretend to escape but hide in an attic, impersonating the ghosts that Legree believes live there.

Legree kills Tom just as George Shelby, the son of his former master, Arthur Shelby, arrives. Shelby knocks Legree to the ground when he sees what the slavemaster has done. He then has Tom buried and helps Cassy and Emmeline escape. Shelby learns that Cassy is Eliza's mother.

At the novel's end Cassy is reunited with Eliza and her family in Canada, but they plan to voyage to Africa and establish a black Christian homeland in Liberia. George Shelby returns to Kentucky and frees his slaves, but they stay on to work for him as free people.

Underground Railroad

The so-called Underground Railroad was a secretive network primarily made up of free African Americans in the northern and upper-southern United States who helped slaves in the South escape to freedom from about 1830 to 1860. No one is certain how it came to be called the Underground Railroad, but terms from the railroad business were used to describe its activities.

Thousands of African-American slaves escaped to freedom in the northern United States or Canada via the Underground Railroad, even though their numbers were not enough to threaten the existence of slavery. More important than the number of slaves who escaped is what the existence of the secret network showed about **slavery** and the true character of Southern slaves. Slaveholders often argued that blacks were inferior to whites and were not capable of living in freedom. The success of the Underground Railroad proved them wrong.

Slaves fleeing bondage through the Underground Railroad (Archive Photos. Reproduced by permission)

Most slaves who escaped did so on their own at first, but once away from the plantations they needed help to keep their hard-won liberty. Many did not have to travel far before finding this help. Hundreds of Underground Railroad networks existed in Ohio, Pennsylvania, and New York, and surprisingly efficient networks—often centered in local black churches—existed in most other Northern states and even in border states like Virginia. Many former slaves lived along the Ohio River, and black communities there offered **fugitive slaves** temporary shelter and then passed them along to other communities farther north.

The Underground Railroad was most effective along the East Coast, with Philadelphia, Pennsylvania, and New York City serving as central distribution points for many underground routes. Leaders such as William Grant Still (1821–1902)—who later recorded the stories of many of the people he helped—directed fugitives to "stations" in upper New York, which in turn provided transportation to Canada. Educated blacks such as Robert Purvis (1810–1898) and William Whipper (1804–1876) arranged for legal and financial assistance as well as valuable contacts among white political leaders who favored **abolition**.

Vigilance committees warned local blacks of kidnapping rings. Black leaders of the Underground Railroad, such as Still and **Harriet Tubman** (c. 1820–1913; called "the Moses of her people"), maintained contact with whites who warned them of slave owners and federal marshals looking for runaway slaves. These leaders used the telegraph to communicate with distant stations.

The most daring and best-organized underground station was run by **free blacks** from Washington, D.C., and Baltimore, Maryland. They used their good reputation among whites to rescue slaves from plantations in Maryland and Virginia, supplying them with free papers and sending them north by land or water routes. One free black used his painting business as a cover to visit plantations and arrange escapes. Another used his carriage service to transport slaves. Others posed as plantation preachers to pass escape plans to their "parishioners." In one case, brave members attacked a slave pen and freed some captives.

The eastern network occasionally worked with white abolitionists (those working to end slavery) like Charles T. Torrey and Thomas Garrett, a leader of the Quaker religious group, which was very active in the abolitionist movement. The network was temporarily disrupted in the 1840s, when race riots in Northern cities and increased Southern investigation forced Washington's most active agents to leave. Still, it is estimated that more than nine thousand fugitive slaves passed through Philadelphia alone between 1830 and 1860 on their way to freedom.

Universal Negro Improvement Association

The Universal Negro Improvement Association (UNIA) was one of the most important, and largest, political and social organizations in African-American history. It was founded by Jamaican-born black-nationalist leader **Marcus Garvey** (1887–1940) in 1914, in Kingston, Jamaica. The UNIA has a simple but powerful motto: One God, One Aim, One Destiny.

The organization was originally formed as a mutual benefit and reform society to improve the lives of people of African descent. Garvey brought the UNIA to the United States in 1916. Established in New York City in 1918, it began to give voice to the new radical movement that arose among blacks after **World War I** (1914–18).

In 1919 membership in the UNIA ballooned as a result of a stock-selling promotion led by Garvey's Black Star shipping line. In the 1920s the UNIA began operating as a sort of provisional (or substitute) government for **Africa**. The organization developed its own national anthem, flag, official publication (*The Negro World*), constitution, and laws.

The UNIA soon became the most forceful voice within the African-American community. It promoted black self-determination—the right of all blacks to determine their own destiny—and the establishing of a black-governed nation in Africa. The document written by the UNIA with the greatest lasting importance was the "Declaration of the Rights of the Negro Peoples of the World," passed at the first UNIA convention in August 1920.

By the mid-1920s the organization had nearly one thousand local divisions throughout the United States and Canada, Central and South America, the West Indies, Africa, and the United Kingdom. Membership at the time was estimated to be in the hundreds of thousands, or perhaps in the millions.

However, when UNIA leader Garvey was sent to prison on charges of mail fraud in 1925, membership started to decline. U.S. president Calvin Coolidge (1872–1933) sent Garvey out of the United States in 1927, which caused the organization to splinter. Garvey tried to revive the organization by starting a new UNIA branch in Jamaica, but the economic collapse of the 1930s caused the organization to lose its source of funding. Garvey made

another attempt to revive the organization in 1935 from London, England. However, a dispute over support for Ethiopian emperor Haile Selassie I (1892–1975) after his country was invaded by Italy proved more than the UNIA could handle. After Garvey died in 1940, loyal members moved the headquarters to Cleveland, Ohio, under the leadership of new president James Stewart. Stewart later moved the UNIA to Liberia, Africa, where it still functioned in the late twentieth century with only a shadow of its former strength. (*See also* **Black Nationalism.**)

Utah

First African-American Settlers: Blacks have resided in Utah continuously since the area was first settled in 1847.

Slave Population: By 1850 approximately sixty African Americans lived in the Utah Territory. The majority were slaves, although laws sanctioning slavery were not enacted until 1852. Although some worked in small shops in Salt Lake City, most worked on small farms. A few slaves escaped and joined wagon trains going west to California and other destinations. Utah did not achieve statehood until 1896.

Free Black Population: Free African Americans migrated to Utah during the pioneer period. The primary objectives of many of these free black migrants were religious; as members of the Church of Jesus Christ of Latter-day Saints, they were in Utah to help build the Mormon Church. Other African Americans came with the expansion and completion of the national railroad and mining and military facilities.

Civil War: In 1862, in the midst of the **Civil War** (1861–65), **slavery** was officially ended when Congress abolished slavery in the territories.

Reconstruction: By the 1890s the small African-American community had numbers sufficient to establish its own churches, newspapers, and political, social, and fraternal organizations. At the turn of the twentieth century, however, discrimination increased with the growth of the black population.

The Great Depression: World War II (1939–45) and the postwar years had dramatic impact on African-American life in the West. Blacks were influenced to relocate to Utah by the growth of railroad centers and defense-related industries.

Civil Rights Movement: The racial climate in Utah gradually improved during the late 1960s and the 1970s, primarily due to the **civil rights** legislation at the federal level. In 1978 the Mormon Church announced that senior leadership positions were open to "all worthy male members of the church without regard to race or color," opening doors for black men aspiring to the priesthood.

Current African-American Population: According to U.S. Census Bureau estimates, the total black population in Utah was 18,677 (0.9 percent of the state population) as of July 1, 1998.

Key Figures: Soldier Charles Young (1864–1922); **Benjamin O. Davis Sr.** (1880–1970), the first African-American general in the U.S. military.

(SEE ALSO **MORMONS.**)

Van Peebles, Melvin

FILMMAKER
August 21, 1932–

Melvin Van Peebles grew up in Illinois and received a bachelor's degree in literature in 1953. After graduation he enlisted in the U.S. Air Force, where he spent three and a half years as a flight navigator. Facing a lack of employment opportunities for blacks at commercial airlines, Van Peebles became a cable car operator in San Francisco, California. He worked there until 1957, when he was fired from his job. He would later become an author and a noted filmmaker.

Van Peebles spent the late 1950s making a number of short films in an unsuccessful attempt to interest Hollywood in his ideas. He immigrated to the Netherlands, where he studied theater and toured as an actor. Van Peebles then moved to Paris, France, to attempt to get his work produced. He wrote five works of fiction that were published in French. He filmed *The Story of a Three Day Pass* in 1967 for $200,000. The film concerns a black U.S. serviceman and the harassment he experiences when his army buddies discover that he has a white girlfriend. It was shown at the 1967 San Francisco Film Festival, where it won the Critics Choice award for best film. The film garnered sufficient attention to earn Van Peebles a studio contract with Columbia Pictures.

In 1969 Van Peebles directed *Watermelon Man*, a farce (a humorous, ridiculous work) about a white racist insurance salesman who wakes up one morning to discover that he has become black. Although the film was a moderate success, Van Peebles found that he disliked working in the studio system. He set out to make his next film, *Sweet Sweetback's Baadasssss Song* (1971), without studio financing. *Sweetback* was one of the first films to portray black heroes in opposition to the white authorities, appealing to black youths' dreams of power.

Van Peebles produced *Ain't Supposed to Die a Natural Death*, a musical Broadway (New York City's main theater district) play, in 1972. In the mid-1970s he wrote two scripts that were produced as television films for NBC: *Just an Old Sweet Song* (1976) and the highly regarded *Sophisticated Gents* (1979).

Van Peebles temporarily set aside entertainment in favor of business, becoming a stock trader at the American Stock Exchange in New York in 1983. At the time, he was the only black trader at the exchange. In the mid-1980s he followed up on his success in stock-trading with two books.

At the end of the decade, Van Peebles returned to entertainment to direct films. In the 1990s his work received renewed attention. His films have been featured at several film festivals, and in 1990 his work was featured

at the Museum of Modern Art in New York. He was awarded an honorary doctorate from Hofstra University in 1994. (*See also* **Film**)

Vaughan, Sarah

JAZZ SINGER
March 29, 1924–April 3, 1990

One of jazz music's first ladies, Sarah Vaughan (Archive Photos. Reproduced by permission)

Nicknamed "Sassy" and "the Divine One," Sarah Vaughan is considered one of America's greatest vocalists. Born in Newark, New Jersey, she began singing and playing organ in the Mount Zion Baptist Church when she was twelve.

In October 1942 she sang "Body and Soul" to win an amateur-night contest at **Harlem's Apollo Theater. Billy Eckstine,** a professional singer, was so impressed that he persuaded his boss to hire Vaughan as a second pianist and singer in early 1943. Later that year, when Eckstine formed his own band, she went with him.

Vaughan made her first records for the Continental label on New Year's Eve 1944, and began working as a solo act the following year at New York's Cafe Society. Following hits on Musicraft (including "It's Magic" and "If They Could See Me Now") and Columbia ("Black Coffee"), her success was ensured. From 1947 through 1952 she was voted top female vocalist in polls in *Down Beat* and *Metronome* **jazz** magazines.

Throughout the 1950s Vaughan recorded pop material for Mercury records, including such hits as "Make Yourself Comfortable" and "Broken-Hearted Melody" and songbooks of classic American songs by George Gershwin and Irving Berlin. In the mid-1960s, Vaughan took a five-year hiatus from recording. By the 1970s her voice had become darker and richer.

By the end of her career, Vaughan had performed in more than sixty countries, in small clubs and in football stadiums, with jazz trios as well as symphony orchestras. She died of cancer in 1990.

Vermont

First African-American Settlers: African Americans have maintained a small presence in Vermont throughout its history; the 1790 census identified 269 blacks in Vermont.

Slave Population: Vermont, despite its constitution of 1777, which banned slavery, did not consistently afford its black residents equal opportunity or the full rights of citizenship. The state joined the Union in 1791.

Free Black Population: Census records reveal stories of the persistence and success of African Americans in Vermont. For instance, Jeremiah Virginia was a Revolutionary War veteran who lived independently with his wife and eight children on a farm in Newbury. Other Vermont blacks were **civil rights** activists, college graduates, and pastors.

Civil War: Some 150 African Americans in Vermont (more than 20 percent of the black population) served the Northern cause in the Civil War (1861–65).

Reconstruction: After the war a number of freedmen journeyed north to settle in Vermont. By 1910 there were 1,621 African Americans in Vermont, double the total in 1900; the population dropped to 572 in 1920.

The Great Depression: The percentage of African Americans in Vermont remained the smallest of any U.S. state; in 1940 there were just 384 blacks in the state.

Civil Rights Movement: Black Vermonters made numerous gains in terms of discrimination and racism. The Vermont Summer of Race Relations, a program that began in the 1940s, invited African-American youths from New York City's **Harlem** neighborhood to stay for two weeks with white Vermont families to promote interracial education. In the 1970s black leaders successfully changed the name of a mountain long known as "Niggerhead Mountain."

Current African-American Population: According to U.S. Census Bureau estimates, the total black population in Vermont was 3,129 (0.5 percent of the state population) as of July 1, 1998.

Key Figures: Clergyman Lemuel Haynes (1753–1833); Alexander Twilight (1795–1857), the first African American to serve in a state legislature.

Vietnam War

The Vietnam War (1959–75) took place in Southeast Asia, between North Vietnam and South Vietnam. North Vietnam was ruled by the Communist Party and wanted to reunite with South Vietnam into one Communist-controlled country. The United States supported South Vietnam's desire to remain an independent non-Communist country. U.S. involvement in the war began in 1961 and ended in 1973.

When not enough men volunteered for **military** service during the Vietnam War, the U.S. government began to use the Selective Service System, or draft. This meant that young men were required to register with a local board and then were selected to serve in the military. Some could get deferments, or permission to be excused from the draft, because they attended college or had political influences. Many of the men who got deferments were wealthy or well educated. This meant that many of the soldiers drafted during the Vietnam War were African Americans who could not afford college. The unfair draft system, along with racial prejudices brought into the services from civilian life, contributed to an increase in tensions between whites and blacks in the military.

The Gesell Committee

In 1962 a committee headed by attorney Gerhard A. Gesell tested the commitment of the armed forces to racial integration. The Gesell

Committee concluded that racial discrimination weakened the morale and performance of military personnel. To eliminate discrimination, the committee recommended that the fight against racism become a responsibility of military commanders. The commanders would direct the campaign for equal treatment and opportunity on military and naval bases and also in nearby communities, where African-American personnel and their families often had only limited access to housing and public accommodations. The committee also recommended that the federal government enforce existing civil rights laws in towns and cities near the bases.

Wartime Expansion

As the United States became more involved in the war, emphasis shifted from ensuring equal treatment and opportunity to preparing for combat. The wartime expansion attracted a large number of recruits, whites as well as blacks, whose attitudes reflected the growing racial hostility in the United States.

As the war intensified after 1965, opposition to U.S. involvement became an important issue among African-American activists. Civil rights leader Rev. **Martin Luther King Jr.** (1929–1968) was outspoken in his opposition to the war, as were many groups in the Black Power movement. In 1967, when heavyweight **boxing** champion **Muhammad Ali** (1942–) refused to be drafted into the army, he was stripped of his title.

Spreading Violence

The assassination of King in 1968 led to a series of racial incidents in South Vietnam. Because the civil rights leader had denounced the war, some white servicemen rejoiced in his death. Sailors at Cua Viet donned makeshift white robes and paraded in imitation of the white terrorist organization the **Ku Klux Klan.** Confederate flags, symbols of **slavery** in the American **Civil War** (1861–65) South, were flown over U.S. military bases in Cam Ranh Bay and Da Nang.

Racial clashes erupted wherever U.S. forces served. In February 1969 rioting broke out at Fort Benning, Georgia, where black soldiers, awaiting discharge after returning from Southeast Asia, attacked white troops. The black soldiers were showing their frustration at being assigned to night maneuvers or menial labor. In Europe violence occurred with such frequency that in 1970 the U.S. Department of Defense sent an interracial team to investigate conditions.

To deal with the causes of these incidents and prevent further clashes, the armed services agreed to make some changes. These included toleration of the clenched-fist Black Power salute, a crackdown on racially offensive terms, and making available products used by African Americans and magazines of interest to them. Additional measures included the removal of references to race from all records reviewed by promotion boards and further emphasis on the recommendations of the Gesell Committee to attack all forms of racial discrimination on military bases and in nearby communities. Finally, the services created discussion groups and councils to improve communication between the races.

African-American soldiers in the field during the Vietnam War (AP/Wide World Photos. Reproduced by permission)

Education in Race Relations

In 1972 the Defense Race Relations Institute opened its doors at Patrick Air Force Base, Florida, and began providing required training in racial issues. Some commanders resisted the efforts of the program. Despite occasional misunderstandings, however, senior officers came to realize the value of the program in promoting racial harmony.

The Impact of the Vietnam War on African Americans

Black Vietnam veterans gained access to government benefits, but these, especially the payments for education, proved less generous than those given to veterans after **World War II** (1939–45). For many African-American officers, including the future chairman of the Joint Chiefs of Staff, **Colin Powell** (1937–), the war provided the opportunity for combat commands and rapid advancement through the military hierarchy. (*See also* **Civil Rights Movement.**)

Virginia

First African-American Settlers: The first Africans imported to the British colonies arrived at Jamestown on the James River in 1619.

Slave Population: In 1670 Virginia ruled that imported Africans were slaves for life. Slaves were primarily employed in the growing of tobacco, the region's main cash crop.

Free Black Population: Records from the seventeenth century indicate that a number of black men and women lived as freeholders or owners of notable amounts of land. Slaves and **free blacks** alike worked as artisans, masons, ironworkers, and blacksmiths. After the **American Revolution** (1775–83) the state's free black population increased from 12,722 to 30,570 owing to changes in political thought and to slaves' purchasing their freedom.

Civil War: Virginia seceded from the Union in 1861, and Richmond was established as the capital of the Confederacy. The state's nonslave western

areas remained loyal and broke away from Virginia, entering the Union as the state of West Virginia in 1863. During the years of the **Civil War** (1861–65) large numbers of blacks fled farms, plantations, and factories, some joining the Union army.

Reconstruction: After the **Civil War**, African-American Virginians found employment as farmers, laborers, coal miners, and dockworkers. Some blacks founded businesses or fought for a full range of social and civil rights. In 1868 a new state constitution established voting rights, and in 1870 public schools for blacks were provided for. By 1910, however, segregation ordinances were in place disenfranchising the black population. Many black Virginians left the state as part of the Great Migration of the early 1900s.

The Great Depression: During the 1940s many African Americans moved to urban areas or left the state altogether. Meanwhile, civil rights efforts increased as black leaders began efforts to desegregate schools.

Civil Rights Movement: A total assault on segregation came in the 1960s with civil rights marches and **sit-ins.** Prohibitions against interracial marriage were overturned in 1967, and black activists forced the repeal of segregation laws.

Current African-American Population: According to U.S. Census Bureau estimates, the total black population in Virginia was 1,362,617 (20 percent of the state population) as of July 1, 1998.

Key Figures: Baptist minister **Adam Clayton Powell Sr.** (1865–1953); Gabriel Prosser (c. 1775–1800), leader of a conspiracy to overthrow the slavery; educator **Booker T. Washington** (c. 1856–1915); James Bland (1854–1911), writer of Virginia's state song, "Carry Me Back to Old Virginny"; **Ella Baker** (1903–1986), founder of the **Student Nonviolent Coordinating Committee (SNCC)**; tennis player **Arthur Ashe** (1943–1993).

(SEE ALSO **GABRIEL PROSSER CONSPIRACY**; **NAT TURNER'S REBELLION**.)

Voodoo

Voodoo—also spelled "Vodou" or "vodoun"—was a traditional religious practice on the West Indian island of Haiti, a French slave colony and major sugar producer during the eighteenth century. Slaves taken to Haiti from the African countries of Dahomey (now the Republic of Benin), Nigeria, Angola, and Zaire introduced much of this practice. The word "vodun" is the most common modern-day term for a traditional spirit or deity among the Fon people of Benin. Haitians prefer to call their religion *Li sevi lwa-yo* ("he, or she, serves the spirits").

Voodoo continues today as a religious practice in Haiti, as well as in Haitian-American communities like those in New York City and Miami, Florida. New Orleans, Louisiana, has the oldest Haitian immigrant community in the United States, dating from the 1700s, but voodoo there is more distant from its Haitian roots.

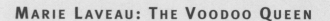

MARIE LAVEAU: THE VOODOO QUEEN

The name Marie Laveau was long associated with voodoo in New Orleans, Louisiana. Scholars believe there were three generations of women called Marie Laveau who worked as spiritual counselors there. The first was a slave brought from Haiti during a slave revolution of the 1700s in which voodoo played a part.

The most famous Marie Laveau, the "voodoo queen of New Orleans," was born in 1827, the granddaughter of this slave woman. Her religion was taken from Haitian voodoo. She kept a large snake on her altar to represent the spirit Danbala Wedo and went into spiritual possession while dancing in Congo Square. She also led an elaborate annual voodoo ceremony on the banks of Lake Pontchartrain on Saint John's Eve (June 24).

But most of her work was done with individual clients, whom she served as spiritual adviser, healer, and supplier of charms (called "gris-gris"). Most New Orleans voodoo in the late twentieth century, like that throughout the South, is limited to these activities.

Haitian voodoo has been represented as a religion obsessed with evil and death, but in reality it is very different. Based on an agricultural way of life, Haitian voodoo centers on loyalty to land, family (including the spirits of the dead), and to the voodoo spirits. Most spirits have a Catholic saint's name and an African name. Priests and priestesses light candles and pour libations (liquids offered to the spirits) each day, wear a favored spirit's color, and make journeys to a shrine or church associated with the spirit. They believe the spirit takes possession of their body and voice and allows them to bless and give spiritual advice to the faithful. They also hold ceremonies with singing, dancing, drumming, and feasting. These ceremonies often include sacrificing an animal.

The main work of voodoo is to enhance and heal relationships. In large Haitian immigrant communities in the United States, hundreds of voodoo healers serve thousands of clients, often practicing from their basements or living rooms. Voodoo "families" provide struggling immigrants with connections to their Haitian roots.

Voodoo, or "hoodoo," as practiced throughout the southern United States, was introduced directly by African slaves from Dahomey, Angola, and Zaire. As with Haitian voodoo, it is usually practiced in addition to Christianity, addressing issues like romantic love and protection of the spirit from spells cast by others. Voodoo healers say one person's illness can be traced to an emotion, such as jealousy, in another. Voodoo has a number of spells, or "cures," using common items and rituals to make one person fall in love with, or be faithful to, another.

The term "voodoo"—like "conjure," "rootwork," and "witchcraft"—is often used to refer to a diverse collection of traditional spiritual practices among descendants of African slaves in the United States.

Walcott, Derek Alton ▪▪▪

POET, PLAYWRIGHT, ESSAYIST
January 30, 1930–

Derek Walcott, winner of the Nobel Prize in literature in 1992, was born along with a twin brother in Castries, Saint Lucia, a small island in the West Indies (the islands of the Caribbean). After graduating from St. Mary's College in Saint Lucia, he continued his education at the University of the West Indies in Kingston, Jamaica.

Walcott's literary career began with three books of poetry published in the Caribbean from 1948 to 1951. The 1950s marked the beginning of his career as a playwright-director in Trinidad (another Caribbean island). His first theater piece, *Henri Cristophe* (1950), a historical play, was followed by a series of folk dramas in verse, the most celebrated of which was the award-winning *Dream on Monkey Mountain*, produced in Toronto, Canada, in 1967. After a brief stay in the United States as a Rockefeller Fellow, Walcott returned to Trinidad in 1959 to become founding director of the Trinidad Theatre Workshop.

Walcott's international debut as a poet came with *In a Green Night: Poems 1948–1960* (1962), followed shortly thereafter by *Selected Poems* (1964). These volumes showcased the qualities that are typical of his verse: excellence in traditional literary forms, the repeated use of myths and themes, and the influences of European and African cultures in a troubled Caribbean landscape. Other published volumes include *In Another Life* (1973), Walcott's book-length self-portrait; *The Star-Apple Kingdom* (1979); *Midsummer* (1984); *Omeros* (1990); and *Tiepolo's Hound* (2000). Walcott's later works are generally myths and histories told in verse.

Although he has described himself as a citizen of "no nation but the imagination" and has lived, written, and taught in various places throughout the world, Walcott has remained faithful to the Caribbean as his standard landscape. This devotion to the history and legends of his homeland is explored in his first collection of essays, *What the Twilight Says* (1998), a volume which includes "The Antilles: Fragments of Epic Memory," the address given by Walcott to the Nobel Academy after winning the 1992 Nobel Prize in literature. Since 1981 Walcott has been a professor of English and creative writing at Boston University. He has continued to publish periodic volumes of poetry, and in 1997 he wrote the lyrics for the singer Paul Simon's *Capeman*.

Walker, Aida Overton ▪▪▪

ENTERTAINER
1880–1914

Aida Overton Walker was the leading African-American female performing artist at the turn of the twentieth century. As a singer and dancer, she became a national, then international, star of authentic black folk culture. Born in New York City, Walker began her career in the chorus of

"Black Patti's Troubadours." She married George William Walker, of the vaudeville comedy team Williams and Walker and soon became the female lead in their series of major musical comedies: *The Policy Players*, *Sons of Ham*, *In Dahomey*, *Abyssinia*, and *Bandanna Land*.

At George Walker's death, she continued in musical theater and vaudeville. She died in New York in 1914 at the age of thirty-four.

Walker, A'Lelia

ENTREPRENEUR
June 6, 1885–August 17, 1931

Through the lavish parties she hosted, A'Lelia Walker made herself the center of social life during the **Harlem Renaissance.** She was born Lelia Walker to Sarah and Moses McWilliams in Vicksburg, Mississippi. (She changed her name to A'Lelia as an adult.) After her father died when she was two, her mother took her to St. Louis, Missouri. She attended public schools there and graduated from Knoxville College, a private black school in Knoxville, Tennessee.

She and her mother then moved to Denver, Colorado, where her mother married C. J. Walker, from whom A'Lelia and her mother took their last names. While in Denver, the Walkers began a hair-care business. **Madam C. J. Walker** developed products that straightened and softened African-American women's hair, and, assisted by her daughter, she quickly created a vast empire.

With her mother's death on May 25, 1919, A'Lelia inherited the bulk of her mother's estate. Although she had the title of director in the Walker business interests, A'Lelia Walker devoted most of her money and attention to social life. She threw parties and established "at-homes," at which she introduced African-American writers, artists, and performers to each other as well as to white celebrities.

When the **Great Depression** came, Walker experienced grave financial difficulties, and she died suddenly on August 17, 1931.

Walker, Alice

NOVELIST
February 9, 1944–

Alice Walker was born in Eatonton, Georgia, the eighth child of sharecroppers, farmers who rented the land they farmed, paying the rent with part of their crops. Blinded in the right eye at age eight, Walker became an introverted child. She would go on to become one of the most famous black authors in the United States.

Walker won a scholarship to **Spelman College** in Atlanta, Georgia, in 1961. Unhappy after two years at Spelman, she transferred to Sarah Lawrence College (Bronxville, New York), and in the summer before her

senior year she traveled to **Africa** to learn more about the cultural traditions of black people. In Africa she became pregnant, and the experience, along with her participation in the **Civil Rights movement,** became the subject of her first book, a collection of poems titled *Once* (1968).

Walker moved to Mississippi in 1965, where she met and married a civil rights lawyer (they were later divorced), had a daughter, Rebecca, in 1969, and wrote her first novel, *The Third Life of Grange Copeland* (1970). While doing research on black folk medicine for a story, Walker first learned of writer **Zora Neale Hurston,** whose beliefs and life history became an inspiration to her. Hurston had all but disappeared from American literary history, in large part because she held views—on black southern rural culture, racism, and discrimination against women—that had been condemned by many leading black intellectuals, including novelist **Richard Wright.** Because Walker drew courage from Hurston's example, she also focused public attention back on Hurston's work.

During her career Walker has published several novels, volumes of poetry, collections of essays, short story collections, and an **autobiography,** *The Same River Twice* (1995). In all these works, she examines the problems and injustices that affect black Americans generally and black women in particular. The most celebrated and controversial of these works is *The Color Purple*, winner of the prestigious Pulitzer Prize for excellence in literature and the National Book Award for the best work of fiction in the United States. *The Color Purple* explores, among other things, marital violence, same-sex relationships, alternative religious practices, and black attitudes about male and female roles in society. Since the early 1980s, Walker has lived in northern California.

Walker, David

CIVIL RIGHTS ACTIVIST, PAMPHLETEER
c. 1785–June 28, 1830

Born free in Wilmington, North Carolina, civil rights activist David Walker traveled extensively in the South and observed the cruelty of **slavery** firsthand. Little is known about his life until he settled in Boston, Massachusetts, where he was living as early as 1826. He operated a clothing store and became a leader in Boston's black community. Walker and his wife, Eliza, had one son, Edwin G. Walker, who later became the first black elected to the Massachusetts legislature.

Walker represented a new generation of black leaders forged by the experience of creating the first extensive free black communities in urban centers of the United States in the half-century after the **American Revolution** (1775–83). The achievement of African Americans in establishing institutions (churches, schools, and mutual aid and friendship societies) and in producing leaders (ministers, educators, businessmen) emboldened some in Walker's generation to challenge the reigning view among whites that African Americans, even if freed, were destined to remain a degraded people, a caste apart, better served by the removal of **free blacks** to Africa, which became the objective of the American Colonization Society (ACS), formed in 1817 by leading statesmen and clergy.

In an address in 1828 delivered before the Massachusetts General Colored Association, Walker laid out a strategy of opposition. Overcoming resistance to organization from within the black community, Walker and others recognized the need for a formal association to advance the race by uniting "the colored population, so far, through the United States of America, as may be practicable and expedient; forming societies, opening, extending, and keeping up correspondences" (*Freedom's Journal*, December 19, 1828). Heralding his famous *Appeal to the Colored Citizens of the World*, Walker sought to arouse blacks to mutual aid and self-help, to cast off passive acquiescence in injustice, and to persuade his people of the potential power that hundreds of thousands of free blacks possessed once mobilized.

Published in 1829, Walker's *Appeal to the Colored Citizens of the World* encouraged black organization and individual activism. For many readers, the most startling aspect of the *Appeal* was its call for the violent revolt of slaves against their masters. Walker also opposed the plans to return blacks to Africa by the ACS.

Walker circulated copies of the *Appeal* through the mails and via black and white seamen, who carried them to southern ports in Virginia, North Carolina, Georgia, and Louisiana. Southern leaders became alarmed and adopted new laws against teaching free blacks to read or write and demanded that Mayor Harrison Gray Otis of Boston take action against Walker. Otis gave assurances that Walker's was an isolated voice, without sympathy in the white community, but noted that Walker had violated no laws. In 1830 Walker died from causes unknown amid suspicion, never confirmed, of foul play.

Walker, Madam C. J.

**ENTREPRENEUR, HAIR-CARE INDUSTRY PIONEER,
PHILANTHROPIST, POLITICAL ACTIVIST**
December 23, 1867–May 25, 1919

Madam C. J. Walker was a legendary businesswoman and civil rights activist. Born Sarah Breedlove to former slaves on a Delta, Louisiana, cotton plantation, she was orphaned by age seven. She lived with her sister in Vicksburg, Mississippi, until 1882, when she married Moses McWilliams. In 1887 Moses McWilliams died, and for the next eighteen years McWilliams worked as a laundress. In 1905, with $1.50 in savings, the thirty-seven-year-old McWilliams moved to Denver, Colorado, to start her own business after developing a formula to treat her problem with baldness—an ailment common among African-American women at the time, brought on by poor diet, stress, illness, damaging hair-care treatments, and scalp disease. In January 1906 she married Charles Joseph Walker, a newspaper sales agent, who helped design her advertisements and mail-order operation.

From 1906 to 1916 Madam Walker traveled throughout the United States, Central America, and the West Indies promoting her business. She settled briefly in Pittsburgh, Pennsylvania, establishing the first Lelia College of Hair Culture there in 1908, then moved the company to Indianapolis, Indiana, in 1910, building a factory and vastly increasing her annual sales.

Madam Walker's business philosophy stressed economic independence for the twenty thousand former maids, farm laborers, housewives, and schoolteachers she employed as agents and factory and office workers. To further strengthen her company, she created the Madam C. J. Walker Hair Culturists Union of America and held annual conventions.

During **World War I**, she was among those who supported the government's black recruitment efforts and war bond drives. She also traveled to Washington to present a petition urging President Woodrow Wilson (1856–1924) to support legislation that would make **lynching** a federal crime.

During the spring of 1919 Madam Walker rewrote her will, directing her attorney to donate five thousand dollars to the **National Association for the Advancement of Colored People's (NAACP)** antilynching campaign and to contribute thousands of dollars to black educational, civic, and social institutions and organizations.

When she died at age fifty-one, she was widely considered the wealthiest black woman in America and was reputed to be the first African-American female millionaire.

Walker's significance is rooted not only in her innovative hair-care system but also in her advocacy of black women's economic independence and her creation of business opportunities at a time when most black women worked as servants and sharecroppers. Having led an early life of hardship, she used her wealth and influence to promote social, political, and economic rights for women and blacks. In 1992 Madam Walker was elected to the National Business Hall of Fame.

Walker, Margaret

WRITER
July 7, 1915–October 1998

Margaret Abigail Walker was born in Birmingham, Alabama, received-her early education in New Orleans, and graduated from Northwestern University, near Chicago, Illinois, at the age of nineteen. In Chicago Walker met and befriended writer **Richard Wright,** and her own poetry matured. By the time she left Chicago for graduate work at the University of Iowa in 1939, she was well on her way to becoming a major poet.

In 1942 Walker completed a collection of poems entitled *For My People*, which won the prestigious Yale Younger Poets Award. She later joined the faculty at Jackson State University in Mississippi, where she met her husband, Firnist James Alexander, and raised their four children. In Mississippi, Walker played an active role in the **Civil Rights movement** and continued to write, eventually publishing a historical novel, *Jubilee* (1966), based on the life and stories of her grandmother. *Jubilee*, one of the first modern novels of **slavery** and **Reconstruction** (post–Civil War rebuilding in the South) told from an African-American point of view, was enormously popular and was translated into seven languages.

Other books followed, including *Prophets for a New Day* (1970) and *October Journey* (1973). In 1979 Walker retired from teaching at Jackson State and continued to work on several projects, including a controversial biography, *Richard Wright: Daemonic Genius*. In 1989 she published a collection of new and earlier poems titled *This Is My Century: New and Collected Poems*. A year later, she published her first volume of essays, *How I Wrote Jubilee and Other Essays on Life and Literature*.

Throughout her long career, Walker received numerous awards and honors for her contribution to American literature, including a 1991 Senior Fellowship from the National Endowment for the Arts.

Waller, Thomas Wright "Fats"

JAZZ PIANIST, ORGANIST, COMPOSER
May 21, 1904–December 15, 1943

Thomas Wright "Fats" Waller was the most popular of **Harlem** pianists. He was one of the most well known and endearing **jazz** musicians of his time. In addition to being a remarkable pianist, Waller was known

for his tasteful use of humor and recreating different styles and songs with his own unique spin.

Born in New York City, Waller lived most of his life there. He started playing piano at a young age and won a talent contest in 1918 at the Roosevelt Theater. Waller left home in 1920 and studied stride (a **ragtime** style) piano with stride experts Russell Brooks and James P. Johnson and also began playing the pipe organ which earned him extra money. He played the pipe organ for silent movies in the 1920s.

Waller became a local celebrity in clubs in **Harlem, New York,** and in 1927 he recorded numerous strides in a New Jersey studio. Among his recordings during this period were "Rusty Pail," "Gladyse," and "Fats Waller Stomp." In the 1930s jazz fanatics fell in love with Waller's music and lovable personality. He continued playing in clubs, recording for films, and composing songs in the 1930s. He also recorded popular hits such as "Ain't Misbehavin'," and "Stayin' at Home." Waller had a unique style of piano playing which was aided by his extremely large hands. He also was the only stride pianist to play the pipe organ as a jazz instrument. Waller was a popular singer as well using an energetic style and often incorporating humorous lyrics (the words in songs). The style of humor that Waller used is called "parody" (poking fun at something). Among the songs he created that highlighted this humorous style were "I'm Crazy 'Bout My Baby" (1931) and "It's a Sin to tell a Lie" (1936).

War. *See* **American Revolution; Civil War; Indian Wars; Korean War; Mexican War; Seminole Wars; Spanish-American War; Vietnam War; World War I; World War II**

Warwick, Dionne

SINGER
December 12, 1941–

Marie Dionne Warwick was one of the most important African-American pop soul artists outside of Motown in the 1960s. **Motown** (slang for Motor Town, which refers to Detroit, Michigan) is considered to be the main city in which modern African-American music developed.

Born in East Orange, New Jersey, Warwick studied voice at the Hartt College of Music. However, she decided to satisfy her passion for gospel music and joined the Drinkard Singers and the Gospelaires. In 1960 she met songwriters Burt Bacharach and Hal David, who helped her get a record contract. Throughout her recording with Scepter Records (1962–71), she worked with Bacharach and David, who wrote songs tailored for her delicate voice and superb diction (ability to pronounce words accurately). Among Warwick's lasting hit songs are "Anyone Who Had a Heart" (1964), "Do You Know the Way to San Jose" (1968), "Then Came You" (1974), and "I'll Never Love This Way Again," which sold one million copies. Later in her career, Warwick donated the proceeds of hit songs such as "That's What Friends Are For" to AIDS (Acquired Immune Deficiency Syndrome)

research. In the 1990s Warwick moved to Brazil and did promotional work for the Psychic Friends Network. She currently resides in Brazil and performs in concerts around the world.

Washington

First African-American Settlers: African-American residence in the state of Washington began with the first settlement party in 1845.

Free Black Population: Several African Americans distinguished themselves during Washington's early years. Missouri landowner George Washington Bush was a successful farmer who was the only black to obtain original title to land in Washington. His son William became the first African American to serve in the state legislature when Washington obtained statehood in 1889. The 1860 territorial census recorded thirty blacks.

Reconstruction: Washington's African-American population did not reach one thousand until hundreds of coal miners were brought into the state during a strike in the late 1880s. Other spurts of population growth occurred during the Gold Rush of the 1890s and during **World War I** (1914–18).

The Great Depression: The 1940 African-American population of fewer than eight thousand quadrupled in response to the **military** buildup for **World War II**, which provided job openings in the state's shipyard operations, aircraft and aluminum manufacturing, and plutonium production. During World War II (1939–45) blacks worked in jobs from which they had previously been barred.

Civil Rights Movement: In the 1960s Washington experienced racial tension in the major cities, which led to efforts to avert violence. Open-housing laws were passed after initial rejections, public accommodation laws were enforced, and job training programs were established.

Current African-American Population: According to U.S. Census Bureau estimates, the total black population in Washington was 198,396 (3 percent of the state population) as of July 1, 1998.

Key Figures: Painter **Jacob Armstead Lawrence** (1917–); musician **Ray Charles** (1930–); producer **Quincy Jones** (1933–); **Jimi Hendrix** (1942–1970), rock guitarist, singer, and songwriter.

Washington, Booker Taliaferro

EDUCATOR, FOUNDER OF TUSKEGEE INSTITUTE
c. 1856–November 14, 1915

African-American educator and leader Booker T. Washington was born a slave but became the most powerful African American of his time as an adviser to Republican presidents Theodore Roosevelt (1858–1919) and William Howard Taft (1857–1930). The founder of Alabama's **Tuskegee Institute,** he was also one of the country's foremost educators during the post–Civil War period.

Washington was born near Hale's Ford, Virginia. He spent his childhood as a houseboy and servant. When slavery was ended in 1865, he moved with his family to Malden, West Virginia, where he worked briefly in the salt and coal mines while attending a local school for African Americans.

Washington earned a degree at **Hampton Institute** in Virginia in 1875, then taught school in Malden and became a local public speaker. In 1881 he founded a school in Tuskegee, Alabama. Beginning with a few shabby buildings, Washington built **Tuskegee Institute** into the best-known African-American school in the country. Its curriculum prepared students for jobs with training in industrial skills and crafts. Washington financed the school's growth with the help of northern philanthropists such as Andrew Carnegie (1835–1919).

Washington's role as a political leader was reflected in a speech delivered in 1895. Often called the **Atlanta Compromise,** it stated Washington's philosophy of racial advancement and political accommodation (compromise, or give-and-take). Washington urged African Americans to accommodate (live with) the segregation and discrimination allowed by law. He said blacks and whites could have separate social lives, while working together for the financial benefit of both groups.

Many whites and African Americans quickly accepted these ideas. Even educator **W. E. B. Du Bois** (1868–1963), later one of Washington's harshest critics, wrote to him praising the speech. Others, however, began criticizing Washington for not directly supporting civil rights legislation and for his support of industrial education rather than academic training. The **National Association for the Advancement of Colored People (NAACP)** and the **National Urban League** later challenged Washington's approach, also pointing to his failure to address the problems of the growing black population in big cities. The defeat of the Republican presidential candidate in 1912 also hurt his political influence. In public, Washington remained faithful to the Atlanta Compromise for the rest of his life; in private, however, he paid the legal fees for cases challenging **Jim Crow** laws discriminating against blacks.

Washington was commended by friend and foes at the time of his death, but his historical reputation has suffered. He has been forgotten by many blacks and whites. However, there has been increased interest in his economic ideas by African-American businesspeople and entrepreneurs.

Washington, Denzel

ACTOR
December 2, 1954–

Denzel Washington is one of the most talented and sought-after actors of his time. As a teen, Washington went through a rebellious period, and his mother sent him to boarding school at Oakland Academy in Windsor, New York. After graduating with a bachelor's degree in journalism from Fordham University in New York in 1978, Washington spent a year at San Francisco's American Conservatory Theater and later performed with the New York Theater.

After refusing to take roles that he deemed degrading, Washington took the part of the idealistic surgeon Dr. Philip Chandler on the popular television drama series *St. Elsewhere* (1982–88).

Despite his consistently powerful performances, it was not until the end of the 1980s that Washington was acknowledged as one of America's leading actors. He appeared as martyred South African activist Stephen Biko in *Cry Freedom* (1987), as a policeman in *The Mighty Quinn* (1989), and as the embittered former slave and Union soldier Trip in *Glory* (1989). Washington received an Academy Award nomination for his work in *Cry Freedom* and in 1990 won an Academy Award for best supporting actor for his performance in *Glory*. That same year, he played the title role in *Richard III* in the New York Shakespeare Festival.

In 1992 Washington played the title role in the film *Malcolm X.* The film received mixed reviews, but Washington's performance as the black nationalist was a critical success, and he received an Oscar nomination as best actor.

Throughout the 1990s Washington continued to act in dramatic, comedic, and action roles. He was nominated for an Academy Award for best

actor after his riveting portrayal of boxer—turned-prisoner Reuben Carter in *The Hurricane* (1999.)

Washington, Dinah ▪▪▪

SINGER
August 19, 1924–December 14, 1963

Known as "the Queen of the Blues," or simply "the Queen," Dinah Washington possessed singing talents that allowed her to cross over from **rhythm and blues (R&B)** to pop.

Born Ruth Jones in Tuscaloosa, Alabama, Washington was raised in Chicago and sang in both Saint Luke's Baptist Church and Sallie Martin's Gospel Group. At age fifteen she won an amateur-night contest and began appearing in local nightclubs. Washington was recommended by an agent to bandleader **Lionel Hampton,** who hired her as a vocalist from 1943 until 1946, when she left to sing solo.

On December 29, 1943, Washington cut her first record for the Keynote label. In 1946 she contracted with Mercury, for which she made over four hundred recordings before signing with Roulette. Between 1949 and 1954 ten of her singles were in the top five on the R&B charts. Following her 1959 breakthrough, "What a Difference a Day Makes," Washington regularly reached the top twenty on the pop charts. She died in 1963 from an overdose of pills and liquor.

Watts, André ▪▪▪

CONCERT PIANIST
June 20, 1946–

André Watts is one of the best piano players of modern times. He is a classical concert pianist, interpreting and playing music written by famous composers.

Watts was born in Nuremberg, Germany, to a Hungarian mother and an African-American father who was a soldier. He started playing the piano at the age of six with the guidance of his mother. He studied at the Philadelphia Academy of Music in Pennsylvania and the Peabody Institute in Baltimore, Maryland. During this period Watts made solo performances with the Philadelphia Orchestra. He played music written by such famous composers as Franz Joseph Haydn (1732–1809), Felix Mendelssohn (1809–1847), and César Franck.

At the age of sixteen Watts became famous when an unexpected opportunity presented itself. He played a concerto (a solo composition written for one or more solo instruments) directed by the famed American conductor Leonard Bernstein in place of the scheduled performer, who was ill. In 1974 Watts began studying with Leon Fleisher and began touring all over the world. Watts is known for his energetic playing style and his ability to play a wide range of music. He is perhaps best know for his interpretation of

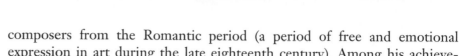

composers from the Romantic period (a period of free and emotional expression in art during the late eighteenth century). Among his achievements are a Grammy Award for most promising classical artist (1964) and the Lincoln Center Medallion (1974).

Weaver, Robert Clifton

ECONOMIST
December 29, 1907–July 19, 1997

Growing up in Washington, D.C., economist Robert Weaver was told by his mother that "the way to offset color prejudice is to be awfully good at whatever you do." He followed her advice and graduated with honors from Harvard (1929), where he also earned a master's degree (1931) and a Ph.D. in economics (1934).

In 1933 Weaver began working for the U. S. Department of the Interior and became an active member of the unofficial "Black Cabinet" that advised President Franklin D. Roosevelt (1882–1945). During **World War II** (1939–45) Weaver held positions on the National Defense Advisory Committee, the War Manpower Commission, and the War Production Board.

After the war Weaver published two studies of discrimination against African Americans, before being chosen in 1955 as New York State's rent commissioner. He was the first African American in the state's history to hold a cabinet office.

After his 1960 election, President John F. Kennedy (1917–1963) made Weaver director of the U.S. Housing and Home Finance Agency, the highest federal position ever held by an African American. However, Weaver had little success in promoting better-designed public housing, low and moderate income housing, and federal rent assistance for the ailing and the elderly.

Kennedy had sought to put Weaver in a new cabinet position, a plan that was twice rejected by Congress. Following the landslide election of Lyndon B. Johnson (1908–1973) in 1964, however, Congress approved a bill to establish the Department of Housing and Urban Development (HUD) and confirmed Weaver as its head. Weaver's skilled administration of HUD would be affected by the financial drain of the **Vietnam War** (1959–75) and by the negative political response to urban rioting from 1965 to 1968.

In 1969 Weaver left the government to become president of City University of New York's (CUNY) Baruch College and then served as Distinguished Professor of Urban Affairs at CUNY's Hunter College. (*See also* **Economics**)

Weems, Carrie Mae

PHOTOGRAPHER
April 20, 1953–

Born in Portland, Oregon, Carrie Mae Weems began taking pictures in 1976 after a friend gave her a camera. In 1979 she began taking classes in art,

folklore, and literature at the California Institute of the Arts. She earned a bachelor's degree in 1981 and a master's degree from the University of California, San Diego, in 1984.

Weems's photographs have followed connected political and cultural themes. The autobiographical series *Family Pictures and Stories* (1978–1984) used the format of a family photo album and included images of relatives at their jobs and at home. The work was a response to the Moynihan Report of ten years earlier, which claimed that female-centered authority in black families was responsible for a general crisis.

In *Ain't Jokin* (1987–1988) Weems questioned racial stereotypes. In 1990 she showed the conflict between a woman's political beliefs and her emotional desires in *Untitled* (Kitchen Table Series). These images showed different interactions between a woman and man from a repeated view of a kitchen table.

Weems created large color still lifes and portraits for *And 22 Million Very Tired and Angry People* (1992). She combined photos of ordinary objects such as an alarm clock, a fan, and a typewriter with text from famous individuals, such as writer **Ntozake Shange** (1948–) and activist **Malcolm X** (1925–65), to educate viewers about political change.

In 1992 Weems exhibited a series of images of the **Gullah** culture of the Sea Islands, located off the coast of South Carolina and Georgia.

Weems has taught photography at several institutions in California and New England. She has also been artist-in-residence at the Visual Studies Workshop in Rochester, New York (1986); the Rhode Island School of Design in Providence (1989–1990); and the Art Institute of Chicago (1990).

Wells-Barnett, Ida Bell

JOURNALIST, CIVIL RIGHTS ACTIVIST
July 6, 1862–March 25, 1931

Ida Wells-Barnett was a groundbreaking journalist and civil rights activist who for years conducted a campaign to put an end to the **lynching** of African-Americans.

Young Ida Wells received her early education in the grammar school of Shaw University in Holly Springs, Mississippi, where she was born. Her schooling stopped when a yellow-fever epidemic claimed the lives of both her parents in 1878 and she assumed responsibility for her seven brothers and sisters. The next year, the family moved to Memphis, Tennessee, with an aunt. There, Wells found work as a teacher.

A turning point in Wells's life occurred on May 4, 1884. While riding a train to a teaching assignment, she was asked to leave her seat and move to a segregated (separated according to race) car. Wells refused, and she was pushed from the railway car. She sued the railroad, and although she was awarded $500 by a lower court, the Tennessee Supreme Court reversed the decision in 1887.

In the same year, she launched her career in journalism, writing of her experiences in an African-American weekly newspaper called *The Living*

Lynch Law in Georgia.

BY

IDA B. WELLS-BARNETT

A Six-Weeks' Record in the Center of Southern Civilization,
As Faithfully Chronicled by the "Atlanta Journal"
and the "Atlanta Constitution."

ALSO THE FULL REPORT OF LOUIS P. LE VIN,

The Chicago Detective Sent to Investigate the Burning of
Samuel Hose, the Torture and Hanging of Elijah Strick-
land, the Colored Preacher, and the Lynching
of Nine Men for Alleged Arson.

Way. In 1892 she became the co-owner of a small black newspaper in Memphis, the *Free Speech*. Her articles on the injustices faced by southern blacks were reprinted in a number of black newspapers.

In March 1892 the lynching of three young black businessmen in a suburb of Memphis focused Wells's attention on the need to address this terrible crime. She argued that most lynchings were prompted by economic competition between whites and blacks.

She urged African Americans in Memphis to move to the western United States, where conditions were said to be more favorable to blacks. She also encouraged African Americans to stop riding segregated streetcars and stop buying from merchants who discriminated against blacks. Her challenges were met by mob violence. In May 1892, while she was out of town, the offices of the *Free Speech* were destroyed by an angry mob of whites.

After her press was destroyed, Wells began to work for the *New York Age*. There, she continued to write extensively on lynching and other African-American issues. Two of her more widely read articles were "Lynching and the Excuse for It" (1901) and "Our Country's Lynching Record" (1913). Perhaps her greatest effort against lynching was her tireless campaign for national antilynching laws. In 1901 she met with U.S. president William McKinley (1843–1901) to convince him of the importance of such legislation.

In 1895 Wells married and in time became the mother of four children. The family settled in **Chicago, Illinois.** Although she was a devoted mother and homemaker, Wells-Barnett's political and reform activities did not stop. She continued to write about racial issues and American injustice. Most of her later work targeted social and political issues in Chicago. In 1930, the year before she died, Wells-Barnett ran unsuccessfully as an independent candidate for the U.S. Senate from Illinois.

West, Blacks in the

The nineteen states of the American West held the promise of social freedom and economic opportunity for thousands of nineteenth- and twentieth-century blacks, beginning with **fugitive slaves** who settled in what would become Texas during the 1830s. As late as 1951 the *Chicago Defender*, the nation's largest black newspaper, urged readers to move west to seek opportunities denied them in the South and Midwest.

Blacks who migrated to the West faced long journeys into unknown territory, as well as possible conflicts with culturally different people, such as European-American settlers, Mexican Americans in the Southwest, Asian Americans on the West Coast, and American Indians throughout the West. Yet they risked these difficulties rather than face the oppression of the South or East.

Blacks in the Early West

In the early 1800s blacks worked as fur traders and trappers and were among the first to explore the Rocky Mountain region. Black trapper Peter Ranne was a member of the first party of Americans to reach California overland, in 1824. One year later Moses Harris became the first non–American Indian to explore the Great Salt Lake region of what would become Utah. Black "mountain men" James Beckwourth (1798–1866) and Edward Rose crossed much of what would become Montana, Idaho, Wyoming, and Colorado.

Wagon trains of white settlers crossing the Rocky Mountains relied on experienced guides like Harris and Beckwourth to lead them. When white farmers moved to the Washington Territory in the 1850s, African-American homesteaders were there to give advice and assistance.

Blacks participated in the "gold rushes" to Idaho, Montana, Colorado, and South Dakota during the mid-1800s. A few blacks found gold on their claims, like John Frazier, who mined $100,000 worth of gold in 1866. Those who did not still managed to make a living. Sarah Campbell, one of the earliest miners to reach the Black Hills of South Dakota, in 1874, never found gold on her claim but earned a good living cooking, washing, and sewing for other miners.

After the **Civil War** (1861–65) and the end of slavery, African Americans migrated to the West by the thousands. Some blacks from the South created black towns such as Boley and Langston in the Oklahoma Territory, Nicodemus in Kansas, and Allensworth in California. The largest of these migrations was led by Benjamin "Pap" Singleton (c. 1809–1892), a Tennessee carpenter who in 1874 distributed a pamphlet praising the political freedom and economic opportunities in Kansas. Because of his efforts, at least twenty-five thousand blacks settled in Kansas between 1874 and 1880.

African-American men worked in the cattle industry in every state and territory of the West before 1900. Blacks made up about nine thousand of the thirty-five thousand cowboys in the West between 1860 and 1895. In 1870 a black Texas trail boss, Bose Ikard, created the Goodnight-Loving Trail from Texas through New Mexico to Colorado. At least 100,000 head of cattle were driven north on this trail over a fifteen-year period.

African-American soldiers after the Civil War were assigned throughout the West to protect homesteaders, capture outlaws, and help keep the peace. Eleven black soldiers earned the Congressional Medal of Honor while serving in the West.

Black Migration in the Twentieth Century

The image of the West as a region of opportunity for African Americans continued into the twentieth century. After 1900, western cities were the destination for most migrants. Between 1900 and 1940 most blacks found work only as dockworkers, railway porters, hotel cooks and waiters, maids, and cannery workers. A few professionals—doctors, lawyers, ministers, and teachers—provided services for black communities and for many whites. In spite of poverty, black communities in cities like Denver, Colorado; San Francisco and Los Angeles, California; and Seattle, Washington, had their own churches, social clubs, political organizations, and chapters of civil rights defense organizations like the **National Association for the Advancement of Colored People (NAACP)** and the **National Urban League**.

During **World War II** (1939–45) thousands of black defense workers found jobs in western shipyards, aircraft factories, and other war-related industries. Between 1940 and 1950 the total number of African Americans in the West grew 49 percent, from 1.3 million to 2 million, with the largest increases in San Francisco, Oakland, and Los Angeles, California.

With this migration racial tension and rivalry grew, as blacks and whites competed for employment and housing. With the rising black population concentrated in segregated neighborhoods, schools also became segregated. The black communities of the West shared many of the same conditions that blacks faced in the eastern and southern ghettos. During the 1960s organizations like the NAACP challenged these problems and, even though they

AFRICAN-AMERICAN SUCCESS STORIES OF THE OLD WEST

Most African Americans found work in the early West, and some became wealthy by being the first in an area to start a particular business. Barney L. Ford, a former slave, migrated to Denver, Colorado, in 1859 and by 1890 had become one of the wealthiest men in the state. A millionaire, he owned a hotel, a dry-goods store, and real estate in Denver and Cheyenne, Wyoming.

Sarah Gammon Bickford owned and operated the water system for Virginia City, Montana, from 1888 to 1931 and became one of the city's most prominent citizens.

William Gross arrived in Seattle, Washington, in 1861 and opened the city's second hotel, as well as a restaurant and barbershop. He later bought a farm that would become the site of Seattle's black community.

Biddy Mason (1818–1891), also a former slave, made a fortune in real estate in Los Angeles, California, during the late 1800s. She donated it to various African-American community institutions and helped to found the First African Methodist Episcopal Church, Los Angeles's oldest black church.

were not always successful, forced political leaders to remove some of the worst examples of discrimination.

The migration of blacks to the West continued into the 1980s, raising the region's total black population by 1990 to 5.3 million. This growth gave greater power and political influence to some black communities and resulted in the election of black mayors such as **Tom Bradley** (1917–1998) in Los Angeles, Wellington Webb (1941–) in Denver, and Norm Rice (1943–) in Seattle. But crime, unemployment, and poverty remain problems that western cities, like those throughout the United States, must solve.

West, Dorothy

WRITER
1912–August 16, 1998

Dorothy West was born in Boston, Massachusetts, where she attended Girls' Latin School and Boston University. Her writing career spanned seventy years, beginning with a story she wrote at the age of seven. When she was barely fifteen, she was selling stories to the *Boston Post*, and before she was eighteen she had shared second place (with writer **Zora Neale Hurston**) in a national writing competition.

In New York, West became friends with several writers associated with the **Harlem Renaissance** (an African-American artistic and cultural movement of the 1920s and 1930s centered in **Harlem, New York**), including **Countee Cullen, Langston Hughes,** and **Wallace Thurman.** As the ren-

aissance ("rebirth" or "revival") faded into the difficult years of the **Great Depression,** West used her own money to launch a literary magazine, *Challenge*, which she edited until the last issue appeared in 1937.

Although often labeled a Harlem Renaissance writer, West actually published most of her work long after the movement had peaked. She published more than sixty short stories throughout her career, including "For Richer, For Poorer," which has been widely included in textbooks and other volumes. The short story was the main focus of her career, but West is best known for her novel *The Living Is Easy* (1948), a portrait of an unprincipled, manipulative woman who lives among New England's black middle class.

For the last four decades of her life, West lived on Martha's Vineyard, an island off the Massachussetts coast, and contributed regular articles and columns to the island's newspaper, the *Vineyard Gazette*. In 1995 she published *The Wedding*, which was made into a television movie in 1998.

Dorothy West (AP/Wide World Photos. Reproduced by permission)

West Virginia

First African-American Settlers: African Americans first entered the western region of the Virginia colony in the 1750s.

Slave Population: Under the impact of the French and Indian Wars (1689–1763), the American Revolution (1775–83), and the westward expansion of the new nation, slavery continued to spread into western Virginia. The number of slaves increased from just over 5,200 in 1790 to almost 20,000 in 1830.

Free Black Population: The population of free blacks was 600 in 1790, rising to 2,200 in 1830. While some blacks worked on large plantations, most labored on small farms, in households, and as laborers in the iron, coal, and salt industries.

Civil War: When Virginia seceded from the Union and joined the Confederacy in 1861, its western delegates voted against secession and petitioned for statehood. When West Virginia gained statehood in 1863, however, it remained a slave state. The population of African Americans dropped from 21,000 in 1860 to 17,000 in 1865.

Reconstruction: Laws instituted in the 1860s and 1870s permitted blacks to testify and serve as witnesses in courts of law and allowed them to vote, but called for segregated schools. The black population increased from 25,800 in 1880 to over 64,000 in 1910, largely because of the growth of the coal industry.

The Great Depression: By 1930 there were nearly 115,000 African Americans in West Virginia. Blacks shouldered a disproportionate share of the hard times during the **Great Depression.** Because of unemployment and the decline of the coal mining industry, the black labor force dropped by over 90 percent in subsequent decades.

Civil Rights Movement: In 1961 most of the state's public accommodations still discriminated against blacks, and as late as 1963 most African-American students continued to receive education in a segregated public school system.

Current African-American Population: According to U.S. Census Bureau estimates, the total black population in West Virginia was 58,095 (3 percent of the state population) as of July 1, 1998.

Key Figures: Martin Delany, the most renowned of the West Virginia blacks to serve in the Civil War.

(SEE ALSO NAT TURNER'S REBELLION.)

Wheatley, Phillis

POET
c. 1753–December 5, 1784

Phillis Wheatley was born, according to her own testimony, in Gambia, West Africa. She was captured as a small child of seven or eight and sold in Boston, Massachusetts, to John and Susanna Wheatley in the summer of 1761. The Wheatleys apparently named the girl, who was covered in a piece of dirty carpet, after the name of the ship that had transported her. Unlike most slave owners of the time, the Wheatleys permitted and even encouraged Phillis to learn to read, and her poetic talent soon began to emerge.

The budding poet first appeared in print in 1767, in the *Newport* [Rhode Island] *Mercury* newspaper, when the author was about fourteen. The poem, "On Messrs. Hussey and Coffin," tells how two men escaped being drowned off Cape Cod in Massachusetts. Much of the poetry that followed deals, as well, with events occurring close to her Boston circle.

In October 1770 Wheatley published an elegy (a poem written to mourn the loss of a person) that was pivotal to her career. The subject of the poem was George Whitefield, a Methodist minister and friend to Selina Hastings, countess of the British estate of Huntingdon. Wheatley's poem was an overnight sensation, and was likely carried back to the countess along with news of Whitefield's death. In the countess, Wheatley found an admirer and supporter—and, after Selina Hastings ensured that the poem was reprinted several times in London, an international reputation.

Wheatley's first collection, titled simply *Poems*, was denied publication in Boston for racist reasons, and Susanna Wheatley sent the volume to a London publisher, where Hastings encouraged its publication. The London publisher, however, wrote back demanding proof that a black girl had written the poems. Phillis was subjected to an oral examination in front of a board of prominent Boston citizens. After interviewing Wheatley, they wrote a declaration that the poems had, in fact, been written by "an uncultivated barbarian." After the book's publication—financed by Selina Hastings—Wheatley became an international celebrity and toured England.

Wheatley was to have been presented at the English court in August 1773 when Susanna Wheatley became ill, and Phillis was called to return to Boston. Some time before October of that year, she was granted her freedom—according to her, "at the desire of my friends in England."

As the **American Revolution** (1775–83) broke out, Wheatley's patriotic feelings began to separate her even more from the Wheatleys, who were

An African-American FIRST

Phillis Wheatley Peters and her newborn child died in a shack on the edge of Boston on December 5, 1784. Her tragic end recalls the misery of her beginning in America, but Wheatley left her country a legacy of firsts: she was the first African American to publish a book, the first woman writer whose publication was urged and nurtured by a community of women, and the first American female author who tried to earn a living by means of her writing.

loyal to the British. Her patriotism is clearly featured in her two most famous Revolutionary War poems, "To His Excellency General Washington" (1775) and "Liberty and Peace" (1784).

In 1778 Wheatley married John Peters, a free African American, by whom she had three children, only one of whom survived. As the nation was caught up in the Revolution, her fortunes began to decline. She published a set of proposals for a new volume of poems in 1779, but the proposals failed to attract subscribers. The new volume—some 300 pages, written over the previous six years—never appeared, and most of its poems are now lost. In February 1999, however, a long-lost poem by Wheatley, "Ocean," was read publicly for the first time in 226 years.

White, Walter Francis

CIVIL RIGHTS LEADER
July 1, 1893–March 21, 1955

Walter White, executive secretary of the **National Association for the Advancement of Colored People (NAACP)** from 1931 to 1955, led the NAACP to become the nation's dominant force in the struggle to influence the federal government to uphold the U.S. Constitution and protect the rights of African Americans.

White was born in Atlanta, Georgia. In 1906, at age thirteen, he stood, rifle in hand, with his father to protect the family's home from a mob of whites who had invaded their neighborhood.

In 1918 the NAACP hired White as assistant executive secretary to investigate **lynching**. White investigated forty-two lynchings, mostly in the Deep South. He also investigated eight race riots that developed during the 1930s and 1940s in such cities as Chicago, Illinois; Philadelphia, Pennsylvania; Washington, D.C.; Omaha, Nebraska; and Detroit, Michigan. In 1931 he became executive secretary of the NAACP.

In August 1946 White helped to create the National Emergency Committee Against Mob Violence. The following month, he led a delegation of labor and civil rights leaders that met with U.S. president Harry S. Truman (1884–1972) to demand federal action to end the problem. Truman responded by creating the President's Committee on Civil Rights.

The NAACP's successful struggle against segregation in the armed forces was one of White's major achievements. In 1940, as a result of the NAACP's intense protests, President Franklin D. Roosevelt (1882–1945) appointed several black officers to high-ranking positions.

White then attempted to get the U.S. Senate to investigate employment discrimination and segregation in the armed services, but the effort failed. He persuaded the NAACP board to express its support for a protest march in Washington, D.C., in demand for jobs for blacks in the defense industries and an end to segregation in the **military**. To avoid the protest, President Roosevelt on June 25, 1941, issued Executive Order 8802 barring discrimination in the defense industries and creating the Fair

Employment Practices Committee. That was the first time a U.S. president acted to end racial discrimination, and the date marked the launching of the **Civil Rights movement.**

In 1945 White represented the NAACP as a consultant to the American delegation at the founding of the United Nations in San Francisco. He urged that the United Nations recognize equality of the races—that it adopt a bill of rights for all people.

During White's time as executive secretary, the NAACP helped win the right to vote for blacks in the South; opposed devices used to discriminate against blacks at the polls; helped to equalize teachers' salaries in the South; and helped end segregation in colleges and universities. Another accomplishment of the NAACP during White's term included playing a large part in the landmark U.S. Supreme Court decision *Brown v. Board of Education of Topeka, Kansas* (1954), which overturned the "separate but equal" doctrine as it applied to public schools.

White wrote *Rope and Faggot: A Biography of Judge Lynch* (1929), a complete study of lynchings; *A Man Called White* (1948), his autobiography; *A Rising Wind* (1945), and other books. White's book about civil rights progress, *How Far the Promised Land?* was published shortly after his death in 1955.

Wideman, John Edgar

NOVELIST
June 14, 1941–

John Edgar Wideman spent much of his early life in Shadyside, an upper-middle-class area of Pittsburgh, Pennsylvania. In 1960 he received a scholarship to the University of Pennsylvania. He was selected to Phi Beta Kappa, a prestigious honor society for high academic achievers, in 1963. Upon graduation, Wideman became only the second African American to be awarded a Rhodes Scholarship, an honor that allowed him to study for three years at Oxford University in England, where he earned a degree in eighteenth-century literature.

After returning to the United States in 1966 and attending the Creative Writing Workshop at the University of Iowa, Wideman taught at the University of Pennsylvania. In 1967 he published his first novel. After publishing a third novel in 1973, Wideman began to be recognized as an author of importance.

In 1975 Wideman left Philadelphia to teach at the University of Wyoming in Laramie. Six years later, he published two books. In 1984 Wideman won the 1984 P.E.N./Faulkner Award, winning over several more established writers.

Wideman was drawn into nonfiction after his brother was convicted of armed robbery and sentenced to life imprisonment. *Brothers and Keepers* (1984) relates the paradoxical circumstances of two brothers: one a successful college professor and author, the other a drug addict.

John Wideman: Selected Works

A Glance Away
(novel, 1967)

Hurry Home
(novel, 1969)

The Lynchers
(novel, 1973)

Damballah
(short story collection, 1981)

Hiding Place
(novel, 1981)

Reuben
(novel, 1987)

Fever
(short story collection, 1989)

Philadelphia Fire
(novel, 1990)

The Stories of John Edgar Wideman
(short story collection, 1992)

Fatheralong: A Meditation on Fathers and Sons
(nonfiction, 1995)

In 1986, after seeing his son, Jake, tried and convicted for the murder of a camping companion, Wideman moved back East to teach at the University of Massachusetts. In the 1990s he continued to publish stories and novels that blended fiction with historical events. Works such as *The Cattle Killing* (1996) portray a violent urban environment and its harsh impact on the African-American community.

Wilberforce University

Founded: Wilberforce University was founded in 1856 by the Methodist Episcopal Church as a school for educating African Americans. It was named for British abolitionist William Wilberforce.

History Highlights:

- 1856: Wilberforce University is established on the site of Tarawa Springs, a former summer resort in Greene County, Ohio. It is run by both the Methodist Episcopal Church and the **African Methodist Episcopal (AME) Church.** An AME school, the Union Seminary, is located in nearby Columbus.

- 1863: Wilberforce and Union Seminary are forced to close because of the Civil War. The AME Church purchases Wilberforce, sells Union Seminary's property, and combines the two institutions. AME Bishop Daniel Payne serves as the first president; he is the first African-American college president in the United States.

- 1867: Several departments are added to the college, including a science department and one in classical studies.

- 1887: Wilberforce begins to receive state funding when a normal and industrial college is opened on its campus. This makes Wilberforce both a private college and a publicly funded school.

- 1893: African-American leader **Hallie Quinn Brown** joins the faculty and remains as a teacher for many years. The university library is named in her honor.

- 1922: Wilberforce introduces its four-year college degree program and is fully accredited in 1943.

- 1947: The normal and industrial department separates from Wilberforce and becomes Wilberforce State College. It is later renamed Central State University and remains a predominantly black school. With the separation comes the removal of state support, which causes financial difficulties.

- 1967: Construction begins on a new campus, located a quarter mile from the old campus.

- 1982: The old campus is sold to the state of Ohio and becomes the location for the National Museum of Afro-American History and Culture Center.

Location: Wilberforce, Ohio

Known For: Wilberforce is the first university owned and operated by African Americans.

Religious Affiliation: African Methodist Episcopal Church

Number of Students (1999–2000): 756

Grade Average of Incoming Freshman: 2.0

Admission Requirements: SAT or ACT scores; four years of English, two years of math, two years of science, one year of social studies, one year of history; interview.

Mailing Address:
Wilberforce University
Office of Admission
1055 N. Bickett Rd.
Wilberforce, OH 45384

Telephone: (800) 367-8568

E-mail: admissions@shorter.wilberforce.edu

URL: http://www.wilberforce.edu

Campus: Wilberforce's 125-acre campus is located eighteen miles from Dayton, Ohio. It includes the Communications Building and the Rembert E. Stokes Learning Resources Center. The library contains over 60,000 documents and houses African Methodist Church archives.

Special Programs: Combined science and engineering program with University of Dayon; CLIMB (Credentials for Leadership in Management and Business), an evening program for adults.

Extracurricular Activities: Student government, student newspaper, the *Mirror*; radio station; four sororities and four fraternities; organizations, including honor societies, National Association of Black Accountants, and a gospel chorus; athletics (men's basketball, cheerleading, cross-country, track-and-field; women's basketball, cheerleading, cross-country, track-and-field).

Wilkens, Leonard Ralph "Lenny"

BASKETBALL PLAYER, COACH
October 28, 1937–

A member of the Professional **Basketball** Hall of Fame, Leonard Randolph "Lenny" Wilkens has enjoyed a long career in the sport. His father died when the boy was just five. Raised by his Irish-American mother, Wilkens mostly attended Catholic schools during his youth.

He earned a basketball scholarship to Providence College, Rhode Island. His NCAA (National Collegiate Athletic Association) play brought him to the attention of professional teams. A first-round draft pick of the St. Louis Hawks, Wilkens began his pro basketball career in 1960. After playing with St. Louis for eight years, he played for the Seattle Supersonics (1968–72), the Cleveland Cavaliers (1972–73), and the Portland Trailblazers

(1974–75). For Seattle and Portland, Wilkens worked as a player-coach, making him only the second African American to coach in the NBA. He was named a National Basketball Association (NBA) all-star nine times during his career has a player.

After finishing his last season in 1975, he stayed with the Trailblazers as head coach. He joined the Supersonics organization the next season, becoming head coach in 1977. Wilkens led the team to an NBA championship in 1979. He stayed with the Sonics until 1986, when he left his job there as general manager to become head coach for Cleveland. After seven seasons with the Cavaliers, he resigned the post and was soon named head coach of the Atlanta Hawks. In the 1994–95 season, he became the all-time most winning coach in the NBA. He announced he was leaving the Hawks in April 2000, and two months later joined the Toronto Raptors as head coach. (*See also* **Basketball**)

Wilkins, Roy Ottoway

CIVIL RIGHTS LEADER, JOURNALIST
August 30, 1901–September 8, 1981

Widely regarded as "Mr. Civil Rights," Roy Wilkins was raised by an aunt and uncle, his legal guardians, in St. Paul, Minnesota. (His mother died when the boy was four, and his father was mostly absent from the family.)

Graduating from University of Minnesota in 1923, Wilkins soon became editor of the *Kansas City Call*, a black newspaper in Missouri. In that role, he was a leader in the fight against Jim Crow, laws and policies that discriminated against African Americans. Already associated with the **National Association for the Advancement of Colored People** (NAACP), in 1930 he became actively involved in the organization's struggle to prevent a self-proclaimed racist from being named to the Supreme Court. Successfully working with the NAACP leadership to block the nomination, Wilkins proved that he could help bring about change. He also forged a friendship with the NAACP head, **Walter White** (1893–1955).

In 1931 Wilkins joined the NAACP's national staff in New York. As assistant secretary, he worked to help overturn the accepted norms of segregation and discrimination—and to fully integrate blacks into American society. When scholar and writer **W. E. B. Du Bois** (1868–1963) argued with NAACP leadership and left the organization in 1934, Wilkins replaced him as editor of the influential magazine, *The Crisis*.

When Walter White died in 1955, Wilkins, who by now had a long and distinguished career with the NAACP, succeeded him as executive secretary (the organization's leader). He rallied the group's nationwide membership of about four hundred thousand people to support the civil rights movement then being led by Dr. **Martin Luther King Jr.** (1929–1968) and James Farmer (1920–).

A powerful and yet practical leader, Wilkins met with many of the nation's presidents, from Franklin D. Roosevelt (1882–1945; president, 1933–45) to Jimmy Carter (1924–; president, 1977–81). He also befriended

Roy Wilkins (left) seated with President Lyndon B. Johnson as he signs the Civil Rights Bill (Corbis Corporation. Reproduced by permission)

President Lyndon B. Johnson (1908–1973; president, 1963–69), whose administration launched many social and economic programs that benefited the African-American community. A vocal critic of Black Power, Wilkins warned that the separatist movement would result in violence and "black death."

In failing health, Wilkins retired from the NAACP in 1976. During his time with the organization, his work witnessed the passage of landmark laws including the Civil Rights Acts of 1957 and 1964, the Voting Rights Act of 1965, and the Fair Housing Act of 1968. (*See also* **Civil Rights Movement**.)

Williams, John Alfred

JOURNALIST, EDUCATOR
1925–

Writer John Alfred Williams was raised in New York. After service in the U.S. Navy in **World War II** (1939–45), he returned to Syracuse, New York, married, and fathered two sons. When his marriage ended in 1952, he turned to writing. He also began a series of jobs in public relations, radio and television, and publishing. In the late 1950s and early 1960s he traveled the world as a correspondent for several magazines and completed two novels.

The diverse characters and plots of Williams's many novels serve to correct history and analyze American life from a black perspective. His characters have the courage to battle their weaknesses as human beings as well as their ambiguous status as blacks in a racist society.

Williams's earlier novels balanced optimism with racial struggle. In *The Angry Ones* (1960) he established major themes: guilt, racial equity, institutionalized racism, black male-black female tensions, blacks in the military, and interracial sex. His novels that followed in the late 1960s and early 1970s presented a bleaker picture of racial issues in a chaotic world. Williams's

John Williams: Selected Works

The Man Who Cried I Am
(1967)

Mothersill and the Foxes
(1975)

In the Junior Bachelor Society
(1976)

!Click Song
(1982)

Jacob's Ladder
(1987)

The King God Didn't Save
(nonfiction, 1970)

If I Stop I'll Die: The Comedy and Tragedy of Richard Pryor
(nonfiction, 1991)

later novels focused more on black unity and suggested hope. By the late 1980s, the author was blending all of the themes of previous works, including hope, despair, betrayal, and optimism. Williams continues to write about the African-American experience, and his work includes fiction and nonfiction writing.

MARY LOU WILLIAMS'S RELIGIOUS MUSIC

During the mid-1950s, jazz pianist Mary Lou Williams (1910–1981) converted from the Baptist faith to Roman Catholicism. She was inspired to write several large-scale works of religious music. One composition, titled *Mary Lou's Mass* (1969) was commissioned by the Vatican (the seat of the Roman Catholic faith). An accompanying dance was created by black choreographer Alvin Ailey (1931–1989).

Williams, Mary Lou

JAZZ PIANIST, ARRANGER
May 8, 1910–May 28, 1981

Called the "Lady who Swings the Band," Mary Lou Williams is considered one of the most important female musicians in jazz history. Born Mary Elfrieda Scruggs, she was raised in Pittsburgh, Pennsylvania. She learned to play piano by ear, performing in public at age six. While in high school, she played in black vaudeville orchestras (vaudeville was a popular variety show).

At sixteen she married saxophonist John Williams (1905–). Settling in Kansas City, Missouri, the couple joined bandleader Andy Kirk's (1898–1992) Clouds of Joy orchestra in 1930. Mary Lou Williams not only played the piano, but also wrote and arranged songs for the orchestra. Her music was ahead of its time, planting the seeds for bebop (a form of modern jazz).

In the mid-1930s the Kirk band moved to New York City. There Williams also arranged songs for such notable bandleaders as **Louis Armstrong** (1901–1971), Earl "Fatha" Hines (1903–1983), and Benny Goodman (1909–1986). In 1942 she left Clouds of Joy to colead a six-piece orchestra with her second husband, trumpeter Harold "Shorty" Baker (1913–1966). After the group and the marriage broke up, Williams began working regularly under her own name. She continued arranging, including for American jazz great **Duke Ellington** (1899–1974), and she wrote songs. In 1945 she performed her *Zodiac Suite* with the New York Philharmonic orchestra.

After touring England and France for two years, Williams retired from music in 1954. But she was coaxed back on stage by fellow musician **Dizzy Gillespie** (1917–1993) in 1957. Through the 1960s, she recorded and performed regularly, including giving recitals and demonstrations on the history of jazz. From 1977 to shortly before her death she worked as an artist in residence at Duke University (North Carolina).

Mary Lou Williams (Corbis Corporation. Reproduced by permission)

Wills, Maurice Morning "Maury"

BASEBALL PLAYER
October 2, 1932–

Credited with changing the game of baseball by turning base-stealing into a fine art, Maury Wills was born and raised in Washington, D.C. Showing great athletic ability, he played all nine positions in baseball. After eight years in the minor leagues, he signed his first major league contract with the Los Angeles Dodgers in June 1959.

Wills combined speed with an ability to read a pitcher's movements to reinvent base-stealing. In September 1962, he stole his ninety-seventh base of the season, breaking baseball legend Ty Cobb's (1886–1961) forty-seven year-old record. Wills tallied a total of 104 stolen bases by the time the season ended. He was named the National League's MVP (most valuable player) and an All-Star, the first of five players (as of 2000) to earn the distinctions in a single season. He led the league in stolen bases six consecutive times (1960–65).

Leaving the Dodgers after the 1966 season, Wills played for the Pittsburgh Pirates and the Montreal Expos. But he returned to Los Angeles in 1969, remaining with the Dodgers through 1972, when he ended his fifteen-year career in the major leagues.

After working as a commentator, winter league manager, and instructor, Wills became manager of the Seattle Mariners in 1980. He was only the third African-American manager in baseball's major leagues. Though he left after one season, he later returned to the sport as a base-running coach. Having battled his own addictions, Wills is a powerful speaker against drugs. (*See also* **Baseball**)

Wilson, August

PLAYWRIGHT
April 27, 1945–

Among the most celebrated American writers working today, August Wilson tells the history and stories of African-American life in his plays. Born Frederick August Kittel, he was raised in a poor, integrated neighborhood in Pittsburgh, Pennsylvania. His German-American father was mostly absent from the family's life. His mother supported her six children with public assistance and by working as a janitor. (In the 1970s August adopted his mother's maiden name, Wilson, as his last name.)

Wilson was in the ninth grade when he dropped out of school. He worked at odd jobs and frequently visited the neighborhood library, where he discovered the works of great black writers such as **Ralph Ellison** (1914–1994) and **Langston Hughes** (1902–1967). He also read books by other great writers, including Welsh poet Dylan Thomas (1914–1953), and he began writing.

In 1968 Wilson co-founded Black Horizons Theatre in Pittsburgh and penned short plays for the theater. In 1977 he moved to St. Paul, Minnesota,

SETTING THE RECORD STRAIGHT

Many news articles about playwright August Wilson mention that he dropped out of school. But not many tell the rest of the story.

In the ninth grade Wilson wrote a twenty-page paper about French emperor Napoleon I (1769–1821). Wishing to give the assignment his best, he rented a typewriter and paid his sister to type the paper for him. When his teacher graded it, he was willing to reward Wilson with an A+ but insisted that the student prove he actually wrote it. Refusing to do so, Wilson collected his paper (which the teacher gave a failing mark) and left school.

Though Wilson did not return to classes he was determined to continue learning. He read everything he could get his hands on at the local library.

A gifted man of letters, Wilson has taught classes at some of the finest schools in the United States, including Dartmouth College in Hanover, New Hampshire.

where his first full-length play, *Jitney*, was produced. It was *Ma Rainey's Black Bottom* (1983) that gained him national attention. Critically and popularly acclaimed, the play chronicles the life of famous blues singer **Gertrude "Ma" Rainey** (1886–1939).

Wilson's next play was *Fences* (1985). It tells the story of a Pittsburgh garbage collector who was a star baseball player in the Negro leagues before player **Jackie Robinson** (1919–1972) broke the color line. *Fences* won a Pulitzer Prize in drama and a Tony Award for best play of the year. (In 2000 Wilson was working on the screenplay for the movie.)

In *The Piano Lesson* (1987), a black brother and sister struggle over a family heirloom, a piano built by their grandfather, a slave. Produced on Broadway (New York's premier theater district) in 1990, it won numerous awards, including a Pulitzer Prize—Wilson's second.

Blessed with a rich imagination, Wilson says he sees stories all around him, and he encourages students to do the same. History is central to his creativity. *Fences* and *The Piano Lesson* are part of a series of ten plays that represent African-American life in the twentieth century (each play is set in a different decade). In 1999 he added *King Hedley II* to the series; it was first performed in Pittsburgh. (*See also* **Drama**)

Wilson, Harriet E. Adams

AUTHOR
c. 1830–1870

Harriet E. Wilson is believed to have written the first novel by an African American published in the United States: *Our Nig; or, Sketches from the Life of a Free Black, in a Two-Story White House, North. Showing That Slavery's Shadows Fall Even There* (1859). The author's name on the book was simply

Playwright August Wilson (left) with Lloyd Richards (AP/Wide World Photos. Reproduced by permission)

"Our Nig"; the book describes the life of an indentured servant (one bound by contract into someone's service, often in payment of travel expenses and food and lodging, for example, for transportation from England to the New World) and condemns Northern whites for the kind of racial prejudice and cruelty more commonly associated with **slavery** and the South. Three letters, presumably written by friends of the novelist, are added to the end of the novel, and it is because of these that the novel has been considered partly autobiographical (about events in the life of the author).

Little is known about Harriet Wilson, though the letters and the end of *Our Nig* provide details of the author's life between 1850 and 1860, when she lived in Massachusetts and worked as a weaver of straw hats. After marrying, giving birth to a son, and being abandoned by her husband, Harriet was rescued by a couple who took in and cared for her and her son. When her health failed, Wilson began writing her novel in an effort to make money: Little is known of Wilson's life after the publication of *Our Nig*. Her son died in New Hampshire in February 1860, and Harriet Wilson died some time between the death of her son and January 1870.

For more than one hundred years, *Our Nig* was barely noticed. In 1983, however, the critic Henry Louis Gates Jr. raised interest in Wilson and the novel by arranging to have the book reprinted.

Wilson, Jackie

RHYTHM-AND-BLUES SINGER
June 9, 1934–January 21, 1984

Singer Jackie Wilson grew up in Detroit, Michigan, during the 1930s and 1940s. As a teenager, he was more interested in boxing than singing, but his mother persuaded him to try a career in music. His clear tenor voice and his friendship with music producer Berry Gordy helped make him a popular local performer and eventually one of the top pop artists of the 1950s.

Wilson began singing as part of several **rhythm-and-blues (R&B)** vocal groups. He made his first recordings as "Sonny" Wilson but was not well-known until 1953, when he joined Billy Ward and his Dominoes. In 1956 he went solo, and the next year he recorded his first hit, "Reet Petite." Wilson became popular with both black and white audiences.

Wilson's promoters tried to pattern him after popular white singer Bing Crosby, resulting in records such as "Night" (1960) and "Alone at Last" (1960), songs based on classical compositions. His more conventional hits from this period include "Doggin' Around" and "A Woman, A Lover, A Friend."

Wilson's ballads and dance numbers are now classics of rock and roll, but originally he was equally famous for his live performances. His sexy dance moves and acrobatic leaps earned him the nickname "Mr. Excitement."

In 1961 Wilson was shot and injured by a fan in New York. Although he recovered, his career began a slow decline. In the 1960s he produced such hits as "Baby Workout" (1963) and "Higher and Higher" (1966), but they never equaled his early successes. Wilson's last hit came in 1968, after which he continued as a popular concert artist. In 1975 Wilson suffered a heart attack and went into a long coma. Eight years later, he died at the age of forty-nine. Wilson was inducted into the Rock and Roll Hall of Fame in 1987.

Oprah Winfrey: Selected Films and Television Movies

The Color Purple
(actress, 1985)

Native Son
(actress, 1986)

The Women of Brewster Place
(ABC-TV, actress and producer, 1989)

Brewster Place
(ABC-TV miniseries, actress and producer, 1990)

There Are No Children Here
(ABC-TV, actress and producer, 1993)

Before Women Had Wings
(ABC-TV, actress and producer, 1997)

Beloved
(actress and producer, 1998)

The Wedding
(ABC-TV, producer, 1998)

David and Lisa
(ABC-TV, producer, 1998)

Winfrey, Oprah Gail

TALK SHOW HOST, ACTRESS, PRODUCER
January 29, 1954–

Oprah Winfrey is a one-woman dynamo who, since the 1980s, has been involved in nearly all areas of the media. As actress, **television** and **film** producer, and host of her daytime television talk show, *The Oprah Winfrey Show*, her influence is far-reaching. Her impact is especially evident by the popularity of Oprah's Book Club, which she started in September 1996 to promote literacy and self-improvement. Oprah's recommended books immediately become best-sellers.

Winfrey was born in Kosciusko, Mississippi, to Vernita Lee and Vernon Winfrey. She lived first with her grandmother, then with her mother in Milwaukee, Wisconsin. It was in Milwaukee that her gift for public speaking was sparked at an early age when she would recite poetry at social teas. During her teen years, Winfrey began to misbehave and was sent to live with her father, a strict disciplinarian, in Nashville, Tennessee. At sixteen she won a speaking contest that awarded her a scholarship to Tennessee State University in Nashville. As a freshman in college she won the Miss Black Tennessee pageant. In 1977 she began her career as a talk-show host in Baltimore, Maryland.

Ophrah Winfrey in action during a taping of her television talk show (AP/Wide World Photos. Reproduced by permission)

In 1984 Winfrey took over as host of *A.M. Chicago*, quickly boosting the show's ratings. In 1986 the show was renamed *The Oprah Winfrey Show*. By 1993 it was seen in ninety-nine percent of U.S. television markets and in sixty-four countries. Since 1986, it has won several Emmy Awards both for best talk show and best talk-show host. In 1986 Winfrey also created her own company, Harpo ("Oprah" spelled backward) Productions.

Winfrey has received numerous awards for her work. She was nominated for an Oscar for her role as Sofia in the 1985 film *The Color Purple* and was inducted into the Television Hall of Fame in 1994. In 1999 Winfrey was listed in *Forbes* magazine as the wealthiest woman entertainer in the United States, based on her earnings of about $725 million. Winfrey is committed to charity and has donated much of her earnings to a variety of causes.

Always seeking new opportunities, in 2000 Winfrey co-founded Oxygen, a television-Internet network for women. In April 2000 she launched her own magazine, *O*.

Wisconsin

First African-American Settlers: In the 1790s the first black families settled in Wisconsin to participate in the fur trade.

Slave Population: The exploitation of lead ores in the southwestern corner of Wisconsin attracted blacks to the territory in the 1820s and 1830s. Some of them were slaves owned by miners from the South and by military officers.

Free Black Population: Some **free blacks** arrived in the state as members of three New York American Indian tribes that had given refuge to escaped Rhode Island slaves. Achievement of statehood in 1848 brought further migration of blacks from both the East and the South to work in service occupations and in industries.

Reconstruction: Until 1910 fewer than 3,000 blacks lived in Wisconsin, accounting for less than 1 percent of the population. Industrial needs in Milwaukee and the state's manufacturing centers during both world wars led to significant recruitment of southern blacks; in 1930 there were 10,739 African Americans residing in the state.

The Great Depression: By 1940 the African-American population in Wisconsin had risen to 12,158 and had more than doubled by 1950 (28,182). Opportunities for housing, jobs, and education continued to be limited for blacks living in Wisconsin's cities; blacks lived principally in isolated neighborhoods of old and substandard housing until the 1960s.

Civil Rights Movement: The 1960s saw legislation and court rulings in favor of desegregation and open housing. A 1967 march lasted two hundred days and was successful in creating an open-housing ordinance. A lawsuit filed in 1965 to fight public school segregation did not reach a successful settlement until 1979.

Current African-American Population: According to U.S. Census Bureau estimates, the total black population in Wisconsin was 290,585 (5 percent of the state population) as of July 1, 1998.

Key Figures: Baseball star **Henry Louis "Hank" Aaron** (1934–); **Oprah Winfrey** (1954–), talk-show host and actress.

(SEE ALSO **SUFFRAGE**; **LYNCHING**.)

Wolfe, George C.

PLAYWRIGHT, DIRECTOR
September 23, 1954–

One of the most important figures in American theater today, George Wolfe was born into a middle-class family in Frankfort, Kentucky. In his youth he read avidly and directed school plays. In 1977 he earned his bachelor's degree in theater from Pomona College in Claremont, California. He continued his studies at New York University, graduating in 1979 with a master's degree in theater.

Wolfe's 1985 musical *Paradise*, about the colonization of America, was produced Off-Broadway. (A select few plays are first performed in New York City's theater district, called Broadway, but many more are premiered in other theaters around the city, or Off-Broadway.) He first met with wide recognition in 1986 with the New York Public Theater production of his play *The Colored Museum*, which explores the stereotypes of African-American culture.

In 1990 Wolfe wrote *Spunk*, a play based on three short stories by African-American writer **Zora Neale Hurston** (c. 1891–1960). The work was widely praised and won Wolfe an Obie (Off-Broadway theater) Award. At the same time he wrote the book for and directed the premiere of *Jelly's Last Jam*, a musical based on the life and music of the great jazz composer **Ferdinand "Jelly Roll" Morton** (1890–1941). Choreographed by and starring **Gregory Hines** (1946–), the play moved to Broadway in 1992 and received three Tony Awards (given for excellence in American theater).

Among Wolfe's biggest sensations was the 1996 dance extravaganza *Bring in 'Da Noise, Bring in 'Da Funk*. Created with phenomenal tap dancer Savion Glover (1974–), the play ran for three years on Broadway and toured nationally, winning four Tony Awards.

In 1993 Wolfe became artistic director of the New York Shakespeare Festival Public Theater (NYSF/PT). In April 2000 *The Wild Party*, an NYSF/PT production based on the book cowritten by Wolfe and Michael John LaChiusa, made its first appearance on Broadway. Set in "jazz-mad" Manhattan, New York, in the 1920s, the musical was directed by Wolfe.

Wonder, Stevie

SINGER, SONGWRITER
May 13, 1950–

Born Stevland Morris on May 13, 1950, in Saginaw, Michigan, Stevie Wonder has been blind since birth. He grew up in Detroit, and by the age

Pop music legend Stevie Wonder (AP/Wide World Photos. Reproduced by permission)

of nine had mastered the harmonica, drums, bongos, and piano. His youthful talent as a musician and composer was discovered by record producer Berry Gordy. Gordy signed him to Hitsville, U.S.A. (later known as Motown Records) in 1961. He was soon dubbed "Little Stevie Wonder" and in 1963 achieved the first of many number one pop singles with "Fingertips—Pt. 2," a live recording featuring harmonica solos. A 1963 album, *Twelve-Year-Old Genius*, was Motown's first number one pop album. From 1964 to 1971 Wonder had several top twenty hits, including "Uptight (Everything's Alright)" (1966), "Mon Cherie Amour" (1969), and "Signed, Sealed, Delivered I'm Yours" (1970).

Wonder's humanitarian interests have charged his music since the early 1970s. This is demonstrated in "Living for the City" (1973), a ghetto-dweller's story; "Happy Birthday" (1980), the anthem for a nationwide appeal to honor the Rev. Dr. **Martin Luther King Jr.**'s birthday as a national holiday; "Don't Drive Drunk" (1984); and "It's Wrong" (1985), a critique of South African apartheid (strict separation of blacks and whites). He has also supported such causes as the elimination of world hunger, AIDS research, and cancer research.

Wonder has been the recipient of more than sixteen Grammys, eighteen gold records, five platinum records, and five gold albums. He was inducted into the Songwriters Hall of Fame in 1982. Wonder continues to record, compose, and perform. He released the album *Natural Wonder* in 1995 and *At the Close of the Century* in 1999.

Woodruff, Hale Aspacio

PAINTER, TEACHER
August 26, 1900–September 10, 1980

A major force in the development of African-American art, Hale Woodruff is known for painting realistic murals (large paintings that cover a wall or ceiling) that comment on society (see **Muralists**). Inspired by his study in 1936 with Mexican muralist Diego Rivera (1886–1957), Woodruff painted several murals, including his 1939 depiction of the 1834 mutiny aboard the slave ship *Amistad*.

Raised in Nashville, Tennessee, Woodruff moved to Indianapolis, Indiana, in 1920. He studied at the John Herron Art Institute. It was there he first saw African art, reproduced in one of the earliest books on the subject. He also worked part-time as a political cartoonist for the black newspaper the *Indiana Ledger*.

From 1927 to 1931 Woodruff lived in France, studying with African-American painter **Henry O. Tanner** (1859–1937) and other master artists. He collected his first objects of African art, which he found in Paris flea markets.

Returning to the United States, Woodruff established the art department at **Atlanta University** in Atlanta, Georgia. He taught painting, drawing, and printmaking. He also helped build a national African-American artistic community by organizing an annual art show for black artists at Atlanta University. Receiving a fellowship (grant) in 1943, Woodruff moved

to New York, where he continued his studies for two years. In 1945 he became a professor at New York University. He was associated with the university until 1970.

Woodruff painted in several different styles. Early in his career he incorporated elements from the art he studied, such as the work of French impressionist Paul Cezanne (1839–1906). In Atlanta he shifted to his own brand of American regionalism, painting the black people and life in the South. After he moved to New York, Woodruff began including elements of African art, and his work became more abstract (representing an idea or figure without appearing realistic). (*See also* **Amistad Mutiny**.)

Woods, Eldrick "Tiger"

GOLFER
December 30, 1975–

Likable, talented, and driven, Tiger Woods is a golf sensation. Born and raised in Cypress, California, he picked up his first golf club by age two. In 1991, when he was fifteen years old, he won his first U.S. Junior Championship. He earned the title two more times before entering California's Stanford University, where he studied accounting. He also continued to play golf, at the college and amateur levels, for the next two years.

After winning an unprecedented three straight U.S. Amateur Championships, Woods turned professional in August 1996. (A serious student, he had planned to complete his studies at Stanford, but with his golf career on the rise, the athlete felt compelled to pursue it fully.) He stunned the golf world by winning two of eight Professional Golfers' Association (PGA) tour events that year. The PGA named him Rookie of the Year.

In 1997 Woods won the prestigious Masters Tournament at Augusta, Georgia. At twenty-one, he was the youngest Masters champion in history. He was also the first African American to claim a major professional golf championship. The sweet victory was just the beginning of Woods's sweep of the four major golf tournaments.

In 1999 Woods won the PGA Tournament. In 2000 he took first place at the U.S. Open. A month later, at historic St. Andrews Golf Course in Scotland (where the game of golf began), he tasted victory again, winning the British Open. The four wins—Masters, PGA, U.S. Open, and British Open—added up to a career "grand slam." Only four other players in history have won golf's grand slam. Woods, at age twenty-four, was not only the youngest to do so, but he also did it in the shortest time. It took him only three years. (The other players, including golf legend Jack Nicklaus [1940–], took between four and thirteen years to sweep the majors.)

Unquestionably a great athlete, Tiger Woods (who is of African-American, Chinese, Cherokee Indian, and Thai descent) has already secured his place in golf history. (*See also* **Golf**)

The dominant golfer of the late twentieth and twenty-first century, Tiger Woods (AP/Wide World Photos. Reproduced by permission)

Woods, Granville T.

INVENTOR
April 23, 1856–January 18, 1910

During his career the brilliant Granville Woods received thirty-five patents, official registrations given to the person who creates (and, therefore, has all rights to) something new. Born in Columbus, Ohio, Woods began working when he was just ten years old. He was an apprentice in a machine shop that repaired railroad equipment. Later he worked as an engineer for the Danniville Southern railroad.

By 1884 Woods had opened his own machine shop in Cincinnati, Ohio. That same year he secured his first patents. One was for a steam-boiler furnace that required less fuel than other models. The other was for a telephone transmitter. Since the telephone had just been invented in 1875 and was still

MAKING TRAIN TRAVEL SAFER

During the late 1880s, Granville Woods (1856–1910) developed numerous inventions that increased railroad safety. For example, in 1887 he patented the Induction Telegraph System, which improved communication between moving trains. His other innovations that helped reduce train collisions included an electromagnetic break and a regulator for electric motors. Since Woods first job was in the railroad industry, it is not surprising that he used his great mechanical mind to make the railways safer. (*See also* **Inventors and Inventions**)

being developed, Woods was able to sell his transmitter to American Bell Telephone Company in Boston. The invention produced clearer voice signals than other transmitters.

Sometimes called the "black Edison," since, like inventor Thomas Edison (1847–1931), he was always busy working out a new idea, Woods continued working on his inventions until 1907, just three years before his death. Sadly, he spent his last years fighting expensive legal battles to protect his patents.

Woods, Tiger. *See* Woods, Eldrick

Woodson, Carter Godwin

HISTORIAN, EDUCATOR
December 19, 1875–April 3, 1950

Historian Carter Woodson was born in New Canton, Virginia. He was the first and only African American born of slave parents to earn a Ph.D. in history. As a boy, Woodson worked on the family farm and as a hired farmworker. Later, he worked as a coal miner in West Virginia.

In 1895, at the age of twenty, Woodson enrolled at Frederick Douglass High School. He completed four years of course work in two years and graduated in 1897. Woodson then enrolled at **Berea College** in Kentucky, a school founded by abolitionists in the 1850s. He graduated in 1903, just a year before Kentucky passed the infamous "Day Law," which prohibited interracial education.

From 1903 to 1907 Woodson was a teacher in the Philippine Islands in eastern Asia. He then enrolled at the University of Chicago (Illinois), where he earned both a bachelor's and a master's degree in European history. In 1912 he received a Ph.D. from Harvard University (Cambridge, Massachusetts). Woodson later taught in the Washington, D.C., public schools; at **Howard University** in D.C.; and at the West Virginia Collegiate Institute.

Woodson devoted his life to the pursuit of truth about African and African-American history. In 1915 he founded the Association for the Study of Negro Life and History. He later founded the *Journal of Negro History*, the *Negro History Bulletin*, and the Associated Publishers. He launched the annual celebration of Negro History Week in February 1926.

With the publication of his first book in 1915, Woodson began a remarkable writing career as a scholar of African-American history. By 1947, when the ninth edition of his textbook *The Negro in Our History* appeared, Woodson had published four academic books, five textbooks, five edited collections of source materials, and thirteen articles, as well as five sociological studies written with other authors.

Within this body of work, Woodson's subject range was very broad. He was among the first to study **slavery** from the slaves' point of view and to compare slavery in the United States and Latin America. Woodson also studied African cultural influences on African-American life.

One of Woodson's major goals was to correct the racism promoted in the work of white scholars. He used new sources and methods to show blacks as major actors in American history, and not as just victims of white oppression and racism. Through this work, Woodson made an immeasurable contribution to the advancement of black history.

World War I

World War I (1914–18) began as a European conflict. When the United States entered the war in 1917, African Americans viewed it as a chance to prove their patriotism and convince whites to grant them full civil rights. Eventually, more than 400,000 blacks served in segregated (racially separated) groups in the U.S. armed forces, mainly as workers.

African-American leaders called on blacks to forget their criticisms of the U.S. government and focus on the fight for democracy. However, even though African Americans were willing to look beyond discrimination, the armed forces were not. The highest-ranking African-American army officer, Lt. Col. Charles Young (1864–1922), was forced into retirement before U.S. troops reported for war. Many African Americans believed he was forced to retire out of fear that white officers and enlisted men would eventually have to serve under his command.

Despite the outstanding record of past African-American regiments, the army did not believe African Americans should participate in combat. Instead, they recruited blacks to serve as laborers. About 89 percent of all blacks who participated in World War I served in units whose work included building training camps and loading supplies.

African-American soldiers who were trained for combat were trained in segregated camps. After their training they served in segregated combat units, usually under the command of white officers. At first the army planned to create a single black division, the 92nd, which was led by a white officer, Charles Ballou. Like many other officers, Ballou did not think

African-American officers were good leaders or that his black soldiers would perform well in combat. His division, as a result, received little training or support and so did not do well in combat. The poor performance of the 92nd Division reinforced white stereotypes (preconceived notions about a group of people) that black soldiers were unsuited for war. The experience also reinforced many African Americans' belief that whites would not allow them to succeed.

The experience of another African-American division, the 93rd, was different. The division was turned over to French leadership almost as soon as it arrived in France, even though American generals rarely allowed white troops to be commanded by foreign officers. The 93rd Division discovered that the French were much more willing to treat African-American soldiers and officers as equals. As a result, the first two African-American war heroes, Needham Roberts and Henry Johnson, came from this division.

African-American women also tried to join the war effort. Adah Thoms (c. 1870–1943), head of the Colored Nurses Association, volunteered her organization to become part of the Nursing Corps. For a long time the army refused. Not until late in the war did the **military** allow the black nurses to serve at two camps in the United States. However, none were permitted to go to Europe.

World War II

World War II (1939–45) was an armed conflict that involved many nations and saw battles all over the world. It began when Germany invaded Poland and England stepped in to try to stop Germany from taking over other countries. The United States sided with England, and although it did not begin active fighting until 1941, the United States was involved in the war in other ways. The United States made guns, airplanes, ships, and other supplies for the war effort.

The Second World War enabled African Americans to enhance their status in both civilian life and **military** service. African-American men and women profited from the manpower crisis, whether in the armed forces or the civilian workforce.

Changes at Home

In 1941 a law was passed making it illegal for companies making products for the war effort to refuse to hire blacks. The law also required that such companies must open training programs to minorities. The law further established a committee to investigate violations.

A million or more blacks found wartime employment, either replacing whites who entered the armed forces or occupying newly created jobs. The wartime job situation intensified the competition for scarce housing and contributed to racial friction and violence in many cities.

Changes in the Military

When World War II began, the U.S. armed forces had a housing policy that segregated black servicemen from white. In 1940 President Franklin D. Roosevelt (1882–1945) and representatives of the War Department and the U.S. Navy met with African-American leaders to talk about better treatment of blacks in the military. This meeting produced a policy of giving black servicemen fair treatment and greater opportunity but still segregated them from white servicemen.

Progress in the Armed Services

In 1941 the organization of a black air squadron was announced. African-American pilots began training at **Tuskegee Institute (University)** in Alabama. The new project produced a trained fighter unit, the 99th Pursuit Squadron, manned by African-American pilots, mechanics, and even clerks. The 99th encountered unique obstacles after it entered combat over the Mediterranean Sea in 1943. The squadron lacked veterans to pass along lessons learned in years of flying. The unit also had gaps in its training. Because of racial segregation, few bases would provide overnight accommodations for black pilots, which eliminated the opportunity for long flights that developed navigating skills. Over the Mediterranean, the 99th learned as they fought. But the 99th squadron improved. By the end of the war, the black 332nd Fighter Group of four squadrons, including the 99th, was escorting bombers from airfields in Italy deep into Germany. The number of African Americans in the wartime Army Air Forces peaked at 145,000, but fewer than a thousand were pilots or members of air crews.

African Americans in the Army Ground and Service Forces

The War Department also decided to create black army divisions with black officers and enlisted men with almost every skill and level of aptitude. The number of African Americans in the army exceeded 700,000 by 1944. They helped build the Alaskan highway, load ships in the United States and unload them overseas, and drive trucks that delivered cargo from the French coast to the U.S. troops advancing toward Germany.

By the end of 1943, the army had sent two black combat units overseas. Other units continued to train, often under white officers who had very bad attitudes toward African Americans. Indifferent leadership and the hatred expressed by local inhabitants contributed to riots by black soldiers at nine military bases during 1943.

WOMEN AND THE WAR EFFORT

World War II did not open employment opportunities for African-American men only. Some 600,000 black women joined the wartime work force. Previously, opportunities for these women existed mainly in domestic or service jobs, but possibilities expanded during the war in sales, clerical occupations, and especially in light industry, where blacks of both sexes provided a ready source of unskilled labor.

Most branches of the armed services recruited women during World War II. Only the U.S. Marine Corps refused throughout the war to accept black women—its women's division remained exclusively white.

The same policy of racial segregation applied to females as to males. As a result, few of the army's almost four thousand African-American women volunteers performed duties related to their skills. The army sent overseas just one unit made up of black women, a postal battalion that served in the United Kingdom under an African-American officer, Major Charity Adams.

When the war began, the army and the navy accepted only white nurses. Eventually, the War Department began to accept black nurses. However, the Army Nurse Corps had only 476 African-American nurses, and they were assigned where they would care for black troops only. The navy, although acknowledging a shortage of five hundred nurses In 1943, admitted just four African-American women. (*See also* **Nursing**.)

In 1944 a German attack resulted in the Battle of the Bulge, where many U.S. soldiers were killed. African-American service troops already in Europe were called on to fill in the ranks—4,500 African Americans signed up to train as riflemen and serve in white rifle companies. This action integrated the battle but not the army.

African Americans in the Navy

The navy moved more slowly than the army to provide broader opportunity and better treatment for African Americans. Secretary of the Navy Frank Knox believed in segregation and remained content to accept blacks as cooks and kitchen helpers in the navy.

Knox continued this practice until 1942, when he established some new policies. As a result, 277 black volunteers could enter the navy each week and, beginning in 1942, train at a segregated camp. The navy intended to assign the African-American graduates of recruit training to advanced courses to learn specialties. Even though fewer blacks volunteered than anticipated, the navy could not easily place them in the general service and instead diverted many of them to duty as workers at naval ammunition depots. To offer carefully selected black enlisted men a chance to become officers, in 1944 the navy established a segregated officer candidate school.

When Knox died in 1944, rigid segregation perished also. James Forrestal succeeded him as secretary of the navy and directed that the serv-

ice integrate the crews of twenty-five ships at the ratio of one black sailor to ten white sailors.

The Coast Guard and the Marines

The U.S. Coast Guard included a few African Americans who manned separate rescue stations or small craft or served in a segregated stewards' branch. To broaden opportunities for African Americans, the Coast Guard manned the weather ship *Sea Cloud* with some twenty blacks in the crew. During successive cruises, the proportion increased until African Americans formed almost a third of the crew, including fifty petty officers and four officers.

In 1942 the Marine Corps began accepting African Americans for the first time since 1798. When the draft swelled the number of black marines, the Corps increased its segregated units by one defense battalion, fifty-one depot companies, and twelve ammunition companies, plus other miscellaneous detachments and a kitchen-helpers branch. In all, some 20,000 African Americans served in the wartime Marine Corps.

Wright, Jay

POET

May 25, 1934–

Jay Wright was born in Albuquerque, New Mexico, and grew up in the care of a couple to whom his father left him at age three. In his early teens Wright went to live with his father, a driver and handyman, in southern California, where Jay soon played both acoustic bass and minor league baseball. From 1954 to 1957 he served in the U.S. Army and was stationed in Germany. Wright graduated from the University of California at Berkeley in 1961 and later attended Rutgers University (New Brunswick, New Jersey).

In 1964 Wright spent a year in Mexico; he returned in 1968 for another three years, this time in the company of his wife, Lois Silber. His poems consistently return to this stay in Guadalajara and Xalapa. In 1971 Wright went to Scotland as a creative writing fellow at Dundee University. Since 1975 he has taught at Yale, the Universities of Utah, Kentucky, and North Carolina at Chapel Hill, and Dartmouth College. He received a MacArthur Fellowship in 1986.

Wright's poems seem to track an endless spiritual quest. In *The Homecoming Singer* (1971), *Elaine's Book* (1988), and *Boleros* (1991), Wright's poems describe the travels of a person to faraway lands, assemble masses of historical and mythological knowledge, and uncover forgotten links between western Europe, Africa, the Caribbean, the Americas, and Asia. Blues and jazz, as well as a number of Caribbean and Latin American song and dance forms, are important in his poetry, and he is likely to combine many different languages in any single poem. His other works include *Explications/Interpretations* (1984), *Dimensions of History* (1976), and *The Double Invention of Komo* (1980). In 1996 Wright received a fellowship for poetic achievement from the Academy of American Poets.

RICHARD WRIGHT'S *NATIVE SON*

R ichard Wright's *Native Son* is now recognized as one of the most important American novels of the twentieth century. The book tells the story of Bigger Thomas, a young black man who accidentally murders a white woman and is eventualy sentenced to death. Thomas's lawyer argues that he is not responsible for his crimes, but Thomas sees his murder and attempted cover-up as liberating, creative acts. A play based on the book was produced by the famous director, producer, and actor Orson Welles. There were two film adaptations, one a Brazilian film in which Wright himself played the part of Bigger Thomas, and *Native Son* (1986), starring Victor Love, but neither was very successful.

Wright, Richard

WRITER
September 4, 1908–November 28, 1960

Richard Wright was the first African-American novelist of international importance, famous for his violent criticism of American racism and the wretched misery and hatred it causes. He was born near Roxie, Mississippi, the son of a sharecropper and a schoolteacher who supported the family when her husband deserted her. Wright's childhood, which he later described in his classic **autobiography,** *Black Boy* (1945), was horrific. His mother was never healthy, and she became completely paralyzed by the time her son was ten years old—as a result, Wright and his family were hopelessly poor.

Wright moved to Chicago, Illinois, in 1927, and his family later joined him. Over the next several years, during the worst of the disastrous **Great Depression,** Wright supported the family through various jobs and wrote when he could find the time. In 1932 he began meeting writers and artists, mostly white, at the Communist-run John Reed Club. Wright found these people eager to showcase African Americans in their movement and became active within the Communist Party, but within a few years he began to suspect they were promoting him only because of his skin color.

In 1937, eager to find a publisher for his work, Wright moved to New York, and the following year he published a collection of short stories, *Uncle Tom's Children*. *Native Son* (1940), Wright's first published novel, called national attention to his talent, although his harsh portrayal of racism was controversial. (In fact, editors had already toned down some of the book—it was not until 1992 that the uncensored version was published.)

In 1942, Wright finally left the Communist Party, dissatisfied with its treatment of African Americans. During the war years, he worked on *Black Boy* (1945), which brought him money and international fame. Wright was invited to France by the French government in 1945, and during the trip he found himself celebrated by French intellectuals. He had married a white

Author Richard Wright (Corbis Corporation.
Reproduced by permission)

woman, Ellen Poplar, in 1941, and the couple had a daughter. He was delighted by France's apparent freedom from racial prejudice and impressed by the central role of literature and thought in French society. Wright moved to Paris permanently in 1947.

As a resident of a country that had colonized large parts of the African continent, Wright now turned his attention to anticolonial questions, eventually writing *Black Power* (1954), in which he supported the idea of Pan-Africanism (an Africa united in its independence from European domination). Over the next several years, he continued to write, lecture, and organize conferences. He died of a heart attack in Paris in November 1960. (*See also* **Black Nationalism**)

Wyoming

First African-American Settlers: The first blacks in what would become Wyoming were the fur trappers and traders James E. Beckwourth and Edward Rose in the early nineteenth century.

Reconstruction: After the **Civil War** (1861–65) many black cowboys rode herd on cattle drives through the region. During the late 1860s many African-Americans migrated to the future state of Wyoming to lay track for the Union Pacific Railroad. Wyoming became the forty-fourth state in 1890. Legislation passed in the late 1800s denied blacks the right to vote, forbade interracial marriages, and mandated segregated schools. In 1900 the total number of African Americans in the state exceeded one thousand for the first time.

The Great Depression: Following the desegregation of the military in the years following **World War II** (1939–45), black troops were stationed in the state. The black population swelled to three thousand in 1950 but returned to two thousand by 1960.

Civil Rights Movement: In 1957 Wyoming passed a civil rights law desegregating public accommodations, and in 1964 it repealed its law against interracial marriage and passed a law against employment discrimination.

Current African-American Population: According to U.S. Census Bureau estimates, the total black population in Wyoming was 4,082 (0.8 percent of the state population) as of July 1, 1998.

Yerby, Frank Garvin

NOVELIST
September 5, 1916–November 29, 1991

Author Frank Yerby was born in Georgia. After earning a master's degree in 1938, he studied education for a year at the University of Chicago while working on the Illinois Federal Writers' Project. He taught at several colleges and universities before moving to Detroit, Michigan, where he worked at an auto assembly plant. Yerby then moved Jamaica, New York, where he worked at Ranger Aircraft until 1945.

Yerby's busy and commercially successful literary career was launched in 1944 when he received the O. Henry Memorial Award for "Health Card," a short story about racial injustice. Some of Yerby's early stories, such as "The Homecoming" (1946), also dealt with social issues, but he later began publishing historical romance novels. Over the course of his career, Yerby was attacked by reviewers and academics for his lack of attention to racial issues, his overuse of white characters, and his reliance on commonplace plots. However, his thirty-two novels were immensely popular with the public, particularly in the 1940s and 1950s.

Yerby's first novel became an immediate best-seller. It sold over two million copies within a few years, was translated into numerous languages, and was made into a film. Yerby then began producing adventure novels, set in various centuries and geographical regions, at the rate of one a year.

Yerby moved to France in the early 1950s, then settled in Madrid, Spain, in 1955. He lived there the rest of his life and wrote novels. Considered by many to be Yerby's masterpiece, *The Dahomean* (1971) is his only work dealing primarily with blacks. Set in the nineteenth century, the novel traces the life of an African who rises to a position of great authority in Dahomean tribal culture, only to be sold into slavery by his own people.

Yerby was awarded an honorary doctor of letters degree by **Fisk University** (Nashville, Tennessee) in 1976 and a doctor of humane letters by Paine College (Augusta, Georgia) in 1977. His last published works were *Devilseed* (1984) and *McKenzie's Hundred* (1985). He died of heart failure in Madrid in 1991.

Young, Albert James Al

POET, NOVELIST, EDUCATOR
1939–

Al Young was raised in poverty in Ocean Springs, Mississippi, and in 1946 moved with his family to Detroit, Michigan. He attended the University of Michigan (1957-61) and the University of California at Berkeley (1961). After traveling around the country and working as a disc jockey, janitor, and musician, he settled in the San Francisco, California, area. Young was awarded a fellowship in creative writing at Stanford University for 1966-67 and taught writing at Stanford while completing *Dancing* (1969), a collection of poetry, and his first novel, *Snakes* (1970).

Young's novels are known for their use of black vernacular (everyday) speech and often concern strange or tough aspects of African-American life. His other novels include *Who Is Angelina?* (1975), *Sitting Pretty* (1976), *Ask Me Now* (1980), and *Seduction by Light* (1988), all of which deal in some way with the importance of love and the black family, the role of music in African-American life, and the power of spirituality. Young is also the author of five books of "musical memoirs," collections of essays, sketches, and critical reviews of jazz and popular music.

Recognized mainly for his fiction and musical memoirs, Young has also published several volumes of poetry as well, including *Heaven: Collected Poems, 1956–1990*. He writes regularly as a freelance journalist for such publications as the *New York Times Book Review* and *Rolling Stone* magazine.

Young, Andrew

POLITICIAN, CIVIL RIGHTS ACTIVIST
October 23, 1932–

An influential leader and politician, Andrew Young in 1972 became the first African-American U.S. representative from Georgia since 1870. He also served as a U.S. ambassador (see **Ambassadors and Diplomats**) to the United Nations and served two terms as mayor of Atlanta, Georgia.

Young grew up in a middle-class family in New Orleans, Louisiana. He attended **Howard University** in Washington, D.C., graduating in 1951. He then studied to become a minister at Hartford Theological Seminary (Connecticut). In 1955 he began preaching in Congregational churches in rural Georgia and Alabama, where he witnessed the severe poverty that shaped the lives of southern blacks. Throughout his career he has worked to put an end to poverty.

In 1957 Young was chosen by the National Council of Churches (NCC) to work for its Youth Division of Christian Education. In 1959 he moved to New York, where he continued working for the organization. He returned to Georgia in 1961, joining the **Southern Christian Leadership Conference** (SCLC), a civil rights organization headed by the Reverend Dr. **Martin Luther King Jr.** (1929–1968). Known for his common sense and moderation, Young became a trusted aide to King and rose through the ranks of the organization.

Turning his attention to politics in 1972, Young was elected to the U.S. House of Representatives. He was reelected to two more two-year terms. In 1977 President Jimmy Carter (1924–; president 1977–81) appointed Young as U.S. ambassador to the United Nations. He served in that position until 1979.

Young mounted a successful campaign for mayor of Atlanta in 1982. Reelected in 1986, he led the city government until 1990. He has remained a leading citizen of Atlanta. In 2000 he became president of the NCC, with which he was associated earlier in his career. In accepting the job, he credited the organization with "laying a wonderful foundation" for his later work in the **Civil Rights movement**, Congress, and the United Nations. Young was also a member of the board of directors of the United Nations Foundation in 2000.

Andrew Young speaking at the Democratic National Convention in 1992 (AP/Wide World Photos. Reproduced by permission)

Young, Coleman Alexander

POLITICIAN
May 18, 1919–November 29, 1997

The first black mayor of Detroit, Michigan, Coleman Young served a record five terms in office. During his twenty years as mayor, several important urban renewal projects were completed, including an elevated rail system; expansion of the civic center; and construction of office, hotel, and retail complexes.

Raised in Detroit, Young took a job at Ford Motor Company after graduating from high school in 1936. He became an organizer for the United Auto Workers (UAW), a labor union (group that protects the interests of workers).

During **World War II** (1939–45) Young joined the Army Air Corps's elite all-black squadron known as the Tuskegee Airmen. After the war he worked for the National Negro Council (NNCL) in Detroit. Some U.S. congressmen believed the NNCL was subversive (secretive and destructive to the government), and Young was asked to appear for questioning in 1951. He did so, but he condemned the members of the congressional Committee on Un-American Activities for their racist views. His remarks angered Detroit labor leaders. As a result, Young found it difficult to find work.

After working as a dry cleaner and later as a salesman, in 1960 Young became a delegate to the convention to rewrite Michigan's constitution. In 1964 he was elected to the Michigan senate. Still a state senator, in 1973 Young launched a campaign to become mayor of Detroit. He narrowly won the election but carried 92 percent of the black vote. He took office in January 1974 and later delivered on his promise to end police brutality. He also worked to revitalize the city's economy.

Considered a gifted speaker and well-liked by the black business community, Young was reelected every time he ran for the mayoral office. He did not seek a sixth term in 1993, and he retired in 1994.

Young, Lester

JAZZ SAXOPHONIST
August 27, 1909–March 15, 1959

One of **jazz** music's great stylists, Lester Young—fondly known as "the Prez" (short for "president")—was one of two tenor saxophonists who helped define the classic years of jazz. (The other was **Coleman Hawkins**, 1904–1969.) Young was well known for his masterful playing and for his sense of humor, storytelling, love of jazz slang, and his porkpie hat (a flat-crowned, wide-brimmed style popular in the 1940s).

Born Willis Lester Young, he grew up outside New Orleans, Louisiana. When he was ten years old, Lester went on tour with his father, carnival bandleader Willis Handy Young, and two of his siblings. The boy learned to play the drums and the saxophone.

After touring the South and Midwest, the Youngs moved to Los Angeles, California. In 1932 Lester returned to the Midwest, where he joined various orchestras. When bandleader **Count Basie** (1904–1984) relocated from Kansas City, Missouri, to New York City in 1936, Young was part of his ensemble. Over the next four years, Young performed on various recordings that are perfect examples of swing-era jazz.

Leading his own band from 1940 to 1943, Young briefly rejoined Basie's orchestra before he was drafted into the U.S. Army in the fall of 1944. Found in possession of illegal drugs, Young spent most of his military service in detention.

From 1946 into the 1950s he toured with the Jazz at the Philharmonic concert series. Praised for his solo work as well as for his flawless backing of singers, Young continued to perform at the height of his abilities until his death in 1959. Among the tributes paid to the Prez was bass player **Charles Mingus**'s (1922–1979) composition "Goodbye Pork Pie Hat."

Zydeco

Zydeco is a style of dance music played by African Americans in the South, particularly in southwestern Louisiana, where many African Americans have French ancestry. The term "zydeco" comes from an old Louisiana song called "Les Haricots Sont Pas Sal's" ("The Green Beans Aren't Salted"). The commonly understood meaning of this is "times aren't good."

Zydeco music began among French settlers who were chased from Canada by the British and arrived in Louisiana during the eighteenth century. Some of the settlers married African Americans and **American Indians,** and the musical traditions of all three cultures were blended. These racially and culturally blended people came to be called **Creoles.** The first zydeco songs date from 1934 and include titles such as "Cajun Negro Fais Dos-Dos Tune," and "Les Haricots Sont Pas Sal's."

In Louisiana, zydeco is played for dancers at nightclubs, dance halls, churches, picnics, and house parties known as "fais-do-do." Zydeco bands

ZYDECO AND CAJUN MUSIC

Zydeco and Cajun (Louisianans descended from French-speaking emigrants from Canada) music have many things in common, but they are different forms. Zydeco tends toward faster tempos, a tight rhythmic structure, and less emphasis on melody. Cajun rhythms are often stiffer, two-step dances or waltzes emphasizing melody.

are usually led by a singer who is accompanied by a fiddle, an accordion, a guitar, and drums. Zydeco is usually sung in the distinctive dialect (language) of the Creole community of Louisiana.

During the 1980s and 1990s zydeco became internationally popular. Important zydeco musicians include accordion player Boozoo Chavis, singer **"Queen Ida" Guillory,** and musicians Rockin' Sidney and Lawrence "Black" Ardoin. One of the most well known zydeco bands at the turn of the century was Buckwheat Zydeco.

A Chronology of African-American History
from 1444 through 2000

1444 Portuguese form the first slave trading company. The Portuguese learn early that slave trade proceeds best in cooperation with Africans.

1482 Sao Jorge de Mina (Elmina) is established. This is the first trading outpost to be built by Portugal on Africa's western coast. It is the first of many permanent trading posts initially dealing with gold and then slaves. Slaves are captured inland and then brought to the outpost. Once there they wait until a ship arrives. Slaves are traded for guns, cowrie shells, mirrors, knives, linens, silk, and beads. This castle or outpost changes ownership several times during the course of the slave trade—owners include the Portuguese, the Dutch, and the English. By the 1700s approximately 30,000 slaves would be deported from Elmina each year.

1510 Spain begins slave trade. King Ferdinand orders the shipment of 250 African slaves from Spain to the West Indies.

1518 Spanish American Colonies are granted a license (*asiento*) for the shipment of African slaves directly from Africa to America.

1619 First African settlers arrive in North America. A Dutch ship reaches Jamestown, Virginia, carrying a cargo of twenty Africans. Fifteen are purchased as indentured servants rather than slaves.

A public school for Native Americans and blacks is established in Virginia.

1621 Dutch form the West India Company. Only members of the company are legally enabled to carry slaves or other goods from Africa to Dutch colonies or elsewhere.

1625 Virginia Court distinguishes between black servitude and black slavery.

1630 Massachusetts enacts a law to protect African slaves who escape from their owners because of abusive treatment.

Virginia restricts relations between blacks and whites.

1638 First black slave arrives in New England.

Maryland passes a law declaring that a servant convicted of running away should be executed. This is the most severe law of its kind.

Slavery is becoming the most common condition of blacks in America. Fewer are accepted as indentured servants. The de facto institution of slavery is well established.

Massachusetts is the first colony to recognize slavery as a legal institution. Virginia passes legislation that requires a servant who escapes for a second time to be branded on the cheek or shoulder with the letter R.

The New England Confederation enters into an intercolonial agreement that a simple statement of certification from any government magistrate can convict a suspected runaway slave.

Eleven blacks petition for freedom in New Netherland. This is probably the first organized black protest in America. They are freed by the Council of New Netherland because they have completed their specified years of servitude.

The first American slave ship sails from Boston. Slaving quickly becomes a major profit-making industry.

1652 Earliest statute for the suppression of slavery in the colonies is noted in the Rhode Island Records. This legislation becomes the first colonial law limiting slavery, but ironically it is never enforced.

New Netherland colony passes legislation regulating the treatment of slaves by their masters.

1655 Elizabeth Key, a slave since birth, sues for her freedom and wins. She is born the daughter of an influential Virginia planter and a slave woman. Her suit is based on three arguments: (1) her father was a free man; (2) she had been baptized, the implication being that a Christian could not be a slave for life; and (3) she had been sold to another planter even after she had served nine years.

1660 English Company of Royal Adventurers is established for trading into Africa. The Royal African will supersede it in 1672.

Maryland and Virginia colonies pass laws concerning black and white servants. White servants can buy their freedom. Black servants become slaves.

1663 First serious slave conspiracy is recorded September 13 in colonial America in Gloucester County, Virginia. The plot by white and black servants to escape from their masters is betrayed by one or more indentured servants.

1664 French West Indies Company is established.

Maryland becomes the first colony to pass legislation prohibiting marriage between black men and white women. Maryland also passes legislation that recognizes slavery as legal. British secure control of New Amsterdam, and the status of black servants is amended to perpetual slavery. Legislation is passed condoning slavery.

1667 British pass legislation entitled "Act to Regulate the Negroes on the British Plantation" that restricts the movement and behavior of blacks.

1668 Virginia's House of Burgesses passes a law stipulating that Christian baptism does not alter a person's condition of bondage or freedom.

1669 Virginia statute is passed that declares it is not a felony for a master or overseer to kill a slave who resists punishment.

The Fundamental Constitutions of Carolina accept slavery as a legal institution.

1670 Virginia passes legislation that disallows lifelong servitude for any black person who has become a Christian before arriving in the colony. The law is passed to address the difficult moral issue raised as Christians enslave other Christians. The law further divides all non-Christian servants into two groups: those coming by sea who "shall be slaves for their lives," and those coming by land who are to serve indentured terms. Almost all Africans come by sea so they are subject to enslavement but Native Americans are not.

1671 An act is passed in Maryland declaring that a slave's conversion to Christianity does not affect his slave status.

1672 Virginia passes a new law that puts a bounty on the heads of fugitive slaves.

British Crown grants a slaving charter to a new corporation, the Royal African Company, to compete with the Dutch and the French.

1682 Movement of slaves is restricted in New York by the General Court. It forbids slaves to leave their owner's property without written permission or to buy or sell goods. Up until this time slaves in New York had been governed by the same judicial processes and criminal code that held for whites.

Slave Law passes in Virginia that prohibits slaves from possessing weapons, leaving their owner's plantations without permission, or lifting a hand against a white person, even in self-defense. Further, the slave law of 1670 is repealed, so the conversion of slaves to Christianity before arriving in the colony no longer keeps them from lifelong servitude.

1684 Slaves are imported into Philadelphia. By 1700 one in every fourteen families in Philadelphia will own slaves.

1688 Quakers pass anti-slavery resolution in Pennsylvania. On February 18, 1688 the Mennonites (Quakers) in Germantown, Pennsylvania adopt the first formal anti-slavery resolution in American history. Although the Quakers are the first religious group to denounce the slave trade and slavery, it becomes a thriving business in Pennsylvania.

1691 First law in Virginia to explicitly restrict intermarriage between blacks and whites is passed.

1692 More slave laws are enacted in Virginia. A new law imposes banishment from the colony of any free white man or woman who marries a black, mulatto, or a Native American. Later the penalty is changed to six months' imprisonment and a fine of 10 pounds. Slaves cannot keep horses, cattle, or hogs. Slaves charged with a capital offense are to be tried without a jury and can be convicted on the testimony of two witnesses under oath. Maryland, Delaware, and North Carolina later copy the Virginia laws.

1693 Philadelphia passes an ordinance restricting the movements of blacks.

1700 Pennsylvania distinguishes slaves as a separate group and laws are passed that apply only to them. Slaves can be put to death for murder, burglary, and rape, and whipped for robbing and stealing.

Judge Samuel Sewell of Massachusetts publishes a statement, entitled *The Selling of Joseph*. He becomes one of the first public officials to denounce slavery. This is the first anti-slavery tract to be distributed in the colonies.

1701 Society for the Propagation of the Gospel is founded as a vehicle to educate slaves and Native Americans. It operates in Virginia, Maryland, North Carolina, Pennsylvania, and New Jersey.

1702 New York passes a law that imposes restraints on slaves, stipulating that no more than three slaves can assemble without the consent of their owners, and that a slave who strikes a free person could be confined for fourteen days and whipped.

1703 According to a census, as many as 43 percent of all whites in New York City own one or more slaves.

1704 Elias Neau opens one of the first schools in the colonies to enroll slaves. It is called the Catechism School for Negroes and is associated with Trinity Church.

1705 Death penalty is imposed for runaway slaves in New York.

Virginia enacts Slave Code called "Act Concerning Servants and Slaves." All existing laws dealing with blacks are collapsed into this slave code. Under this law, slaves are attached to the soil, so that the heir to a plantation is entitled to purchase the inherited interests of others in the slaves.

1706 New York passes legislation requiring that the legal status for children would be determined by the condition of the mother. A similar measure is in effect in North Carolina and Georgia, and it becomes the law in other parts of South as well.

1707 White mechanics in Philadelphia form a guild to protest unfair labor competition from black slaves.

1708 Slaves revolt in Newton, Long Island, New York. Seven whites are killed during the revolt. Three slaves and one Native American are hanged and one black woman is burned alive.

1711 Escaped slaves arm themselves and raid various plantations and farms in South Carolina. The slaves' leader is a Spanish black named Sebastian who is finally captured.

1712 New York denies slaves access to courts.

South Carolina adopts model Slave Code.

Slaves revolt in New York City on April 7. Nine whites are killed and at least twelve slaves are executed. The Catechism School for Negroes at Trinity Church is closed because slave owners believe that the French

founder, Elias Neau, is inciting slaves to revolt. More restrictive slave codes are enacted.

Pennsylvania passes a law preventing the importation of slaves into the colony by imposing a duty of 20 pounds per head. However, the law is repealed in England.

1713 Quakers develop a manumission plan. Protests by Quakers seriously curtail the slave market activity in Philadelphia leading to legislative action that attempts to prohibit slavery in the colony.

1716 First slaves arrive in French Louisiana.

1720 Slaves revolt in Charleston, South Carolina. Many slaves are banished, some are hanged, and others are burned alive.

1721 The "Negro Watch" is created in Charleston, South Carolina to allay the fears of the white population of possible slave revolts. Patrols are set up to stop slaves on sight and to shoot them if they do not stop when ordered.

1722 Slave plot to kill whites is uncovered. About 200 slaves gather at a church near Rappahannock, Virginia to attack whites who had abused them. Although the plot is revealed all the slaves escape.

1723 Virginia Assembly passes legislation that disfranchises free blacks. This law is enacted as a result of the slave conspiracy. It is felt that free blacks should be punished even if they were not involved in the plot.

1724 Slave codes are enacted in Louisiana. Slave owners can legally punish runaway slaves by cutting off their ears, hamstringing them, or branding them.

1725 First Church of Colored Baptists is established. Black slaves are granted the right to have a separate Baptist church in Williamsburg, VA.

1726 Pennsylvania passes laws that further curtail the activities of slaves. Racial intermarriage is banned.

1729 Maryland passes a law that permits brutal punishments upon conviction of slaves for certain crimes. These punishments include hanging, decapitation, and severing the body into four quarters for display in public places.

1732 Slave mutiny occurs aboard a ship commanded by Captain John Major of Portsmouth, New Hampshire. The entire crew is killed. Interestingly only those uprisings resulting in the death of captain or crewmembers are documented. Little is known of uprisings that failed and of the large numbers of slaves thrown overboard.

1733 Spanish pass decree stating that any slave who escapes to Spanish territory would be considered free. Many slaves attempt to escape to Florida-especially St. Augustine.

Georgia, the last of thirteen colonies, is established. It is a haven for the indebted and oppressed. The Trustees of the colony disapprove of slavery.

1734 Slaves overtake the crew and captain of the slave ship *Dolphin*. All are killed in an explosion.

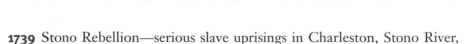

1739 Stono Rebellion—serious slave uprisings in Charleston, Stono River, and St. John's Parish, South Carolina. Groups of slaves seek freedom in St. Augustine. Many whites are killed along the route.

1740 South Carolina declares lifelong slavery for all blacks.

Fifty slaves are hanged in Charleston after alleged insurrection plots are uncovered.

1741 Soldiers from Georgia destroy an established settlement that housed fugitive slaves from South Carolina.

A series of suspicious fires and reports of slave conspiracies lead to general hysteria in New York City. According to some accounts, 13 conspirators were burned alive, 18 hanged, and 80 more deported. Another account stated that as many as 400 whites took part in the uprising and 125 blacks were arrested. It was later revealed that there was no evidence of a conspiracy or slave revolt.

1744 An Anglican missionary, Samuel Thomas, opens a school for blacks in South Carolina.

1750 Quaker abolitionist Anthony Benezet schools blacks in his home.

Georgia permits slavery so that the colony's growth will parallel that of the others.

1751 Virginia passes legislation giving the churchwardens of any parish the power to sell blacks or slaves residing one month if they had been emancipated without the consent of the governor and council.

1753 Benjamin Franklin presents the argument that "slavery is poor economic policy" in his book, *Observations Concerning the Increase of Mankind and the Peopling of Countries*.

1754 The twenty-two-year-old free black man Benjamin Banneker, considered to be the first African-American man of science, constructs the first clock made in the North American colonies. He makes the clock entirely from seasoned wood.

The Quaker abolitionist John Woolman publishes "Some Considerations on the Keeping of Negroes; Recommended to the Professors of Christianity of Every Denomination," a moral plea to other Quakers to emancipate their slaves. Fellow Quaker Anthony Benezet pens the first draft of *An Epistle of Caution and Advice, Concerning the Buying and Keeping of Slaves*, the Quakers's first official denunciation of slavery—both the slave trade and, more significantly, slaveholding.

1756 Blacks serve as scouts, wagoners, and laborers with British forces during the French and Indian War. Black militiamen serve with units from almost every colony. Many blacks receive praise for their bravery in the battles of Fort Duquesne, Fort Cumberland, and the Plains of Abraham outside Quebec City.

1758 Quakers in Philadelphia take steps to abolish slavery. They cease buying and selling slaves.

1760 "An Evening Thought: Salvation by Christ, with Penitential Cries" by the slave Jupiter Hammon is the first poem by a black person to be published in North America.

The *Narrative of the Uncommon Sufferings, and Surprizing Deliverance of Briton Hammon, A Negro Man* is the first slave narrative to be published in North America.

1763 Black chimney sweeps in Charleston form the first union-type organization. They refuse to work until the city increases their wages.

1766 Anthony Benezet, a schoolteacher from Philadelphia, writes *A Caution and Warning to Great Britain and Her Colonies, in a Sharot Representation of the Calamitous State of the Enslaved Negroes in the British Dominions.* He is one of the great pre-Revolutionary abolitionists.

1769 Thomas Jefferson tries without success to introduce a bill to the Virginia House of Burgesses that would emancipate African slaves.

1770 Crispus Attucks is the first person to be killed fighting the British at the Boston Massacre, becoming one of the first casualties of the American Revolution.

1772 Slavery is abolished in England.

1773 Phillis Wheatley, a 20-year-old slave, publishes her *Poems on Various Subjects, Religious and Moral*, making her the first African-American—and only the third American woman—to publish a volume of poetry.

Massachusetts slaves petition the legislature for freedom on January 6.

Black Baptist church is organized at Silver Bluff, South Carolina. This is probably the first black Baptist church under black leadership established in the colonies.

Caesar Hendricks of Massachusetts takes his master to court and asks to be freed. An all-white jury renders a verdict in his favor.

1774 The Society of Friends rule at their yearly meeting that Quakers who buy or sell slaves should be disowned and those who refuse to emancipate their slaves should be barred from leadership in the Society.

Connecticut, Massachusetts, and Rhode Island prohibit the importation of slaves.

Virginia Convention of 1774 passes a resolution condemning slavery.

Continental Congress pledges to end slave trade. The resolution is a powerful statement, but it proves to mean very little since the desire to gain wealth through slavery is still a potent force in America.

1775 Continental Navy recruits blacks. A recruitment poster in Newport calls for "ye able backed sailors, men white or black to volunteer for naval service in ye interest of freedom." About 2,000 blacks serve in the Continental Navy during the Revolution.

The first abolitionist society—the Society for the Relief of Free Negroes Unlawfully Held in Bondage, and for Improving the Condition of the African Race—is formed in Pennsylvania.

April 19—Blacks are among the minutemen who defeat the British at Concord. African Americans serve as minutemen before they are allowed into the regular army.

May—The Committee on Safety of the Continental Congress permits free blacks, but not slaves, to serve in the Continental Army.

June 17—Black soldiers—Salem Poor, a free black, and Peter Salem, a slave—fight the British heroically at the Battle of Bunker Hill.

July—despite the battle heroics of soldiers such as Poor and Salem, Gen. George Washington bars blacks from joining the army.

November 7—Lord Dunmore, royal governor of Virginia, issues a proclamation promising freedom to slaves willing to fight with the British. Dunmore's action will later be characterized in the Declaration of Independence as "exciting domestic insurrections."

December 31—General Washington reverses his earlier decision barring blacks from enlisting when the British start recruiting slaves for the British army.

Thomas Paine publishes *Slavery in America*—an indictment against the institution of slavery.

Benjamin Rush publishes *An Address to the Inhabitants of the British Settlements in America, Upon Slavekeeping*. He argues that blacks are not intellectually and morally inferior; that slavery is not necessary for the economic development of the South; and that slavery is not a Christian institution.

1776 New York and other colonies pass a law allowing any white man who is drafted to serve in the Continental Army to send a free black in his place. The number of whites who took advantage of this is unknown because a large number of blacks—slave and free—volunteered to serve their country.

The Declaration of Independence, written by Thomas Jefferson, himself the owner of over 175 slaves at the time, asserts that all persons "are created equal; that they are endowed by their creator with certain unalienable rights; that among these are life, liberty, and the pursuit of happiness." These words would later provide fuel for anti-slavery movements in the States.

Quakers refusing to free their slaves are disowned from the Society of Friends.

1777 Vermont becomes the first state to abolish slavery in its constitution.

Parting Ways, one of the earliest free black settlements in America, is established near Plymouth, MA. Cato Howe, a black Revolutionary War veteran, is given 94 acres of land by the town. The grant specifies that the land has to be cleared and settled by Howe and three others who participated in the war.

1778 The Continental Army enlists blacks for three-year terms. They serve in integrated units. Eventually all-black units emerge, such as the company from Connecticut referred to as the "Colonials" and a company from Boston called the "Bucks of America" whose members are slave volunteers and commanded by a black. Black soldiers, including Prince Whipple and Oliver Cromwell, were members of the regiment that crossed the Delaware River with Washington. By the end of the Revolutionary war 5,000 black soldiers and 2,000 blacks had fought bravely for their country.

First Rhode Island Regiment, an entirely black army unit, holds the line against three times as many British at Newport in the battle of August 29—the only battle fought in Rhode Island.

1779 Jean Baptiste Point Du Sable establishes the first permanent settlement at a site that would become Chicago.

November 12—twenty slaves petition the New Hampshire legislature to abolish slavery.

Rhode Island passes anti-slavery legislation including the prohibition of slave trade and the kidnapping of slaves.

1780 Pennsylvania passes the Gradual Abolition Act, the first abolition act in the United States.

Paul Cuffe and six other free blacks petition against taxation without representation. They refuse to pay their taxes because they are denied the right to vote.

The state constitution of Massachusetts effectively ends slavery in the state with the words, "All men are born free and equal, and have certain natural, essential, and unalienable rights; among which may be reckoned the right of enjoying and defending their lives and liberties."

Lemuel Haynes is commissioned to preach in the Congregational Church. He is the first black minister of this church.

James Armistead is granted permission by his owner to serve in the Continental Army. He becomes one of the most important spies of the American Revolution. Lafayette is his commander. After the war Armistead returns to being a slave. Although Lafayette writes a letter urging for his freedom, it is not until 1786 that the Virginia General Assembly intervenes and grants it.

1783 It is estimated that 20,000 blacks leave with the British troops after the Revolutionary War. Some are brought to freedom in England, Nova Scotia, and Jamaica. Others are taken to the British West Indies and sold back into slavery.

Black populations reach one million in the colonies. More than half of all slaves reside in Virginia.

1784 Connecticut and Rhode Island pass gradual emancipation statutes.

Methodist Episcopal Churches in America denounce slavery and issue a mandate to members to free slaves. The adopted regulations are defeated and suspended a year later.

March 1—Jefferson's congressional committee proposes banning slavery everywhere in the United States after 1800. The proposal is narrowly defeated.

1785 The Rhode Island Society for Abolishing the Slave Trade is founded in Providence. Its purpose is to organize anti-slavery activities, assist free blacks in finding employment, discourage slave trade, provide education, and register deeds of manumission.

New York establishes Society for Promoting the Manumission of Slaves. It publicizes laws relating to slavery, distributes anti-slavery literature, and sponsors lectures by noted abolitionists.

Rev. Richard Allen, founder of the African Methodist Episcopal Church, is seized by a trader who makes a sworn affidavit that Allen is an escaped slave. Slavers frequently come north to kidnap freed blacks. Allen is freed after many prominent Philadelphians testify on his behalf. The slave trader is imprisoned for perjury.

Runaway slaves led by a person trained in military tactics by the British continue to harass and alarm residents of Savannah. They refer to themselves as the "King of England's soldiers."

1787 The U.S. Constitution legitimizes the institution of slavery in the laws of the United States and allows for the continuation of the African slave trade until 1808.

British establish a colony of free blacks in Sierra Leone in West Africa. Paul Cuffe, a mulatto ship captain from Massachusetts, establishes trade between the United States and Sierra Leone. He is a visible leader of the project to resettle many blacks there. The movement is continued by the American Colonization Society.

Blacks in Massachusetts, including Prince Hall, petition the General Court for funds to return to Africa. The petition is refused, but it is the first recorded effort by blacks to return to their homeland.

Richard Allen and Absalom Jones establish Philadelphia's Free African Society. The society is organized as a mutual aid society, a church, and a political structure.

Prince Hall establishes the Negro Masonic Order in the United States. This becomes the first black self-help fraternal institution in the United States.

Three-fifths Compromise is included in the U.S. Constitution. It allows the states to count three-fifths of the black population in determining political representation in the House of Representatives.

The Northwest Ordinance forbids the expansion of slavery into the area north and west of the Ohio River.

The London Society, an anti-slavery group, is organized.

New York Manumission Society establishes the African Free School. It is the first free secular school for blacks in the city.

1788 The Delaware Society for Promoting the Abolition of Slavery and for the Relief and Protection of Free Blacks and People of Colour Unlawfully Held in Bondage is organized.

New Jersey legislature passes an anti-slavery law that stipulates the confiscation of ships involved in the slave trade and prohibits the removal of slaves over twenty-one years of age rom the state.

Pennsylvania passes an act to fine slave owners 50 pounds when slave family members are separated for a distance greater than ten miles without the consent of family members.

Andrew Bryan, a slave, establishes the First African Baptist Church in Savannah, GA. He remains a slave until his owner's death when he purchases his freedom.

Free blacks in Massachusetts protest the forcible exportation of blacks from Boston to Martinique. This prompts the Assembly to review the issue and declare slave trade illegal.

1792 Benjamin Banneker, a noted astronomer, inventor, and mathematician, becomes the first Black to publish an almanac—*Benjamin Banneker's Pennsylvania, Delaware, Maryland and Virginia Almanack and Ephemeris, for the Year of our Lord, 1792*. It is the first scientific book written by a black man. Banneker's heralded almanacs are published annually for the next ten years.

1793 Eli Whitney invents the cotton gin, a device that—by making cotton a much more profitable crop—contributes to the spread and entrenchment of slavery in the South.

The Fugitive Slave Act makes it a criminal offense to harbor a runaway slave or to interfere with the return of a slave to his or her owner.

1794 Bowdoin College is founded in Brunswick, Maine. It becomes a center for abolitionist sentiment for the Civil War.

First African Methodist Episcopal Church is founded by Richard Allen in Philadelphia.

France abolishes slavery in its colonial territories.

Amos Fortune, former slave, becomes a leading businessman in Jaffrey, New Hampshire. He founds the Jaffrey Social Library.

1795 Plans for a slave revolt in Point Coupee, Louisiana, are uncovered. Twenty-five slaves are executed.

1796 The African Methodist Episcopal Zion Church becomes the first black Methodist Church in New York City.

A grand jury in Charlotte, North Carolina accuses Quakers of inciting slave unrest and arson.

1797 First recorded anti-slavery petition to Congress. Four black slaves in North Carolina petition Congress in protest against a state law that requires illegally freed slaves to be returned to their masters. The slaves had been freed by their Quaker masters, who purchased them for the purpose of freeing them, though the practice is illegal.

1798 Joshua Johnson, portrait painter, advertises in the Baltimore Intelligencer. He calls himself a "self taught genius." Johnson paints portraits of some of the most successful and influential white families in Maryland and Virginia.

1799 New York passes a gradual emancipation law providing that all children born of slaves should be freed after reaching the age of twenty-eight.

1800 South Carolina becomes the clearing-house for slaves bound for plantations throughout the South. Two-fifths of the slaves who arrive in America during the early 1800s will pass through here.

Gabriel Prosser Conspiracy. On August 30 Prosser organizes 1,000 slaves and sets out to attack Richmond, Virginia with plans to establish his own government. Two house slaves betray the plot. Prosser and his family are hung on October 30 along with twenty-four other conspirators.

1801 Slave trade is reopened in the Louisiana Territory and flourishes.

Georgia passes a law with severe penalties for freeing slaves.

1802 The Ohio State Constitution prohibits slavery and involuntary servitude in the state. Blacks have the right to live in the state and receive the protection of its laws. However, they do not have the privileges of citizens.

France reinstitutes slavery.

1803 Free black settlement is established in Isle Breville, LA. Louis Metoyer, architect, designs the Melrose plantation house.

South Carolina passes legislation to reopen slave trade from South America and the West Indies.

Twenty blacks are arrested and convicted for burning eleven houses in New York City. They were planning to burn the entire city. Rioting follows their arrest.

1804 The Ohio General Assembly becomes the first in the country to enact laws intended to restrict the rights of free blacks. All blacks are required to produce certificates of freedom from a U.S. court before they can settle in the state.

1805 Virginia passes laws requiring all freed slaves to leave the state.

1806 John Parrish publishes *Remarks on the Slavery of the Black People*. This is one of the most complete treatments of slavery and the principles of democracy.

1807 George Bell, Nicholas Franklin, and Moses Liverpool, three former slaves, build the first schoolhouse for African-American children in Washington, D.C.

Congress passes a law that bars the importation of new slaves from Africa into the United States.

Louisiana legislature passes a law that defines slaves as "real estate."

1808 Federal law prohibiting the importation of new slaves into the United States goes into effect.

Louisiana court declares slave marriages illegal.

Peter Williams, Jr. publishes *An Oration on the Abolition of the Slave Trade; Delivered in The African Church, in the City of New York, January 1, 1808*. This is one of the first black anti-slavery speeches.

1809 Rev. Thomas Paul establishes the Abyssinian Baptist Church in New York City.

1810 Tom Molineaux becomes the first African American to compete for the heavyweight championship. He fights Englishman Tom Crib and is defeated after fighting thirty-nine rounds.

1811 Slave trade is reopened in the Louisiana Territory and flourishes.

Delaware passes a law that prevents free blacks from entering the state.

Pointe Coupee Revolt—five hundred slaves march toward New Orleans burning plantations on the way. Approximately 65 slaves are killed and their heads are displayed along the road from New Orleans as a deterrent to other slaves in the region.

Paul Cuffe makes his first trip to the English colony of Sierra Leone with a crew of nine black sailors. He becomes intrigued with the possibilities of beginning a three-way trade between the United States, England, and Sierra Leone.

1812 Free blacks fight in the War of 1812. At least 15 percent of all seamen during the war are black. Andrew Jackson calls upon free blacks to volunteer for the army.

Illinois Territory prohibits free blacks from immigrating into the territory.

James Forten along with Richard Allen and Absalom Jones help raise a volunteer regiment of African Americans to help defend Philadelphia from the British.

1815 Black veterans returning from the War of 1812 carry the news of freedom for blacks in Canada.

Blacks fight in the Battle of New Orleans, the last battle of the War of 1812.

1816 African Methodist Episcopal Church is established nationally.

U.S. troops attack and destroy a settlement of about three hundred fugitive slaves and about twenty Native Americans at Fort Blount on Apalachicola Bay, FL. This marks the beginning of other attacks to recapture runaway slaves.

The American Colonization Society is established to resettle free black Americans outside the territorial limits of the United States.

1817 Morris Brown is ordained a deacon in the African Methodist Episcopal Church.

Richard Allen leads blacks in Philadelphia in a protest against the efforts of the American Colonization Society.

1818 Georgia passes legislation prohibiting manumissions regardless of cause, reason, circumstance, or method in an effort to restrict or eliminate its free black populations. Other Southern states pass similar statutes.

Battle of Suwannee takes place in Florida. It is one of several battles of the First Seminole War between U.S. troops and Seminoles and blacks. Intent on gaining territory for annexation and setting a precedent for the destruction of runaway-slave communities as a deterrent for further defection, U.S. troops set fire to villages and crops and capture Seminole Indians and Maroons.

1819 Congress passes the Anti-Slave Trade Act to curtail slave smuggling.

1820 Boston opens an elementary school for black children. Earlier Primus Hall established a separate school in his home in 1798.

The state of Maine grants the right to vote and the right to an education to all male citizens regardless of race.

U.S. Army prohibits blacks and mulattoes from enlisting.

Daniel Coker publishes his journal on procolonization, *Journal of Daniel Coker*.

Congress enacts the Missouri Compromise. This permits Missouri to enter the Union as a slave state and Maine as a free state.

1821 Alabama introduces slave-hunting patrols to prevent the escape of slaves.

The American Colonization Society purchases Cape Mesurado in Africa. It is located 225 miles south of Sierra Leone.

The Genius of Universal Emancipation begins publication in Mount Pleasant, Ohio. It is one of first abolitionist journals to be published.

Suffrage is extended to free black males in New York.

1822 Plans for one of the most elaborately planned slave revolts are uncovered—the Denmark Vesey Conspiracy. The plot reportedly involved 9,000 slaves near Charleston, SC.

July—South Carolina State legislature passes laws to restrict the movement of free blacks. These laws are enacted in response to the Denmark Vesey affair.

James Varick is ordained as the first black bishop of the independent African Methodist Episcopal Zion Church.

1823 The U.S. Circuit Court in Washington, D.C. rules that if a slave is moved to a free state, the slave is free. The Court also rules that inhumane treatment of a slave is an indictable offense under common law.

Alexander Lucius Twilight becomes the first black to graduate from an American college.

Mississippi legislature prohibits blacks (free or slave) from congregating. It also prohibits educating blacks.

The Black Republic of Liberia is founded. The American Colonization Society believes that racial problems in America can be solved only by encouraging free blacks to emigrate.

1824 Illinois legislature rejects a proposal to establish slavery in the state.

Virginia expands its slave codes.

The Hardscrabble riots take place in Providence, Rhode Island. The riots leave black neighborhoods destroyed.

1827 Samuel Cornish and John Brown Russwurm begin publication of the first black newspaper, *Freedom's Journal*.

Slavery is abolished in New York state.

Publication of Nathaniel Paul's *An Address, Delivered on the Celebration of the Abolition of Slavery, in the State of New York, July, 1827*, one of the most important African-American orations regarding the abolition of slavery in New York.

Publication of Robert Roberts's *The House Servant's Directory, or a Monitor for Private Families . . .*, the first cookbook written by an African American.

Morris Brown is ordained a deacon in the African Methodist Episcopal Church.

1828 Thomas D. Rice paints his face black and portrays a character called "Jump Jim Crow" on stage. Daniel Alexander Payne opens school for blacks in Charleston, SC.

1829 Georgia passes legislation that prohibits the education of slaves and free blacks.

Fearing the rapid growing African-American population, whites in Cincinnati insist on more rigid enforcement of the Black Laws and demand a bond payment. White mobs attack blacks who can not pay the bond. A three-day riot ensues and many blacks are killed and their communities are burned.

David Walker, a free black man, publishes a radical anti-slavery pamphlet *Appeal to the Coloured Citizens of the World.*

George Moses Horton, a poet and slave, publishes his first book of poetry.

1830 Josiah Henson escapes with his wife and family to Canada. Once there he begins working as conductor on the Underground Railroad.

Louisiana passes legislation making it a crime punishable by imprisonment or death to distribute abolitionist literature.

The first National Negro Convention, chaired by Richard Allen, meets at the Bethel AME Church in Philadelphia. Thirty-eight delegates devise ways to better their condition and respond to mob action against blacks created by colonization propaganda.

1831 Mississippi passes a law requiring freed slaves to leave the state within 90 days or be in danger of being sold back into slavery.

The first issue of William Lloyd Garrison's *the Liberator* is published. This is the most celebrated anti-slavery paper.

Nat Turner leads the most significant slave revolt in U.S. Turner's Rebellion claims more lives than any similar uprising. Some suggest that this uprising represents the first major battle of the long war to end slavery.

1832 A group of black women in Boston organize the African-American Female Intelligence Society for the purpose of educating "women of color."

Virginia enacts a law imposing the death penalty for both slaves and free blacks for certain offenses, including the rape of a white woman, the beating of a white person, and inciting rebellion.

Pennsylvania rejects a petition from free blacks to admit their children to public schools.

First female anti-slavery society is organized by a group of black women in Salem, MA.

Maria Miller Stewart, abolitionist and feminist, delivers a public lecture in Boston. She is the first African-American woman to do so.

The New England Anti-Slavery Society is founded. It is first group to demand the unconditional and immediate abolition of slavery.

1833 Alabama prohibits free blacks and slaves to preach.

American Anti-Slavery Society is established.

1834 Vermont Anti-Slavery Society is formed by Quakers and others opposed to slavery.

A meeting of the American Anti-Slavery Society in New York is broken up by a proslavery mob.

Slavery is abolished throughout British colonies. Over 700,000 people are freed.

White mobs march into the black section of Philadelphia and commit acts of violence. Homes are burned, wrecked, and pulled down.

James G. Birney publishes *Letter on Colonization*, a powerful anticolonization tract.

1835 The Second Seminole War begins. During the course of the war over 1,500 American soldiers are killed and the Florida Seminoles, both Indian and black, are decimated and moved to the West.

A mob of white citizens use oxen to pull the Noyes Academy, an integrated school, into a swamp just outside of Canaan, NH.

William Lloyd Garrison is paraded through the streets of Boston at the end of a rope after a proslavery mob disrupted a meeting of the Boston Female Anti-Slavery Society. City officials are quickly denounced for the lack of protection they provide abolition meetings.

President Andrew Jackson recommends a law prohibiting the circulation of anti-slavery materials by mail.

1836 The Grimkè sisters—Sarah and Angelina—both publish abolitionist tracts. Angelina wrote *Appeal to the Christian Women of the South*, and her sister wrote *Epistle to the Clergy of the Southern States*.

Louisiana has more free black residents than any other southern state.

Alexander Lucius Twilight is elected to a one-year term in the Vermont state legislature.

The Women's Anti-Slavery Society in New York bars blacks from membership. Although the group works to abolish slavery, it is clear that the mixing of whites and blacks in public is not one of its goals.

Texas state constitution officially legalizes slavery.

Richard Hildreth publishes *The Slave: or Memoirs of Archy Moore*, the first American abolitionist novel.

1837 James McCune Smith, first African American to earn a medical degree, returns to New York and opens a medical practice.

The Weekly Advocate is first published in New York City. It is founded by Philip A. Bell and Robert Sears. Several months later Samuel Cornish takes editorial control and renames it the *Colored American*.

Cotton prices fall by nearly one-half on the New Orleans market. Many businesses fail. Since slaves are tied to cotton production, any major drop in the price of cotton forces farmers on marginal land and large plantation owners to sell their slaves in order to pay off debts.

Hosea Easton publishes *A Treatise on the Intellectual Character, and Civil and Political Condition of the Colored People of the U. States; And the Prejudice Exercised Towards Them*, the first full-length work on racial prejudice by an African American.

1838 Robert Purvis, a leading abolitionist, is given the honorary title of president of the Underground Railroad.

John C. Calhoun, advocate of states' rights, introduces resolutions in the U.S. Senate that affirm slavery as a legal institution.

The first black magazine, *Mirror of Liberty*, is published by David Ruggles.

Frederick Douglass escapes to freedom with the aid of Anna Murray, a free African-American woman.

1839 Samuel Ringgold Ward embarks on a career as an orator on abolition. He becomes known as the "black Daniel Webster."

The Amistad Mutiny occurs off the northern coast of Cuba in July. It is the best-known slave mutiny in U.S. history. The mutiny is led by a black man called Joseph Cinque.

Charles Bennet Ray becomes the editor of the *Colored American*.

Theodore Dwight Weld publishes *American Slavery As It is: Testimony of a Thousand Witnesses*. It is one of the most factual books written on the nature of slavery.

A group of moderate abolitionists form the Liberty Party in New York. Two black abolitionists—Samuel Ringgold Ward and Henry Highland Garnet—are among the founders.

1840 World Anti-Slavery Convention takes place in London. Women delegates are denied seats. Charles Lenox Remond creates a sensation by chastising the assembly for their exclusionary policy and by withdrawing from the proceedings.

1841 The U.S. Supreme Court rules that African mutineer Joseph Cinque and his fellow slaves from the Amistad mutiny are free. Justice Joseph Story rules that they were kidnapped free men and thus have the same rights as other kidnapped persons.

The Liberty Party holds a national convention in New York City to reaffirm its militant anti-slavery position.

Street skirmishes in Cincinnati escalate into five days of anti-black rioting.

1842 Violence breaks out between Irish and free blacks seeking coal-mining jobs in Pennsylvania.

After five years of fighting the Second Seminole War ends.

Prigg v. Commonwealth of Pennsylvania—the U.S. Supreme Court rules that owners are able to recover their fugitive slaves from any state, and the states could neither help nor hinder the slaves.

Charles Lenox Remond becomes the first black to address the Massachusetts House of Representatives.

1843 Norbert Rillieux receives a patent for inventing the multiple effect vacuum pan evaporator.

The United States and Britain, according to the terms of the Webster-Ashburton Treaty, jointly agree to patrol Africa's west coast to intercept vessels involved in smuggling slaves to their territories.

The Vermont legislature blocks enforcement of the Fugitive Slave Act of 1793.

Henry Highland Garnet attends the National Convention of Colored Men and delivers his provocative "Address to the Slaves of the United States of America."

African Americans hold a state convention in Detroit, Michigan to discuss many of the problems confronting free blacks in the state. They draft a strongly worded petition against oppression and a call for blacks to defend their liberties.

1844 Macon Bolling Allen is admitted to the bar in the state of Maine, although he never practiced law there.

African Americans in Boston hold mass meetings to protest segregated "Jim Crow" schools and other instances of inequality.

1845 Frederick Douglass publishes his *Narrative of the Life of Frederick Douglass*, and follows with a successful speaking of tour of Great Britain.

Florida joins the Union as a slave state and Iowa joins as a free state.

African Americans living in Massachusetts maintain a high degree of political and legal equality with whites. They are able to send their children to the public schools in Salem, New Bedford, Nantucket, Worcester, and Lowell. Only Boston maintains segregated schools.

William A. Leidesdorff is the first African American to become a diplomat. He is named vice-consul to the Mexican territory of Yerba Buena (San Francisco).

1846 The New Jersey legislature finally passes a law to abolish slavery. Blacks continue to protest the segregation of schools in Boston.

Sojourner Truth joins the anti-slavery circuit, traveling with Abby Kelly Foster, Frederick Douglass, William Lloyd Garrison, and British M.P. George Thompson.

The American Missionary Association is founded in New York. It is both a missionary and an abolitionist society.

1847 David John Peck becomes the first African American to graduate from an American medical school.

Frederick Douglass and Martin Robinson Delany begin publishing the *North Star*, an abolitionist newspaper.

1848 A posse of slavecatchers arrive in Marshall, Michigan, seeking the Crosswaite family. They are jailed long enough for the fugitive slaves to flee across the border to Canada.

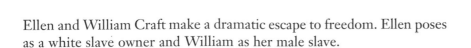

Ellen and William Craft make a dramatic escape to freedom. Ellen poses as a white slave owner and William as her male slave.

Charles L. Reason becomes the first black professor at a predominantly white university.

Mary Ellen Pleasant arrives in San Francisco during the Gold Rush. She opens a restaurant and boarding house where many prominent Californians stay.

John Van Surly De Grasse receives a medical degree with honors from Bowdoin College.

The legendary black explorer James Pierson Beckwourth discovers a pass in the Sierra Nevada, which is used by many pioneers to enter California, named Beckwourth Pass in his honor.

1849 Three states—Connecticut, New Jersey, and Ohio—hold conventions to discuss the conditions of free blacks and slaves.

Harriet Ross Tubman escapes from slavery, leaving behind her husband, who refused to accompany her. Shortly after her escape, Tubman becomes involved in the abolition movement and the Underground Railroad where she conducts over 300 African-American men, women, and children to freedom.

Publication of *Narrative of Henry Box Brown, Who Escaped from Slavery Enclosed in a Box 3 Feet Long and 2 Wide*, an account by an escaped slave.

Roberts v. City of Boston—court ruling that justifies the constitutionality of "Jim Crow" schools and the separate-but-equal doctrine later confirmed in Plessy v. Ferguson (1896). The case against the court's verdict was argued by abolitionist Charles Sumner and by Robert Morris, the nation's second licensed African-American lawyer.

1850 The phrase "sold down the river" becomes part of the American lexicon. During this time, slaves from older slave states could be sold to masters in the newer areas of the Cotton Belt along the Mississippi River where the living conditions were much harsher.

The narrative of Sojourner Truth is published.

Compromise of 1850 is adopted. The legislation contains five separate acts that affect African Americans. These include a new Fugitive Slave Law, the admissions of slaves into some of the new western territories, the admission of California to the Union as a free state, and the prohibition of the public sale of slaves in Washington, D.C.

Henry Walton Bibb publishes his autobiography, *Narrative of the Life and Adventures of Henry Bibb, an American Slave*.

1851 Emancipated slaves in Virginia lose or forfeit their rights if they remain in the state more than twelve months after being granted their freedom.

William Cooper Nell publishes the pioneering historical work *Services of Colored Americans in the Wars of 1776 and 1812*.

The debut of Elizabeth Taylor Greenfield takes place before the Buffalo Musical Association. The Buffalo press dubs her "the Black Swan."

1852 Martin Robinson Delany publishes *The Condition, Elevation, Emancipation and Destiny of the Colored People of the United States, Politically Considered*. This work is cited for its nationalism and advocacy of emigration out of the United States.

Frederick Douglass delivers his "Independence Day Address." This is the first deliverance of a fully realized black declaration of inevitable independence.

Harriet Beecher Stowe's *Uncle Tom's Cabin* is published.

1853 Mary Ann Shadd Cary publishes the *Provincial Freeman*, a weekly Canadian newspaper. She is generally acknowledged to be the first woman newspaper publisher in Canada and the first black newspaper-woman in North America.

Publication of William Wells Brown's *Clotelle, or The President's Daughter*, the first novel published by an African American.

Sarah Mapps Douglass accepts a position with the Quaker-sponsored Institute for Colored Youth.

At Boston's Howard Athenaeum Sarah Parker Remond refuses to vacate a seat in the "whites-only" gallery during an opera. She is arrested and thrown down the stairs. She subsequently wins $500 in damages in a civil suit.

The National Council of Colored People is established.

1854 Frances Ellen Watkins Harper publishes her volume of verse, *Poems of Miscellaneous Subjects*. Many of the pieces in this volume deal with the horrors of slavery.

The Republican Party is founded, and its major goal is the abolition of slavery.

Anthony Burns, a fugitive slave, is arrested and held in jail. His arrest prompts Boston's Vigilance Committee to stage a mass protest meeting. A militant faction within meeting decides to lead an armed attack to rescue Burns. Federal troops suppress the mob. Burns is returned to his master, but his freedom is purchased the following year. This case encouraged many states to pass personal liberty acts that would block the enforcement of the Fugitive Slave Acts.

Congress passes the Kansas-Nebraska Act. Settlers in these territories would be allowed to choose whether to permit slavery there.

James A. Healy is ordained a Catholic priest in Notre Dame Cathedral in Paris. He is the first black American ordained a Catholic priest.

Delegates from eleven states convene in Cleveland, Ohio to discuss and develop a national plan for black emigration. One of the most outspoken emigrationists is Martin Robinson Delany.

Frederick Douglass publishes *My Bondage and My Freedom*.

Kansas elects a proslavery legislature. Several thousand men from Missouri cross into Kansas and vote in the territorial election.

John Mercer Langston becomes one of the first African Americans elected to public office.

The governor of Massachusetts signs a bill ending "Jim Crow" schooling in Boston.

Kansas settlers opposing slavery hold a convention and petition for admission to the Union as a free state. They declare that the territorial proslavery legislation is illegal because Missourians supporting slavery voted in the election.

1855 Biddy Bridget Mason escapes from captivity and arranges to have her owner put on trial for owning slaves in California. Biddy and her family are manumitted. She settles in Los Angeles, where she works as a midwife and nurse.

1856 California's first black newspaper is founded and edited by Mifflin W. Gibbs.

James H. Adams, the governor of South Carolina, argues for the repeal of 1807 law prohibiting slave trade into the United States.

Wilberforce University is founded by the African Methodist Episcopal Church.

Bleeding Kansas—abolitionists and proslavery groups battle. Slavery supporters burn the Free State Hotel, wreck the newspaper, and ransack homes. John Brown and his followers retaliate by shooting and killing five slaveholding settlers.

Governor Daniel Woodson, a proslavery advocate, declares Kansas to be in a state of open insurrection.

1857 Disunion Convention meets in Worcester, MA. Delegates adopt the slogan "No union with slaveholders." The convention supports a split between slave states and free states.

James Buchanan is sworn in as the fifteenth president. In his inaugural speech he calls for tolerance of slavery for the purpose of keeping the states united.

Dred Scott v. Sanford—the U.S. Supreme Court rules that blacks are not citizens of the United States, thus upholding the Fugitive Slave Law and denying Congress the power to prohibit slavery in any federal territory. The Court declares that blacks have no rights that a white man is required to respect.

In response to the Dred Scott decision New Hampshire passes legislation that does not deprive any person—regardless of color—of citizenship.

Publication of Frank J. Webb's *The Garies and Their Friends*, the second novel by an African American.

1858 Voters in the Kansas Territory reject the proslavery constitution.

Arkansas requires free blacks to choose either exile or enslavement.

John Brown holds an anti-slavery convention in Chatham, Canada. The group draws up a constitution for a nation of liberated slaves to be set up in the mountains of Virginia. Brown plans to provoke a general slave uprising and lead slaves and free blacks into the mountains. His first strike is to be Harpers Ferry, VA.

Abraham Lincoln and Stephen A. Douglas complete their final debate while campaigning for the U.S. Senate. Douglas supports a state's right to choose whether or not to allow slavery, and Lincoln argues that all people are born with the right to life, liberty, and the pursuit of happiness.

William Wells Brown's *The Escape: or, A Leap for Freedom. A Drama, in Five Acts*, is the first play published by an African American.

1859 Martin R. Delany signs a treaty with the Alake of Abeokuta, in what is now western Nigeria, providing for the settlement of educated African Americans. Before the first group of settlers can leave for West Africa the Civil War breaks out.

A survey of the free black population is published in this year stating that 2,900 black men served on board whaleboats. African Americans could find work in this industry and were paid wages according to rank—not color. Integration varied from vessel to vessel.

Mississippi resolves to secede from the Union if a Republican is elected president.

"Aunt" Clara Brown journeys to Colorado with a wagon train of gold prospectors. She opens a laundry in Central City, serves as a nurse, and organizes the city's first Sunday school.

John Brown raids Harpers Ferry. He attacks and seizes arms from the United States Arsenal. He is captured and stands trial for treason. Brown is found guilty of murder and conspiring with slaves to create an insurrection.

Publication of Harriet E. Wilson's *Our Nig: or; Sketches from the Life of a Free Black in a Two-Story White House, North, Showing that Slavery's Shadows Fall Even There*, perhaps the first novel written by an African-American woman.

1860 The Republican Party nominates Abraham Lincoln as its presidential candidate.

The Democratic Party is split over the issue of slavery. It breaks into two separate political entities.

Congress adopts a set of resolutions sponsored by southern congressmen clarifying the status of slavery.

A slave conspiracy is uncovered in Plymouth, NC. The insurrection is planned by a small group of slaves who hope to encourage hundreds of others to join them. A slave betrays them.

Lincoln is elected president of the United States.

South Carolina secedes from the Union. Federal troops move to Fort Sumter several days after the secession. In response to this federal action, the South Carolina militia seizes other federal installations in Charleston.

1861 The remaining Southern states follow South Carolina in seceding from the Union and join the Confederacy.

April 12—Confederate forces open fire on Fort Sumter in Charleston harbor. This act begins the Civil War.

After the attack on Fort Sumter, President Lincoln calls for 75,000 volunteers to serve in the Union army. Although many free blacks try to enlist, they are not allowed to participate.

May 6—the Confederate Congress officially declares war on the United States.

May 23—General Benjamin Butler declares that slaves who enter his lines are "contraband." Since Virginia claims to be a foreign country, the Fugitive Slave Act cannot be enforced. In two months' time about 900 runaway slaves seek their freedom behind his lines. Butler uses the former slaves to build roads and fortifications, unload vessels, and store provisions.

August 6—Congress passes the first Confiscation Act. Any runaway slave who has been used to aid the Confederacy can be granted freedom once under the control of the Union army.

August 30—General John C. Frèmont issues a proclamation of emancipation, freeing the slaves in Missouri. On September 2, President Lincoln declares this null and void.

Mary S. Peake becomes the first teacher to be hired in the first American Missionary Association's school.

September 25—the Secretary of the Navy authorizes the enlistment of slaves to fight in the Civil War.

Harriet A. Jacobs publishes *Incidents in the Life of a Slave Girl*, the most comprehensive antebellum autobiography by an African-American woman.

1862 Lincoln meets with Frederick Douglass and other black leaders to discuss the emigration of free blacks to Central America. He asks the black leaders to recruit volunteers for a government-sponsored colonization project. Douglass is outraged by Lincoln's request. He responds, "This is our country as much as it is yours, and we will not leave it."

Jefferson Davis is elected president of the Confederacy.

Nashville becomes the first Confederate state capital to fall under the control of Union forces.

Susie Baker King Taylor joins the First South Carolina Volunteer Regiment, an all black regiment. She becomes the unit laundress and volunteer nurse.

Lincoln recommends a plan to Congress that would offer aid to any state promising gradual abolition of slavery.

Free blacks in New York organize a National Freedmen's Relief Association to help slaves adjust to their new freedom. Similar associations are established in Chicago, Cincinnati, and Philadelphia.

Penn School is established for freed slaves on St. Helena Island off South Carolina within weeks after its capture by Union troops. African Americans are trained in agriculture and home economics.

Contraband slaves and free blacks seeking protection and freedom swell the Union forces.

Slavery is abolished in the District of Columbia. Slave owners are to be compensated at the rate of $300 per slave.

New Orleans, the largest seaport in the South, falls into Union hands.

Union troops take Norfolk, Virginia, and it becomes a center for black refugees from the countryside.

The First South Carolina Volunteer Regiment is officially mustered.

Robert Smalls, a black navy pilot, is pressed into service by the Confederate government. He is made wheelsman of the steamboat the Planter. While the white crew members are on shore, Smalls seizes the opportunity to steer the ship, containing his family and a small group of other slaves, to Union lines.

President Lincoln signs a bill outlawing slavery in the territories but not in the states.

Congress authorizes an act that allows the use of blacks in the Union army.

1863 Frederick Douglass becomes a major recruiter for the Union army. After meeting several times with Lincoln, he advises blacks to join in large numbers as an expression of their patriotism. In the March issue of *Douglass' Monthly*, he publishes "Men of Color, to Arms!"—a call for black recruitment.

The first clash between officially recruited black Union troops and Confederate soldiers occurs at the Battle of Hundred Pines. The black soldiers hold their ground and repel Confederate troops.

The Emancipation Proclamation is issued. Its purpose is to deplete Southern manpower reserve in slaves. It frees only those slaves residing in the territory in rebellion. It does not abolish slavery in loyal states. Floods of fugitive slaves begin to enter Union lines in Virginia, Tennessee, and along the southern coast.

Representatives from Freedmen's Aid Societies in Boston, New York, and Philadelphia lead a missionary expedition to aid contraband slaves in Hilton Head, South Carolina.

Daniel Alexander Payne is named president of Wilberforce University, the first black-controlled college in the United States.

The U.S. War Department establishes the Bureau of Colored Troops to handle all recruitment of black regiments.

Harriet Tubman serves the Union cause as a spy and guide. She receives a formal commendation from the secretary of war for her work in the Sea Islands as a nurse and daring scout.

Draft riot erupts in New York City. The Colored Orphan Asylum is burned down, almost 100 people are killed, and many blacks flee the city. Immigrant workers vent their racial prejudices and economic fears upon the city's black population.

The Fifty-fourth Massachusetts Volunteers lead the charge against Fort Wagner, South Carolina. It is the first black regiment raised in the North, and they display extreme bravery in their assault of the fort.

Black troops protest discriminatory wages. The Fifty-fourth regiment refuses pay for eighteen months rather than accept less wages.

1864 William Walker, a black sergeant in the Third South Carolina Regiment is shot by order of a court-martial for leading a protest against unequal pay for black soldiers.

Three black regiments fight in a battle in Olustee, Florida. Three hundred of the black soldiers are killed.

Rebecca Lee graduates from the New England Female Medical College. She becomes the first African-American woman to work as a physician.

April 12 Fort Pillow in west Tennessee is the site of one of the most controversial battles of the Civil War. About three hundred black troops, many of whom attempted to surrender, and their family members are massacred by the Confederate troops.

The First Kansas Colored Volunteers storm the Confederate lines at Poison Spring, Arkansas. They suffer heavy casualties. Those who are captured are murdered. African-American troops are not taken prisoner as their white counterparts are.

Black soldiers participate in the ten-month siege started in Petersburg, Virginia. Grant wants a quick engagement to cut off rail supplies to Richmond, but Lee wants to prolong the siege, hoping the North will tire of the casualties and accept a peace settlement. Twelve hundred of the sixty-three hundred casualties are black soldiers. The engagement ends one week before the final Southern surrender.

The Battle for Chaffin's Farm, Richmond, VA—General Benjamin Butler uses nine black regiments in this battle. The Union forces are victorious. More than 500 black soldiers are killed or wounded, and nine receive the Congressional Medal of Honor for bravery during the battle.

A group of 150 black men hold a convention in Syracuse, New York to discuss the future of their race. Frederick Douglass is elected as their chairman. They establish the National Equal Rights League and elect John Mercer Langston as the president.

1865 Fewer than a hundred African Americans become officers in the Union army, and not one black receives a naval commission. Major Martin Robinson Delany serves as a surgeon, as does Alexander Thomas Augusta.

By the end of the Civil War the Union army has more than 386,000 African Americans enlisted. Nearly 37,000 blacks died during the war.

The Tennessee State Convention of Negroes convenes in Nashville. A petition is submitted to the U.S. Senate protesting the seating of the Tennessee delegates in Congress until the state legislature secures the rights of blacks as freemen.

African Americans in Norfolk, Virginia hold mass meetings and demand equal rights and ballots.

The Freedman's Savings and Trust Company, the first bank for blacks, opens in Washington, D.C.

Patrick Frances Healy receives his Ph.D. from the University of Louvain in Belgium.

Illinois repeals its black laws.

John Sweat Rock becomes the first black lawyer admitted to practice before the U.S. Supreme Court.

Henry Highland Garnet is invited to deliver a memorial sermon in the U.S. House of Representatives commemorating passage of the Thirteenth Amendment.

Black troops of the Fifty-fifth Massachusetts Regiment march into Charleston, and are greeted with the cheers of the city's black population.

Congress establishes the Bureau of Refugees, Freedmen and Abandoned Lands. It is created to help blacks adjust to their new freedom.

Jefferson Davis signs a bill authorizing the use of 300,000 slaves as soldiers in the Confederate army. The order comes too late to influence the outcome of the war.

Appomattox Courthouse—Robert E. Lee surrenders to Ulysses S. Grant. The Civil War is over.

President Johnson reveals his reconstruction plan. Reconstruction began long before the Confederacy's final surrender. Lincoln introduced a Reconstruction Plan in December of 1863.

Planters meet to fix wages and set conditions of employment regarding blacks. These meetings take place in Virginia counties and other states where black labor is plentiful.

June 19—Union forces arrive in Galveston, and the news spreads rapidly throughout the state. African Americans are declared free and celebrate emancipation on this day, known as Juneteenth.

Mississippi establishes black codes restricting the rights and movement of blacks in response to President Johnson's Restoration program. Legislatures in other southern states begin to formalize such black codes.

Committee on Reconstruction is established, and slavery is made illegal in the United States.

Fisk Free School opens in Nashville, TN. It is established by E. M. Cravath, and E. P. Smith of the American Missionary Association and John Ogden of the Freedman's Bureau to produce qualified black teachers. In 1867 it is incorporated as Fisk University.

1866 Ku Klux Klan is formed by Confederate army veterans in Pulaski, Tennessee to resist Reconstruction in Confederate states.

Sharecropping system is adopted throughout the South. Freedmen, who could not buy or rent land, were willing to work for a "share" of the crop.

Congress passes the Southern Homestead Act, which opens federal lands in Florida, Alabama, Mississippi, Louisiana, and Arkansas for

homesteading. About 4,000 black families bought land; few were able to hold on to it because they lacked capital.

A delegation of black leaders, including Frederick Douglass, meets with President Andrew Johnson. They present their views on the personal safety and protection of the rights of African Americans, and they solicit the president's views. Johnson is opposed to any federal laws to protect freed slaves and feels that the states have to solve problems within their own boundaries.

Civil Rights Bill of 1866 grants blacks the rights and privileges of American citizenship.

Race riot erupts in Memphis after a white policeman confronts a group of black men and strikes one. The policeman is then struck by a black man. News of the incident spreads through the city and a large mob of whites roam through the black community setting fires to schools, churches, and homes. Many blacks are beaten, wounded, or killed.

Eight of the former Confederate states enact laws to limit the freedom of the black labor force.

1867 Rebecca Cole becomes the second black woman to receive an M.D. and accepts an invitation to work with Elizabeth Blackwell in the New York Infirmary for Women and Children.

Howard University is chartered. It soon becomes an education center for free blacks.

Morehouse College is founded. It is noted for its rigorous academic standards.

Nebraska becomes the thirty-seventh state and black settlers flock there because the land is cheap.

Congress passes several Reconstruction Acts to provide for political participation of blacks in southern state politics.

The Knights of the White Camellia are founded. It becomes one of the largest terrorist organizations in the Reconstruction South.

1868 Francis Lous Cardozo becomes South Carolina's secretary of state. John W. Menard of Louisiana is elected the first black congressman, but he is never seated.

South Carolina Constitutional Convention meets in Charleston. It is the first assembly of its kind to have a black majority.

Hampton Institute is founded by Samuel Chapman Armstrong. It is an agricultural and industrial college for blacks.

Pinckney B. S. Pinchback and James J. Harris become the first African-American delegates to attend a Republican convention.

Alabama, Florida, Louisiana, North Carolina, and South Carolina are readmitted to the Union.

Fourteenth Amendment is ratified, declaring blacks full citizens.

1869 George L. Ruffin becomes the first black person to earn a law degree from Harvard University.

The Union Pacific Railroad employs three hundred black workers.

President Grant appoints Ebenezer Don Carlos Bassett U.S. minister to Haiti and the Dominican Republic.

1870 Alonzo J. Ransier is elected lieutenant governor of South Carolina. He becomes the first African American to hold a high executive post in South Carolina.

Benjamin S. Turner is elected to Congress. He is the first black congressman from Alabama.

Robert Brown Elliott is elected to the House of Representatives from South Carolina. He serves on several key committees, including the Committee on Education and Labor.

James W. Smith becomes the first black student admitted to West Point. However he does not graduate. He is court-martialed and forced to leave the academy.

The *New Era* newspaper, edited by John Sella Martin, is founded.

The last of the former Confederate states are readmitted to the Union.

Jefferson Franklin Long becomes the first Georgian seated and the second African American to ever serve in the House of Representatives.

The Fifteenth Amendment, granting blacks the right to vote, is ratified.

Congress passes the first Enforcement Act to enforce the Fifteenth Amendment because terrorist tactics are being used throughout the South to keep blacks from voting.

Robert Carlos DeLarge is elected U.S. Representative from South Carolina.

Jonathan Jasper Wright becomes the only African American to serve on a state supreme court in South Carolina during Reconstruction.

Joseph H. Rainey is elected to the House of Representatives from South Carolina. He is the first African American member of the House.

1871 A group of black farmers form the Alabama Negro Labor Union to consider the plight of black workers in the state.

Ku Klux Klan massacres thirty blacks in Meridian, MS.

The Forty-second Congress convenes with five black congressmen: Joseph H. Rainey, Robert Carlos DeLarge, Robert Brown Elliott, Benjamin S. Turner, and Joseph T. Wells.

Jefferson F. Long becomes the first black to address the House. He spoke in opposition to granting leniency for ex-Confederates. "If this House removes the disabilities of disloyal men by modifying the test-oath," he warns, "I venture to prophesy you will again have trouble from the very same men who gave you trouble before."

Congress passes the Second Enforcement Act or the Ku Klux Klan Act—giving federal officers and courts control of voter registration and voting in congressional elections. The law is designed to enforce the Fifteenth Amendment.

James Milton Turner is appointed U.S. Minister to Liberia. He becomes the first black American diplomat to an African country.

Josiah Thomas Walls takes his seat in the House of Representatives to become Florida's first black Congressman.

Congress passes the Third Enforcement Act, regarding Klan conspiracy as rebellion against the United States and giving broad powers to the president to suspend the writ of habeas corpus and declare martial law in rebellious areas.

The Federal government's campaign against the Klan is a success. Klansmen are convicted for murder, violence, and interferance with the rights of black and Republican voters.

P. B. S. Pinchback becomes Lieutenant governor of Louisiana.

1872 Republicans win a slate of state offices in South Carolina. Elected officials include Henry E. Hayne, Francis L. Cardozo, Henry W. Purvis, and Richard H. Gleaves.

Richard Harvey Cain is elected to the House of Representatives.

African Americans win several major offices in Louisiana including: C. C. Antoine, P. G. Deslonde, W. B. Brown.

Charlotte E. Ray graduates from Howard University's Law School, becoming the first African-American woman to receive a law degree from any law school in the nation.

Five hundred Klansmen are arrested in South Carolina as part of the anti-Klan campaign. Only fifty-five are convicted in federal court.

Congress passes the Amnesty Act that allows all but a few hundred Confederate leaders to hold elective offices.

Freedman's Bureau is closed.

James Thomas is elected to Congress. He is the second black representative from Alabama.

P. B. S. Pinchback becomes acting governor of Louisiana during the impeachment of Gov. Henry Clay Warmoth.

1873 Macon B. Allen is elected judge of the Inferior Court of Charleston, SC.

Seven African Americans are elected to the Forty-third U.S. Congress. They are Richard Harvey Cain, Alonzo J. Ransier, James Thomas Rapier, Josiah T. Walls, and John R. Lynch. U. S. Supreme Court begins to chip away at the power of the Fourteenth Amendment in a series of decisions in the *Slaughterhouse Cases*. The court rules that the Fourteenth Amendment protects federal civil rights, not the civil rights belonging exclusively to the states.

In Mississippi African Americans are elected to offices on the local and state level including lieutenant governor.

Mifflin W. Gibbs is elected city judge in Little Rock, Arkansas, thereby becoming the first African-American judge in the United States.

1874 In Louisiana, after a disputed gubernatorial election, white and black factions fight for control of the government. Riots and armed confrontations break out at Liberty Place in New Orleans, at the Conshattau Massacre in Red River parish, and at the Colfax Massacre in Grant Parish—where more than sixty black men, women, and children are killed.

Edward Alexander Bouchet becomes the first black to graduate from Yale University with honors as well as being elected to Phi Beta Kappa national honor society.

Jeremiah Haralson is elected to the U.S Congress representing Alabama.

John A. Hyman becomes the first African American congressman from North Carolina.

Robert Smalls is elected to the U.S. Congress. Throughout his career, he made significant contributions as a soldier and politician.

Blanche K. Bruce is elected the first African-American senator from Mississippi.

Freedman's Bank fails after years of mismanagement. The bank's monetary losses are especially tragic because they represented one of the first attempts of the newly freed slaves to grasp economic security and equal citizenship.

Patrick Francis Healy is installed as president of Georgetown University.

Sixteen blacks are lynched in Tennessee.

Democrats and KKK members start a riot in Vicksburg, MS. Seventy-five blacks are killed.

1875 Oliver Lewis wins the Kentucky Derby. Black jockeys dominate horseracing at this time.

Tennessee adopts Jim Crow Laws.

Grant sends federal troops to Vicksburg, MS. White Democrats and the KKK continue to use intimidation tactics against blacks and Republicans.

Congress passes the Civil Rights act of 1875 prohibiting discrimination in public accommodations.

James Healy is named the first black Catholic Bishop of Portland, Maine.

First convention of black journalists convenes in Cincinnati, Ohio. J. Stella Martin, Mifflin Gibbs, and Henry Turner are among those who attend.

Racial conflicts erupt in Mississippi in September. White Democrats and KKK members attack and kill blacks and Republicans.

November—Democrats win many state and local government elections throughout the South. Their strategy to suppress the black vote through violence, economic intimidation, and murder is successful at restoring white supremacy. The reconstruction governments in South Carolina and Louisiana are defeated.

1876 Edward Bouchet becomes the first African American to be awarded a doctorate by a major American university.

President Grant sends federal troops to South Carolina to restore order after widespread racial rioting and white terrorism erupts.

United States v. Reese—Supreme Court rules that the Fifteenth Amendment does not confer the right to suffrage but only allows the government to provide a punishment for denying the vote to anyone based on race, color, or previous condition of servitude.

Supreme Court denies punishment to the people who had broken up a black political meeting in Louisiana. In the case of the *United States v. Cruikshank*, the court decides that the right of suffrage is not a necessary attribute of citizenship and that the right to vote in the states comes from the states.

Terrorism and race riots erupt in South Carolina.

1877 The Forty-fifth Congress convenes with three African Americans. Blanche K. Bruce is a senator for Mississippi, and Richard Cain and Robert Smalls are representatives from South Carolina.

Frederick Douglass becomes the first black to receive a major government appointment when he is named U.S. Marshall for the District of Columbia.

Henry Ossian Flipper becomes the first black graduate of West Point.

Federal troops withdraw from Southern states.

1878 James A. Bland, a songwriter, publishes "Carry Me Back to Ole Virginny." He is considered to be one of the most successful composers of popular songs in the United States at this time.

Publication of James Monroe Trotter's *Music and Some Highly Musical People*, the first historical survey of black music by an African American.

Supreme Court overturns a Louisiana law prohibiting racial segregation in the *Hall v. De Cut* decision.

1879 Due to escalating violence, thousands of blacks leave the South and migrate to the North and West.

Benjamin "Pap" Singleton organizes mass migrations to Kansas.

John M. Langston and Richard T. Greener are convinced that they should migrate to the West because the federal government will not actively support blacks in the South.

White terrorists, fearing the loss of cheap labor, set up a military-style blockade on the Mississippi River to prevent African Americans from migrating to Kansas.

Whites meet with African Americans throughout the South, and they promise to improve conditions for blacks in order to keep them from leaving.

Exodusters are about 20,000 southern African Americans who migrate spontaneously to Kansas from Mississippi, Louisiana, Texas, Kentucky, and Tennessee in the spring of 1879.

Mary Eliza Mahoney becomes the first African American woman to graduate from the nursing program in the United States.

1880 The first successful agricultural cooperative association settlement is established in the Sea Islands off the coast of South Carolina.

Southern University and the Agricultural and Mechanical College are chartered in New Orleans for blacks.

In *Strauder v. West*, the Supreme Court rules it unconstitutional to exclude blacks from jury duty.

1881 The Forty-seventh Congress convenes with two black representatives—Robert Smalls and John R. Lynch.

Publication of John Patterson Smapson's *Mixed Races: Their Environment, Temperament, Heredity, and Phrenology*, the first full-length study of phrenology by an African American.

Henry Highland Garnet is appointed minister to Liberia.

Tuskegee University is founded, and Booker T. Washington is recommended to organize the school.

1882 Lewis H. Latimer patents his most important invention—a carbon filament that increased the brightness and longevity of the light bulb.

A bill is proposed in the U.S. Congress to use federal lands to equalize educational opportunities for blacks and whites in the South. It is defeated.

Gray v. Cincinnati and Southern Railroad Company—a federal court rules that separation of races on trains is legal as long as accommodations are equal.

Vigilantism continues in the South—forty-nine blacks are lynched. The *Chicago Tribune* begins recording lynching.

George Washington Williams publishes his two-volume *History of the Negro Race in America, 1619-1880*. It is the first serious work in this field.

John Fox Slater creates the Slater Fund when he donates one million dollars for the schooling of former slaves and their children in the South.

1883 Isaac Murphy, a black jockey, wins a remarkable 51 out of 133 races.

Jan E. Matzaliger receives a patent for an automatic shoe laster that revolutionizes the American shoe industry.

George L. Ruffin, the first black to earn a law degree from Harvard University, is appointed city judge of the District Court of Charlestown. He is the first black to hold this position.

U. S. Supreme Court declares the Civil Rights Act of 1875 unconstitutional.

Forty-eighth Congress convenes with two African Americans James E. O'Hara of North Carolina and Robert Smalls of South Carolina.

Black citizens in Ohio meet for a State Convention to discuss continued white terrorism in the South.

1884 Benjamin Tucker Tanner establishes the *A.M.E. Church Review*, a quarterly journal focusing on African American issues.

The Medical Chirurgical Society of the District of Columbia, the first African American medical society, is established.

Black newspapers publish letters and advertisements encouraging migration to and settlement in the West.

Moses Fleetwood Walker makes his debut as a catcher on the Toledo team of the American Baseball Association. He is the first black player in major league baseball.

T. Thomas Fortune, a prominent black journalist, establishes the New York Freeman.

1885 Frank Thompson organizes the best of the all-black professional baseball teams—the Cuban Giants.

Forty-ninth Congress convenes with two black representatives—James O'Hara and Robert Smalls.

George Washington Williams is named United States minister to Haiti.

Lynching continues in Louisiana.

Augustus Tolton, the son of two escaped slaves, is ordained a Catholic priest. He is considered by some to be the first fully black ordained priest. The Healy brothers who were ordained before him were the sons of an Irish father and a mulatto mother.

1887 Fiftieth Congress convenes with no black members.

Lynching continues in the South. Seventy are reported in this year. The black press continues to report these acts of oppression.

Granville T. Woods patents an Induction Telegraph System.

New York Age editor T. Thomas Fortune calls for the formation of the National Afro-American League. The league's goals are to seek the elimination of disfranchisement, lynching, segregation on railroads and in public accommodations, and abuse of black prisoners.

1888 Mound Bayou, Mississippi, considered by many to be the first all African American town, is founded by Isaiah Thornton Montgomery and Benjamin Green.

Henry P. Cheatham is elected to the Fifty-first Congress as a representative from North Carolina.

Sixty-nine lynchings are reported this year.

John M. Langston is elected to the U.S. Congress from Virginia but is denied his seat until 1890 when the House adjudicates in his favor.

The Capital Savings Bank of Washington, D.C. opens. It is the first African-American commercial bank.

1889 Number of lynchings reported this year escalates to ninety-four.

Charles Young graduates from West Point. He is the third African American to graduate from the military academy.

The Fifty-first Congress convenes with three black congressmen—Henry P. Cheatham, John M. Langston, and Thomas E. Miller.

1890 The "Grandfather clause" is introduced into Mississippi's constitution to keep blacks from voting. Voting is restricted to those who are descendants of persons who had voted prior to 1866. In addition, a poll tax and literacy tests are adopted. This is the first attempt to eliminate black voting. By World War I almost all the ex-Confederate states had adopted some form of black disfranchisement.

Edwin P. McCabe and his wife, Sarah, move to Oklahoma and together with Charles Robbins and William L. Eagleson found Langston City, an all-black community.

The lynching of black Americans continues—eighty-five are reported this year.

T. Thomas Fortune becomes a key figure in the National Afro-American League, an early and important vehicle for civil rights agitation. He is elected secretary at the 1890 meeting.

Thomas E. Miller leaves his congressional seat. Miller's election is contested by his white opponent, and the South Carolina Supreme Court rules in the Democrat's favor.

1891 The Georgia legislature passes laws to segregate streetcars.

Lynchings continue to increase. There are 113 reported this year.

Daniel Hale Williams establishes Provident Hospital in Chicago. It is the first black-owned hospital in the United States, and it has an interracial staff of doctors.

The Fifty-second Congress convenes with only one black congressman—Henry P. Cheatham, NC.

1892 William H. Lewis is the first African American selected for Walter Camp's All-American football team.

There are 161 lynchings reported this year.

Ida B. Wells-Barnett becomes editor and co-owner of the *Memphis Free Speech*.

The Baltimore Afro-American newspaper is first published. This newspaper is now the oldest family-owned black publication in America.

Paul Laurence Dunbar publishes his first book, *Oak and Ivy.*

1893 Henry Ossawa Turner, painter and illustrator, begins depicting genre scenes of African-American life. His best know genre study is *The Banjo Lesson,* which depicts an older musician teaching his art to a young boy.

The Fifty-third Congress convenes with the only black member George W. Murray from South Carolina.

Daniel Hale Williams performs the first successful open-heart surgery.

1894 Harry T. Burleigh, singer and composer, becomes the baritone soloist in St. George's Episcopal Church in New York.

1895 Mary Church Terrell becomes the first African American to serve on the Washington, D.C. School Board.

Frederick Douglass, abolitionist, journalist, orator, and social reformer, dies. He fully understood and vividly personified his people's struggle

from slavery to freedom; from obscurity and poverty to recognition and respectability.

W. E. B. Du Bois becomes the first African American to receive a doctorate in history at Harvard University.

Black lynchings continue—there are 113 reported this year.

Booker T. Washington delivers his famous "Atlanta Compromise" speech. It is the best single statement of Washington's philosophy of racial advancement and his political accommodation with the predominant racial ideology of this time.

South Carolina adopts a new constitution that includes an "Understanding Clause" designed to strip blacks of any remaining political rights.

Austin M. Curtis becomes the first black physician on the medical staff of Chicago's Cook County Hospital.

1896 George Washington Carver becomes the director of the agricultural department at Tuskegee Normal and Industrial Institute.

Justice John Marshall Harlan of the Supreme Court writes a dissenting opinion of the Jim Crow laws. He states that Jim Crow laws deprive black citizens of equal protection of the law.

Lynching of blacks continues—seventy-eight blacks are lynched this year.

The National Association of Colored Women is founded. Mary Church Terrell is elected the first president. The organization is mainly concerned with educational and health issues and ending the practice of lynching.

Plessy v. Ferguson—the Supreme Court upholds an 1890 Louisiana statute that required railroads to provide separate but equal accommodations for blacks and whites, and forbade persons from riding in cars not assigned to their race. This ruling gave constitutional sanction to virtually all forms of racial segregation in the United States until after World War II.

Paul Laurence Dunbar's third collection of verse, *Lyrics of Lowly Life*, is published.

1897 George Henry White is the only black congressman. He attempts to introduce the country's first anti-lynching legislation. Andrew J. Beard, inventor, receives a patent for his most important invention—a car coupler for automatically hooking railroad cars together.

One hundred and twenty-three blacks are lynched this year.

The American Negro Academy is founded to promote African-American literature, science, art, and higher learning.

A Trip to Coontown, a musical comedy written by Bob Cole, is produced, directed, and managed by blacks. It runs for three years.

1898 Black troops fight in the Spanish-American War.

There are 101 lynchings reported this year.

Samuel W. Rutherford organizes the National Benefit Life Insurance Company in Washington, D.C.

Race riot erupts in Wilmington, North Carolina, and eight blacks are killed when white supremacists drive black officeholders out of office.

South Carolina passes legislation requiring racial segregation within trains.

Louisiana introduces a grandfather clause that specifies that a person could register to vote if his father or grandfather had been eligible to vote on January 1, 1867, or if he or an ancestor had served in either the Confederate army or the Union army.

1899 John Merrick and associates open the North Carolina Mutual and Provident Insurance Company.

Eight blacks are massacred in Palmetto, Georgia.

Charles W. Chesnutt publishes *The Conjure Woman*, the first book of serious fiction by an African American to garner commercial success.

W. E. B. Du Bois publishes *The Philadelphia Negro*, the most significant sociological inquiry written by an African American up to this time.

Scott Joplin releases one of his finest works, "Maple Leaf Rag."

Lynching continues—eighty-five blacks are reported lynched this year.

1900 Louis Armstrong is born in New Orleans.

Black congressman George H. White introduces the first bill in Congress that would make lynching a federal crime. It never comes to a vote.

Booker T. Washington organizes the National Negro Business League in Boston, MA.

The Black National Anthem is performed for the first time on February 12 at a celebration of Lincoln's birthday. Called "Lift Ev'ry Voice and Sing." The anthem is written by the African-American poet and political leader James Weldon Johnson with his brother John Rosamond Johnson.

Virginia passes legislation segregating trains and calls a new constitutional convention aimed at erasing Reconstruction-era civil rights gains.

One hundred six blacks are reported lynched in this year.

1901 The *Boston Guardian* is founded. Published by William Monroe Trotter and George Forbes, the newspaper is a response to the more conservative politics of Booker T. Washington.

Booker T. Washington publishes *Up From Slavery: An Autobiography*.

1902 Virginia establishes a literacy test and a poll tax that effectively disenfranchises the African-American population.

1903 W. E. B. Du Bois publishes *The Souls of Black Folk: Essays and Sketches*, which famously asserts that "the problem of the Twentieth Century is the problem of the color line." The book also openly attacks Booker T. Washington's position that blacks should give up the right to vote and to a liberal education in return for white friendship and support.

Maggie Lena Walker opens the St. Luke Penny Savings Bank in Richmond, Virginia, becoming the first African-American woman in America to own and operate a bank.

Boley, Oklahoma, is founded. It is one of many black towns formed in the South as a response to escalating racism.

1904 Mary McLeod Bethune establishes the Daytona Educational and Industrial Institute for girls. It is the first black school in Florida to offer education beyond the elementary grades.

George Poage, representing the Milwaukee Athletic Club is the first African-American Olympic medalist, winning a bronze medal in the 400-meter hurdles race at the St. Louis games.

The National Liberty Party, the first nationally based black political party, is formed. They choose Iowa editor George Edwin Taylor as their presidential candidate; after he gains only a few votes, the party disappears.

Whites in Statesboro, Georgia, lynch two African-American men accused of murdering a white family. The white mob then turns on the rest of the African-American population, beating them and burning homes.

Oscar DePriest is elected to the Cook County Board of Commissioners in Chicago, Illinois.

1905 New York is the site of a race riot between the African-American community and the predominantly Irish police. The riot arises out of tensions over police brutality against African Americans.

The Chicago Defender is founded by Robert Sengstacke Abbott, a journalist and lawyer from Georgia. *The Defender,* although muckraking and sensationalistic, is mainly concerned with issues of racial justice.

The Niagara Movement, led by W.E.B. Du Bois, is formed in Fort Erie, Canada. The protest group's goal is to challenge the dominant accommodationist ideas of Booker T. Washington. Although the movement lasts for only five years, many of its goals and tactics are adopted by the National Association for the Advancement of Colored People (NAACP), which forms in 1909.

1906 The National Association for the Protection of Colored Women is founded. It addresses the problems facing the great numbers of southern African-American women who migrate to the North.

The first African-American Greek letter fraternity, Alpha Phi Alpha, is founded at Cornell University in Ithaca, New York.

In Atlanta, Georgia, a race riot erupts and lasts for several days. Gangs of white males attack African Americans in response to unsubstantiated newspaper reports of black attacks on white women. The riots leave the city's race relations tense for years to come.

In Brownsville, Texas, a racial incident occurs when suspicion falls on African American soldiers from the Twenty-fifth Infantry Division for a shooting that left one white man dead and two others wounded. President Theodore Roosevelt has three companies of African-

American troops dishonorably discharged in retaliation for not giving up the guilty parties. The discharges are formally reversed in 1972 by the U.S. Army.

1907 Alain Locke becomes the first African-American Rhodes scholar. He will go on to become one of the leading figures in the Harlem Renaissance.

Oklahoma passes legislation segregating streetcars.

The U.S. Supreme Court upholds the right of railroads to segregate passengers traveling between states, even when the laws of the state in which the train is traveling do not allow segregation.

Wendell P. Dabney starts *the Union*, a newspaper for African Americans, in Cincinnati, Ohio.

George Henry White, a former slave and congressman, incorporates the People's Savings Bank to serve the banking needs (especially loans) of the residents of Whitesboro, New Jersey, an all-black town that White had helped found a few years earlier.

1908 At the London Olympics, John Baxter Taylor is the first African-American gold medalist, running on the 1600-meter relay team.

The first African-American sorority, Alpha Kappa Alpha, is established at Howard University in Washington, D.C., just two years after the first African-American fraternity was formed at Cornell University.

Jack Johnson becomes the first African-American heavyweight boxing champion by defeating then-champion Tommy Burns in Sydney, Australia.

In *Berea College v. Kentucky*, the U.S. Supreme Court upholds a state statute requiring segregation in private institutions.

The all-black town of Allensworth is founded in Tulare County in California by Colonel Allen Allensworth, a former slave and the highest-ranking African American in the U.S. Army. It is the westernmost town of its kind.

Springfield, Illinois, hometown of Abraham Lincoln, is the site of a massive weeklong race riot, which begins when a white woman falsely accuses a black man of raping her. (The woman later confesses that a white man had beaten her.) The violence is so shocking that it leads to the formation of the National Association for the Advancement of Colored People (NAACP) the next year.

1909 The National Association of Colored People (NAACP) is formed in New York City in response to the violent race riot the previous year in Springfield, Illinois. The NAACP is made up of white "neo-abolitionists" and black intellectuals (led by W.E.B. Du Bois) opposed to Booker T. Washington's accommodationism.

The National Association of Colored Graduate Nurses (NACGN) is founded. At the time, African-American nurses are not allowed in the American Nurses Association and have little access to training and hospital positions.

On April 6, Matthew Henson reaches the North Pole on an expedition led by explorer Robert Peary, with whom Henson had made five previous unsuccessful attempts.

The *New York Amsterdam News*, which becomes the leading black paper in New York City for most of the twentieth century, is founded by James H. Anderson.

1910 Oklahoma introduces literacy and property qualifications for voters—effectively disfranchising blacks—but includes a grandfather clause that exempts most whites.

Sickle-cell anemia, a genetic blood disorder that affects blacks almost exclusively, is named by J.B. Herrick when he describes the bent shape of the blood cells of an anemic patient. (The name "sickle-cell disease" is now preferred to the older "sickle-cell anemia.")

Heavyweight champion Jack Johnson's defeat of the white boxer Jim Jeffries causes riots across the country when a film of the fight is shown, revealing whites' deep fears of black male power.

The first issue of W. E. B. Du Bois' *The Crisis: A Record of the Darker Races* is published.

President William Taft appoints William H. Lewis assistant attorney general of the United States, the first African American to hold this government position.

The decade begins with a reported sixty-seven lynchings of African Americans during this year.

1911 The National Urban League is founded with the merger of the National League for the Protection of Colored Women, the Committee for Improving Industrial Conditions of Negroes in New York, and the National League on Urban Conditions Among Negroes. The League provides professional social services to the black community

W.E.B. Du Bois publishes his first novel *The Quest of the Silver Fleece*, a study of the cotton industry seen through the fate of a young black couple.

1912 Claude McKay publishes his first book of poetry, *Songs of Jamaica*; his second, *Constab Ballads*, comes out later in the year.

W.C. Handy publishes his first blues song, the popular "Memphis Blues."

1913 James Weldon Johnson anonymously publishes his first and only novel, *The Autobiography of an Ex-Colored Man*. Many readers take it for a true autobiography.

Arthur A. Schomberg publishes *Racial Integrity: A Plea for the Establishment of a Chair of Negro History in our Schools and Colleges, etc.*

Rosa Parks, future civil rights leader, is born on February 4.

Harriet Tubman, an important leader of the Underground Railroad, dies on March 10.

Dr. Daniel Hale Williams is the first African American to become a member of the American College of Surgeons. In 1893, Williams had performed the operation for which he is best known—the first successful open-heart surgery.

1914 In Kingston, Jamaica, West Indies, Marcus Garvey founds the Universal Negro Improvement Association (UNIA), which will become incorporated in New York in 1918. Its motto is "One God, One Aim, One Destiny."

African-American inventor Garrett Morgan wins a patent for the first "gas mask," a device that allows firefighters to breath in smoke-filled buildings and protects engineers, chemists, and workers who labor near noxious fumes and dust.

The Spingarn Medal, named for former NAACP chairman Joel E. Spingarn, is instituted to honor annually the exemplary achievements of an African American man or woman.

W.C. Handy publishes the blues song for which he is best known, "St. Louis Blues."

The U.S. Supreme Court outlaws grandfather clauses in the Oklahoma case *Guinn v. United States*. Grandfather clauses were devices used by southern legislatures to limit African-American suffrage following Reconstruction.

1915 Oklahoma passes a law segregating telephone booths, the nation's first such law.

D.W. Griffith's *The Birth of a Nation* is released. The film, inspired by two overtly racist novels written by Thomas Dixon, opens to critical praise and popular success, prompting the NAACP to launch an unsuccessful campaign to have the filmed banned from theaters.

Lincoln Motion Pictures, the second black film company, is formed—partly as a protest against racist attitudes on exhibit in D.W. Griffith's hugely successful *Birth of a Nation*.

On Thanksgiving Day, in Georgia, William Joseph Simmons, along with fifteen of his friends, revives the then-dormant Ku Klux Klan.

Booker T. Washington dies on November 14 in Tuskegee, Alabama.

1916 The annual NAACP meeting having been canceled out of respect for the late Booker T. Washington (he died the year before), the Amenia Conference held in Amenia, NY brings together both the followers of Booker T. Washington and the NAACP (led by W.E.B. Du Bois) in an independent conference.

The first issue of Carter G. Woodson's *Journal of Negro History* is published.

Garrett Morgan's patented gas masks are worn when he and others enter a smoke-filled tunnel under Lake Erie to rescue workers trapped by an underground explosion.

1917 The New York City Fifth Avenue March takes place on July 28. Thousands of African Americans march in protest of lynchings and racial inequalities.

In August, a violent confrontation between the black 24th Infantry and Houston, Texas residents leads to the eventual hanging of nineteen African-American soldiers.

The U.S. Supreme Court, in *Buchanan v. Warley*, rules that laws requiring segregation of residential neighborhoods violate the Fourteenth Amendment.

The United States enters World War I. Eventually, more than 400,000 African Americans will serve in segregated units in the U.S. armed forces, mainly as laborers in the United States and France, although a small percentage will serve in two combat divisions.

During the massive spurt of black migration after the beginning of World War I, a bloody riot erupts in the wake of a failed labor strike in the steel and mining town of East St. Louis, Illinois, leaving dozens of African Americans dead and many more injured.

James Weldon Johnson publishes his first book of poetry *Fifty Years and Other Poems*.

1918 African-American filmmaker and novelist Oscar Micheaux directs his first film, *The Homesteader*, based on his third novel (published in 1917).

A race riot in Philadelphia, Pennsylvania leaves four African Americans dead and many injured.

1919 The U.S. Supreme Court, in *Strauder v. West Virginia*, rules that blacks should be admitted to juries.

In rural Phillips County, Arkansas, a white deputy sheriff fires shots into a meeting of the Progressive Farmers and Householders Union, a self-help organization for African-American farmers. When union members return fire, wounding the deputy, a furious race riot breaks out and hundreds of blacks are killed. No whites are arrested for rioting, but a dozen blacks are convicted of murder at a mob-dominated trial. (Following an appeal by the NAACP, their sentences are overturned in 1923 by the U.S. Supreme Court in *Moore v. Dempsey*.)

Delilah Beasley publishes *The Negro Trail-Blazers of California*, a meticulously researched chronicle of the role of African Americans in the Far West.

William Monroe Trotter, at the Paris Peace Conference, argues unsuccessfully that guarantees of racial equality be included in the Treaty of Versailles.

Claude Barnett founds the Associated Negro Press (ANP), the first national news service for African-American newspapers.

James Weldon Johnson coins the term "Red Summer" to describe the period during which twenty-five race riots and incidents occurred. Red Summer convinces many African Americans that their participation in the war for democracy did not mean that white domination in America would disappear.

The most serious riot of Red Summer takes place in Chicago, Illinois, starting on July 27 and lasting a week. When a black man unwittingly crosses an invisible color line in the water at Chicago's segregated

Twenty-Ninth Street beach, whites stone him and he drowns. The ensuing violence leaves fifteen whites and twenty-three blacks dead; the injured number over 500. Property damage is assessed at over $1,000,000 and thousands of blacks are left homeless by the widespread bombing and arson.

The NAACP publishes its report *Thirty Years of Lynching in the United States, 1889-1918*.

A decade high of seventy-six lynchings of African Americans are reported by the end of the year.

1920 The Nineteenth Amendment to the Constitution is ratified. It enfranchises women voters.

James Weldon Johnson becomes the first African-American secretary of the NAACP.

The first international convention of Marcus Garvey's Universal Negro Improvement Association (UNIA) is held in August in Harlem.

Fritz Pollard becomes the first African-American coach in the American Professional Football Association (APFA), which would later become the National Football League (NFL). He leads his team the Akron Pros to an undefeated season and a championship win.

The National Negro Baseball League is organized by Andrew "Rube" Foster. The league is composed of six teams from midwestern cities with large African-American populations. The league enjoys great popularity until it folds in 1931 during the Great Depression.

Mamie Smith's recording of "Crazy Blues" sparks the blues craze of the 1920s upon its release.

Charles Gilpin appears on Broadway in Eugene O'Neill's *The Emperor Jones* and is named one of the ten people who had done the most for the American theater by the Drama League of New York, the first African American so honored.

1921 In an effort to disfranchise blacks, Louisiana adopts a new constitution that includes a poll tax and an "understanding clause."

On May 31, a race riot erupts in Tulsa, Oklahoma when an African-American bootblack is falsely accused of raping a white woman. Death reports range from 36 to 175, and 11,000 blacks are left homeless when the black neighborhood is leveled by bombs.

The first all-black musical, Eubie Blake and Noble Sissle's *Shuffle Along*, opens in New York City.

Lynchings of African Americans reach a decade high of fifty-nine in this year.

1922 African-American aviator Bessie Coleman receives an international pilot's license in France—the first African-American woman to do so—and returns to the United States to become an exhibition flyer known as "Brave Bessie."

Claude McKay publishes *Harlem Shadows*, which includes his acclaimed poem "If We Must Die."

The U.S. House of Representatives passes the Dyer Anti-Lynching Bill, but Republicans in the Senate vote to abandon the bill.

The first all-black professional basketball team, the Renaissance Big Five, nicknamed the Harlem Rens, is organized.

African-American inventor Garrett Morgan receives a patent for the first three-way automatic traffic signal. He will sell the invention to General Electric the following year.

1923 The first issue of the National Urban League's magazine *Opportunity*, edited by Charles Spurgeon Johnson, appears in January.

In *Moore v. Dempsey*, the U.S. Supreme Court rules that mob-dominated trials violate federal due-process guarantees. The decision overturns the death penalties of twelve African Americans convicted in the 1919 Arkansas race riot trial.

Jean Toomer's *Cane* is published, a pivotal work of the Harlem Renaissance.

Bessie Smith, considered by many to have been the greatest blues singer of all time, records her first songs, "Down Hearted Blues" and "Gulf Coast Blues."

Marcus Garvey, leader of the Universal Negro Improvement Association (UNIA), is sentenced to a five-year prison term on a single count of mail fraud. In this same year, Garvey's wife edits and publishes a volume of sayings and speeches titled *Philosophy and Opinions of Marcus Garvey*.

1924 Paul Robeson appears in his only "race" movie, Oscar Micheaux's *Body and Soul*.

At the Paris Olympics, William Dehart Hubbard wins the gold medal in the broad jump.

Jessie Redmon Fauset's *There Is Confusion* is published. It is one of the earliest novels of the Harlem Renaissance.

1925 Alain Locke publishes *The New Negro*, an influential anthology that combines literature with arts and social commentary, and helps define the "New Negro" movement.

African-American entertainer Josephine Baker creates a sensation when she appears in Paris in *La Revue Negre*.

Harlem Renaissance poet Countee Cullen publishes his first book, *Color*.

Labor and civil rights leader A. Philip Randolph organizes the all-black Brotherhood of Sleeping Car Porters union to bargain with the Pullman Company. After 12 years of ignoring the Brotherhood, the Pullman Company finally recognizes it as a certified bargaining agent in 1937.

Dr. Ossian Sweet, defended by Clarence Darrow, is acquitted of murder. In self-defense, Sweet had shot and killed a man when a mob came to drive him out of the middle-class white neighborhood he had just moved into.

The National Negro Bar Association is formed in Des Moines, Iowa. (It later becomes the National Bar Association.)

1926 In February, Negro History Week is established by African-American historian Carter G. Woodson. (In the early 1970s, it will become a month-long celebration called Black History Month.)

The lavish Savoy Ballroom opens on March 12 in Harlem. Every black big band of note will eventually play at the Savoy.

Mordechai W. Johnson becomes the first African-American president of Howard University.

Black intellectuals are split in their reaction to white writer Carl Van Vechten's novel *Nigger Heaven*, with its incendiary title and its message that blacks' preoccupation with cultural improvement is a misguided affectation that will cost the race its vitality.

In *Corrigan v. Buckley*, the U.S. Supreme Court rejects the NAACP's challenge to restrictive covenants—provisions put in deeds to prohibit the sale of real estate to blacks—maintaining that they were private agreements and therefore did not violate the Fourteenth Amendment.

Violette Neatley Anderson becomes the first black woman admitted to practice law before the U.S. Supreme Court.

Langston Hughes publishes his first book of verse, *The Weary Blues*.

The Harlem Globetrotters basketball team is organized by Abe Saperstein in Chicago, Illinois.

1927 James Weldon Johnson publishes *God's Trombones: Seven Sermons in Verse*.

The *Cleveland Call & Post*, a black newspaper still in existence in the late 1990s, is formed by the merger of two smaller journals.

Sadie T.M. Alexander becomes the first black female graduate of the University of Pennsylvania Law School and the first African-American woman to enter the bar and practice law in Pennsylvania.

In *Nixon v. Herndon*, the U.S. Supreme Court strikes down a Texas law forbidding blacks to vote in Democratic primary elections as a violation of the Fourteenth Amendment.

After serving 33 months in a penitentiary for mail fraud, Marcus Garvey's sentence is commuted, thanks to an extensive petition campaign. Garvey is deported to Jamaica upon his release.

On December 4, Duke Ellington and his band debut at Harlem's all-white Cotton Club.

1928 Bill "Bojangles" Robinson, the most famous of all African-American tap dancers, appears on Broadway in the all-black revue, *Blackbirds of 1928*, tapping up and down a flight of stairs—a dance that would become his signature "stair dance."

Oscar DePriest of Chicago, Illinois is elected to Congress as the first African-American U.S. Representative in twenty-eight years and the first from a northern state.

The number of lynchings of African Americans drops to a low of seven.

1929 Wallace Thurman's first novel, *The Blacker the Berry*, is published. The novel deals with the problems of a dark-skinned woman who struggles with intraracial schisms caused by colorism.

A new Atlanta University is created when three historically black schools (Morehouse College, Spelman College, and Atlanta University) affiliate.

The stock market crashes on October 29, ushering in the Great Depression. Blacks will be particularly hard hit by the Depression.

1930 The NAACP successfully campaigns against President Herbert Hoover's nomination of Judge John J. Parker—a known racist who had spoken against black suffrage—to the U.S. Supreme Court.

Master W. Fard establishes the Temple of Islam in a black neighborhood in Detroit to house what he called the "Lost-Found Nation of Islam," later to be known simply as the Nation of Islam.

Paul Robeson triumphs on Broadway singing his stirring rendition of "Ol' Man River" in Jerome Kern and Oscar Hammerstein II's Show Boat.

1931 In Scottsboro, Alabama, a group of nine African-American youths traveling in a freight train are charged with raping two white women. Despite the lack of credible evidence, an all-white jury finds the nine guilty and they receive the death penalty. The U.S. Supreme Court twice overturns the death penalty convictions, but five of the nine serve long prison terms nonetheless.

In Camp Hill, Alabama, a riot erupts when a group of white farmers—led by the local sheriff—opens fire on a meeting of a black farmer's union.

1932 In *Nixon v. Condon*, the U.S. Supreme Court rules that Texas's state Democratic Party committee rules barring blacks from party primaries are unconstitutional. Texas responds by severing legal ties to the state Democratic Party convention, which subsequently votes to exclude black voters.

In one of the Scottsboro case appeals, *Powell v. Alabama*, the U.S. Supreme Court rules that defendants in capital cases must receive more than a pro forma defense. (One Scottsboro attorney had been drunk at the original trial.)

Sterling Brown's book of poems, *Southern Road*, is published.

1933 James Weldon Johnson publishes his autobiography, *Along This Way*.

Katharine Dunham dances her first leading role in Ruth Page's ballet *La Guiablesse*. She would come to be known for the "Katherine Dunham Technique," which combined African and Caribbean styles of movement with the techniques of ballet and modern dance.

Oklahoma City is segregated and martial law is established by executive order to prevent "bloodshed" when blacks move into white neighborhoods. It is a disingenuous order designed to perpetuate segregation of residential neighborhoods. The state Supreme Court reverses the order in 1935 in *Allen v. Oklahoma City*.

The NAACP holds a second Amenia Conference (the first was in 1916). The goal is to revitalize the organization, whose agenda for social advancement has been severely disrupted by the Great Depression. The meeting is later deemed a failure by many due to a lack of both real leadership and vision in the proposals.

1934 Chicago's Arthur Mitchell becomes the first black Democrat elected to Congress when he defeats black Republican Congressman Oscar DePriest.

The Southern Tenant Farmer's Association, a rare interracial labor organization, is formed in Arkansas when eleven whites and seven blacks meet to address the crisis facing tenant farmers in cotton agriculture. All agree that success against the planters can only be achieved if they preserve interracial unity.

Mary McLeod Bethune starts the National Council of Negro Women.

Elijah Muhammad establishes the national headquarters of the Nation of Islam in Chicago, with himself as the new leader. (Master Fard, the former leader of the Nation of Islam, had mysteriously disappeared.)

1935 In *Grovey v. Townsend*, the U.S. Supreme Court approves the Texas white primary, ruling that the state's Democratic party is a private organization and its exclusion of black voters is not an impermissible state action.

On March 19, a riot erupts in Harlem when a false rumor spreads that a white shopkeeper had beaten a black boy for shoplifting. By the end of the riot, three blacks are dead, 200 are wounded, and damage is estimated at $2 million (mostly to white-owned property). Mayor Fiorello La Guardia appoints a biracial Mayor's Commission on Conditions in Harlem to investigate the event.

Jazz vocalist Ella Fitzgerald is discovered when she performs in an amateur competition at Harlem's Apollo Theater. Fitzgerald is hired by Chick Webb as vocalist for his band and she makes her first recording with them later that year.

In the second of the Scottsboro case appeals, Powell v. Alabama, the U.S. Supreme Court agrees with the defense argument that African Americans had been systematically excluded from Alabama juries, and returns the case to Alabama for retrial.

W. E. B. Du Bois publishes *Black Reconstruction: An Essay Toward a History of the Part Which Black Folk Played in the Attempt to Reconstruct Democracy in America, 1860-1880.*

Chemist Percy L. Julian develops physostigmine, a drug effective in the treatment of the eye disease glaucoma.

The NAACP wins an important victory in the U.S. Supreme Court decision in *Hollins v. Oklahoma*, which overturned a death-penalty rape conviction because of systematic racial prejudice in jury selection.

NAACP lawyer Charles H. Houston successfully represents Donald Murray in his suit to gain admission to the all-white University of Maryland Law School. Murray becomes the first African American in the twentieth century to integrate a state university in the South.

1936 Track-and-field athlete Jesse Owens wins four gold medals at the Berlin Olympics. Adolf Hitler refuses to shake Owens's hand.

The Nation Negro Congress (NNC) is formed, with A. Philip Randolph as its first president. The participation of the Communist Party in the NNC later became a liability, causing even Randolph to abandon the organization.

1937 William Hastie is appointed federal judge of the U.S. District Court for the Virgin Islands. Hastie is the first African American to be appointed a federal judge.

Joe Louis defeats Jim Braddock to become the boxing heavyweight champion, only the second black to become heavyweight champion and the first even permitted to fight since Jack Johnson lost the title in 1915.

Boxer Henry Armstrong holds the championship titles in the feather-weight, lightweight, and welterweight divisions simultaneously, the first fighter to achieve this feat.

Sterling Brown publishes two studies of the African-American presence in American literature, *The Negro in American Fiction and Negro Poetry and Drama*.

Zora Neale Hurston publishes the novel for which she is best known, *Their Eyes Were Watching God*.

1938 In *Lane v. Wilson*, the U.S. Supreme Court invalidates Oklahoma's 1915 twelve-day voter registration limit, noting the Fifteenth Amendment forbids "sophisticated as well as simpleminded modes of discrimination."

Lionel Hampton performs with Benny Goodman's Quartet at Carnegie Hall. This famous concert, along with other engagements and recordings, solidifies his position as jazz's most influential vibraphonist.

Richard Wright's first book, *Uncle Tom's Children: Four Novellas*, is published.

Crystal Dreda Bird Fauset is elected to the Pennsylvania House of Representatives, the first African-American woman elected to a state legislature.

The U.S. Supreme Court in *Missouri* ex rel. *Gaines v. Canada* orders the University of Missouri, which has no black graduate school, to admit African-American student Lloyd Gaines, arguing that scholarships to out-of-state schools do not constitute equal admission.

1939 Hattie McDaniel becomes the first African American to win an Oscar for her performance as "Mammy" in the Civil War epic *Gone with the Wind*.

Opera contralto Marian Anderson is refused access (for racial reasons) to Constitution Hall for a Washington, D.C. concert by the Daughters of the American Revolution (DAR). Anderson responds by giving an Easter Sunday outdoor recital—introduced by Secretary of the Interior Harold Ickes—on the steps of the Lincoln Memorial before a crowd of 75,000. The scandal prompts Eleanor Roosevelt to resign her DAR membership.

Jane Bolin is named justice of the New York City Domestic Relations Court, becoming the first black woman judge in the United States.

Edward Franklin Frazier publishes his pioneering study, *The Negro Family in the United States*, which demonstrates that the internal problems of black families were socially created within and by Western civilization, not by the failure of Africans to live up to American standards.

1940 Employers and labor unions in defense-related industries are free to practice systematic and overt discrimination against African Americans during this time.

Federal antilynching legislation is introduced during the Seventy-sixth Congress but legislation is never enacted.

Virginia General Assembly selects James A. Bland's "Carry Me Back to Old Virginny" as the state song.

Roosevelt and representatives from the War and Navy departments meet with three African American leaders: A. Philip Randolph, Walter White, and T. Arnold Hill. This meeting produces a policy of giving black servicemen better treatment and greater opportunity within the confines of racial segregation.

Col. Benjamin O. Davis, Sr. receives a promotion to brigadier general and becomes the first African American to attain this rank. At the same time Col. Campbell C. Johnson becomes an aide to the director of the Selective Service System, and William H. Hastie is appointed a special advisor to the Secretary of War on matters pertaining to black soldiers.

Native Son, Richard Wright's first published novel, becomes a Book-of-the-Month selection.

The American Negro Theatre is founded by Abram Hill and Frederick O'Neal in Harlem, New York.

The Cotton Club is closed. Most of the renowned jazz performers of the period appeared at the Cotton Club, including Louis Armstrong, Ethel Waters, and dancers Bill "Bojangles" Robinson, and the Nicholas Brothers.

Hansberry v. Lee—the Supreme Court declares that it is illegal for whites to bar African Americans from white neighborhoods. The plaintiff in this case is Carl Hansberry, a prominent real estate broker and father of Lorraine Hansberry, who moved his family to an all-white neighborhood. Her play *A Raisin in the Sun* is based on this incident.

The Selective Service and Training Act of 1940 is passed outlawing "discrimination against any person on account of race or color" in administering the draft. But it contains loopholes that perpetuate segregation despite the ban on discrimination.

U.S. Supreme Court rules that Edgar Smith's conviction was unconstitutional and his sentence void because blacks had been systematically excluded from jury service. Smith is released from jail in January 1941.

1941 Jesse Locker, a black Republican, is elected to the city council of Cincinnati, OH.

Joe Louis remains the undefeated world heavyweight champion. Following the Schmeling fight in 1938, Louis embarked on a remarkable string of title defenses, winning seventeen fights in four years, fifteen by knockout. His only serious challenge came from Billy Conn in 1941, who outboxed the champion for twelve rounds before succumbing to Louis's knockout punch in the thirteenth.

The NAACP, the Urban League, and other organizations support A. Philip Randolph's call for a march on Washington to demand jobs and integration of the military. Randolph threatens a massive demonstration of 100,000 African Americans to be held on July 1. In response Roosevelt issues Executive Order 8802, which specifies that defense contracts bar discrimination and open training programs to minorities, and set up a Fair Employment Practice Committee to investigate violations. The march is canceled.

African-American pilots begin training at segregated facilities at Tuskegee Institute. The Tuskegee experiment produces a trained fighter unit, the 99th Pursuit Squadron, manned by African-American pilots, mechanics, and clerks.

The Golden Gate Male Quartet, a gospel group, performs at the President's Inaugural Concert at Constitution Hall in Washington, D.C. They were the only black entertainers to perform.

NAACP lobbies successfully for a Navy officer-training program for African Americans.

District of Columbia Bar Association votes to remove restrictions to the use of its library, which is housed in a federally owned building. Black lawyers, who had been prohibited from using the library, filed a suit against the association. After considering the cost of moving, the association voted to change their policy.

U.S. Supreme Court rules in *Mitchell v. United States* that segregated coach laws for interstate travel are illegal. Arthur W. Mitchell argues the case himself before the high court.

The National Urban League sponsors an hour-long national radio program to encourage equal employment opportunities for blacks in the defense program. Many famous black entertainers participate in the program.

The NAACP with the help of Aline Black and Melvin Alston, two teachers from Norfolk, Virginia, successfully challenge the constitutionality of unequal pay for teachers based on race. Black and Alston are reinstated to their positions by the city board of education.

The governor of Georgia, Eugene Talmadge, an outspoken racist, orders all public schools to ban all books on evolution, adolescence, and blacks from their libraries.

Adam Clayton Powell, Jr. is elected to the New York City Council. He is the first African American to serve on the council.

The National Negro Opera Company is established in Pittsburgh, Pennsylvania by Mary Cardwell Dawson.

Dorie Miller becomes the first African-American war hero of World War II. He shoots down four Japanese planes during the attack on Pearl Harbor.

1942 Black press launches the Double V Campaign seeking victory over tyranny abroad and racial segregation at home.

African Americans enlist in large numbers; however, all of the four major services adhere to the 10 percent black participation quota set in 1940. Blacks are primarily segregated and assigned only to certain areas.

Hugh Mulzac becomes the first of three African Americans to serve as a wartime ship's captain when he takes command of the *USS Booker T. Washington*.

William Levi Dawson is elected to the House of Representatives from Chicago, Illinois.

James Farmer becomes the first executive director of the Congress for Racial Equality.

Benjamin O. Davis, Jr. is promoted to the rank of major and is given command of the 99th Pursuit Squadron.

Chicago-based publisher John H. Johnson creates the *Negro Digest*. It published general articles about African-American life with an emphasis on racial progress.

Sarah Vaughan sings "Body and Soul" and wins an amateur-night contest at Harlem's Apollo Theater.

Publication of Margaret Walker's *For My People*, the first volume by an African-American woman to garner national recognition in literary competition.

1943 William H. Hastie resigns from his position as assistant to secretary of war, disgusted by the Army's reluctance to lower racial barriers. Hastie decides that he can fight segregation more effectively outside the constraints of an official position.

Detroit Riot of 1943—many African Americans and whites move to Detroit seeking employment in defense industries. The city is unprepared to handle the influx, and racial tensions are exacerbated by competition for jobs and housing. Violence erupts and quickly spreads throughout the city, and military police are finally brought in to restore order. A Fact-Finding Committee blames the riots on blacks' "militant appeals for equality." However, the mayor sets up an Interracial Committee—the first of its kind in the nation—with authority to investigate complaints and to use the courts to enforce antidiscrimination laws.

The Navy, admitting a shortage of 500 nurses, accepts four African-American women to that specialty.

The 99th Pursuit Squadron—the first African American Army Air Corps unit—flies its first combat mission over the Mediterranean island of Pantelleria.

Paul Robeson opens in the starring role of Othello on Broadway.

Indifferent leadership and hatred expressed by local inhabitants contribute to riots by black soldiers at nine military bases during this year.

1944 Navy assigns predominantly black crews to man a patrol craft PC 1264 and the destroyer escort USS Mason.

Adam Clayton Powell, Jr. is elected to the U.S. House of Representatives from Harlem. He is the first African-American Congressman from the Northeast.

Smith v. Allwright—Supreme Court declares an all-white Texas Democratic primary unconstitutional. The Court states that blacks cannot be barred from voting in the Texas Democratic primaries.

Due to a shortage of troops after the casualties from the Battle of the Bulge, Lt. Gen. John C. H. Lee persuades Gen. Eisenhower to call for volunteers among the predominantly black service units to retrain as riflemen. Forty-five hundred African Americans sign up, undergo training, and serve in sixty-man platoons that join two-hundred-man white rifle companies. This improvised racial policy integrates the fighting but not the army.

1945 Colonel Benjamin O. Davis, Jr. is appointed commander of the 477th Composite Group.

The premier issue of *Ebony* magazine is published. It becomes the largest circulation African-American periodical.

Benjamin Quarles has an essay accepted by the Mississippi Valley Historical Review. It is the first from a black historian to appear in a major historical journal.

1946 Alabama passes the Boswell amendment requiring prospective voters to be able to "interpret" the state constitution.

Race riots break out in Alabama, Tennessee, and Pennsylvania—nearly 100 blacks are injured.

Sugar Ray Robinson wins the world welterweight boxing title in a fifteen-round decision over Tommy Bell.

The NAACP Legal Defense and Education Fund brings a series of cases before the Supreme Court—*Sipuel Board of Regents of the University of Oklahoma, McLaurin v. Oklahoma, and Sweatt v. Painter.*

Harry S. Truman appoints a national committee on civil rights to investigate racial injustices and recommend action.

Morgan v. Virginia—Supreme Court prohibits segregation in interstate bus travel.

Jackie Robinson joins the Montreal Royals of the International League, the top farm club in the Dodger system. He breaks the color line when he moves to the Dodgers in 1947. He becomes the first African American to play major league baseball.

1947 Charles S. Johnson becomes the first black president of Fisk University.

Larry Doby becomes the second African American to play major league baseball. He is recruited by the Cleveland Indians—making him the first black player in the American League.

The Congress of Racial Equality (CORE) decides to test the Morgan decision with the Journey of Reconciliation—sixteen men (eight white and eight black) travel by bus through the region challenging segregated seating arrangements that relegated blacks to the back of the bus. The arrest of four of the protesters in Chapel Hill, North Carolina catapults CORE and the Journey of Reconciliation to national attention.

Truman appoints Edith S. Sampson as an alternate to the United Nations, making her the first black U.S. delegate to the organization.

1948 Ralph J. Bunche is appointed acting mediator for the U.N. Special Commission on Palestine after the assassination of Folke Bernadotte by Jewish militants. Bunche negotiates with both sides and arranges an armistice. His actions earn him the 1950 Nobel Prize for Peace.

Roy Campanella joins Jackie Robinson on the Brooklyn Dodgers. He becomes the major league's first African-American catcher.

The Supreme Court of California declares the state law prohibiting interracial marriages unconstitutional.

The Supreme Court rules in *Sipuel v. University of Oklahoma* that a state must provide legal education for blacks at the same time it is offered to whites.

Shelley v. Kramer—Supreme Court rules that courts cannot enforce restrictive housing covenants, which restricted certain homes or tracts of land from use and occupancy by blacks.

President Truman issues Executive Order 9981 to end discrimination in the armed forces.

Satchel Paige becomes the first black baseball player to pitch for the American League.

Nat King Cole becomes the first African American to have his own network radio show.

1949 Wesley A. Brown becomes the first African American to graduate from the U.S. Naval Academy.

William H. Hastie leaves his position of governor of the Virgin Islands to take a seat as judge on the Third Circuit Court of Appeals.

President Truman signs an order banning federal housing aid in areas where racial or religious bias is found.

Robert McFerrin, Sr. performs in William Grant Still's *Troubled Island* with the New York City Opera Company.

1950 The Korean War begins. Segregation still persists. The largest African-American combat unit, the 24th Infantry, which traces its regimental lineage to the post-Civil War reorganization of the Army, goes to war in July 1950. Black troops share in the first American victory.

Prolific writer Gwendolyn Brooks is awarded the Pulitzer Prize for poetry. She is the first African American to win a Pulitzer Prize.

Ralph Bunche, scholar and United Nations diplomat, is awarded the Nobel Peace Prize for his brilliant negotiation of an armistice in the Arab-Israeli War of 1948.

The University of Texas is ordered by the U.S. Supreme Court to admit Heman Sweatt to its law school. In *Sweatt vs. Painter*, Thurgood Marshall argues the speciousness of the separate-but-equal doctrine. The decision weakens segregation generally.

1951 Paul Robeson and William L. Patterson present a petition to the United Nations, charging the U.S. government with genocide. It charges the United States with genocide by "deliberately inflicting on [African Americans] conditions of life calculated to bring about their physical destruction" through executions, lynchings, and terrorism.

Sugar Ray Robinson knocks out Jake La Motta and becomes the middleweight champion.

In Washington, D.C., Mary Church Turrell, a prominent civil rights and women's rights activist for fifty years, joins the sit-ins challenging racial segregation in restaurants and public accommodations. Partially as a result of this, the Municipal Court of Appeals outlaws segregation in restaurants in the District of Columbia.

Governor Adlai Stevenson of Illinois dispatches the National Guard to quell a race riot in Cicero, Illinois. More than 3,000 whites were protesting a black family's residence at a home in an all-white community.

1952 For the first time, no lynchings of blacks are reported in the United States.

The University of Tennessee admits its first black student.

Dorothy Maynor becomes the first black artist to perform commercially in Constitution Hall.

Boxer Archie Moore wins the light heavyweight crown.

Ralph Ellison publishes his novel *Invisible Man*, which receives the National Book Award the following year.

1953 James Baldwin publishes his first novel *Go Tell It on the Mountain*.

Earl Warren becomes Chief Justice of the United States Supreme Court. The "Warren Court" era begins.

Percy Lavon Julian, chemist and educator, founds Julian Laboratories, Inc., a pharmaceutical company. It is successful. When he retires, he holds more than 130 chemical patents.

Rufus Early Clement is elected to the Atlanta Board of Education by a sweeping majority making him the first African American to be elected to public office in Atlanta since Reconstruction.

Hulin Edwin Jack is elected Manhattan borough president. He is the first black to hold this office.

1954 The case of the century, *Brown v. Board of Education of Topeka*. It is actually five similar (school desegregation) cases, which the Supreme Court decides to hear as one. The trial lasts about one year. Going against the advice of some of his colleagues, Thurgood Marshall uses "sociological evidence" and argues that separate-but-equal is the psychological abuse of black youngsters. On May 17 Chief Justice Earl Warren reads the famous verdict, saying, "In the field of public education, separate but equal has no place. " The verdict precipitates a backlash, and the formation of a wave of defensive groups who denounce the decision. Many Southern leaders and communities are defiant.

Benjamin O. Davis, Jr., is appointed general in the U.S. Air Force, making him the first African American to hold this rank.

Charles C. Diggs, Jr. is elected to the U.S. House of Representatives from Michigan. He is the first black Congressman from the state.

The U.S. Supreme Court rules in *District of Columbia v. John R. Thompson Co., Inc.* that discrimination in Washington, D.C. restaurants is illegal.

1955 A. Philip Randolph becomes a vice-president of the newly merged AFL-CIO.

Emmett Till, a fourteen-year old black adolescent who allegedly made sexual advances toward a white woman, is kidnapped and murdered. Two white men tried for his murder are acquitted. The trial, receiving national attention, highlights the unequal administration of justice.

In Montgomery, Alabama, Rosa Parks refuses to give up her seat on a segregated bus and provokes the Montgomery Bus Boycott. More than fifty thousand African Americans participate in the boycott, which is led by the twenty-six-year old Martin Luther King, Jr.

Roy Wilkins becomes executive secretary of the NAACP.

The Interstate Commerce Commission prohibits segregation in public vehicles operating in interstate travel.

Marian Anderson appears at the Metropolitan Opera.

Ray Charles releases his breakthrough hit "I've Got a Woman."

1956 Autherine Lucy enters the University of Alabama. Lucy is accepted by the University of Alabama in 1952; however, her acceptance is rescinded when the school administration discovers she is not white. Three years go by. In the wake of the U.S. Supreme Court *Brown* decision, the university is ordered by a federal District Court to admit her. There are protests. She is suspended from the school on the grounds that her own safety is in jeopardy. The NAACP protests the suspension, and the federal court orders that the school reinstate her as well as undertake measures to protect her. Shortly thereafter, Lucy is expelled from the university on the grounds that she has maligned its officials by taking them to court. The NAACP, this time around, feeling that further legal action is pointless, does not contest this decision. In 1992 the University of Alabama names an endowed fellowship in her honor.

Sammy Davis, Jr. appears in the lead role in *Mr. Wonderful* on Broadway.

Nat King Cole gets his own television show. (The program was canceled, however, because of difficulty in finding sponsors for it.)

Floyd Patterson knocks out forty-three-year-old champion Archie Moore to take the light-heavyweight crown.

In some quarters white resistance to school integration grows. Segregationists use a variety of stratagems to circumvent court-ordered

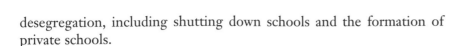

desegregation, including shutting down schools and the formation of private schools.

1957 Hank Aaron is named the National League's Most Valuable Player.

Federal troops escort nine black students to class in Little Rock, Arkansas. Governor Orval Faubus of Arkansas, using the Arkansas National Guard and under pretense of maintaining order, obstructs the integration of the city's Central High School. Supreme Court justices and others are shocked at his blatant defiance of a Supreme Court decision. President Eisenhower orders one thousand federal troops into Little Rock, to halt the obstruction of desegregation and to protect the nine black teenagers who wish to attend Central High.

The Southern Christian Leadership Conference, a network of nonviolent civil rights activists drawn mainly from black churches, is formed.

Senator Strom Thurmond of South Carolina speaks against the pending civil rights bill and sets a record for filibuster.

The Civil Rights Act of 1957 becomes law. President Eisenhower signs the first civil rights act since reconstruction. The act creates a commission to monitor civil rights violations and authorizes the Justice Department to guard black voting rights through litigation against discriminatory voter registrars.

Althea Gibson becomes the first black to win the Wimbledon and the U.S. singles.

1958 Governor J.P. Coleman of Mississippi proclaims that blacks in Mississippi are not ready to vote.

NAACP Youth Council chapters in Wichita and Oklahoma City stage "sit-downs" at lunch-counters.

The state of Alabama imposes a $100,000 fine on the already financially strapped NAACP, for refusing to provide its membership lists to an Alabama judge. It is a clear attempt to undermine and even bring to a halt civil rights progress in the state. Through legal maneuvers, the NAACP is kept out of Alabama until 1964.

Alvin Ailey starts his own dance theater company. The Alvin Ailey American Dance Theater begins as repertory company of seven dancers devoted to both modern dance classics and new works created by Ailey.

The Supreme Court unanimously rejects an appeal by the Little Rock school board for a delay in the racial integration of Central High School.

1959 School desegregation is getting mixed reviews and having mixed results. Whites continue to use various ploys to thwart integration. In some places school districts open their desegregated public schools without any disturbance.

Lorriane Hansberry's *A Raisin in the Sun* is produced and is a huge critical and commercial success. She wins the New York Drama Critics Circle Award and other awards.

Berry Gordy, Jr., forms Motown Records.

1960 Black college students attempting to integrate a Woolworth lunch counter in Greensboro, North Carolina spearhead a sit-in movement that spreads rapidly throughout the South. Reacting to this upsurge in student activism, Ella Baker, Southern Christian Leadership Conference official, invites student protest leaders to an Easter weekend conference in Raleigh, NC. The student leaders, believing that existing civil rights organizations are overly cautious, agree to form a new group, the Student Non-Violent Coordinating Committee (SNCC). Marion S. Berry, Jr. is elected as chairman.

Black Americans at the Olympics in Rome win medals in major events: Cassius Clay, Willie McClure, and Eddie Crooks bring home gold; Wilma Rudolph wins three gold medals in track; and Rafer Johnson wins gold for the decathlon.

Martin Luther King, Jr., is arrested at a student initiated protest in Atlanta. Presidential candidate John F. Kennedy intervenes to secure his release from jail.

A. Philip Randolph forms the Negro American Labor Council as a vehicle through which to pressure the labor federation to act against segregated and discriminatory unions.

Wilma Rudolph is chosen as the United Press Athlete of the Year, and the next year is designated Woman Athlete of the Year by the Associated Press.

Six years after the Supreme Court prohibited segregation in the schools, only a small percentage of the schools in the South have begun to integrate.

President Eisenhower signs the Voting Rights Act. This law is sometimes called the Civil Rights Act of 1960.

Dionne Warwick meets Burt Bacharach and Hal David and begins her solo career.

A major race riot erupts after blacks move onto a section of the Biloxi beach reserved for whites only. City officials blame the NAACP for inciting the violence.

A federal court ends restrictions against black voting in Fayette Country, TN.

Harry Belafonte wins an Emmy for his television special "Tonight with Harry Belafonte." He becomes the first African American to win an Emmy.

W. E. B. Du Bois visits Ghana for the inauguration of Kwame Nkrumah as its first president. He accepts an invitation from Nkrumah to return and start work on an Encyclopedia Africana.

Gomillion v. Lightfoot—the Supreme Court rules that the Fifteenth Amendment rights of Tuskegee blacks had been violated when the Alabama legislature redefined the city limits to exclude blacks and give whites political control. This is a major triumph over segregationists who tried to crush the political power of the black population.

1961 President Kennedy appoints Thurgood Marshall as judge of the Second U.S. Circuit Court of Appeals.

Adam Clayton Powell, Jr. becomes the chairman of the powerful House Education and Labor Committee.

Oscar Robertson is voted NBA Rookie of the Year. He averaged 30.5 points per game in this first season in the National Basketball Association.

Robert Weaver is appointed director of the U.S. Housing and Home Finance Agency, at the time the highest federal position ever held by an African American.

President Kennedy appoints Clifton R. Wharton, Sr. U.S. ambassador to Norway. He is the first black to attain this position by rising through the ranks of the foreign service.

Whitney Young, Jr. is selected to be executive director of the National Urban League.

Congress of Racial Equality mounts its most militant challenge to segregation—the Freedom Rides. The Freedom Rides are protests against segregated interstate buses and terminals in the South. Seven white and six black activists including James Farmer participate in the Freedom Rides.

Jackie Robinson is inducted into the Baseball Hall of Fame. He becomes the first black member.

1962 The Albany Movement is organized to abolish discrimination in all public facilities in Albany, Georgia. It is supported by the Southern Christian Leadership Conference, the Student Non-Violent Coordinating Committee, NAACP, and the Congress of Racial Equality, and led by Martin Luther King, Jr. Many of the demonstrators are beaten and jailed, including Dr. King, who leaves Albany without a victory.

Edward W. Brooke III is elected attorney general for the state of Massachusetts. He becomes the highest-ranking African-American official in New England.

Wilt Chamberlain scores 100 points in a single game against the New York Knickerbockers.

Marvin Gaye releases his debut solo album on Motown.

Augustus Hawkins is elected to the House of Representatives. He is the first black representative from California.

Leroy Johnson is elected to the Georgia Senate. He becomes the first black legislator in Georgia since Reconstruction.

James Meredith tries to enroll at the University of Mississippi but his admission is blocked by the governor. The Kennedy administration dispatches federal marshals to escort Meredith to classes. To quell subsequent rioting, U.S. troops police the campus. They remain there until 1963 when Meredith graduates.

Carl Stokes becomes the first black Democrat elected to the Ohio House of Representatives.

Mal Goode is selected as news commentator on ABC-TV. He is the first African American on network television news.

Sonny Liston wins the world heavyweight boxing championship from Floyd Patterson.

President John F. Kennedy signs an executive order prohibiting racial discrimination in housing built or purchased with federal assistance.

1963 W. E. B. DuBois renounces his U.S. citizenship and officially becomes a citizen of Ghana.

Thomas Bradley is elected to the Los Angeles city council. He is the first black official in Los Angeles.

Elston Howard of the New York Yankees becomes the first black player in the American League to win the Most Valuable Player award.

President Kennedy declares the black struggle for civil rights a "moral issue." He calls on Congress to strengthen voting rights and create job opportunities for African Americans.

Sidney Poitier becomes the first African American to win an Academy Award for best actor for his performance in *Lilies of the Field.*

Bayard Rustin coordinates the March on Washington.

The U.S. Supreme Court rules in several cases that help bolster the civil rights movement. It rules that segregation in courtrooms is unconstitutional, state and local governments cannot interfere with peaceful sit-ins for racial integration of public places of business, and the court prohibits an indefinite delay in the desegregation of public schools.

Medgar Evers, NAACP field secretary, is murdered in the doorway of his home in Jackson, MS. His alleged assailant is acquitted by a hung jury.

The March on Washington is held to advance the civil rights bill then before Congress. Several hundred thousand African Americans and whites attend. They gather on the steps of the Lincoln Memorial and listen to Martin Luther King, Jr. deliver his "I Have a Dream" speech.

Four young black girls are killed when a bomb explodes in the Sixteenth Street Baptist Church. Martin Luther King, Jr., gives a eulogy at a joint funeral for three of the girls and urges African Americans to keep up their struggle despite the murders.

1964 Congress passes the Civil Rights Act of 1964. President Johnson signs the bill in the presence of Martin Luther King, Jr.

Congress passes the Economic Opportunity Act. Some of the programs in this legislative package include Head Start, Upward Bound, and college work-study educational programs.

John Conyers, Jr. is elected to Congress as a representative from Michigan.

John Hope Franklin is selected to chair the department of history at the University of Chicago.

The Mississppi Freedom Democratic Party is established to serve as an alternative party that will allow black and white Mississippians to be in a party that shares the same views as the national organization.

Malcolm X breaks with the Black Muslim movement. No longer bound by Elijah Muhammad's religious structures, he is free to develop his own philosophy of the black freedom struggle.

Constance Baker Motley is elected to the New York State Senate. She is the first African American elected to this body.

Martin Luther King, Jr. receives the Nobel Peace Prize.

Race riots occur throughout the country. In Harlem violence erupts over police brutality. The rebellion continues for four nights and spreads to Brooklyn's Bedford-Stuyvesant neighborhood. Race riots also erupt in Chicago, Jersey City, Rochester, and Philadelphia.

Carl T. Rowan is appointed director of the United States Information Service by President Johnson. He is the first black to hold this post.

The Twenty-fourth Amendment to the U.S. Constitution is ratified. The amendment eliminates poll-tax requirement in national elections.

Cassius Clay wins the world heavyweight championship by defeating Sonny Liston.

Three young men who had been working on black voter registration are declared missing and presumed murdered in Mississippi. They are James E. Chaney, Michael Schwerner, and Andrew Goodman. President Johnson sends 200 naval personnel to assist in the search for the missing men. Their bodies are found buried near Philadelphia, MS.

Bob Hayes is awarded a gold medal at the Olympic Games in Tokyo for the 100-meter dash.

1965 Julian Bond is denied his seat in the Georgia House of Representatives because he opposes the U.S. involvement in Vietnam. The Supreme Court orders Bond seated in December of 1966.

President Johnson names Thurgood Marshall to be solicitor general of the United States. This is the highest judicial position ever held by an African American.

Bill Cosby becomes the first African American to star in a television series, *I Spy*.

President Johnson creates the cabinet-level Council on Equal Opportunity.

James Earl Jones receives an Obie for his performance in the title role of *Othello* at the New York Shakespeare Festival.

President Johnson appoints Robert C. Weaver to head the Department of Housing and Urban Development. He is the first African American to become a Cabinet member.

Martin Luther King, Jr. leads a successful voting rights campaign in Selma, AL. Demonstrations had begun early in 1965 and reached a turning point on March 7, when a group of demonstrators began a march from Selma to the state capitol in Montgomery. State troopers attack the marchers with tear gas and clubs on the outskirts of Selma. The police assault on the marchers increases national support. President Johnson reacts by introducing the Voting Rights Act of 1965.

Malcolm X is shot down by assassins as he speaks at the Audubon Ballroom in Harlem.

Patricia Roberts Harris is appointed U.S. ambassador to Luxembourg. She becomes the first African-American woman to be an ambassador of the United States.

Muhammad Ali defeats Floyd Patterson for the world heavyweight boxing title.

1966 Arthur Ashe becomes the first black man to win one of the preeminent Grand Slam titles in tennis.

Emmett Ashford begins his first year in the major leagues officiating at the opening-day game in Washington, D.C. He is the first African American to umpire in the major leagues.

Huey P. Newton and Bobby Seale found the Black Panther Party for Self-Defense. The party expanded from its base in Oakland, California to become a national organization.

Stokely Carmichael is elected SNCC chairman. He proffers an outspoken, militant stance that helps distance SNCC from the moderate leadership of competing civil rights organizations. He is the chief architect and spokesperson for the new Black Power ideology.

President Lyndon B. Johnson names Andrew F. Brimmer to the Board of Governors of the Federal Reserve Bank.

Edward W. Brooke, III is elected U.S. Senator from Massachusetts. He is the first popularly elected African-American member of the Senate.

Yvonne Brathwaite Burke is elected to the first of her three two-year terms in the California State Assembly. She is the first black assemblywoman in California.

Barbara Jordan becomes the first black since 1883 elected to the Texas Senate.

Samuel Proctor Massie, Jr. becomes the first African American to join the faculty of the U.S. Naval Academy at Annapolis.

Frank Robinson wins the American League's Most Valuable Player award—making him the first player to win the award in both major leagues.

Floyd B. McKissick becomes national director of CORE.

Constance Baker Motley, first African-American woman to be elected to the New York State Senate and to be elected borough president of Manhattan, becomes the first black woman to be appointed as a federal judge.

James Meredith sets out on a "walk against fear" from Memphis to Jackson, MS. On the second day out he is shot by an assailant and wounded. His attack sparks outrage and the major civil rights organizations carry on the march to Jackson. This procession is marked by

Stokely Carmichael's call for black power and a resulting rift between the moderate and militant wings of the movement.

1967 The Black Power Conference is held in Newark, NJ. It is an assembly of over 1,000 delegates who meet to discuss the most pressing issues of the day.

Morgan Freeman makes his Broadway debut in an all-black production of *Hello Dolly*.

Nineteen men are indicted in the murders of civil rights workers James C. Chaney, Michael Schwerner, and Andrew Goodman who were slain in 1964. Twelve are acquitted.

Major Robert Lawrence is selected for the Department of Defense's Manned Orbital Laboratory program. He dies six months later in a plane crash.

There are urban riots in Newark and Detroit.

Thurgood Marshall becomes the first black Supreme Court Justice.

Carl Burton Stokes is elected mayor of Cleveland, Ohio. He is the first elected black mayor of a major American city.

Adam Clayton Powell, Jr. is expelled from the House of Representatives. It is the first time since 1919 that the House had expelled one of its members. Powell vows to fight the case all the way to the Supreme Court. However, he wins a special election to fill his own vacant seat.

H. Rap Brown becomes Stokely Carmichael's successor as National Chairman of SNCC where he continues a militant stance.

Supreme Court rules that states cannot interfere with or prevent inter-racial marriages.

The Organziation of Black-American Culture (OBAC) is founded. In its most dramatic public statement, members of the visual arts workshop paint the Wall of Respect, a Black Power mural depicting various historical and contemporary black heroes such as Muhammad Ali, W. E. B. Du Bois, Malcolm X, Marcus Garvey, Nina Simone, Amiri Baraka, and Gwendolyn Brooks.

1968 William Lacy Clay wins a congressional election to become the first black congressman from Missouri.

In his second term President Johnson appoints more blacks to federal positions than any previous president.

Eartha Kitt criticizes the war in Vietnam at a White House luncheon. As a result she loses bookings and is vilified by conservatives.

Former Congressman Adam Clayton Powell, Jr. goes on a speaking tour of college campuses, rallying black and white students to fight for equality and end the American involvement in Vietnam.

The Kerner Report—the result of a seven-month study by the National Commission on Civil Disorders to pinpoint the cause of racial violence in American cities in the late 1960s—is released to President Johnson. Stating that discrimination and segregation are deeply embedded in

American society, the reports warns that America is "moving toward two societies, one black, one white—separate and unequal."

Eldridge Leroy Cleaver publishes Soul on Ice. It is a collection of autobiographical and political essays that articulate the sense of alienation that many black nationalists feel.

Dr. Martin Luther King, Jr. goes to Memphis to take part in a strike by black sanitation workers and is assassinated as he stands on the balcony of the Lorraine Motel. Rioting breaks out in different parts of the city as blacks expressed their rage in the streets.

The Rev. Ralph Abernathy is unanimously elected to succeed Martin Luther King, Jr. as head of SCLC.

Arthur R. Ashe, Jr. wins the U.S. amateur men's singles championship and the U.S. Open championship.

Huey Newton is convicted on manslaughter charges and sentenced to two to fifteen years in prison. His conviction is later overturned by the Court of Appeals because of procedural errors.

Wyomia Tyus wins a gold medal in the 100-meter race in the 1968 Olympics making her the first person to win this race in two consecutive Olympics.

Tommie Smith and John Carlos, medal winner sprinters, offer the Black Power salute during the playing of the U.S. national anthem at the 1968 Summer Olympics in Mexico.

1969 James Charles Evers gains national prominence when he is elected mayor of Fayette, MS. Evers's victory helped open the way for many black candidates who desired political office.

James Earl Jones wins the Tony award for *The Great White Hope*.

The U.S. Department of Justice sues the state of Georgia for its refusal to desegregate schools.

Arthur Mitchell forms the Dance Theatre of Harlem.

Moneta Street becomes the first African American to win the Pulitzer Prize in photography.

Alexander v. Holmes—Supreme Court rules that Mississippi's continued operation of segregated schools is unconstitutional. It also rejects the Nixon administration's appeal to delay desegregating thirty Mississippi schools districts.

The Black Panther Party's clashes with police decimate its leadership. Cleaver leaves for exile to avoid returning to prison. Bobby Seale is arrested for conspiracy to incite rioting at the 1968 Democratic Convention in Chicago. In May, Connecticut officials charge Seale and seven other Panthers with murder in the slaying of party member Alex Rackley. In New York twenty-one Panthers are charged with plotting to assassinate policemen and blow up buildings. Nearly all the charges brought against Panther members either do not result in convictions or are overturned on appeal. The prosecutions absorbed much of the party's resources.

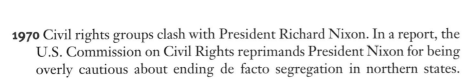
1970 Civil rights groups clash with President Richard Nixon. In a report, the U.S. Commission on Civil Rights reprimands President Nixon for being overly cautious about ending de facto segregation in northern states. Also, the NAACP denounces Nixon's nomination of G. Harold Carswell of Florida, whom they believe to be racist, as an associate justice of the Supreme Court. His nomination is defeated. Later in the year the NAACP denounces the Nixon administration as "anti-Negro."

Marxist philosopher Angela Davis is placed on the FBI's Ten Most Wanted List. In San Rafael, California, three Soledad Prison inmates are being tried for the murder of a prison guard. The brother of one of the defendants enters the courtroom, and holding the room at gunpoint, distributes weapons to the three defendants. There is a dramatic shootout resulting in four deaths. During the investigation several of the guns are traced to Davis. Distrustful of the judicial system, Davis goes into hiding.

A serious effort to collect and preserve forgotten music scores by black composers begins at the Music Library of Indiana University at Bloomington.

The first celebration of Martin Luther King, Jr., Day. Public schools are closed in many cities.

Essence: The Magazine for Today's Black Woman appears and is successful almost immediately.

1971 Jesse Jackson founds People United to Save Humanity (Operation PUSH). As head of PUSH he undertakes an agenda of negotiating black employment agreements with white businesses. Jackson also articulates the organization's other agenda—to promote black educational excellence and black self-esteem.

Swann v. Charlotte-Mecklenburg. The U.S. Supreme Court votes unanimously to direct school authorities in North Carolina to achieve "the greatest possible degree of actual desegregation." In effect, the Supreme Court rules in favor of busing to achieve integration.

The Attica Prison Uprising. Starting in early summer 1971, prisoners at the Attica Correctional Facility in upstate New York have been organizing and demanding more humane prison conditions. In September more than 1,200 black and Latino inmates seize control of the prison. Governor Nelson Rockefeller authorizes a raid. State police retake the prison, killing ten hostages and twenty-nine prisoners.

Shaft, starring Richard Roundtree as a black private eye, opens in theaters and becomes the best-known work of the "blaxploitation" film genre.

1972 Barbara Jordan of Texas is elected to the U.S. House of Representatives, becoming the first African-American woman elected to Congress from the South.

Eight thousand African Americans from every region of the United States attend the first National Black Political Convention in Gary, Indiana. The convention approves a platform that demands reparations for slavery, proportional congressional representation for blacks, the elimination of capital punishment, increased federal spending to combat drug trafficking, a reduced military budget, and a guaranteed income of $6,500 for a family of four.

President Nixon proposes a moratorium on all court-ordered busing.

National People's Action (NPA) is established from a coalition of community-based organizations. Its purpose is to focus national attention on redlining and other housing discrimination policies, in part by identifying discriminatory lenders. NPA, assisted by the NAACP and the National Urban League, attempts to form partnerships (with the government and the private sector) dedicated to the eradication of discrimination in lending practices.

1973 The secretary of the U.S. Army rescinds the dishonorable discharges given to 167 African-American soldiers after the Brownsville, Texas, incident of 1906. Soldiers of the Twenty-fifth Infantry had been involved in a riot with city police and merchants, during which some 250 rounds of ammunition were fired into several Brownsville buildings. One man was killed and two were wounded. President Theodore Roosevelt had discharged the soldiers without trial. The Army finds that this action had been improper. Only one of the soldiers is still alive.

Forty years of medical experimentation on human subjects comes to light and becomes the worst medical scandal in U.S. history. The Tuskegee Syphilis Experiment (1932-1972) was a study conducted by the U.S. Public Health Service. It involved observing the effects of untreated syphilis on several hundred black men living in rural Alabama. The study proceeded without the informed consent of the participants. The study is still ongoing in 1972 when a whistle-blower inside the PHS leaks the story to the press. Health officials try to defend their actions but public outrage silences them as they agree to end the experiment.

Coleman Young is elected mayor of Detroit and becomes one of the most powerful leaders in the state.

Thomas Bradley is elected mayor of Los Angeles, America's third largest city.

Marian Wright Edelman, who started her career as a lawyer working with the poor in Mississippi, founds the Children's Defense Fund, an advocacy organization for children.

1974 Julius Erving, the "greatest slam dunker of all time," is selected the Most Valuable Player by the American Basketball Association.

In Boston, violence erupts between supporters and opponents of public school desegregation. As court-ordered busing of black students to white schools in South Boston begins, whites riot outside the schools and attack black students. Boston becomes a national symbol of resistance to busing.

In Kansas City, in tribute to the city's historical role as a regional political and cultural center, civil rights activist Horace Peterson III opens an archives/museum, the Black Archives of Mid-America.

The Kentucky state legislature passes a law that makes victims of discrimination eligible for financial compensation for embarrassment and/or humiliation.

1975 Physicist Shirley Ann Jackson is a visiting scientist at the European Center for Nuclear Research (CERN), where she concentrates on theories of strongly interacting elementary particles.

Elijah Muhammad dies. Wallace Deen Muhammad is named his father's successor as supreme minister of the Nation of Islam. In short order Wallace shocks the movement by announcing an end to its racial doctrines and black-nationalist teachings. He disbands the Fruit of Islam and the Muslim Girls Training, elite internal organizations, and moves his followers toward orthodox Sunni Islam.

WGPR-TV in Detroit, the first black-owned television station, goes on the air for the first time.

The Voting Rights Act of 1975, an expansion of the voting rights act of ten years prior, passed by Congress and signed by President Ford, abolishes all literacy requirements for voting.

1976 At the Montreal Summer Olympics Edwin Moses wins the 400-meter hurdles in world-record time.

President Gerald Ford presents the Medal of Freedom to Jesse Owens, for his "inspirational life" and for his contribution to the ideals of freedom and democracy. Owens won four gold medals at the 1936 Olympic Games in Berlin, upsetting his Nazi hosts (as well as racists on both sides of the Atlantic), and disputing Adolf Hitler's belief in Aryan racial superiority.

The Afro-American Historical and Cultural Museum opens in Philadelphia.

The federal courts order the Omaha (Nebraska) Public School Districts to use busing to integrate their schools.

President-elect Jimmy Carter appoints Andrew Young as the United States Ambassador to the United Nations.

1977 Alberta Hunter, one of the best-known blues singers of the 1920s and a popular band singer throughout the World War II era, is coaxed back to the nightclub circuit after three decades of hiatus. She becomes a hit all over again, in New York City.

Toni Morrison publishes *Song of Solomon* and becomes a highly regarded novelist.

Roots, the television miniseries dramatization of Alex Haley's novel of black history, is one of the greatest successes in the history of television. Close to 130 million Americans follow the 300-year saga chronicling the travails of African Americans in their trajectory from Africa to Emancipation.

Filmmaker William Miles releases his first film, *Men of Bronze*, launching his career as a filmmaker. The film demonstrates his passion for uncovering the history of forgotten black Americans through archival film footage and historic photographs.

Reggie Jackson, in the sixth game of the 1977 World Series against the Los Angeles Dodgers, hits three consecutive homeruns thrown by three different pitchers, all on the first pitch.

The Congressional Black Caucus establishes TransAfrica. Headed by Randall Robinson, TransAfrica becomes the major lobbying body in Washington on behalf of the Anti-Apartheid Movement in South Africa.

1978 Warrington Hudlin, George Cunningham, and Alric Nembhard, Yale classmates, found a nonprofit organization, the Black Filmmakers Foundation. Based in New York City, the organization provides administrative and networking support to black filmmakers, and publishes a semiannual journal on black film, *Black Face*. The foundation distributes the early films of such notable filmmakers as Spike Lee, Bill Duke, and John Singleton.

Louis Farrakhan, who had expected to be chosen as Elijah Muhammad's successor, leads a schismatic group and resurrects the old Nation of Islam. Farrakhan's Nation retains the black-nationalist and separatist doctrines that were part of the teachings of Elijah Muhammad.

U.S. Representative Augustus Freeman Hawkins coauthors with Hubert Humphrey the Humphrey-Hawkins Full Employment and Balanced Growth Act. In its original form, the legislation requires that the federal government provide jobs for all people who cannot find work in the private sector. The bill that passes, however, has considerably weaker language and provisions.

The U.S. Supreme Court rules in a 5 to 4 decision, in Regents of the University of *California v. Bakke*, that the University of California must admit Allan Bakke to its medical school. Bakke had charged that he was rejected because preference was given to minority students with lower scores. The Court rules that race CAN be considered in admissions decisions, but that schools cannot apply rigid quotas for minorities.

1979 Patricia Harris is chosen by President Jimmy Carter to become Secretary of Health, Education, and Welfare—renamed the Department of Health and Human Services in 1980. She serves until 1981.

Segregation of schools is still widespread. The United States Commission on Civil Rights issues a report stating that 46 percent of the nation's minority students still attend segregated schools. The report also states that only token integration has been implemented in historically segregated areas.

The Congressional Black Caucus sets up an "action alert communications network." The network is designed to exert pressure on white congressional representatives of select areas to vote with the Caucus.

Andrew Young resigns his position as Ambassador to the United Nations after it is reported that he has held unauthorized talks with representatives of the Palestine Liberation Organization.

1980 In *Mobile v. Bolden*, the U.S. Supreme Court rules that electoral failure of black candidates is insufficient proof of voting discrimination.

In *Rome v. United States*, the U.S. Supreme Court rules that the Voting Rights Act's preclearance strictures apply even to measures which unintentionally lead to discrimination.

In May, rioting erupts in Miami, Florida when four Dade County policemen—with extensive histories of citizen complaints and internal

review probes—are acquitted by an all-white, all-male jury of the shooting death of Arthur McDuffie, a black motorist. After two days of rioting, eighteen are dead (eight whites and ten blacks) and property damage is estimated at $80 million.

Vernon E. Jordan, Jr, executive director of the National Urban League, is shot in the back. One suspect is tried in relation to the shooting—charged with violating Jordan's civil rights, not attempted murder—but is acquitted. Vernon resigns in 1981.

Maurice "Maury" Wills is named manager of the Seattle Mariners, becoming only the third black manager in major league baseball.

At the height of his popularity, comedy great Richard Pryor sets himself on fire while freebasing cocaine and nearly dies.

The U.S. Civil Rights Commission endorses racially based employment quotas in a report entitled "Civil Rights in the 1980s: Dismantling the Process of Discrimination."

Earvin "Magic" Johnson, Jr. leads the Los Angeles Lakers to the National Basketball Association (NBA) Championship, the first of five championship wins in the decade.

Willie Brown makes a successful bid to become speaker of the California state assembly. He is the first African American to hold this position.

1981 Samuel Pierce becomes secretary of Housing and Urban Development (HUD) under President Ronald Reagan, the only African American in Reagan's cabinet. Pierce would have an undistinguished tenure in the position, and though Pierce himself would not be charged with any wrongdoing, several of his close associates would serve prison terms for fraud, bribery, and lying to Congress.

Pam Johnson becomes publisher of the *Ithaca Journal* in upstate New York. She is the first African-American woman to control a mainstream daily newspaper.

The Reagan administration fights vigorously against a third extension of the Voting Rights Act of 1965. Nevertheless, the Act is not only extended, but it is also amended to address the wide range of strategies designed to circumvent it, effectively nullifying the Mobile decision of 1980.

Acquired Immune Deficiency Syndrome (AIDS) first receives national media attention. Although the disease is widely regarded to be a disease affecting mainly white gay men, it would become clear by the end of the decade that African Americans could no longer deny the extent to which it was affecting their community. (Cultural taboos against homosexuality are often cited as the reason for the denial among blacks.)

1982 President Ronald Reagan restores the federal tax exemptions for segregated private schools that had been ended in 1970. The next year, the U.S. Supreme Court would overturn this decision, ruling that it violated the Civil Rights Act of 1964.

Voting Rights Act is extended twenty-five years. States are required to eliminate procedures with discriminatory effect and to draw electoral district lines to maximize minority voting strength. Numerous black-majority electoral districts will be created in succeeding years.

Andrew Young is elected mayor of Atlanta, Georgia.

Michael Jackson releases his album *Thriller*, which sells more than 40 million copies, making it the best-selling album of all time.

Charles Fuller wins the Pulitzer Prize for Drama (along with a host of other awards) for *A Soldier's Play*, about the investigation of a black sergeant's murder at an army base in Louisiana during World War II.

Clarence Thomas is appointed chair of the Equal Employment Opportunity Commission. Known for his conservative views, Thomas would go on to be confirmed as a justice of the Supreme Court in 1991 after controversial confirmation hearings in which former assistant Anita Hill would charge that Thomas had sexually harassed her when she had worked for him.

Baseball great Frank Robinson is inducted into the Baseball Hall of Fame. Robinson holds the distinction of being the only player to be named Most Valuable Player in both the National League and the American League.

1983 The U.S. Supreme Court rules that private schools that discriminate on the basis of race are not eligible for tax-exempt status.

Guion Stewart Bluford becomes the first African American in space when he joins the eighth Challenger shuttle flight in August.

Alice Walker's *The Color Purple* wins both the Pulitzer Prize and the National Book Award.

Gloria Naylor's novel *The Women of Brewster Place*, about the lives of seven black women who live on one ghetto street, wins the American Book Award for best first novel.

Lou Gossett, Jr. wins the Best Supporting Actor Academy Award for his role as a drill sergeant in *An Officer and a Gentleman*. He is only the third black actor to win an Oscar.

Harold Washington is elected mayor of Chicago, the city's first African-American mayor.

Vanessa Williams is the first African American to be crowned Miss America. She will be stripped of her crown when nude photographs that she posed for surface during her reign.

Jesse Jackson announces on the television program *60 Minutes* that he will run for the Democratic nomination for the Presidency. He will garner an impressive 3.3 million votes out of the approximately 18 million cast.

President Ronald Reagan signs into law a bill making Martin Luther King, Jr.'s birthday a national holiday.

Harvey Gantt, W. Wilson Goode, and James A. Sharp, Jr. become the first black mayors of Charlotte, North Carolina, Philadelphia, Pennsylvania, and Flint, Michigan, respectively.

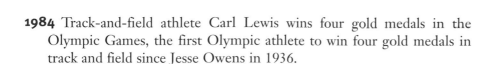

1984 Track-and-field athlete Carl Lewis wins four gold medals in the Olympic Games, the first Olympic athlete to win four gold medals in track and field since Jesse Owens in 1936.

Benjamin Hooks, executive director of the NAACP, leads a 125,000-person March on Washington to protest the "legal lynching" of civil rights by the Reagan administration.

Rap artists Run-D.M.C. release the first gold rap album, the eponymously named Run-D.M.C.

Recording artist Prince produces, writes, scores, and stars in the film *Purple Rain*. The soundtrack wins an Oscar for best original music score, as well as three Grammys and three American Music Awards.

On April 1, Motown superstar Marvin Gaye is shot to death by his father in Los Angeles.

The Cosby Show premieres on NBC in the fall. The show, which features Bill Cosby as Cliff Huxtable, an obstetrician living with his wife and four children in a brownstone in New York City, breaks new ground by representing the daily lives of an African-American upper-middle-class family, which had been rarely seen on American television.

Michael Jordan, playing for the Chicago Bulls, is named the National Basketball Association's Rookie of the Year.

In November, Randall Robinson and other activists begin an anti-apartheid vigil in front of the South African embassy in Washington, D.C. The vigil, which raises awareness about the evils of apartheid and expresses opposition to President Reagan's policy of constructive engagement, lasts over fifty-three weeks.

1985 A constitutional amendment to grant full voting privileges to residents of the District of Columbia fails to achieve ratification by the required three-quarters of states.

Popular talk-show host Oprah Winfrey is nominated for a Best Supporting Actress Oscar for her performance in Steven Spielberg's adaptation of the Alice Walker novel, *The Color Purple*.

In a final showdown with police, eleven members of the countercultural group MOVE are killed when a bomb is dropped on their headquarters in Philadelphia. MOVE's philosophy—rejecting the "man-made" or "unnatural" and refusing to subscribe to "man's laws"—brought its members into conflict with social workers concerned over children and neighbors who complained of garbage, fecal odors, and rat infestations.

1986 African-American scientist-astronaut Ronald McNair is killed when the ill-fated space shuttle *Challenger* explodes shortly after liftoff on January 28. In February, the Massachusetts Institute of Technology names the building that houses its Center for Space Research after McNair.

A mob of white men attack three black men in Howard Beach, a predominantly white neighborhood in Queens, New York.

Mike Tyson wins the World Boxing Council heavyweight title in Las Vegas, Nevada, becoming the youngest heavyweight champion in history.

August Wilson's play *Fences* receives the Pulitzer Prize. (The play wins the Tony Award for best play in 1987.) Set in 1957, the play is about the frustrations felt by a garbage collector who was once a star player in the Negro Leagues before Jackie Robinson broke baseball's color line. Wilson will win a second Pulitzer in 1990 for his play *The Piano Lesson*.

1987 Rita Dove wins the Pulitzer Prize in Poetry for her book *Thomas and Beulah*. In 1993, Dove would have the distinction of becoming the first African-American woman Poet Laureate of the United States.

Kurt Schmoke becomes the first black mayor of Baltimore, Maryland.

In Wappingers Falls, New York, fifteen-year-old Tawana Brawley claims that she has been kidnapped, sexually assaulted, physically defiled, and verbally abused by four white men—two off-duty policemen, a New York assistant prosecutor, and a utility worker. Her supporters include Alton Maddox, Jr., and C. Vernon Mason, her lawyers, and the Rev. Al Sharpton. A grand jury report later concludes that the entire incident was a hoax.

1988 At the Seoul Olympic Games, track-and-field athlete Florence Griffith Joyner, popularly known as "Flo Jo," wins three gold medals, tying Wilma Rudolph's 1960 record. Her sister-in-law Jackie Joyner-Kersee wins the gold medal in the heptathlon—the most demanding event in women's track and field—making her "America's best all-around female athlete."

Ice skater Debi Thomas is the first African American to win a medal in a Winter Olympics at Calgary, a bronze.

Novelist Toni Morrison wins the Pulitzer prize for *Beloved*, a novel that deals with the legacy of slavery in the years following the Civil War.

Jesse Jackson makes a strong showing in the Democratic presidential primaries, coming in either first or second in thirty-one out of thirty-six primaries, and accruing almost seven million votes out of a total of twenty-three million cast.

Donald Payne of Newark becomes New Jersey's first African-American congressman.

1989 Having led the Washington Redskins to a victory over the Denver Broncos, Doug Williams is named Most Valuable Player in Super Bowl XXII. He is the first African American ever to start as quarterback in a Super Bowl game.

Barbara Harris becomes the first female bishop (and the first female African-American bishop) of the Protestant Episcopal Church.

Ronald Brown is chosen to be chair of the Democratic National Committee, the first African American to chair a major political party.

African-American men in Boston, Massachusetts, are randomly searched and intimidated by the police after a white man Charles Stuart falsely claims that his pregnant wife was murdered by a young black

man. Stuart would later commit suicide when he became a suspect in the case.

Bill White is named president of the National Baseball League, the first African American to head a major professional sports league.

Colin Powell, a newly promoted four star general, is nominated by President George Bush to become the first African-American chair of the Joint Chiefs of Staff, the highest military position in the armed forces. Powell becomes a national hero after the successful conclusion of the war in the Persian Gulf in 1991.

In the predominantly white neighborhood of Bensonhurst, New York, a group of whites shoot and kill black sixteen-year-old Yusuf Hawkins who has come to the neighborhood to look at a used car. Protest marches in the wake of the incident are plagued by violence between protesters and hostile residents of the neighborhood. Five whites are eventually convicted and sentenced for the killing.

David Dinkins wins the New York City Democratic mayoral primary against incumbent Edward Koch and then defeats Republican Rudolph Giuliani to become the city's first African-American mayor.

Douglas Wilder is elected governor of Virginia, the first African-American state governor.

Spike Lee releases his controversial and highly successful film *Do the Right Thing*. The film explores the tensions between an Italian-American family that owns a pizzeria in the Bedford-Stuyvesant neighborhood of Brooklyn and the economically depressed black community that patronizes it.

When Alvin Ailey dies in December leaving his American Dance Theater without an artistic director, former Ailey dancer Judith Jamison is chosen for the position.

The Centers for Disease Control report that in the United States, African Americans are twice as likely as whites to contract AIDS; that more than one-half of all women with the disease are African American; that about 70 percent of babies born with the disease are African American; and that nearly one-fourth of all males with the disease are African American.

1990 The Medger Evers murder case is reopened. Bryon De La Beckwith, a white supremacist who had been tried twice before for the murder, is brought to trial again and convicted.

Floyd Flake, U.S. representative of New York is indicted on charges of misappropriating thousands of dollars from a federally subsidized housing complex built by his church. He is also charged with evading taxes. Flake is subsequently cleared of all wrongdoing.

Gary Franks becomes the first black Republican to win a House seat in Connecticut in fifty years.

Conrad Harper is elected president of the New York City Bar Association.

James Usry, the mayor of Atlantic City, is indicted on charges of bribery and corruption associated with the gaming resort. Usry is the first black mayor of Atlantic City. He pleads not guilty to all charges.

President Bush names Arthur Fletcher to head the Civil Rights Commission.

Leander Jay Shaw, Jr. is appointed chief justice of the Florida Supreme Court. He becomes the first black to attain this position in the state.

Walter Mosley publishes *Devil in a Blue Dress*, the first of his "Easy Rawlins" detective novels.

John Edgar Wideman wins the P.E.N./Faulkner Award for the second time for his novel *Philadelphia Fire*. He received his first award for *Sent for You Yesterday* in 1984. He is the first author to receive this prestigious award twice.

Marion S. Barry, Jr., mayor of Washington D.C., is convicted of cocaine possession and serves a six-month prison sentence.

Lee Patrick Brown becomes the first black commissioner of the New York Police Department.

Denzel Washington receives an Academy Award for his performance in *Glory*.

The U.S. Senate passes the Civil Rights Bill of 1990, but President Bush vetoes the bill because it is a "quota" bill. The Senate fails by one vote to overturn Bush's veto.

Maxine Moore Waters is elected to represent a wide area of South Central Los Angeles in the U.S. House of Representatives.

Amid charges that it had not given the community sufficient notice, the federal government closes Freedom National Bank. The bank had been losing money for several years.

Itabari Njeri is awarded the American Book Award for her book *Every Good-bye Ain't Gone*.

Whoopi Goldberg wins an Academy for Best Supporting Actress in the film *Ghost*.

1991 Rickey Henderson becomes the all-time stolen base leader when he breaks Lou Brock's mark of 938 career steals.

President Bush nominates Clarence Thomas, a conservative, to replace Thurgood Marshall on the Supreme Court. Thomas's confirmation hearings are acrimonious. Many national organizations including the NAACP and the Congressional Black Caucus voice opposition to his nomination. The Senate Judiciary Committee is deadlocked on his nomination and sends it to the Senate floor without a recommendation. Shortly thereafter information is leaked to the media about the testimony of Anita Hill, a former assistant of Thomas, who claimed that he had sexually harassed her. The committee reopens hearings and the questioning of becomes a national television event. Despite the damaging allegations, Thomas is confirmed.

Miles Davis, one of the most influential jazz musicians in America during the 1950s and 1960s, dies.

Quincy Jones wins six Grammy awards for his album *Back on the Block*.

Police officers in Los Angeles stop a car driven by an African American named Rodney King. The four officers proceed to kick and beat him with clubs, fracturing his skull and one of his legs. A witness records King's beating on videotape. The tape is broadcast throughout the country. Within two weeks the police officers are indicted on charges that include assault with a deadly weapon.

While excavating a site for a new office building, workers discover an African American Burial Ground in Manhattan. The cemetery is one of the oldest and largest black cemeteries known in the United States.

Willy T. Ribbs becomes the first African American to qualify for the Indy 500.

The National Civil Rights Museum opens at the Lorraine Motel in Memphis, the site of the assassination of Martin Luther King, Jr.

Robert L. Johnson offers shares in Black Entertainment Television. The initial public offering on the New York Stock Exchanges sells 4.2 million shares.

Magic Johnson retires from professional basketball after testing positive for HIV.

Riots break out between blacks and Jews in Crown Heights, Brooklyn, when young black boy is killed by a car driven by a Jewish driver.

1992 Gregory Hines receives a Tony award for best actor in a Broadway musical for *Jelly's Last Jam*.

Carol Moseley-Braun becomes the first black woman to hold a seat in the U.S. Senate.

Riots break out in Los Angeles after the four white police officers who had beaten Rodney King are acquitted.

Terry McMillan publishes *Waiting to Exhale*. It becomes a bestseller within the first week of its release.

Arthur Ashe reveals that he is suffering from AIDS, which he contracted through blood transfusions.

Mike Tyson is found guilty of raping a young woman and is sentenced to serve six years in the Indiana Youth Center.

Michael Jordan is named the NBA's Most Valuable Player.

The Federal Reserve issues its second annual report on lending discrimination, stating that mortgage applications from blacks and Hispanic Americans are rejected about twice as often as those from whites and Asian Americans.

Spike Lee releases his film *Malcolm X*, which is based on Alex Haley's biography of the slain civil rights leader.

1993 Hazel Rollins O'Leary is confirmed as secretary of energy in the Clinton administration. She becomes the first woman ever to hold this post. Clinton also appoints Clifton R. Wharton, Jr. as Deputy Secretary of State, Mike Espy as head of the Agriculture Department, Ron Brown as Secretary of Commerce, Jesse Brown as Veterans Affairs Secretary, and Joycelyn Elders as Surgeon General.

Maya Angelou writes a poem for President Clinton's inauguration.

Thurgood Marshall, Supreme Court Justice for twenty-four years, dies. His extraordinary contributions to American life are memorialized in an outpouring of popular grief and adulation greater than that expressed for any previous justice.

Michael Jordan announces his retirement from basketball.

Benjamin Chavis is named the seventh director of the NAACP.

Police Sergeant Stacey C. Koon and Officer Laurence M. Powell are found guilty of violating Rodney King's civil rights after being tried again in federal court.

Toni Morrison becomes the first African American to win a Nobel Prize for literature.

Senator Carol Moseley-Braun is one of two women elected to the Senate Judiciary Committee. Braun was inspired to run partly as a result of angry feelings over the Anita Hill-Clarence Thomas Hearings in 1991.

Colin Powell retires from the Army at the end of his second term as chair of the Joint Chiefs of Staff.

David Dinkins is defeated by Rudolph Giuliani in his bid for reelection.

David Satcher is appointed director of the federal Centers for Disease Control.

1994 The Florida legislature agrees to pay up to $150,000 to each survivor of the Rosewood Massacre. On New Year's Day in 1923, a white woman claimed that she had been assaulted by a black man. A white mob marched to the small, black community of Rosewood in search of the man. Failing to find him they proceeded to burn nearly every house. Many people fled the violence.

Joycelyn Elders resigns as U.S. Surgeon General after making controversial statements on sex education and drug use.

Benjamin Franklin Chavis joins the Nation of Islam as an organizer and close adviser to Minister Louis Farrakhan after resigning from the NAACP.

Stanley Crouch wins the prestigious Guggenheim "genius" award.

Carl McCall is elected New York Stare Comptroller.

1995 Mike Tyson is released after serving three years in prison.

O. J. Simpson is acquitted of the murder of his ex-wife Nicole Brown Simpson and her friend Ron Goldman. Simpson's criminal trial lasted over eight months.

Bob Watson is hired to be the General Manager of the New York Yankees. He is the first African American to hold this position.

Colin Powell publishes his memoir *My American Journey*.

The Million Man March—Louis Farrakhan of the Nation of Islam organizes this march as an opportunity for black men to take responsibility for their lives and communities. Many turn out for the march. It stimulates black voter registration and political activism.

Eubie Blake is featured on a U.S. postage stamp.

1996 Arthur Ashe is honored in his native Richmond by the erection of a statue on Monument Avenue, the city's central thoroughfare.

Nikki McCray dominates the women's basketball competition at the 1996 Olympics.

Harry Belafonte produces and stars in a television special *Harry Belafonte and Friends.*

Ron Brown and his party are killed in an airplane crash while on a trip to Croatia.

Kweisi Mfume is sworn in as the head of the NAACP.

Carl Lewis wins the long jump in the 1996 Olympics, thus tying an Olympic record with nine gold medals.

1997 Debbie Allen fulfills a decades-long dream by producing Steven Spielberg's film *Amistad.*

Mike Tyson is suspended from boxing for biting Evander Holyfield's ears during a boxing match.

Bill Cosby's life is shattered when his son Ennis is robbed and murdered in Los Angeles. Later this year he becomes the target of an extortion plot by Autumn Jackson, who threatens to reveal that Cosby is her father unless he pays her. Cosby admits to an extramarital affair with Jackson's mother, but he denies that he is her father. DNA testing confirms his assertion.

Tiger Woods, a twenty-one-year-old African American, astounds the golf world by shooting a record low score to win the Masters Tournament.

Malcolm X's widow, Betty Shabazz, is badly burned in a fire set by her grandson. She dies three weeks later.

Lee Brown is elected mayor of Houston.

1998 Julian Bond is elected Chair of the Board of the NAACP.

Mike Tyson's boxing suspension is lifted.

Charles Burnett directs *The Wedding*, a television adaptations of Dorothy West's novel.

Vernon Jordan testifies before a grand jury investigating Clinton's relationship with Monica Lewinsky.

James Byrd, Jr. is beaten and dragged to his death in Jasper, Texas, by two white supremacists. The horror of his death shocks the country.

Kwame Tuore (Stokely Carmichael) dies of prostate cancer. He spent the last thirty years of his life in Guinea where he continued his work in political education and promoting the goal of a unified socialist Africa.

Ruby Dee and Ossie Davis celebrate their fiftieth wedding anniversary by publishing a joint memoir, *With Ossie and Rudy Dee: In This Life Together.*

Richard Pryor becomes the first recipient of the Kennedy Center's Mark Twain prize for humor.

1999 Michael Jordan retires from basketball for a second and final time after leading the Chicago Bulls to their sixth NBA championship.

A long-lost poem by Phillis Wheatley, "Ocean," is read publicly for the first time in 226 years.

President Clinton grants Henry O. Flipper a presidential pardon fifty-nine years after his death. Flipper was court-martialed in 1881 on falsified thievery charges.

February—Amadou Diallo, a young African immigrant, is shot and killed by four New York City policemen in the doorway of his Bronx apartment building. Forty-one shots are fired. Local residents protest over police brutality. Rallies are held everyday outside of police headquarters until the police officers are indicted for murder. Many prominent citizens are arrested daily, including: David Dinkins, Carl McCall, Ossie Davis, Ruby Dee, and Susan Sarandon.

The federal government investigates the New Jersey State Police and New York City Police department for their policies of "racial profiling."

Maurice Ashley becomes the first African-American Grandmaster chess player. An estimated 600 players worldwide hold the Grandmaster title—approximately forty-five are U.S. players.

April—a protest led by the relatives of victims of police brutality from across the country is held in Washington, D.C. The protesters intend to mobilize and organize to fight for social, economic, and racial justice.

Louis Farrakhan is seriously ill with cancer and is hospitalized.

Lincoln Center celebrates Duke Ellington's 100th birthday with a centennial year tribute honoring his contributions to jazz and classical music.

2000 South Carolina Governor Jim Hodges signed a bill that officially instituted a Martin Luther King, Jr. holiday for state workers in South Carolina, the last state in the nation to proclaim the event as a state holiday.

L. A. Reid took over as president and CEO of Arista Records.

Tennis player, Venus Williams won the Women's singles at Wimbledon, making her only the second African-American to do so.

Denzel Washington wins the Golden Globe award for Best Performance by an Actor in a Dramatic Motion Picture for *The Hurricane.*

Tiger Woods becomes the youngest player to achieve a "grand slam," winning all four major golf championships (the British Open, the Masters, the PGA Championship, and the U.S. Open).

Gustavas A. McLeod becomes the first man to pilot an open-cockpit plane to the North Pole.

Christopher Paul Curtis wins the Newbery Medal and the Coretta Scott King Author award for his book, *Bud, Not Buddy*. This marks the first time that one book has won both awards. This is also the first time since 1976 that a black writer has won the Newbery award.

Three sisters, Joetta Clark-Diggs, Hazel Clark, and Jearl Miles-Clark, become the first family to win all three spots on the U.S. Olympic team for the womens' 800 meter track event.

The South Carolina Senate votes to remove the Confederate flag, a symbol to many of the South's history of slavery, from the dome of the State Capitol Building.

Marion Jones becomes the first African-American woman to win 5 medals in one Olympic Games, held in Sydney, Australia. She won 3 gold and 2 bronze.

Glossary

abolition the ending of slavery.

activist someone who takes an active part in working for a political party or other organization.

affirmative action a program that seeks to address past discrimination through active measures to ensure equal opportunity, for example, in education or employment.

apartheid the past governmental policy in the Republic of South Africa of separating the races in society.

bebop a type of modern jazz that evolved in the mid-1940s. It involves extensive improvisation and unusually accented rhythms.

big band a large band that usually features a mixture of ensemble (group) playing and solo improvisation typical of jazz or swing music.

Black codes laws passed to regulate the rights of free African Americans around the time of the Civil War.

Black Muslim a member of a chiefly black American group, the Nation of Islam, that professes Islamic religious beliefs.

black nationalism a movement by militant black people to achieve separatism from white people and to establish self-governing black communities.

boycott to refuse to have dealings with (a person, store, or organization) to express disapproval or to force acceptance of certain conditions.

Broadway the leading theater district of New York City.

call-and-response a way of singing chorus songs, found especially in church music. The leader sings a line (the "call") and the audience responds with another.

choreographer someone who creates new dances.

communism a form of government whose system requires common ownership of property for the use of all citizens. All profits are to be equally distributed and prices on goods and services are usually set by the state. Communism was the official doctrine of the former USSR.

civil disobedience refusal to obey laws in an effort to bring about changes in governmental policy or legislation. It is marked by the use of passive resistance or other nonviolent means.

civil rights the right of all invididuals to be treated as equals under the laws of their country.

desegregation the removal of restrictions that keep people of a particular race separate from other groups, socially, economically, and, sometimes, physically.

diaspora the breaking up and scattering of a people from their homeland.

discrimination treatment or consideration based on race or class rather than individual merit.

disfranchisement the taking away of a legal right, especially the right to vote.

emancipation the freeing of persons from bondage or slavery. (*See also* manumission.)

Emancipation Proclamation President Abraham Lincoln's executive order abolishing, or doing away with, slavery in the Confederacy (the Southern states).

ensemble a group of things or people acting or taken together as a whole, especially a group of musicians who play together regularly.

free blacks free people of African descent, known alternatively as free Negroes, free blacks, free people of color, or simply free people.

fugitive slaves runaway slaves who escaped to free states in the North or to Canada, often by way of the Underground Railroad.

Great Depression the severe U.S. economic crisis of the 1930s, believed to have been brought on by the stock market crash of 1929. At its worst sixteen million people—one-third of the labor force— were unemployed. The policies of the New Deal helped to relieve the crisis.

Great Migration the huge migration of African Americans from the rural South to the industrial North in the early 1900s.

Harlem Renaissance a flowering of American-American literature and culture in the 1920s, centered in New York City's Harlem area. Some of the black writers of this period produced fine original works about African-American life, attracting white readers and publishers.

homestead to settle and farm land. The Homestead Act, passed by Congress in 1862, promised ownership of a 160-acre tract of public land to a citizen or head of a family who had resided on and cultivated that tract for five years.

improvisation playing or singing in a way that departs from the written structure of a song by changing the melody, harmony, rhythm, etc.; or simply creating music spontaneously without any original foundation.

integration the brining of people of different racial or ethnic groups into unrestricted and equal association, as in society or an organization. (*See also* segregation.)

jazz a style of music, born around 1895, combining elements of ragtime, marching band music, and the blues. It is characterized by a strong but flexible rhythmic understructure with solo and ensemble improvisations on basic tunes and chord patterns.

Jim Crow the systematic practice of discriminating against and suppressing black people.

manumission the act of releasing from slavery. (*See also* emancipation.)

Middle Passage the transport of slaves to the Caribbean or the Americas the middle portion of a three-step passage into slavery. The first step was the capturing of slaves by slave traders, who placed them in holding pens. The third step was the selling of the slaves in the New World and their being transported to their place of servitude.

migration to move from one location to another.

militant having a combative character; aggressive, especially in the service of a cause.

Negro leagues Any of several "black only" U.S. baseball leagues of the first half of the twentieth century. Two of the "majors" were the Negro National League and the Negro American League.

porter a person employed to carry burdens, especially an attendant who carries travelers' baggage at a hotel or transportation station.

racism the belief that race accounts for differences in human character or ability and that a particular race is superior to others.

ragtime a style of jazz characterized by elaborately syncopated rhythm in the melody and a steadily accented accompaniment.

rap a type of popular music that originated in the mid-1970s among African-American and Hispanic performers in New York City. It consists of chanted, often improvised street poetry accompanied by disco or funk music.

rhythm and blues a type of popular music with a strong beat and jazz influence, developed by African-Americans in the 1940s and 1950s.

scat jazz singing in which improvised, meaningless syllables are sung to a melody.

segregation the practice of separating the races, as in schools, housing, and work. (See also integration.)

separatism the withdrawal of dissenters or those discriminated against from a larger social, political, or religious group. (*See also* black nationalism.)

sharecropping a farming arrangement whereby a farmer rents land to farm and gives part of the crop as the rent.

sit-in the act of occupying the seats or an area of a segregated establishment to protest racial discrimination.

slave trade the transportation of black Africans beginning in the 1700s to other countries to be sold as slaves—people owned as property and forced to work for their owners with no pay.

Spingarn Medal the highest award bestowed by the National Association for the Advancement of Colored People (NAACP), given each year for the most distinguished service of any black person in advancing the cause of blacks in the United States.

stereotype an oversimplified conception, opinion, or image of a group or category of people.

Underground Railroad a secret cooperative network that aided fugitive slaves in reaching sanctuary in the free states or in Canada in the years before the abolition of slavery in the United States.

white supremacist one who believes that the white race is superior to all others and is thereby entitled to rule over them.

A List of Suggested Resources

GENERAL SOURCES: BOOKS, VIDEOS, SOUND RECORDINGS, MAGAZINE ARTICLES, AND MULTIMEDIA

Alexander, Amy. *Fifty Black Women Who Changed America.* Carol Pub. Group, 1998.

Appiah, Kwame Anthony, and Henry Louis Gates, Jr., eds. *Microsoft Encarta Africana 2000* [multimedia optical discs]. Microsoft, 1999.

Aptheker, Herbert. *American Negro Slave Revolts.* International Publishers, 1993.

Asante, Molefi K. *The African-American Atlas: Black History and Culture—An Illustrated Reference.* Macmillan, 1998.

Ashe, Arthur. *A Hard Road to Glory: A History of the African-American Athlete.* Penguin USA, 1993.

Astor, Gerald. *The Right to Fight: A History of African Americans in the Military.* Presidio, 1998.

Bearden, Romare. *A History of African-American Artists from 1792 to the Present.* Pantheon Books, 1992.

"Black History in Words and Pictures." *Ebony*, Feb. 1998.

"Black History Trails." *Ebony*, Feb. 1999.

Black Shadows on a Silver Screen: The Black Film Industry from 1915–1950 [videorecording]. Republic Pictures Home Video, 1986.

Bogle, Donald. *Blacks in American Films and Television: An Encyclopedia.* Garland, 1988.

Boyd, Herb, ed. *Autobiography of a People: Three Centuries of African American History Told by Those Who Lived It.* Doubleday, 2000.

Bradley, David, ed. *The Encyclopedia of Civil Rights in America.* M.E. Sharpe, 1998.

Carson, Clayborne, et al. *The Eyes on the Prize Civil Rights Reader.* Viking, 1991.

A Century of Black Cinema [videorecording]. Passport Video, 1997.

Cohen, David, ed. *The African Americans* [photographs]. Viking Studio Books, 1993.

Eyes on the Prize: America's Civil Rights Years, 1954–1965. PBS Video, 1987; and *Eyes on the Prize: America at the Racial Crossroads.* PBS Video, 1989 [videorecordings].

Haskins, James. *Black Dance in America: A History Through its People.* HarperTrophy, 1992.

Hawkins, Walter L. *African American Biographies: Profiles of 558 Current Men and Women.* McFarland, 1992.

Hine, Darlene Clark, ed. *Facts on File Encyclopedia of Black Women in America.* Facts on File, 1997.

Kranz, Rachel. *Biographical Dictionary of African Americans.* Facts on File, 1999.

Lanning, Michael Lee. *The African-American Soldier: From Crispus Attucks to Colin Powell.* Carol Pub. Group, 1997.

Martin, Waldo E., ed. *Civil Rights in the United States.* Macmillan Reference USA, 2000.

Murphy, Larry G., ed. *Encyclopedia of African American Religions.* Garland, 1993.

The New York Public Library African American Desk Reference. Wiley, 1999.

Newman, Richard, and Marcia Sawyer. *Everybody Say Freedom: Everything You Needed to Know About African-American History.* Penguin, 1996.

Pinkney, Andrea Davis. *Let It Shine: Stories of Black Women Freedom Fighters.* Harcourt Brace Jovanovich, 2000.

Salzman, Jack, David Lionel Smith, and Cornel West, eds. *Encyclopedia of African-American Culture and History.* Macmillan Library Reference, 1995.

"A Short Course in Black History." *U.S. News & World Report*, Feb. 2, 1998.

Smith, Jessie Carney, ed. *Black Heroes of the 20th Century.* Visible Ink Press, 1998.

Smith, Jessie Carney, and Joseph Palmisano, eds. *Reference Library of Black America.* Gale Group, 2000.

Smith, Valerie, ed. *African American Writers.* Maxwell Macmillan, 1993.

Southern, Eileen. *The Music of Black Americans: A History.* W.W. Norton, 1997.

Stretch Your Wings: Famous Black Quotations for Teens. Little Brown, 1999.

Thompson, Kathleen, and MacAustin, Hilary, eds. *The Face of Our Past: Images of Black Women from Colonial America to the Present.* Indiana University Press, 1999.

"The 20 Most Important Events in African American History." *Ebony*, Dec. 1999.

Williams, Juan. *Eyes on the Prize: America's Civil Rights Years, 1954–1965.* Penguin Books, 1988.

Young, Henry J. *Major Black Religious Leaders, 1755–1940.* Abingdon, 1977.

Zinn, Howard. *A People's History of the United States: 1492–Present.* HarperCollins, 1999.

GENERAL SOURCES: WEBSITES

"African American History Resources." *Montgomery County (MD) Public Schools Website.*
http://www.mcps.k12.md.us/curriculum/socialstd/
African_Am_bookmarks.html

"The African American Journey." *PBS Online.*
http://www.pbs.org/aajourney/

"African American Literature and History." *Internet School Library Media Center.*
http://falcon.jmu.edu/~ramseyil/afroamer.htm

"African American Mosaic." *Library of Congress.*
http://lcweb.loc.gov/exhibits/african/intro.html

"African American Odyssey." *Library of Congress.*
http://memory.loc.gov/ammem/aaohtml/exhibit/aointro.html

"African-American Pioneers." *African Genesis.*
http://afgen.com/pioneer.html

"African American Writers: Online E-texts." *Internet School Library Media Center.*
http://falcon.jmu.edu/~ramseyil/afroonline.htm

Africana.com.
http://www.africana.com/ms/encarta.htm

"Africans in America." *PBS Online.*
http://www.pbs.org/wgbh/aia/

Afro-American Almanac.
http://toptags.com/aama/

Black Facts Online.
http://www.blackfacts.com/

"Black History." *The New York Institute for Special Education.*
http://www.nyise.org/blackhistory/index.html

Black History Museum.
http://www.afroam.org/history/history.html

"Black History-Related Postage Stamps." *ThinkQuest.*
http://library.thinkquest.org/10320/Blk_Hist.htm

The Civil Rights Movement (1954–1968).
http://www.educ.wsu.edu/97fall/workspac/tl/303/section1/stoda/index.htm

Education First: Black History Hotlist!
http://www.kn.pacbell.com/wired/BHM/bh_hotlist.html

Encyclopaedia Britannica Guide to Black History.
http://blackhistory.eb.com/

The Faces of Science: African Americans in the Sciences.
http://www.princeton.edu/~mcbrown/display/faces.html

"Gateway to African American History." *Office of International Information, U.S. Department of State.*
http://usinfo.state.gov/usa/blackhis/

"Historic Documents and Books on the Internet: African American." *Ethnic Studies Project, University of Southern California.*
http://www.usc.edu/isd/archives/ethnicstudies/historicdocs/

"Images of African Americans from the 19th Century." *New York Public Library Schomburg Center.*
http://digital.nypl.org/schomburg/images_aa19/

National Civil Rights Museum.
http://www.midsouth.rr.com/civilrights/

"Prominent African Americans: Past and Present." *African American Web Connection.*
http://www.aawc.com/paa.html

INDIVIDUAL ENTRIES

Abdul-Jabbar, Kareem

"Abdul-Jabbar, Kareem." *Current Biography*, Feb. 1997.

Abdul-Jabbar, Kareem. *Kareem*. Random House, 1990.

Abdul-Jabbar, Kareem. *A Season on the Reservation: My Sojourn with the White Mountain Apache*. W. Morrow, 2000.

Kareem: Reflections from Inside [videorecording]. CBS/Fox Video Sports, 1989.

Abernathy, Ralph

Abernathy, Donzaleigh. *Partners to History: Martin Luther King, Jr., Ralph David Abernathy, and the Civil Rights Movement*. General Publishing, 1998.

Abernathy, Ralph. *And the Walls Came Tumbling Down: An Autobiography*. Harper and Row, 1989.

Applebome, Peter. "Rights Leaders Denouncing New Book by Ex-King Aide." *New York Times*, Oct. 13, 1989.

Reef, Catherine. *Ralph David Abernathy*. Dillon Press, 1995.

Severo, Richard. "Ralph D. Abernathy, 64, Rights Pioneer." *New York Times*, Apr. 18, 1990 (obituary).

Abolition Movement

Altman, Linda Jacobs. *Slavery and Abolition in American History*. Enslow Publishers, 1999.

Chittenden, Elizabeth F. *Profiles in Black and White: Stories of Men and Women Who Fought Against Slavery*. Scribner, 1973.

Currie, Stephen. *The Liberator: Voice of the Abolitionist Movement*. Lucent Books, 2000.

Lowance, Mason, ed. *Against Slavery: An Abolitionist Reader*. Penguin Books, 2000.

Quarles, Benjamin. *Black Abolitionists*. Da Capo Press, 1991.

Revolution [videorecording]. PBS Video, 1998.

Affirmative Action

Beyond Black and White: Affirmative Action in America [videorecording]. PBS Video, 1999.

Eisaguirre, Lynne. *Affirmative Action: A Reference Handbook*. ABC-CLIO. 1999.

Africa

Altman, Susan. *The Encyclopedia of African-American Heritage*. Facts On File, 1997.

Piersen, William Dillon. *From Africa to America: African American History from the Colonial Era to the Early Republic, 1526–1790*. Twayne Publishers, 1996.

Salley, Columbus. *The 100 Must Reads for African-Americans: From the African Past to Today*. Carol Pub. Group, 1997.

African American Origins

African-American Heritage [videorecording]. Schlessinger Video Productions, 1997.

Altman, Susan. *The Encyclopedia of African-American Heritage*. Facts On File, 1997.

Asante, Molefi K. *The African-American Atlas: Black History and Culture—An Illustrated Reference*. Macmillan, 1998.

Diggs, Ellen Irene. *Black Chronology: From 4000 B.C. to the Abolition of the Slave Trade.* G.K. Hall, 1983.

Smith, Jessie Carney, and Joseph Palmisano, eds. *Reference Library of Black America.* Gale Group, 2000.

Wright, Donald R. *African Americans in the Colonial Era: From African Origins Through the American Revolution.* Harlan Davidson, 1990.

Ailey, Alvin

Ailey, Alvin. *Revelations: The Autobiography of Alvin Ailey.* Carol Pub. Group, 1995.

Dunning, Jennifer. *Alvin Ailey: A Life in Dance.* Addison-Wesley, 1996.

Lewis-Ferguson, Julinda. *Alvin Ailey, Jr.: A Life in Dance.* Walker, 1994.

A Tribute to Alvin Ailey [videorecording]. Kultur, 1990.

Ali, Muhammad

Ali, Muhammad. *The Greatest, My Own Story.* Random House, 1975.

Freedman, Suzanne. *Clay v. United States: Muhammad Ali Objects to War.* Enslow Publishers, 1997.

Hauser, Thomas. *Muhammad Ali: His Life and Times.* Simon and Schuster, 1991.

Remnick, David. *King of the World: Muhammad Ali and the Rise of an American Hero.* Random House, 1998.

"Muhammad Ali." *International Boxing Hall of Fame.*
http://www.ibhof.com/ali.htm

Amistad Mutiny

Amistad [videorecording]. DreamWorks, 1998.

Chambers, Veronica. *Amistad Rising: A Story of Freedom.* Harcourt Brace Jovanovich, 1998.

Jurmain, Suzanne. *Freedom's Sons: The True Story of the Amistad Mutiny.* Lothrop, Lee and Shepard Books, 1998.

Myers, Walter Dean. *Amistad: A Long Road to Freedom.* Dutton Children's Books, 1998.

Owens, William A. *Black Mutiny: The Revolt on the Schooner Amistad.* Black Classic Press, 1997.

"Amistad." *Dreamworks/Penguin Putnam.*
http://www.penguinputnam.com/amistad/

Anderson, Marian

Alexander, Amy. *Fifty Black Women Who Changed America.* Carol Pub. Group, 1998.

Anderson, Marian. *My Lord, What a Morning: An Autobiography.* Viking Press, 1956.

Broadwater, Andrea. *Marian Anderson: Singer and Humanitarian.* Enslow Publishers, 2000.

Keiler, Allan. *Marian Anderson: A Singer's Journey.* Scribner, 2000.

Marian Anderson: A Life in Song.
http://www.library.upenn.edu/special/gallery/anderson/index.html

Angelou, Maya

Angelou, Maya. *I Know Why the Caged Bird Sings.* Bantam Books, 1993.

King, Sarah E. *Maya Angelou: Greeting the Morning.* Millbrook Press, 1994.

Maya Angelou: Rainbow in the Clouds [videorecording]. PBS Video, 1992.

Pettit, Jayne. *Maya Angelou: Journey of the Heart.* Lodestar Books, 1996.

Spain, Valerie. *Meet Maya Angelou*. Random House, 1994.

Apollo Theatre

Fox, Ted. *Showtime at the Apollo*. Da Capo Press, 1993.

Helbling, Mark Irving. *The Harlem Renaissance: The One and the Many*. Greenwood Press, 1999.

Schiffman, Jack. *Harlem Heyday: A Pictorial History of Modern Black Show Business and the Apollo Theatre*. Prometheus Books, 1984.

Armstrong, Louis

Armstrong, Louis. *Satchmo: My Life in New Orleans*. Da Capo Press, 1986.

Collier, James Lincoln. *Louis Armstrong: An American Success Story*. Macmillan, 1985.

McKissack, Pat. *Louis Armstrong: Jazz Musician*. Enslow Publishers, 1991.

Orgill, Roxanne. *If I Only Had a Horn: Young Louis Armstrong*. Houghton Mifflin, 1997.

Artists (General)

Bearden, Romare. *A History of African-American Artists from 1792 to the Present*. Pantheon Books, 1992.

Butler, Jerry. *A Drawing in the Sand: The Story of African American Art*. Zino Press Children's Books, 1998.

Hacker, Carlotta. *Great African Americans in the Arts*. Crabtree Pub. Co., 1997.

Kindred Spirits: Contemporary African-American Artists [videorecording]. PBS Video, 1992.

Lewis, Samella S. *African American Art for Young People*. Unity Works Press, 1991.

Sullivan, George. *Black Artists in Photography, 1840–1940*. Cobblehill Books, 1996.

Ashe, Arthur

Arthur Ashe: Citizen of the World [videorecording]. HBO Sports, 1994.

Ashe, Arthur. *Days of Grace: A Memoir*. Knopf, 1993.

Ashe, Arthur. *A Hard Road to Glory: A History of the African-American Athlete*. Penguin USA, 1993.

Weissberg, Ted. *Arthur Ashe*. Chelsea House, 1991.

Athletes (General)

African-American Sports Greats: A Biographical Dictionary. Greenwood Press, 1995.

Ashe, Arthur. *A Hard Road to Glory: A History of the African-American Athlete*. Penguin USA, 1993.

Barry, James P. *The Berlin Olympics, 1936: Black American Athletes Counter Nazi Propaganda*. Franklin Watts, 1975.

Hunter, Shaun. *Great African Americans in the Olympics*. Crabtree Pub. Co., 1997.

The Journey of the African-American Athlete [videorecording]. HBO Home Video, 1996.

Rediger, Pat. *Great African Americans in Sports*. Crabtree Pub. Co., 1996.

Negro Baseball Leagues.
http://www.blackbaseball.com/

Attucks, Crispus

Lanning, Michael Lee. *The African-American Soldier: From Crispus Attucks to Colin Powell*. Carol Pub. Group, 1997.

Millender, Dharathula H. *Crispus Attucks, Black Leader of Colonial Patriots.* Aladdin Books, 1986.

Authors and Literature (General)

African-American Literature: An Anthology. NTC Publishing Group, 1998.

Bloom, Harold, ed. *Black American Poets and Dramatists of the Harlem Renaissance.* Chelsea House, 1995.

Bloom, Harold, ed. *Major Black American Writers Through the Harlem Renaissance.* Chelsea House, 1995.

Caroling Dusk: An Anthology of Verse by Black Poets of the Twenties. Carol Pub. Group, 1993.

Giant Steps: The New Generation of African American Writers. Perennial, 2000.

Our Souls Have Grown Deep Like the Rivers: Black Poets Read Their Work [sound recording]. Rhino/Word Beat, 2000.

Rand, Donna. *Black Books Galore! Guide to Great African American Children's Books.* Wiley, 1998.

Rollock, Barbara. *Black Authors and Illustrators of Children's Books: A Biographical Dictionary.* Garland, 1992.

Selected African American Writing from 1760 to 1910. Bantam Books, 1995.

Smith, Valerie, ed. *African American Writers.* Maxwell Macmillan, 1993.

Swanson, Meg, ed. *Playwrights of Color.* Intercultural Press, 1999.

Toussaint, Pamela. *Great Books for African-American Children.* Plume, 1999.

The Vintage Book of African American Poetry. Vintage Books, 2000.

Wilkinson, Brenda Scott. *African American Women Writers.* J. Wiley, 2000.

Wilson, Sondra Kathryn, ed. *The Messenger Reader: Stories, Poetry, and Essays from The Messenger Magazine.* Modern Library, 2000.

"African American Writers: Online E-texts." *Internet School Library Media Center.*
http://falcon.jmu.edu/~ramseyil/afroonline.htm

Baldwin, James

Baldwin, James. *Go Tell it on the Mountain.* Modern Library, 1995.

Baldwin, James. *Notes of a Native Son.* Beacon Press, 1990.

Gottfried, Ted. *James Baldwin: Voice from Harlem.* Franklin Watts, 1997.

James Baldwin: Author [videorecording]. Schlesinger Video Productions, 1994.

Kenan, Randall. *James Baldwin.* Chelsea House, 1994.

Black English

Brasch, Walter M. *Black English and the Mass Media.* University Press of America, 1984.

Dillard, J.L. *Black English: Its History and Usage.* Random House, 1972.

Rickford, John R. *Spoken Soul: The Story of Black English.* John Wiley and Sons, 2000.

Black History Month

Black History Month Resource Book. Gale Research, 1993.

Carter, Polly. *Harriet Tubman and Black History Month.* Silver Burdett Press, 1990.

"Why February Was Chosen to Celebrate Black History." *Jet*, Feb. 14, 1994.

Black Muslims

Banks, William. *The Black Muslims.* Chelsea House, 1997.

Barbosa, Steven, ed. *American Jihad: Islam after Malcolm X.* Doubleday, 1994.

Brown, Kevin. *Malcolm X: His Life and Legacy.* Millbrook Press, 1995.

Halasa, Malu. *Elijah Muhammad: Religious Leader.* Chelsea House, 1990.

Haskins, James. *Louis Farrakhan and the Nation of Islam.* Walker and Co., 1996.

Black Panther Party

Brown, Elaine. *A Taste of Power: A Black Woman's Story.* Pantheon, 1992.

Cleaver, Eldridge. *Soul on Ice.* Laurel/Dell, 1992.

Foner, Philip S., ed. *The Black Panthers Speak.* Da Capo Press, 1995.

Jones, Charles E., ed. *The Black Panther Party.* Black Classic Press, 1998.

Newton, Huey P. *To Die for the People: The Writings of Huey P. Newton.* Random House, 1972.

Seale, Bobby. *Seize the Time: The Story of The Black Panther Party and Huey P. Newton.* Black Classic Press, 1991.

"The Black Panther Party." *The Black History Museum.* http://www.afroam.org/history/Panthers/panther-lead.html

Black Power

Carmichael, Stokely. *Black Power: The Politics of Liberation in America.* Vintage Books, 1992.

Cwiklik, Robert. *Stokely Carmichael and Black Power.* Millbrook Press, 1993.

McWorter, Gerald A. *Malcolm X for Beginners.* Writers and Readers Publishing, 1990.

Newton, Huey P. *Revolutionary Suicide.* Writers and Readers Publishing, 1995.

Bond, Julian

Eyes on the Prize: America's Civil Rights Years, 1954–1965. PBS Video, 1987; and *Eyes on the Prize: America at the Racial Crossroads* [videorecordings]. PBS Video, 1989.

Neary, John. *Julian Bond: Black Rebel.* Morrow, 1971.

White, Jack E. "It's Still White Supremacy: Julian Bond Restores the Focus of the N.A.A.C.P." *Time,* July 27, 1998.

Brown, John

Barrett, Tracy. *Harpers Ferry: The Story of John Brown's Raid.* Millbrook Press, 1994.

Cox, Clinton. *Fiery Vision: The Life and Death of John Brown.* Scholastic, 1997.

John Brown's Holy War [videorecording]. PBS Video, 2000.

Stein, R. Conrad. *John Brown's Raid on Harpers Ferry in American History.* Enslow Publishers, 1999.

Brown v. Board of Education Case

Kraft, Betsy Harvey. *Sensational Trials of the Twentieth Century.* Scholastic Press, 1998.

Mauro, Tony. *Illustrated Great Decisions of the Supreme Court.* CQ Press, 2000.

Rochelle, Belinda. *Witnesses to Freedom: Young People Who Fought for Civil Rights.* Puffin Books, 1997.

Tackach, James. *Brown v. Board of Education.* Lucent Books, 1997.

Tushnet, Mark V. *Brown v. Board of Education: The Battle for Integration.* Franklin Watts, 1995.

Carpetbaggers
See RECONSTRUCTION.

Carver, George Washington
Carver, George Washington. *George Washington Carver in His Own Words.* University of Missouri Press, 1987.

Coil, Suzanne M. *George Washington Carver.* Franklin Watts, 1990.

McKissack, Pat. *George Washington Carver: The Peanut Scientist.* Enslow Publishers, 1991.

Mitchell, Barbara. *A Pocketful of Goobers: A Story about George Washington Carver.* Carolrhoda Books, 1986.

Nicholson, Lois. *George Washington Carver.* Chelsea House, 1994.

Chamberlain, Wilt
Chamberlain, Wilt. *A View From Above.* Villard Books, 1991.

Frankl, Ron. *Wilt Chamberlain.* Chelsea House, 1994.

Litsky, Frank. "Wilt Chamberlain Is Dead at 63; Dominated Basketball in the 60's." *New York Times*, Oct. 13, 1999.

Civil Rights Acts of 1960 and 1964
Allison, Robert J., ed. *American Social and Political Movements 1945–2000: Pursuit of Liberty.* St. James Press, 2000.

Berman, Daniel M. *A Bill Becomes a Law: Congress Enacts Civil Rights Legislation.* Macmillan, 1966.

Whalen, Charles W. *The Longest Debate: A Legislative History of the 1964 Civil Rights Act.* Seven Locks Press, 1985.

Civil Rights Movement
Allison, Robert J., ed. *American Social and Political Movements 1945–2000: Pursuit of Liberty.* St. James Press, 2000.

Davis, Townsend. *Weary Feet, Rested Souls: A Guided History of the Civil Rights Movement.* W.W. Norton, 1998.

Dunn, John M. *The Civil Rights Movement.* Lucent Books, 1998.

Eyes on the Prize: America's Civil Rights Years, 1954–1965. PBS Video, 1987; and *Eyes on the Prize: America at the Racial Crossroads* [videorecordings]. PBS Video, 1989.

Fradin, Dennis B. *Ida B. Wells: Mother of the Civil Rights Movement.* Clarion Books, 2000.

Henry, Christopher E. *Forever Free: From the Emancipation Proclamation to the Civil Rights Bill of 1875.* Chelsea House, 1995.

Humanitarians and Reformers. Macmillan Library Reference USA, 1999.

Kasher, Steven. *The Civil Rights Movement: A Photographic History, 1954–68.* Abbeville Press, 1996.

Levy, Peter B. *The Civil Rights Movement.* Greenwood Press, 1998.

Voices of the Civil Rights Movement: Black American Freedom Songs, 1960–1966 [sound recording]. Smithsonian Folkways, 1997.

Weber, Michael. *Causes and Consequences of the African-American Civil Rights Movement.* Raintree Steck-Vaughn, 1998.

Weisbrot, Robert. *Freedom Bound: A History of America's Civil Rights Movement.* W.W. Norton, 1990.

Wexler, Sanford. *An Eyewitness History of the Civil Rights Movement.* Checkmark Books, 1999.

Winters, Paul A., ed. *The Civil Rights Movement.* Greenhaven Press, 2000.

The Civil Rights Movement (1954–1968).
http://www.educ.wsu.edu/97fall/workspac/tl/303/section1/stoda/index.htm
National Civil Rights Museum.
http://www.midsouth.rr.com/civilrights/

Civil War

Africans in America: America's Journey Through Slavery [videorecording]. PBS Video, 1998.

The American Civil War: A Multicultural Encyclopedia. Grolier Educational Corp., 1994.

Biel, Timothy L. *The Civil War.* Lucent Books, 1991.

Carter, Alden R. *The Civil War: American Tragedy.* Franklin Watts, 1992.

The Civil War [videorecording]. PBS Video, 1989.

Collier, Christopher. *Slavery and the Coming of the Civil War, 1831–1861.* Benchmark Books, 1998.

Cromie, Alice. *A Tour Guide to the Civil War.* Rutledge Hill Press, 1990.

Golay, Michael. *The Civil War.* Facts on File, 1992.

Historical Times Illustrated Encyclopedia of the Civil War. HarperPerennial, 1991.

Kallen, Stuart A. *The Civil War and Reconstruction: A History of Black People in America, 1830–1880.* Abdo and Daughters, 1990.

Naden, Corinne J. *Why Fight? The Causes of the American Civil War.* Raintree Steck–Vaughn, 2000.

Smith, Carter, ed. *Prelude to War: A Sourcebook on the Civil War.* Millbrook Press, 1993.

Civil War, African Americans in the

Black, Wallace B. *Slaves to Soldiers: African-American Fighting Men in the Civil War.* Franklin Watts, 1997.

Brooks, Victor. *African Americans in the Civil War.* Chelsea House, 2000.

Glory [videorecording]. RCA/Columbia Pictures Home Video, 1990.

Haskins, James. *Black, Blue, and Gray: African Americans in the Civil War.* Simon and Schuster Books for Young Readers, 1998.

Lanning, Michael Lee. *The African-American Soldier: From Crispus Attucks to Colin Powell.* Carol Pub. Group, 1997.

The Massachusetts 54th Colored Infantry [videorecording]. PBS Video, 1991.

Mettger, Zak. *Till Victory Is Won: Black Soldiers in the Civil War.* Lodestar Books, 1994.

Trudeau, Noah Andre. *Like Men of War: Black Troops in the Civil War, 1862–1865.* Little Brown, 1998.

Cleaver, Eldridge

Cleaver, Eldridge. *Soul on Ice.* Dell, 1968.

"Eldridge Cleaver, Ex-Black Panther, Author, Political Conservative, Dies." *Jet*, May 18, 1998.

"A Fiery Soul Set Free: Eldridge Cleaver's Radical Journey Ends." *Newsweek*, May 11, 1998.

Johnson, Charles. "A Soul's Jagged Arc." *New York Times Magazine*, Jan. 3, 1999.

Core (Congress of Racial Equality)

Farmer, James. *Lay Bare the Heart: An Autobiography of the Civil Rights Movement.* New American Library, 1985.

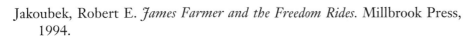

Jakoubek, Robert E. *James Farmer and the Freedom Rides*. Millbrook Press, 1994.

Cosby, Bill

Cortina, Betty. "Bill Cosby: Crossover Comic, TV Pioneer, America's Favorite Dad." *Entertainment Weekly*, Nov. 1, 1999.

Herbert, Solomon J. *Bill Cosby, Entertainer*. Chelsea House, 1991.

Rosenberg, Robert. *Bill Cosby: The Changing Black Image*. Millbrook Press, 1991.

Schuman, Michael. *Bill Cosby: Actor and Comedian*. Enslow Publishers, 1995.

Smith, Ronald L. *Cosby: The Life of a Comedy Legend*. Prometheus Books, 1997.

Cullen, Countee

Caroling Dusk: An Anthology of Verse by Black Poets of the Twenties. Carol Pub. Group, 1993.

Cullen, Countee. *My Soul's High Song: The Collected Writings of Countee Cullen, Voice of the Harlem Renaissance*. Doubleday, 1991.

"Countee Cullen." *The Academy of American Poets*.
http://www.poets.org/poets/index.cfm

Countee Porter Cullen (1903–1946) Teacher Resource File.
http://falcon.jmu.edu/~ramseyil/cullen.htm

Davis, Angela

Alexander, Amy. *Fifty Black Women Who Changed America*. Carol Pub. Group, 1998.

Davis, Angela Yvonne. *Angela Davis: An Autobiography*. International Publishers, 1988.

Davis, Angela Yvonne. *The Angela Y. Davis Reader*. Blackwell, 1998.

Diseases and Epidemics

Bell, Geneva. *My Rose: An African American Mother's Story of AIDS*. Pilgrim Press, 1997.

Haskins, James. *Sports Great Magic Johnson*. Enslow Publishers, 1992.

Miss Evers' Boys [videorecording]. HBO Home Video, 1997.

Silverstein, Alvin. *Sickle Cell Anemia*. Enslow Publishers, 1997.

Douglass, Frederick

Douglass, Frederick. *Escape from Slavery: The Boyhood of Frederick Douglass in His Own Words*. Knopf, 1994.

Douglass, Frederick. *Life and Times of Frederick Douglass*. Citadel Press, 1983.

Girard, Linda Walvoord. *Young Frederick Douglass: The Slave Who Learned to Read*. A. Whitman, 1994.

Jackson, Garnet. *Frederick Douglass, Freedom Fighter*. Modern Curriculum Press, 1993.

Kerby, Mona. *Frederick Douglass*. Franklin Watts, 1994.

McKissack, Pat. *Frederick Douglass: Leader Against Slavery*. Enslow Publishers, 1991.

"American Visionaries: Frederick Douglass." *Frederick Douglass National Historic Site*.
http://www.cr.nps.gov/csd/exhibits/douglass/

Dred Scott Case

Ehrlich, Walter. *They Have No Rights: Dred Scott's Struggle for Freedom*. Greenwood Press, 1979.

Finkelman, Paul. *Dred Scott v. Sandford: A Brief History with Documents.* Bedford Books, 1997.

Fleischner, Jennifer. *The Dred Scott Case: Testing the Right to Live Free.* Millbrook Press, 1997.

Herda, D.J. *The Dred Scott Case: Slavery and Citizenship.* Enslow Publishers, 1994.

Lukes, Bonnie L. *The Dred Scott Decision.* Lucent Books, 1997.

Du Bois, W.E.B.

Cavan, Seamus. *W.E.B. Du Bois and Racial Relations.* Millbrook Press, 1993.

Du Bois, W.E.B. *The Souls of Black Folk.* Modern Library, 1996.

Lewis, David L. *W.E.B. Du Bois—Biography of a Race, 1868–1919.* H. Holt, 1993.

McDaniel, Melissa. *W.E.B. DuBois: Scholar and Civil Rights Activist.* Franklin Watts, 1999.

Rowh, Mark. *W.E.B. Du Bois: Champion of Civil Rights.* Enslow Publishers, 1999.

Ellington, Edward Kennedy "Duke"

Collier, James Lincoln. *Duke Ellington.* Collier Books, 1993.

Ellington, Duke. *Music Is My Mistress.* Doubleday, 1973.

Frankl, Ron. *Duke Ellington.* Chelsea House, 1988.

Lawrence, A.H. *Duke Ellington and His World: A Biography.* Schirmer Books, 1999.

On the Road with Duke Ellington [videorecording]. Direct Cinema, 1980.

Ellison, Ralph

Bishop, Jack. *Ralph Ellison.* Chelsea House, 1988.

Ellison, Ralph. *Flying Home and Other Stories.* Random House, 1996.

Ellison, Ralph. *Invisible Man.* Modern Library, 1994.

Gates, Henry Louis, Jr. "The Last Sublime Riffs of a Literary Jazzman." *Time,* June 28, 1999.

Emancipation Proclamation

Henry, Christopher E. *Forever Free: From the Emancipation Proclamation to the Civil Rights Bill of 1875.* Chelsea House, 1995.

Roberts, Russell. *Lincoln and the Abolition of Slavery.* Lucent Books, 2000.

Tackach, James. *The Emancipation Proclamation.* Lucent Books, 1999.

Young, Robert. *The Emancipation Proclamation: Why Lincoln Really Freed the Slaves.* Maxwell Macmillan, 1994.

Evers, Medgar

Evers-Williams, Myrlie. *For Us, the Living.* Banner Books, 1996.

Ghosts of Mississippi [videorecording]. Columbia TriStar Home Video, 1997.

Morris, Willie. *The Ghosts of Medgar Evers: A Tale of Race, Murder, Mississippi, and Hollywood.* Random House, 1998.

Nossiter, Adam. *Of Long Memory: Mississippi and the Murder of Medgar Evers.* Addison-Wesley, 1994.

Farmer, James

See CORE.

Farrakhan, Louis

Alexander, Amy. *The Farrakhan Factor: African-American Writers on Leadership, Nationhood, and Minister Louis Farrakhan.* Grove Press, 1998.

Cottman, Michael H. *Million Man March.* Crown, 1995.

Haskins, James. *Louis Farrakhan and the Nation of Islam.* Walker and Co., 1996.

Levinsohn, Florence Hamlish. *Looking for Farrakhan.* Ivan R. Dee, 1997.

Magida, Arthur J. *Prophet of Rage: A Life of Louis Farrakhan and His Nation.* Basic Books, 1996.

Film and Television, African Americans in

Black Shadows on a Silver Screen: The Black Film Industry from 1915–1950 [videorecording]. Republic Pictures Home Video, 1986.

Bogle, Donald. *Toms, Coons, Mulattoes, Mammies, and Bucks: An Interpretive History of Blacks in American Films.* Continuum Publishing Group, 1994.

A Century of Black Cinema [videorecording]. Passport Video, 1997.

Color Adjustment [videorecording]. California Newsreel, 1991.

Diawara, Manthia, ed. *Black American Cinema.* Routledge, 1993.

Gray, John. *Blacks in Film and Television: A Pan-African Bibliography of Films, Filmmakers, and Performers.* Greenwood Press, 1990.

Grimes, William. "Can a Film Be Both Racist and Classic?" *New York Times,* Apr. 27, 1994.

Hill, George H. *Ebony Images: Black Americans and Television.* Daystar Pub. Co., 1986.

James, Darius. *That's Blaxploitation!* St. Martin's Griffin, 1995.

"Jet Celebrates 45 Years of the Hottest Black Music, TV and Movie Stars." *Jet,* Nov. 3, 1997.

Martinez, Gerald. *What it Is, What it Was! The Black Film Explosion of the '70s in Words and Pictures.* Hyperion, 1998.

Mico, Ted, et al., eds. *Past Imperfect: History According to the Movies.* H. Holt, 1995.

Parker, Janice. *Great African Americans in Film.* Crabtree Pub. Co., 1997.

Sampson, Henry T. *Blacks in Black and White: A Source Book on Black Films.* Scarecrow Press, 1995.

That's Black Entertainment [videorecording]. OnDeck Home Entertainment, 1997.

Zook, Kristal Brent. *Color by Fox: The Fox Network and the Revolution in Black Television.* Oxford University Press, 1999.

Folklore

Abrahams, Roger D., ed. *African-American Folktales: Stories from Black Traditions in the New World.* Pantheon Books, 1999.

Hamilton, Virginia. *The People Could Fly: American Black Folktales.* Random House, 2000.

Haskins, James. *Moaning Bones: African-American Ghost Stories.* Lothrop, Lee and Shepard/Morrow, 1998.

Lester, Julius. *Black Folktales.* Grove Press, 1970.

Raw Head, Bloody Bones: African-American Tales of the Supernatural. Scribner, 1991.

Food

Jones, Wilbert. *African-American Holiday Cooking.* Birch Lane, 1999.

Mack-Williams, Kibibi. *Food and Our History.* Rourke Press, 1995.

Webster, Cassandra Hughes. *Mother Africa's Table: A Collection of West African and African American Recipes and Cultural Traditions.* Main Street/Doubleday, 1998.

Franklin, Aretha

Aretha Franklin, the Queen of Soul [videorecording]. Pacific Arts Video, 1989.

Bego, Mark. *Aretha Franklin, the Queen of Soul.* St. Martin's Press, 1989.

Franklin, Aretha. *Aretha: From These Roots.* Villard, 1999.

Gourse, Leslie. *Aretha Franklin: Lady Soul.* Franklin Watts, 1995.

Sheafer, Silvia Anne. *Aretha Franklin: Motown Superstar.* Enslow Publishers, 1996.

Freedmen's Bureau [Bureau of Refugees, Freedmen, and Abandoned Lands]

Bentley, George R. *A History of the Freedmen's Bureau.* Octagon Books, 1970.

Berlin, Ira. *Slaves Without Masters: The Free Negro in the Antebellum South.* Vintage Books, 1976.

Hansen, Joyce. *Bury Me Not in a Land of Slaves: African-Americans in the Time of Reconstruction.* Franklin Watts, 2000.

King, Wilma. *Children of the Emancipation.* Carolrhoda Books, 2000.

McFeely, William S. *Yankee Stepfather: General O.O. Howard and the Freedmen.* W.W. Norton, 1970.

"Freedom Summer"

Belfrage, Sally. *Freedom Summer.* University Press of Virginia, 1990.

Murder in Mississippi: The Price of Freedom [videorecording]. Films for the Humanities and Sciences, 1994.

Walter, Mildred Pitts. *Mississippi Challenge.* Aladdin Paperbacks, 1996.

Winters, Paul A., ed. *The Civil Rights Movement.* Greenhaven Press, 2000.

Garvey, Marcus

Archer, Jules. *They Had a Dream: The Civil Rights Struggle, from Frederick Douglass to Marcus Garvey to Martin Luther King, and Malcolm X.* Puffin Books, 1996.

Garvey, Marcus. *Message to the People.* Majority Press, 1986.

Lawler, Mary. *Marcus Garvey.* Chelsea House, 1987.

Marcus Garvey: Black-Nationalist Leader [videorecording]. Schlessinger Video Productions, 1994.

Gates, Henry Louis, Jr.

Appiah, Kwame Anthony, and Henry Louis Gates, Jr., eds. *Microsoft Encarta Africana 2000* [multimedia optical discs]. Microsoft, 1999.

Gates, Henry Louis. *Colored People: A Memoir.* Vintage Books, 1995.

Gates, Henry Louis. *Wonders of the African World.* Knopf, 1999.

Wonders of the African World [videorecording]. PBS Video, 1999.

Gay and Lesbian African Americans

Haskins, James. *Bayard Rustin: Behind the Scenes of the Civil Rights Movement.* Hyperion Press, 1997.

Kenan, Randall. *James Baldwin.* Chelsea House, 1994.

Ruff, Shawn Stewart, ed. *Go the Way Your Blood Beats: An Anthology of Lesbian and Gay Fiction by African-American Writers.* H. Holt, 1996.

Singer, Bennett L., ed. *Growing Up Gay/Growing Up Lesbian: A Literary Anthology.* New Press, 1994.

Gibson, Althea

Biracree, Tom. *Althea Gibson.* Chelsea House, 1989.

Davidson, Sue. *Changing the Game: The Stories of Tennis Champions Alice Marble and Althea Gibson.* Seal Press, 1997.

Gibson, Althea. *I Always Wanted to Be Somebody*. Harper, 1958.

Goldberg, Whoopi

Adams, Mary Agnes. *Whoopi Goldberg: From Street to Stardom*. Dillon Press, 1993.

Caper, William. *Whoopi Goldberg: Comedian and Movie Star*. Enslow Publishers, 1999.

Gaines, Ann. *Whoopi Goldberg*. Chelsea House, 1999.

Goldberg, Whoopi. *Book*. Avon, 1998.

Griffith Joyner, Florence

Aaseng, Nathan. *Florence Griffith Joyner: Dazzling Olympian*. Lerner Publications, 1989.

Brennan, Christine. "So Fast, So Cool." *New York Times Magazine*, Jan. 3, 1999.

Connolly, Pat. "An Athlete to Remember, for a Variety of Reasons." *New York Times*, Sept. 27, 1999.

Haley, Alex

Bloom, Harold, ed. *Alex Haley and Malcolm X's The Autobiography of Malcolm X*. Chelsea House, 1999.

Haley, Alex. *Alex Haley's Queen: The Story of an American Family*. W. Morrow, 1993.

Haley, Alex. *Roots*. Doubleday, 1976.

Roots [videorecording]. Warner Home Video, 1992.

Shirley, David. *Alex Haley*. Chelsea House, 1993.

Hamer, Fannie Lou

Colman, Penny. *Fannie Lou Hamer and the Fight for the Vote*. Millbrook Press, 1993.

Mills, Kay. *This Little Light of Mine: The Life of Fannie Lou Hamer*. Dutton, 1993.

Rubel, David. *Fannie Lou Hamer: From Sharecropping to Politics*. Silver Burdett Press, 1990.

Harlem Renaissance

Against the Odds: The Artists of the Harlem Renaissance [videorecording]. PBS Video, 1990.

Bloom, Harold, ed. *Black American Poets and Dramatists of the Harlem Renaissance*. Chelsea House, 1995.

Bloom, Harold, ed. *Major Black American Writers Through the Harlem Renaissance*. Chelsea House, 1995.

Caroling Dusk: An Anthology of Verse by Black Poets of the Twenties. Carol Pub. Group, 1993.

Cullen, Countee. *My Soul's High Song: The Collected Writings of Countee Cullen, Voice of the Harlem Renaissance*. Doubleday, 1991.

Helbling, Mark Irving. *The Harlem Renaissance: The One and the Many*. Greenwood Press, 1999.

Hughes, Langston. *The Big Sea: An Autobiography*. Thunder's Mouth Press, 1986.

Hurston, Zora Neale. *Dust Tracks on a Road, an Autobiography*. HarperPerennial, 1996.

Jacques, Geoffrey. *Free Within Ourselves: The Harlem Renaissance*. Franklin Watts, 1996.

Kallen, Stuart A. *The Twentieth Century and the Harlem Renaissance: A History of Black People in America, 1880–1930.* Abdo and Daughters, 1990.

Marks, Carole. *The Power of Pride: Stylemakers and Rulebreakers of the Harlem Renaissance.* Crown Publishers, 1999.

Watson, Steven. *The Harlem Renaissance: Hub of African-American Culture, 1920–1930.* Pantheon Books, 1995.

Wilson, Sondra Kathryn, ed. *The Messenger Reader: Stories, Poetry, and Essays from The Messenger Magazine.* Modern Library, 2000.

"Harlem, New York." *Africana.com.* http://www.africana.com/tt_020.htm

Hemings, Sally

Lanier, Shannon, and Jane Feldman. *Jefferson's Children: The Story of One American Family.* Random House, 2000.

Lewis, Neil A. "Study Finds Strong Evidence Jefferson Fathered Slave Son." *New York Times*, Jan. 27, 2000.

Randolph, Laura B. "Who Was Sally Hemings?" *Ebony*, June 1999.

Truscott, Kucian K. "Jefferson's Children: A Descendant of the Author of the Declaration of Independence Challenges His Family to Embrace the Offspring of a Slave." *Life*, July 1, 1999.

Holiday, Billie

Alexander, Amy. *Fifty Black Women Who Changed America.* Carol Pub. Group, 1998.

Hacker, Carlotta. *Great African Americans in Jazz.* Crabtree, 1997.

Holiday, Billie. *Lady Sings the Blues.* Lancer Books, 1972.

Margolick, David. *Strange Fruit: Billie Holiday, Cafe Society, and an Early Cry for Civil Rights.* Running Press, 2000.

Holidays

Eklof, Barbara. *For Every Season: The Complete Guide to African-American Celebrations.* HarperCollins, 1997.

Jones, Wilbert. *African-American Holiday Cooking.* Birch Lane, 1999.

Winchester, Faith. *African-American Holidays.* Bridgestone Books, 1996.

Hughes, Langston

Hughes, Langston. *The Big Sea: An Autobiography.* Thunder's Mouth Press, 1986.

Hughes, Langston. *The Collected Poems of Langston Hughes.* Knopf, 1994.

Hughes, Langston. *Pictorial History of the Negro in America.* Crown Publishers, 1983.

McKissack, Pat. *Langston Hughes: Great American Poet.* Enslow Publishers, 1992.

Meltzer, Milton. *Langston Hughes.* Millbrook Press, 1997.

Hurston, Zora Neale

Hurston, Zora Neale. *Dust Tracks on a Road, an Autobiography.* HarperPerennial, 1996.

Hurston, Zora Neale. *Their Eyes Were Watching God.* Perennial Classics, 1998.

Lyons, Mary E. *Sorrow's Kitchen: The Life and Folklore of Zora Neale Hurston.* Collier Books, 1993.

McKissack, Pat. *Zora Neale Hurston, Writer and Storyteller.* Enslow Publishers, 1992.

Witcover, Paul. *Zora Neale Hurston*. Chelsea House, 1991.

Interracial Families and Racially Mixed People
An American Love Story [videorecording]. New Video Group, 1999.

Funderburg, Lise. *Black, White, Other: Biracial Americans Talk about Race and Identity*. W. Morrow, 1994.

Gay, Kathlyn. *The Rainbow Effect: Interracial Families*. Franklin Watts, 1987.

Kandel, Bethany. *Trevor's Story: Growing Up Biracial*. Lerner Publications, 1997.

Rosenberg, Maxine B. *Living in Two Worlds*. Lothrop, Lee and Shepard Books, 1986.

Secret Daughter [videorecording]. PBS Video, 1996.

Sollors, Werner, ed. *Interracialiam: Black-White Intermarriage in American History, Literature, and Law*. Oxford University Press, 2000.

Woodson, Jacqueline. *The House You Pass on the Way*. Delacorte Press, 1997.

Jackson, Jesse
Frady, Marshall. *Jesse: The Life and Pilgrimage of Jesse Jackson*. Random House, 1996.

Haskins, James. *I Am Somebody! A Biography of Jesse Jackson*. Enslow Publishers, 1992.

Jackson, Jesse. *Straight from the Heart*. Fortress Press, 1987.

Jakoubek, Robert E. *Jesse Jackson*. Chelsea House, 1991.

McKissack, Pat. *Jesse Jackson: A Biography*. Scholastic, 1989.

Jackson State Shootings
Nelson, Jack. *The Orangeburg Massacre*. Ballantine Books, 1970.

Spofford, Tim. *Lynch Street, The May 1970 Slayings at Jackson State College*. Kent State University Press, 1988.

"Ten Days Later . . ." *60s Activism*. http://www.kenyon.edu/khistory/60s/webpage.htm

"30 Years Ago Today: Jackson State Deaths Recalled." *Associated Press Release*, May 14, 2000. Reproduced at http://www.commondreams.org/headlines/051400-03.htm

Walker, Linda B. "Jackson State and Kent State—Alive in History." *Akron Beacon Journal*, May 4, 2000. Reproduced at http://www.ohio.com/ksu/docs/015337.htm

Jim Crow Laws
Collier, Christopher. *Reconstruction and the Rise of Jim Crow, 1864–1896*. Benchmark Books, 1998.

George, Charles. *Life Under the Jim Crow Laws*. Lucent Books, 2000.

Litwack, Leon F. *Trouble in Mind: Black Southerners in the Age of Jim Crow*. Knopf, 1998.

Rasmussen, R. Kent. *Farewell to Jim Crow: The Rise and Fall of Segregation in America*. Facts on File, 1997.

Johnson, James Weldon
Bond, Julian, and Sondra Kathryn Wilson, eds. *Lift Every Voice and Sing: A Celebration of the Negro National Anthem*. Random House, 2000.

Johnson, James Weldon. *Autobiography of an Ex-Colored Man*. W.W. Norton, 1999.

Johnson, James Weldon. *Lift Ev'ry Voice and Sing*. Scholastic, 1995.

McKissack, Pat. *James Weldon Johnson: "Lift Every Voice and Sing"*. Childrens Press, 1990.

Tolbert-Rouchaleau, Jane. *James Weldon Johnson*. Chelsea House, 1988.

Jordan, Michael

Greene, Bob. *Rebound: The Odyssey of Michael Jordan*. Viking, 1995.

Halberstam, David. *Playing for Keeps: Michael Jordan and the World He Made*. Random House, 1999.

Jordan, Michael. *For the Love of the Game: My Story*. Crown Publishers, 1998.

Kornbluth, Jesse. *Michael Jordan*. Simon and Schuster, 1996.

Lazenby, Roland. *Blood on the Horns: The Long Strange Ride of Michael Jordan's Chicago Bulls*. Andrews McMeel, 1998.

Michael Jordan, His Airness [videorecording]. PolyGram Video, 1999.

Joyner-Kersee, Jackie

Cohen, Neil. *Jackie Joyner-Kersee*. Little Brown, 1992.

Green, Carl R. *Jackie Joyner-Kersee*. Maxwell Macmillan, 1994.

Joyner-Kersee, Jacqueline. *A Kind of Grace: The Autobiography of the World's Greatest Female Athlete*. Warner Books, 1997.

King, Martin Luther, Jr.

Abernathy, Donzaleigh. *Partners to History: Martin Luther King, Jr., Ralph David Abernathy, and the Civil Rights Movement*. General Publishing, 1998.

Branch, Taylor. *Parting the Waters: America in the King Years, 1954–63*. Simon and Schuster, 1988.

Carson, Clayborne, et al. *The Eyes on the Prize Civil Rights Reader*. Viking, 1991.

Eyes on the Prize: America's Civil Rights Years, 1954–1965. PBS Video, 1987; and *Eyes on the Prize: America at the Racial Crossroads*. PBS Video, 1989 [videorecordings].

King, Martin Luther, Jr. *Strength to Love*. Harper and Row, 1963.

King, Martin Luther, Jr. *Stride Toward Freedom*. Harper and Row, 1958.

The Martin Luther King, Jr. Center for Nonviolent Social Change. http://www.thekingcenter.com/

Martin Luther King, Jr. National Historic Site. http://www.nps.gov/malu/

Martin Luther King, Jr., Papers Project at Stanford University. http://www.stanford.edu/group/King/

Ku Klux Klan

Cook, Fred J. *The Ku Klux Klan: America's Recurring Nightmare*. J. Messner, 1989.

Meltzer, Milton. *The Truth about the Ku Klux Klan*. Franklin Watts, 1982.

Stanton, Bill. *Klanwatch: Bringing the Ku Klux Klan to Justice*. Penguin, 1992.

Wade, Wyn Craig. *The Fiery Cross: The Ku Klux Klan in America*. Simon and Schuster, 1987.

Kwanzaa

The Celebration of Kwanzaa: Echoes of Africa [videorecording]. MVP Home Entertainment, 1996.

Ford, Juwanda G. *K is for Kwanzaa: A Kwanzaa Alphabet Book*. Scholastic, 1997.

Kwanzaa Music [sound recording]. Rounder Records, 1994.

Riley, Dorothy Winbush. *The Complete Kwanzaa: Celebrating Our Cultural Harvest.* HarperCollins, 1995.

Walton, Darwin McBeth. *Kwanzaa.* Raintree Steck-Vaughn, 1999.

Washington, Donna L. *The Story of Kwanzaa.* HarperCollins, 1996.

Labor and Labor Unions

Honey, Michael K. *Black Workers Remember: An Oral History of Segregation, Unionism, and the Freedom Struggle.* University of California Press, 1999.

Patterson, Lillie. *A. Phillip Randolph: Messenger for the Masses.* Facts on File, 1995.

Santino, Jack. *Miles of Smiles, Years of Struggle: Stories of Black Pullman Porters.* University of Illinois Press, 1989.

Struggles in Steel: The Fight for Equal Opportunity [videorecording]. California Newsreel, 1996.

Lee, Spike

Bernotas, Bob. *Spike Lee: Filmmaker.* Enslow Publishers, 1993.

Hardy, James Earl. *Spike Lee.* Chelsea House, 1996.

Lee, Spike. *Best Seat in the House: A Basketball Memoir.* Crown Publishers, 1997.

Lee, Spike. *By Any Means Necessary: The Trials and Tribulations of the Making of Malcolm X.* Hyperion, 1992.

McDaniel, Melissa. *Spike Lee: On His Own Terms.* Franklin Watts, 1998.

Liberia

Borzendowski, Janice. *John Russwurm.* Chelsea House, 1989.

Hope, Constance Morris. *Liberia.* Chelsea House, 1987.

Levy, Patricia. *Liberia.* M. Cavendish, 1998.

Smith, James Wesley. *Sojourners in Search of Freedom: The Settlement of Liberia by Black Americans.* University Press of America, 1987.

Louis, Joe

Barrow, Joe Louis. *Joe Louis: 50 Years an American Hero.* McGraw-Hill, 1988.

Louis, Joe. *Joe Louis, My Life.* Ecco Press, 1997.

Mead, Chris. *Champion: Joe Louis, Black Hero in White America.* Scribner, 1985.

Marsalis, Wynton

Ellis, Veronica Freeman. *Wynton Marsalis.* Raintree Steck-Vaughn, 1997.

Gourse, Leslie. *Wynton Marsalis: Skain's Domain, a Biography.* Schirmer Books, 1999.

Malone, Margaret Gay. *Jazz is the Word: Wynton Marsalis.* Benchmark Books, 1998.

Marsalis, Wynton. *Sweet Swing Blues on the Road.* W.W. Norton, 1994.

Marshall, Thurgood

Aldred, Lisa. *Thurgood Marshall.* Grolier, 1990.

Greene, Carol. *Thurgood Marshall: First African-American Supreme Court Justice.* Childrens Press, 1991.

Haskins, James. *Thurgood Marshall: A Life for Justice.* H. Holt, 1992.

Hess, Debra. *Thurgood Marshall: The Fight for Equal Justice.* Silver Burdett Press, 1990.

Thurgood Marshall, Supreme Court Justice [videorecording]. Schlessinger Video Productions, 1992.

McKay, Claude

Bloom, Harold, ed. *Black American Poets and Dramatists of the Harlem Renaissance.* Chelsea House, 1995.

McKay, Claude. *A Long Way from Home.* Arno Press, 1969.

McKay, Claude. *The Passion of Claude Mckay; Selected Poetry and Prose, 1912–1948.* Schocken Books, 1973.

Our Souls Have Grown Deep Like the Rivers: Black Poets Read Their Work [sound recording]. Rhino/Word Beat, 2000.

Million Man March

Best, Felton O., ed. *Black Religious Leadership from the Slave Community to the Million Man March: Flames of Fire.* Edwin Mellen Press, 1998.

Cottman, Michael H. *Million Man March.* Crown, 1995.

Sadler, Kim Martin, ed. *Atonement: The Million Man March.* Pilgrim Press, 1996.

Terry, Roderick. *One Million Strong: A Photographic Tribute of the Million Man March and Affirmations for the African-American Male.* Duncan and Duncan, 1996.

"The Million Man March." *The Black History Museum.* http://www.afroam.org/history/million/millman.html

Morrison, Toni

Century, Douglas. *Toni Morrison.* Chelsea House, 1994.

Kramer, Barbara. *Toni Morrison, Nobel Prize-Winning Author.* Enslow Publishers, 1996.

Morrison, Toni. *The Bluest Eye.* Plume Books, 1994.

Morrison, Toni. *Tar Baby.* New American Library, 1987.

Toni Morrison [videorecording]. Home Vision, 1987.

Muhammad, Elijah

Clegg, Claude Andrew. *An Original Man: The Life and Times of Elijah Muhammad.* St. Martins Press, 1997.

Elijah Muhammad: Religious Leader [videorecording]. Schlessinger Video Productions, 1994.

Evanzz, Karl. *The Messenger: The Rise and Fall of Elijah Muhammad.* Pantheon Books, 1999.

Halasa, Malu. *Elijah Muhammad: Religious Leader.* Chelsea House, 1990.

Murray, Anna Pauline (Pauli)

Murray, Pauli. *Pauli Murray: The Autobiography of a Black Activist, Feminist, Lawyer, Priest and Poet.* University of Tennessee Press, 1989.

Murray, Pauli. *Proud Shoes: The Story of an American Family.* Harper and Row, 1987.

Murray, Pauli. *Song in a Weary Throat: An American Pilgrimage.* Harper and Row, 1987.

Music

Allen, William Francis. *Slave Songs of the United States.* Dover, 1995.

Ayazi-Hashjin, Sherry. *Rap and Hip Hop: The Voice of a Generation.* Rosen Pub. Group, 1999.

Baraka, Imamu Amiri. *Blues People: Negro Music in White America.* Greenwood Press, 1980.

Bluesland: Portraits of Thirteen Major American Blues Masters. Dutton, 1991.

Bond, Julian, and Sondra Kathryn Wilson, eds. *Lift Every Voice and Sing: A Celebration of the Negro National Anthem.* Random House, 2000.

Broughton, Viv. *Black Gospel: An Illustrated History of the Gospel Sound.* Sterling, 1985.

Caldwell, Hansonia L. *African American Music: A Chronology, 1619–1995.* Ikoro Communications, 1995.

Chappell, Kevin. "How Blacks Invented Rock and Roll." *Ebony,* Jan. 1997.

Courlander, Harold. *Negro Folk Music U.S.A.* Dover, 1992.

Davis, Angela Yvonne. *Blues Legacies and Black Feminism: Gertrude "Ma" Rainey, Bessie Smith, and Billie Holiday.* Pantheon Books, 1998.

Dicaire, David. *Blues Singers: Biographies of 50 Legendary Artists of the Early 20th Century.* McFarland, 1999.

Fernett, Gene. *Swing Out: Great Negro Dance Bands.* Da Capo Press, 1993.

Fong-Torres, Ben. *The Motown Album: The Sound of Young America.* St. Martin's Press, 1990.

Friedwald, Will. *Jazz Singing: America's Great Voices from Bessie Smith to Bebop and Beyond.* C. Scribner's Sons, 1990.

George, Nelson. *Hip Hop America.* Penguin Books, 1999.

Hacker, Carlotta. *Great African Americans in Jazz.* Crabtree, 1997.

Harris, Sheldon. *Blues Who's Who: A Biographical Dictionary of Blues Singers.* Arlington House, 1979.

Hasse, John Edward, ed. *Jazz: The First Century.* William Morrow, 2000.

Hasse, John Edward, ed. *Ragtime: Its History, Composers, and Music.* Schirmer Books, 1985.

Jasen, David A. *That American Rag: The Story of Ragtime from Coast to Coast.* Schirmer Books, 2000.

"Jet Celebrates 45 Years of the Hottest Black Music, TV and Movie Stars." *Jet,* Nov. 3, 1997.

Johnson, Anne E. *Jazz Tap: From African Drums to American Feet.* Rosen Pub. Group, 1999.

Jones, K. Maurice. *Say It Loud! The Story of Rap Music.* Millbrook Press, 1994.

Kernan, Michael. "Conveying History Through Song." *Smithsonian,* Feb. 1999.

Lovell, John. *Black Song: The Forge and the Flame; the Story of How the Afro-American Spiritual Was Hammered out.* Paragon House, 1986.

Move the Crowd: Voices and Faces of the Hip-Hop Nation. MTV Books/Pocket Books. 1999.

Newman, Richard. *Go Down Moses: A Celebration of the African-American Spiritual.* Clarkson Potter, 1998.

Rediger, Pat. *Great African Americans in Music.* Crabtree Pub. Co., 1996.

Roots of Rhythm [videorecording]. New Video Group, 1997.

Say Amen, Somebody [videorecording]. Pacific Arts Video Records, 1984.

Southern, Eileen. *Biographical Dictionary of Afro-American and African Musicians.* Greenwood Press, 1982.

Southern, Eileen. *The Music of Black Americans: A History.* W.W. Norton, 1997.

The Story of Gospel Music [videorecording]. CBS/Fox Video, 1996.

Tate, Eleanora E. *African American Musicians.* J. Wiley, 2000.

That Rhythm—Those Blues [videorecording]. PBS Video, 1988.

That's Black Entertainment [videorecording]. OnDeck Home Entertainment, 1997.

Voices of the Civil Rights Movement: Black American Freedom Songs, 1960–1966 [sound recording]. Smithsonian Folkways, 1997.

Waller, Don. *The Motown Story.* Scribner, 1985.

Ward, Geoffrey C. *Jazz: An Illustrated History.* Knopf, 2000.

Warren, Gwendolyn Sims. *Ev'ry Time I Feel the Spirit: 101 Best-Loved Psalms, Gospel Hymns, and Spiritual Songs of the African-American Church.* Owl Books, 1999.

Whitall, Susan. *Women of Motown: An Oral History.* Avon Books, 1998.

NAACP (National Association for the Advancement of Colored People)

Finch, Minnie. *The NAACP, Its Fight for Justice.* Scarecrow Press, 1981.

Greenberg, Jack. *Crusaders in the Courts: How a Dedicated Bunch of Lawyers Fought For the Civil Rights Revolution.* Basic Books, 1994.

Hughes, Langston. *Fight for Freedom: The Story of the NAACP.* Norton, 1962.

McDaniel, Melissa. *W.E.B. DuBois: Scholar and Civil Rights Activist.* Franklin Watts, 1999.

Ovington, Mary White. *The Walls Came Tumbling Down.* Schocken Books, 1970.

Wilkins, Roy. *Standing Fast: The Autobiography of Roy Wilkins.* Viking Press, 1982.

Nation of Islam

See BLACK MUSLIMS.

National Urban League

Dickerson, Dennis C. *Militant Mediator—Whitney M. Young, Jr.* University Press of Kentucky, 1998.

Mann, Peggy. *Whitney Young, Jr., Crusader for Equality.* Garrard Pub. Co., 1972.

Parris, Guichard, and Lester Brooks. *Blacks in the City: A History of the National Urban League.* Little Brown, 1971.

Weiss, Nancy J. *Whitney M. Young, Jr., and the Struggle for Civil Rights.* Princeton University Press, 1989.

Negro History Week

Bader, Barbara. "History Changes Color." *Horn Book Magazine*, Jan.–Feb. 1997.

Bennett, Lerone. "Still on the Case: Carter G. Woodson, Father of Black History." *Ebony*, Feb. 1999.

"Carter G. Woodson: February, 1926." *Jet*, Feb. 6, 1995.

Negro National Anthem

See JOHNSON, JAMES WELDON.

Odell Waller Case

Sherman, Richard B. *The Case of Odell Waller and Virginia Justice, 1940–1942.* University of Tennessee Press, 1992.

"What Legal Case Brought Issues of Race and Class to Public Attention?" *Africana.com.*
http://www.africana.com/bl_fact_82.htm

O'Neal, Shaquille

Castello, Bob. *Meet Shaquille O'Neal: An Unauthorized Biography.* Publications International, 1993.

Gutman, Bill. *Shaquille O'Neal.* Pocket Books, 1998.

O'Neal, Shaquille. *Shaq Attaq!* Hyperion, 1993.

Owens, Jesse

Baker, William J. *Jesse Owens: An American Life*. Free Press, 1986.

Barry, James P. *The Berlin Olympics, 1936: Black American Athletes Counter Nazi Propaganda*. Franklin Watts, 1975.

Jesse Owens: Champion Athlete [videorecording]. Schlessinger Video Productions, 1994.

Owens, Jesse. *Blackthink; My Life as Black Man and White Man*. Morrow, 1970.

Owens, Jesse. *Jesse: The Man Who Outran Hitler*. Ballantine Books, 1983.

Parks, Rosa

Celsi, Teresa Noel. *Rosa Parks and the Montgomery Bus Boycott*. Millbrook Press, 1991.

DeWitt, Lynda. "Rosa Parks: When I Was a Kid." *National Geographic World*, Feb. 1998/

Greenfield, Eloise. *Rosa Parks*. HarperCollins, 1996.

Hull, Mary. *Rosa Parks: Civil Rights Leader*. Chelsea House, 1994.

Parks, Rosa. *Rosa Parks: My Story*. Scholastic, 1994.

Passing

Ellison, Ralph. *Juneteenth*. Vintage, 1999.

Jordan, June. "Passing," in *A Way Out of No Way: Writings about Growing Up Black in America*. Ballantine Books, 1997.

Larsen, Nella. *Passing*. Penguin Books, 1997.

"Black or White?" *The Black History Museum*.
http://www.afroam.org/history/bnw/bwmain.html

Plessy v. Ferguson Case

Fireside, Harvey. *Plessy v. Ferguson: Separate But Equal?* Enslow Publishers, 1997.

Harrison, Maureen, and Steve Gilbert, eds. *Landmark Decisions of the United States Supreme Court*. Excellent Books, 1991.

Mauro, Tony. *Illustrated Great Decisions of the Supreme Court*. CQ Press, 2000.

Politics and Politicians (General)

Dudley, Karen. *Great African Americans in Government*. Crabtree Pub. Co., 1997.

Gomes, Ralph C., and Linda Faye Williams, eds. *From Exclusion to Inclusion: The Long Struggle for African American Political Power*. Greenwood Press, 1992.

Haskins, James. *Distinguished African American Political and Governmental Leaders*. Oryx Press, 1999.

Smith, Jessie Carney, and Joseph Palmisano, eds. *Reference Library of Black America*. Gale Group, 2000.

Powell, Adam Clayton, Jr.

Haskins, James. *Adam Clayton Powell: Portrait of a Marching Black*. Dial Press, 1974.

Haygood, Will. *King of the Cats: The Life and Times of Adam Clayton Powell, Jr.* Houghton Mifflin, 1993.

Jakoubek, Robert E. *Adam Clayton Powell, Jr.* Chelsea House, 1988.

Powell, Adam Clayton. *Adam by Adam: The Autobiography of Adam Clayton Powell, Jr.* Dial Press, 1971.

Powell, Colin

Banta, Melissa. *Colin Powell.* Chelsea House, 1994.

Colin Powell: A Soldier's Campaign [videorecording]. A&E Home Video, 1995.

Finlayson, Reggie. *Colin Powell.* Lerner Publications, 1997.

Haskins, James. *Colin Powell: A Biography.* Scholastic, 1995.

Powell, Colin L. *My American Journey.* Random House, 1995.

Schraff, Anne E. *Colin Powell: Soldier and Patriot.* Enslow Publishers, 1997.

Prejudice and Racism

Ben Jelloun, Tahar. *Racism Explained to My Daughter.* New Press, 1999.

Berry, Joy Wilt. *Every Kid's Guide to Overcoming Prejudice and Discrimination.* Children's Press, 1987.

Black Is—Black Ain't: A Personal Journey Through Black Identity [videorecording]. California Newsreel, 1995.

Bridging Racial Divisions [videorecording]. New York Bureau for At-Risk Youth, 1997.

Cole, Jim. *Filtering People: Understanding and Confronting Our Prejudices.* New Society Publishers, 1990.

Ethnic Notions: Black People in White Minds [videorecording]. California Newsreel, 1987.

Finkenstaedt, Rose L.H. *Face-to-Face: Blacks in America; White Perceptions and Black Realities.* W. Morrow, 1994.

Grant, R.G. *Racism: Changing Attitudes 1900–2000.* Raintree Steck-Vaughn, 2000.

Helmreich, William B. *The Things They Say Behind Your Back.* Doubleday, 1982.

Kronenwetter, Michael. *United They Hate: White Supremacist Groups in America.* Walker and Co., 1992.

McKissack, Pat. *Taking a Stand Against Racism and Racial Discrimination.* Franklin Watts, 1990.

Roberts, Diane. *The Myth of Aunt Jemima: Representations of Race and Region.* Routledge, 1994.

Shaughnessy, Diane. *Let's Talk About Racism.* PowerKids Press, 1997.

Shipler, David K. *A Country of Strangers: Blacks and Whites in America.* Knopf, 1997.

Race, Scientific Theories of

Cavalli-Sforza, L.L. *The Great Human Diasporas: The History of Diversity and Evolution.* Addison-Wesley, 1995.

Diamond, Jared M. *Guns, Germs, and Steel: The Fates of Human Societies.* W.W. Norton, 1997.

Lampton, Christopher. *Human Race.* Franklin Watts, 1989.

Shipman, Pat. *The Evolution of Racism: Human Differences and the Use and Abuse of Science.* Simon and Schuster, 1994.

Wolpoff, Milford H., and Rachel Caspari. *Race and Human Evolution.* Simon and Schuster, 1997.

Racism

See PREJUDICE AND RACISM.

Randolph, A. Philip

Cwiklik, Robert. *A. Philip Randolph and the Labor Movement*. Millbrook Press, 1993.

Hanley, Sally. *A. Philip Randolph*. Chelsea House, 1989.

Patterson, Lillie. *A. Philip Randolph: Messenger for the Masses*. Facts on File, 1995.

Wright, Sarah. *A. Philip Randolph: Integration in the Workplace*. Silver Burdett Press, 1990.

Reconstruction

Collier, Christopher. *Reconstruction and the Rise of Jim Crow, 1864–1896*. Benchmark Books, 1998.

Kirchberger, Joe H. *The Civil War and Reconstruction: An Eyewitness History*. Facts on File, 1991.

Naden, Corinne J. *Civil War Ends: Assassination, Reconstruction, and the Aftermath*. Raintree Steck-Vaughn, 2000.

Smith, John David. *Black Voices from Reconstruction, 1865–1877*. Millbrook Press, 1996.

Ziff, Marsha. *Reconstruction Following the Civil War in American History*. Enslow Publishers, 1999.

Religion

Best, Felton O., ed. *Black Religious Leadership from the Slave Community to the Million Man March: Flames of Fire*. Edwin Mellen Press, 1998.

Billingsley, Andrew. *Mighty Like a River: The Black Church and Social Reform*. Oxford University Press, 1999.

Murphy, Larry G., ed. *Encyclopedia of African American Religions*. Garland, 1993.

Smith, Jessie Carney, and Joseph Palmisano, eds. *Reference Library of Black America*. Gale Group, 2000.

Washington, James Melvin, ed. *Conversations with God: Two Centuries of Prayers by African Americans*. HarperPerennial, 1995.

Weisenfeld, Judith, and Richard Newman, eds. *This Far by Faith: Readings in African-American Women's Religious Biography*. Routledge, 1996.

Young, Henry J. *Major Black Religious Leaders, 1755–1940*. Abingdon, 1977.

Revolutionary War, African Americans in the

Cox, Clinton. *Come All You Brave Soldiers: Blacks in the Revolutionary War*. Scholastic Press, 1999.

Lanning, Michael Lee. *The African-American Soldier: From Crispus Attucks to Colin Powell*. Carol Pub. Group, 1997.

Millender, Dharathula H. *Crispus Attucks, Black Leader of Colonial Patriots*. Aladdin Books, 1986.

Wright, Donald R. *African Americans in the Colonial Era: From African Origins Through the American Revolution*. Harlan Davidson, 1990.

Robeson, Paul

Ehrlich, Scott. *Paul Robeson*. Chelsea House, 1988.

Holmes, Burnham. *Paul Robeson: A Voice of Struggle*. Raintree Steck-Vaughn, 1995.

Larsen, Rebecca. *Paul Robeson, Hero Before His Time*. Franklin Watts, 1989.

Robeson, Paul. *Here I Stand*. Beacon Press, 1988.

Wright, David K. *Paul Robeson: Actor, Singer, Political Activist*. Enslow Publishers, 1998.

Paul Robeson Centennial Celebration.
http://www.cs.uchicago.edu/cpsr/robeson/

Robinson, Jackie

Falkner, David. *Jackie Robinson, from Baseball to Birmingham*. Simon and Schuster, 1995.

Frommer, Harvey. *Rickey and Robinson: The Men Who Broke Baseball's Color Barrier*. Macmillan, 1982.

Hine, Darlene Clark. *The Path to Equality: From the Scottsboro Case to the Breaking of Baseball's Color Barrier, 1931–1947*. Chelsea House, 1995.

Jackie Robinson [videorecording]. A&E Home Video, 1994.

Rampersad, Arnold. *Jackie Robinson: A Biography*. Knopf, 1997.

"Jackie Robinson." *The Black History Museum*.
http://www.afroam.org/history/Robinson/intro.html

Rudolph, Wilma

Krull, Kathleen. *Wilma Unlimited: How Wilma Rudolph Became the World's Fastest Woman*. Harcourt Brace Jovanovich, 1996.

Sherrow, Victoria. *Wilma Rudolph: Olympic Champion*. Chelsea House, 1995.

Wilma Rudolph [videorecording]. Schlessinger Video Productions, 1995.

Rustin, Bayard

Haskins, James. *Bayard Rustin: Behind the Scenes of the Civil Rights Movement*. Hyperion Press, 1997.

Haughton, Buzz. "Bayard Rustin—Civil Rights Leader." *Quaker Studies*, Fall 1999. Reproduced at
http://www2.gol.com/users/quakers/bayard_rustin.htm

"Rustin, Bayard". *Current Biography*, Oct. 1987.

Scientists (General)

Aaseng, Nathan. *Black Inventors*. Facts on File, 1997.

Great Black Innovators [videorecording]. Knowledge Unlimited, 1995.

Haber, Louis. *Black Pioneers of Science and Invention*. Harcourt Brace Jovanovich, 1991.

Kessler, James H., ed. *Distinguished African American Scientists of the 20th Century*. Oryx Press, 1996.

McKissack, Pat. *African-American Scientists*. Millbrook Press, 1994.

Sertima, Ivan Van, ed. *Blacks in Science: Ancient and Modern*. Transaction, 1994.

The Faces of Science: African Americans in the Sciences.
http://www.princeton.edu/~mcbrown/display/faces.html

SCLC (Southern Christian Leadership Conference)

Garrow, David J. *Bearing the Cross: Martin Luther King, Jr., and the Southern Christian Leadership Conference*. W. Morrow, 1986.

Weisbrot, Robert. *Marching Toward Freedom, 1957–1965: From the Founding of the Southern Christian Leadership Conference to the Assassination of Malcolm X*. Chelsea House, 1994.

"Scottsboro Boys"

Harrison, Maureen, and Steve Gilbert, eds. *Landmark Decisions of the United States Supreme Court*. Excellent Books, 1991.

Haskins, James. *The Scottsboro Boys*. H. Holt, 1994.

Hine, Darlene Clark. *The Path to Equality: From the Scottsboro Case to the Breaking of Baseball's Color Barrier, 1931–1947*. Chelsea House, 1995.

Horne, Gerald. *Powell v. Alabama: The Scottsboro Boys and American Justice*. Franklin Watts, 1997.

"The Scottsboro Boys." *The Black History Museum*.
http://www.afroam.org/history/scott/scotts.html

Shakur, Assata (Joanne Chesimard)

Shakur, Assata. *Assata, an Autobiography*. Lawrence Hill Books, 1987.

White, Evelyn. "Prisoner in Paradise." *Essence*, June 1997.

Williams, Evelyn. *Inadmissible Evidence*. Lawrence Hill Books, 1993.

Skin Color

Griffin, John Howard. *Black Like Me*. Penguin Books, 1996.

Lerner, Marguerite Rush. *Color and People: The Story of Pigmentation*. Lerner Publications Co., 1971.

Newman, Gerald. *Racism: Divided by Color*. Enslow Publishers, 1995.

A Question of Color [videorecording]. California Newsreel, 1992.

Russell, Kathy. *The Color Complex: The Politics of Skin Color Among African Americans*. Anchor Books, 1993.

"Black or White?" *The Black History Museum*.
http://www.afroam.org/history/bnw/bwmain.html

Slave Narratives

Govenar, Alan B. *African American Frontiers: Slave Narratives and Oral Histories*. ABC-CLIO, 2000.

I Was a Slave: True Life Stories Told by Former American Slaves in the 1930's. American Legacy Books, 1995.

Slave Narratives. Penguin Putnam, 2000.

Slavery Time When I Was Chillun. Putnam, 1997.

Voices from Slavery: 100 Authentic Slave Narratives. Dover, 2000.

Washington, Booker T. *Up From Slavery*. Doubleday, 1998.

"American Slave Narratives: An Online Anthology." *American Hypertext Workshop, University of Virginia*.
http://xroads.virginia.edu/~hyper/wpa/wpahome.html

Slave Revolts

See also TURNER, NAT.

Aptheker, Herbert. *American Negro Slave Revolts*. International Publishers, 1983.

Katz, William Loren. *Breaking the Chains: African-American Slave Resistance*. Atheneum, 1990.

McKissack, Pat. *Rebels Against Slavery, American Slave Revolts*. Scholastic, 1999.

Wepman, Dennis. *The Struggle for Freedom: African-American Slave Resistance*. Facts On File, 1996.

"Black Resistance." *The Black History Museum*.
http://www.afroam.org/history/slavery/index.html

Slave Trade

Haskins, James. *Bound for America: The Forced Migration of Africans to the New World*. Lothrop, Lee and Shepard Books, 1999.

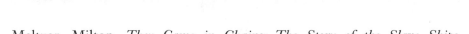

Meltzer, Milton. *They Came in Chains: The Story of the Slave Ships.* Benchmark Books, 2000.

Phillips, Caryl. *The Atlantic Sound.* Knopf, 2000.

Reynolds, Edward. *Stand the Storm: A History of the Atlantic Slave Trade.* I.R. Dee, 1993.

Ship of Slaves: The Middle Passage [videorecording]. A&E Video, 1997.

Thomas, Hugh. *The Slave Trade: The Story of the Atlantic Slave Trade, 1440–1870.* Simon and Schuster, 1997.

Slavery

Africans in America: America's Journey Through Slavery [videorecording]. PBS Video, 1998.

Collier, Christopher. *Slavery and the Coming of the Civil War, 1831–1861.* Benchmark Books, 1998.

Currie, Stephen. *Life of a Slave on a Southern Plantation.* Lucent Books, 2000.

Gutman, Herbert G. *The Black Family in Slavery and Freedom, 1750–1925.* Vintage Books, 1977.

Jacobs, Harriet A. *Incidents in the Life of a Slave Girl.* Penguin Books, 2000.

Kolchin, Peter. *American Slavery, 1619–1877.* Hill and Wang, 1993.

Miller, Randall M., and John David Smith, eds. *The Dictionary of Afro-American Slavery.* Greenwood Press, 1988.

Oakes, James. *The Ruling Race: A History of American Slaveholders.* Knopf, 1982.

Stowe, Harriet Beecher. *Uncle Tom's Cabin, Or, Life among the Lowly.* Barnes and Noble Books, 1995.

White, Deborah G. *Ar'n't I a Woman? Female Slaves in the Plantation South.* Norton, 1999.

Smith, Bessie

Alexander, Amy. *Fifty Black Women Who Changed America.* Carol Pub. Group, 1998.

Davis, Angela Yvonne. *Blues Legacies and Black Feminism: Gertrude "Ma" Rainey, Bessie Smith, and Billie Holiday.* Pantheon Books, 1998.

Feinstein, Elaine. *Bessie Smith.* Penguin, 1985.

Friedwald, Will. *Jazz Singing: America's Great Voices from Bessie Smith to Bebop and Beyond.* C. Scribner's Sons, 1990.

Jones, Hettie. *Big Star Fallin' Mama; Five Women in Black Music.* Viking Press, 1974.

SNCC (Student Non-violent Coordinating Committee)

Freedom on My Mind [videorecording]. California Newsreel, 1994.

Lewis, John. *Walking with the Wind: A Memoir of the Movement.* Simon and Schuster, 1998.

Zinn, Howard. *SNCC, the New Abolitionists.* Beacon Press, 1964.

Television, African Americans in

See FILM AND TELEVISION, AFRICAN AMERICANS IN.

Till, Emmett

"Remembering Emmett Till." *Jet*, Sept. 13, 1999.

Whitfield, Stephen J. *A Death in the Delta: The Story of Emmett Till.* Free Press, 1988.

"Till, Emmett Louis." *Africana.com.*
http://www.africana.com/tt_150.htm

Truth, Sojourner

Gilbert, Olive. *Narrative of Sojourner Truth.* Dover Publications, 1997.

Krass, Peter. *Sojourner Truth.* Chelsea House, 1988.

McKissack, Pat. *Sojourner Truth: Ain't I a Woman?* Scholastic, 1992.

Painter, Nell Irvin. *Sojourner Truth.* W.W. Norton, 1996.

Shumate, Jane. *Sojourner Truth and the Voice of Freedom.* Millbrook Press, 1991.

Tubman, Harriet

Bentley, Judith. *Harriet Tubman.* Franklin Watts, 1990.

Elish, Dan. *Harriet Tubman and the Underground Railroad.* Millbrook Press, 1993.

Petry, Ann Lane. *Harriet Tubman: Conductor on the Underground Railroad.* Harper Trophy, 1996.

Taylor, Marian. *Harriet Tubman.* Chelsea House, 1991.

A Woman Called Moses [videorecording]. Xenon Home Video, 1992.

Turner, Nat

Barrett, Tracy. *Nat Turner and the Slave Revolt.* Millbrook Press, 1993.

Bisson, Terry. *Nat Turner.* Grolier, 1988.

Goldman, Martin S. *Nat Turner and the Southhampton Revolt of 1831.* Franklin Watts, 1992.

Oates, Stephen B. *The Fires of Jubilee: Nat Turner's Fierce Rebellion.* Harper and Row. 1975.

Styron, William. *The Confessions of Nat Turner.* Vintage Books, 1992.

Tuskegee Airmen

Francis, Charles E. *The Tuskegee Airmen: The Men Who Changed a Nation.* Branden Pub., 1997.

Harris, Jacqueline L. *The Tuskegee Airmen: Black Heroes of World War II.* Dillon Press, 1995.

Homan, Lynn M. *The Tuskegee Airmen.* Arcadia, 1998.

McKissack, Pat. *Red-Tail Angels: The Story of the Tuskegee Airmen of World War II.* Walker and Co., 1995.

The Tuskegee Airmen [videorecording]. HBO Home Video, 1995.

"The Sky Was the Limit." *The Black History Museum.*
http://www.afroam.org/history/tusk/tuskmain.html

"Tuskegee Experiment"

Jones, James H. *Bad Blood: The Tuskegee Syphilis Experiment.* Free Press, 1992.

Miss Evers' Boys [videorecording]. HBO Home Video, 1997.

"The Troubling Legacy of The Tuskegee Syphilis Study." *University of Virginia Health Sciences Library Collection.*
http://www.hsc.virginia.edu/hs-library/historical/apology/

Underground Railroad

Bial, Raymond. *The Underground Railroad.* Houghton Mifflin, 1995.

Gorrell, Gena K. *North Star to Freedom: The Story of the Underground Railroad.* Delacorte Press, 1997.

Hamilton, Virginia. *Many Thousand Gone: African Americans from Slavery to Freedom.* Knopf, 1993.

Haskins, James. *Get on Board: The Story of the Underground Railroad.* Scholastic, 1993.

The Underground Railroad.
http://education.ucdavis.edu/NEW/STC/lesson/socstud/railroad/contents.htm

United States Constitution
Africans in America: America's Journey Through Slavery [videorecording]. PBS Video, 1998.

Banfield, Susan. *The Fifteenth Amendment: African-American Men's Right to Vote.* Enslow Publishers, 1998.

Johnson, Charles Richard, and Patricia Smith. *Africans in America: America's Journey Through Slavery.* Harcourt Brace Jovanovich, 1999.

Schleichert, Elizabeth. *The Thirteenth Amendment Ending Slavery.* Enslow Publishers, 1998.

Stiller, Richard. *Broken Promises: The Strange History of the Fourteenth Amendment.* Random House, 1972.

Urban Riots
Conot, Robert E. *Rivers of Blood, Years of Darkness: The Unforgettable Classic Account of the Watts Riot.* W. Morrow, 1968.

Fires in the Mirror [videorecording]. PBS Video, 1993.

Salak, John. *The Los Angeles Riots: America's Cities in Crisis.* Millbrook Press, 1993.

Upton, James N. *Urban Riots in the 20th Century: A Social History.* Wyndham Hall Press, 1989.

Vesey, Denmark
Edwards, Lillie J. *Denmark Vesey.* Chelsea House, 1990.

Egerton, Douglas R. *He Shall Go Out Free: The Lives of Denmark Vesey.* Madison House, 1999.

Robertson, David. *Denmark Vesey.* Knopf, 1999.

Vietnam War, African Americans in the
Freedman, Suzanne. *Clay v. United States: Muhammad Ali Objects to War.* Enslow Publishers, 1997.

Lanning, Michael Lee. *The African-American Soldier: From Crispus Attucks to Colin Powell.* Carol Pub. Group, 1997.

Super, Neil. *Vietnam War Soldiers.* Twenty-First Century Books, 1993.

Taylor, Clyde. *Vietnam and Black America: An Anthology of Protest and Resistance.* Anchor Press, 1973.

Westheider, James E. *Fighting on Two Fronts: African Americans and the Vietnam War.* New York University Press, 1997.

Voting
Lusane, Clarence. *No Easy Victories: Black Americans and the Vote.* Franklin Watts, 1996.

Rubel, David. *Fannie Lou Hamer: From Sharecropping to Politics.* Silver Burdett Press, 1990.

Scott, William R. *Upon These Shores: Themes in the African-American Experience, 1600 to the Present.* Routledge, 2000.

Walter, Mildred Pitts. *Mississippi Challenge.* Bradbury Press, 1992.

Winters, Paul A., ed. *The Civil Rights Movement.* Greenhaven Press, 2000.

Walker, Alice
Gentry, Tony. *Alice Walker.* Chelsea House, 1993.

Kramer, Barbara. *Alice Walker: Author of The Color Purple.* Enslow Publishers, 1995.

Lazo, Caroline Evensen. *Alice Walker.* Lerner Publications, 1999.

Walker, Alice. *The Color Purple.* Pocket Books, 1985.

Walker, Alice. *The Same River Twice.* Scribner, 1996.

Washington, Booker Taliaferro

McKissack, Pat. *Booker T. Washington: Leader and Educator.* Enslow Publishers, 1992.

McLoone, Margo. *Booker T. Washington: A Photo-Illustrated Biography.* Bridgestone Press, 1997.

Nicholson, Lois. *Booker T. Washington.* Chelsea House, 1997.

Washington, Booker T. *Up From Slavery.* Doubleday, 1998.

Wells-Barnett, Ida B.

Fradin, Dennis B. *Ida B. Wells: Mother of the Civil Rights Movement.* Clarion Books, 2000.

Freedman, Suzanne. *Ida B. Wells-Barnett and the Antilynching Crusade.* Millbrook Press, 1994.

Lisandrelli, Elaine Slivinski. *Ida B. Wells-Barnett: Crusader Against Lynching.* Enslow Publishers, 1998.

Wells-Barnett, Ida B. *The Memphis Diary of Ida B. Wells.* Beacon Press, 1995.

West, African Americans in the

The African American West: A Century of Short Stories. University Press of Colorado, 2000.

The Black West [videorecording]. Turner Home Entertainment, 1993.

Katz, William Loren. *The Black West.* Simon and Schuster, 1996.

Sanford, William R. *Bill Pickett: African-American Rodeo Star.* Enslow Publishers, 1997.

Savage, W. Sherman. *Blacks in the West.* Greenwood Press, 1976.

Schlissel, Lillian. *Black Frontiers: A History of African American Heroes in the Old West.* Simon and Schuster, 1995.

Wukovits, John F. *The Black Cowboys.* Chelsea House, 1997.

Williams, Serena

Howard, Johnette. "Bragging Rights." *Tennis,* Nov. 1999.

Price, S.L. "Father Knew Best." *Sports Illustrated,* Sept. 20, 1999.

"Serena Williams." *ESPN.com.*
http://espn.go.com/tennis/s/wta/profiles/swilliams.html

"Serena Williams Wins at U.S. Open; First Black Female Champion since 1958." *Jet,* Sept. 27, 1999.

Williams, Venus

Aronson, Virginia. *Venus Williams.* Chelsea House, 1999.

Howard, Johnette. "Bragging Rights." *Tennis,* Nov. 1999.

Teitelbaum, Michael. *Grand Slam Stars: Martina Hingis and Venus Williams.* HarperActive, 1998.

"Venus Williams." *ESPN.com.*
http://espn.go.com/tennis/s/wta/profiles/vwilliams.html

Winfrey, Oprah

Brooks, Philip. *Oprah Winfrey: A Voice for the People.* Franklin Watts, 1999.

Nicholson, Lois. *Oprah Winfrey.* Chelsea House, 1994.

Ward, Kristin. *Learning about Assertiveness from the Life of Oprah Winfrey.* PowerKids Press, 1999.

Winfrey, Oprah. *Oprah Winfrey Speaks: Insight from the World's Most Influential Voice.* Wiley, 1998.

Winfrey, Oprah. *The Uncommon Wisdom of Oprah Winfrey: A Portrait in Her Own Words.* W. Morrow, 1996.

Wooten, Sara McIntosh. *Oprah Winfrey: Talk Show Legend.* Enslow Publishers, 1999.

Woods, Tiger

Durbin, William. *Tiger Woods.* Chelsea House, 1998.

Gutman, Bill. *Tiger Woods: Golf's Shining Young Star.* Millbrook Press, 1998.

Rosaforte, Tim. *Tiger Woods: The Makings of a Champion.* St. Martin's Press, 1997.

Tiger Woods: Son, Hero and Champion [videorecording]. CBS Video, 1997.

Woods, Earl. *Playing Through: Straight Talk on Hard Work, Big Dreams, and Adventures with Tiger.* HarperCollins, 1998.

Tiger Woods Official Golf Website.
http://www.tigerwoods.com/

World War I, African Americans in

Barbeau, Arthur E. *The Unknown Soldiers: African-American Troops in World War I.* Da Capo Press, 1996.

Cooper, Michael L. *Hell Fighters: African American Soldiers in World War I.* Lodestar Books, 1997.

Lanning, Michael Lee. *The African-American Soldier: From Crispus Attucks to Colin Powell.* Carol Pub. Group, 1997.

Men of Bronze [videorecording]. Pacific Arts Video, 1977.

World War II, African Americans in

Fletcher, Marvin E. *America's First Black General: Benjamin O. Davis, Sr., 1880–1970.* University Press of Kansas, 1989.

Garza, Hedda. *Without Regard to Race: The Integration of the U.S. Military After World War II.* Franklin Watts, 1995.

Howell, Ann Chandler. *Tuskegee Airmen: Heroes in Flight for Dignity, Inclusion and Citizenship Rights.* Chandler/White Publishing, 1994.

Lanning, Michael Lee. *The African-American Soldier: From Crispus Attucks to Colin Powell.* Carol Pub. Group, 1997.

McGowen, Tom. *Lonely Eagles and Buffalo Soldiers: African Americans in World War II.* Franklin Watts, 1995.

"This Is Our War." *The Black History Museum.*
http://www.afroam.org/history/OurWar/intro.html

Wright, Richard

Richard Wright: Black Boy [videorecording]. California Newsreel, 1994.

Urban, Joan. *Richard Wright.* Chelsea House, 1989.

Wright, Richard. *Black Boy: A Record of Childhood and Youth.* HarperPerennial, 1993.

Wright, Richard. *Native Son.* HarperCollins, 1998.

X, Malcolm

Bloom, Harold, ed. *Alex Haley and Malcolm X's The Autobiography of Malcolm X.* Chelsea House, 1999.

Brown, Kevin. *Malcolm X: His Life and Legacy.* Millbrook Press, 1995.

Davis, Lucille. *Malcolm X: A Photo-Illustrated Biography.* Bridgestone Books, 1998.

Malcolm X [videorecording]. Warner Home Video, 2000.

Malcolm X. *The Autobiography of Malcolm X.* Ballantine Books. 1999.

Myers, Walter Dean. *Malcolm X: A Fire Burning Brightly.* HarperCollins, 2000.

Young, Andrew

Roberts, Maurice. *Andrew Young, Freedom Fighter.* Children's Press, 1983.

Westman, Paul. *Andrew Young, Champion of the Poor.* Dillon Press, 1983.

Young, Andrew. *An Easy Burden: The Civil Rights Movement and the Transformation of America.* HarperCollins, 1996.

Young, Andrew. *A Way Out of No Way: The Spiritual Memoirs of Andrew Young.* T. Nelson Publishers, 1994.

Young, Whitney

See NATIONAL URBAN LEAGUE.

Index

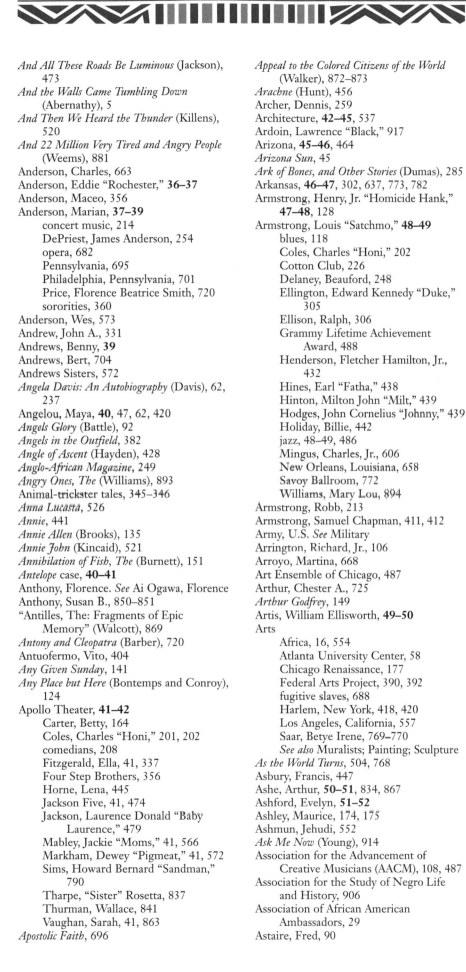

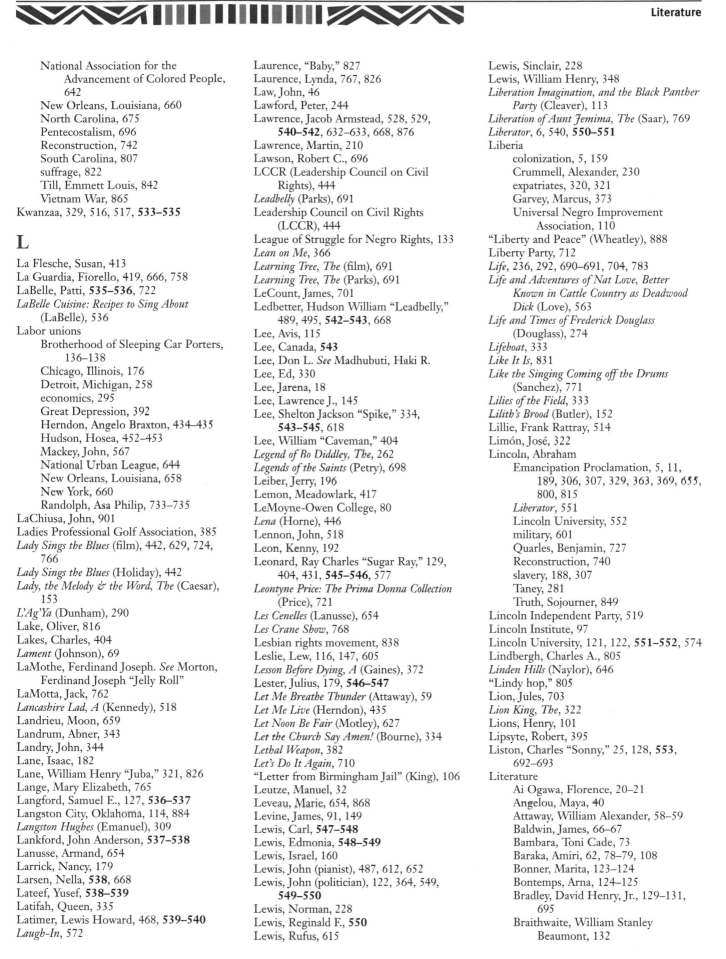